RELIGIOUS INFORMATION SOURCES: A WORLDWIDE GUIDE

Garland Reference Library of the Humanities (Vol. 1593)

Religious Information Systems Series, Vol. 2

Other volumes in the series:

Religious Bodies in the United States: A Directory
by J. Gordon Melton

Magic, Witchcraft and Paganism in America: A Bibliography
Second Edition
by J. Gordon Melton and Isotta Poggi

The African-American Holiness Pentecostal Movement:
An Annotated Bibilography
by Sherry Sherrod DuPree

Holy Ground: A Study of the American Camp Meeting
by Kenneth O. Brown

The Cult Controversy: A Guide to Sources
by J. Gordon Melton

RELIGIOUS INFORMATION SOURCES: A WORLDWIDE GUIDE

by
J. Gordon Melton
and
Michael A. Köszegi

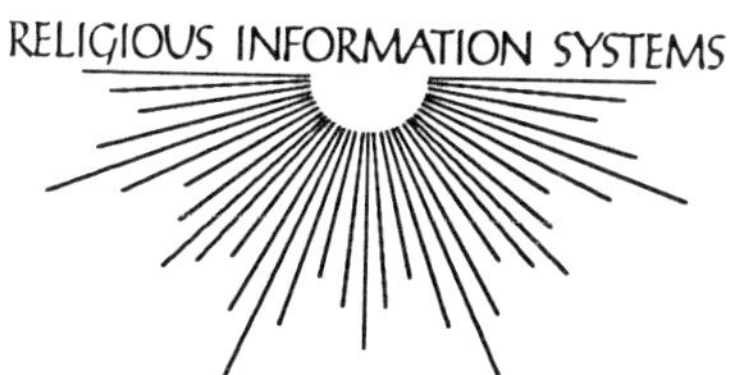

Garland Publishing, Inc.
New York & London
1992

Library of Congress Cataloging-in-Publication Data

Melton, J. Gordon

Religious information sources: a worldwide guide / compiled by J. Gordon Melton and Michael A. Köszegi.

p. cm. — (Garland reference library of the humanities; v. 1593) (Religious information systems; vol. 2)

Includes indexes.

ISBN 0-8153-0859-0

1. Religion—Bibliography. 2. Religion—Information services. I. Köszegi, Michael A. II. Title. III. Series. IV. Series: Religious information series; vol. 2.

Z7751.M45 1992
[BL48]
016.2—dc20 91-47697
CIP

Printed on acid-free, 250-year-life paper
Manufactured in the United States of America

TABLE OF CONTENTS

Part 3: **Africa and the Middle East**

Part 4: **The Americas, Europe and Oceania**

III. Issues in Comparative Religion

Part 1: **Forming the Religious Life**

Part 2: **The Interaction of Religious Communities**

IV. Christianity

V. Christianity: Issues in Christian Studies

VI. Christian Historical Studies

VII. Christian Denominational Family Traditions

INTRODUCTION

Religious Information Sources: A Worldwide Guide (*RIS*) is simply what its name suggests, a comprehensive guide to the many sources of information in the broad field of religion. Broken down into numerous sections, it provides a quick and handy reference to anyone working in a particular field, from women's religious studies to Islamic studies to metaphysical religion, pointing them to the spectrum of published information sources and the variety of available resource centers specializing in the area. It attempts worldwide coverage, though with a distinct North American emphasis, and coverage of the entire field of religious studies, though with an English-language bias. In compiling the text, we began by asking the question, "Where can I find information on [any given field of interest in religion?]" and then proceeded to structure the text to answer that query. For example, in the area of Buddhism, we asked, "What books summarize data about Buddhism and where can I turn for more information?" The answer led to a number of reference books, bibliographies, some professional associations which study Buddhism, and several archival collections.

RIS is designed to assist the broad spectrum of people with questions about religion from the professor and graduate student in religious studies interested in getting a handle upon resources in the field, to the reference librarian trying to assist an individual needing help, to anyone seeking information about religion.

Our generation benefits from the tremendous abundance of information that is available to us for the first time. At the same time we suffer from the problems created by that over-abundance. So much information, from so many different sources, surrounds us that we find it easy to become overwhelmed by it and unable to stay ahead of its rapid growth. We also find ourselves missing valuable material, directly relevant to our own particular special interests, because we were unaware of its publication or how to obtain a copy. It is easy to miss valuable storehouses of information simply because we are either unaware that it exists or how to locate it. While probably no worse than other broad areas of knowledge, religion seems to be especially blessed and cursed by the information overload. This volume attempts to address that issue. It is neither a book about religion nor even a book about books on religions (even though bibliography is an important component of the text). Rather, it is a guide to information sources, many of which happen to be found in books, but increasingly includes many more that are not.

Over the years of creating reference books and building a resource library in American religion, the Institute for the Study of American Religion had informally built its own list of resources. As our work expanded to include Canada and Europe, and as we began to look at Africa and the Pacific Rim for future projects, and as calls increased looking for various bits of obscure information, that resource list expanded. We began to see the need for a general sourcebook to aid us in gaining an overview of the whole field of religion and religions. The need was further stimulated as we became painfully aware of large vacuums in religious information.

The original plan for *RIS* called for limiting it to English-language sources. That plan was quickly abandoned as, first, we encountered areas in which the best sources were in other languages, and, second, as we recalled the essential encyclopedic and bibliographic work being done in Europe. Hence while we retain the original English-language emphasis, we have incorporated numerous non-English sources, especially the standard French, German, Spanish, and Italian ones. It is hoped that in future editions of *RIS* more comprehensive coverage of European and Asian sources can be incorporated into the body of the text.

The Organization of *Religious Information Sources: A Worldwide Guide*

The assembling of the numerous sources cited below suggested several different possible arrangements. In the end we decided upon one which went from the more abstract and general to the more concrete and particular. Thus the very first section of *Reliegious Information Sources* deals with the abstract concept of "religion" and with the major academic disciplines which have turned their attention to its study—philosophy, psychology, science, and sociology. Some issues to which a significant amount of contemporary interdisciplinary scholarly attention has been directed are also highlighted—the communal life, religious conversion, the evolution/creation debate, religious healing, millennialism, mysticism and spirituality, and the status and role of women in religion.

The second section of *RIS* concerns the world's religions. They are grouped according to traditional geographical areas, though all of the major religions have now diffused around the world. Within each broad geographic area, the religious traditions are listed alphabetically. Material on Buddhism, Hinduism, Islam, and Judaism in North America is grouped in each chapter for easy access (consult the table of contents to locate a particular religion). In the chapters on religion in Europe and in North America, we have also included sources on atheism and related schools of thought (the religiously non-religious), an important religious community routinely neglected by religious reference books. There is also a chapter of materials on New Religious Movements.

The third section concerns Christianity. Christianity's placement in a separate section is not to be taken as a value judgment on its importance, rather it is the simple acknowledgment that the greatest number of sources in religious studies relate primarily to Christianity and to the many areas of Christian church life. The initial sources cited in this section concern the more general sources on the Christian community and some of the major issues to which it has given attention—the arts, the Bible, ecumenism, ethics, social concerns, theology, worship.

Christian church history, about which numerous reference tools have been created, is covered in a subsection under Christianity. Sources are divided into the large historical eras beginning with Patristics (concerning the age of the Fathers), the Medieval Period, the European Reformation era, and several chapters on the modern period in Europe and North America. Christianity, like other major religious traditions, is divided into various factions usually thought of as denominational families. These denominations are treated separately in a section following the section on church history. The denominations are a particularly important factor in religious studies as they maintain and support the great majority of religious archives and religious resource centers (libraries) in North America.

The final section concerns another large but frequently neglected area of religious life, the psychic, esoteric, and metaphysical world. This neglect grows out of a lingering Christian distrust of the occult which has manifested until quite recently in scholarly circles by an unwillingness to consider the area one of legitimate study. That situation has changed significantly in the last generation as academic associations concerned with the occult have appeared and solid reference tools have been published.

Locating Religious Information Sources

First, it should be noted that every metropolitan area in North America has at least one large collection of religious materials which can be found in the libraries of the seminaries and Bible colleges whose primary purpose is training leaders for a particular religious group. Within many large metropolitan areas one can find a variety of schools oriented around different religious persuasions and thus with libraries that include very different books and materials. In North America, Chicago has the greatest number of seminary and religious libraries; however, seminary complexes can also be found in Boston, New York City, Washington, D.C., Atlanta, Dubuque (Iowa), Dallas-Fort Worth, Denver, and San Francisco-Berkeley.

Almost all of the seminaries of the larger Christian and Jewish groups will have a basic religious reference collection. To find the schools in your neighborhood, look in the yellow pages of the phone book or consult the *Yearbook of American and Canadian Churches*. In addition, most universities, especially those with religious studies departments, will have a representative religious collection that will contain a selection of the source materials listed in this book. Most reference librarians are happy to assist non-university persons with their inquiries.

Types of Information Sources

For each section and chapter of *RIS*, we have tried to anticipate the different kinds of source materials which might be required. In terms of reference books, the most obvious are the encyclopedias and bibliographies. However, we have also sought out guides to periodical literature, biographical dictionaries, atlases, and directories. Those few reference tools which do not fit into these broad categories are listed under "general sources." Where no source materials of a particular type have been located, that section is, of course, left blank.

Besides the printed sources, most areas of concern are blessed with one or more associations of professionals who study that area and consider the theoretical issues it raises for society and culture. There being no readily available central directory listing such organizations, which range from the very comprehensive American Academy of Religion to the more informal Hermetic Studies Association, we have supplied such a listing. In addition, there are numerous centers dedicated to fostering research and study of a particular area of religious research. They are scattered across the continent and, with few exceptions, little known beyond a small circle of specialists. An attempt to locate and list these centers, and apologies to those we did not find, has been made below. Finally, libraries and archival centers which house the collections of materials in specialized areas are also cited below.

The professional associations, research/resources centers, and archival collections are listed in the relevant chapters below just as is the print material. Thus to locate centers for Islamic studies, look in the chapter on Islam, and for centers on ancient Christianity look in the chapter on Patristics.

Finally, each chapter lists any relevant non-print media including microphotography sources (microfilm and microfiche), computer data bases, and CD-ROM discs. This is one of the most rapidly changing areas of source material production.

Reference Books

The most obvious and accessible sources of information are reference books. Their number and scope increase annually, not to mention the new editions that regularly appear of some of the more popular reference books. They include encyclopedias, dictionaries, directories, bibliographies, periodical indices, and biographical directories. For each topic considered below, a comprehensive list of available English-language reference books has been compiled. For many topics an exhaustive list is included below, but for a few, such as the Bible and theology, the list is somewhat selective. Some older books which still contain useful information or have important historical value in the development of an area of study are also listed. Reference books are grouped under five labels.

Encyclopedias and Dictionaries——include those books which attempt to survey a specific area be it the whole field of religion or Shi'a Islam. While ideally encyclopedias and dictionaries serve different functions, in practice they grade into each other in a complex fashion and are difficult to separate. Hence they are listed together.

Biographical Materials——include biographical dictionaries and "Who's Who"-type volumes which offer basic biographical data about individual religious leaders and figures. Biographical dictionaries grade into works of collective biography, but are distinguished by a primary focus upon data and information.

Directories——are an increasingly important reference tool but a type of reference source frequently overlooked in bibliographies of reference material. Such directories allow researchers to locate centers of a particular religious community, stay in touch with colleagues in their field, or learn who is doing work in a related area of interest. The old out-of-date directories become basic source material for sociological analysis and for tracking the progress through time of different organizations.

Bibliographies——are the essential tools for keeping up with the production of new material in various fields of endeavor as the amount of material geometrically increases from year to year and decade to decade (with no sign of slowing down). There is at present no on-going indexing service for religious bibliographies (though many are listed in *Religion Index One*), an obvious need to be filled in the future.

Guides to Periodical Literature——serve to index periodicals and list serials. There are hundreds of scholarly periodicals in religion appearing annually and tens of thousands of religious periodicals. A number of specialized indexing services are available, some covering a particular religious tradition, and others covering selected periodicals from across the field.

Materials not Included in *RIS*

It should be noted that *RIS* attempts to provide in one volume broad coverage of the major sources of information in religion. To accomplish this goal, some boundaries had to be drawn. The first decision was to exclude those general reference books which also gave some coverage to religion. Standard reference books such as the *Book Review Digest*, *Readers Guide to Periodical Literature*, or *Who's Who* give some coverage to religion. Reference books about different countries frequently include a chapter about religion in the area. To include such sources would have tripled the size of this work, without significantly increasing its effectiveness. Readers who need some orientation to such basic secular reference materials might begin with the Gorman's *Theological and Religious Reference Materials* (cited below as item #43).

In like measure, books primarily about languages, especially those languages heavily identified with religious studies such as Hebrew, Coptic, Sanskrit, or Latin, are seen as a separate specialized concern in their own right, and not included in this volume. In like measure some areas tangential to religious studies, such as mythology, were excluded, though the decision to include them in future editions is still open.

Finally, in choosing materials for this volume, the concern has been with information sources rather than religious teaching material. Some books generally thought of as reference books, but which function primarily as religious teaching tools, rather than sources of information about religion and religions, were omitted from consideration. Thus we have deleted any citations to Bible commentaries, concordances, and handbooks. We have also not included history texts concerning any single religion or a group of related religions, though we have included sources to locate such books.

Religious Research

Organizations which focus research on religion are considered in each chapter under three main headings.

Professional Associations—frequently include the most knowledgeable people on any given topic and serve as think tanks for the field. Religion is such a vast field, that numerous such organizations have arisen to focus consideration, study, and dialogue on particular areas of concern. The American Academy of Religion is by far the most comprehensive organization for religious scholars in North America and holds its annual meeting jointly with the Society for Biblical Studies. The sections of the Academy give focus to many areas of religious studies, and a number of organizations not officially associated with the AAR choose to hold their meeting at the same time as the AAR thus taking advantage of the gathering of scholars.

Research/Resource Centers—provide a focus for scholarly research and dialogue often in very specialized areas of concern. They are often related to specialized library and/or archival collections at a college or university, sponsor conferences, and/or publish a journal in the field.

Archival Collections—can be found across North America. Many are often unheralded collections of significant religious resources. Most denominational and religious groups have some kind of archival depository.

The larger denominations will often have several designated centers. While the locations of such archival centers is not a secret, it is also rarely included in denominational profiles and can be some of the most difficult information to uncover.

Compiling *RIS*

The compiling of this *RIS* moved through several phases. An initial list of entries for inclusion was made from the files of the American Religions Collection and the Reference collection of the University of California-Santa Barbara. The University is home to the largest religious studies department at a secular university in the western United States and the University had built one of the most comprehensive religious reference collections in the world. The files of the American Religions Collection include coverage of religious studies centers, organizations, and archives. Its collection is further supplemented by the nearby collection of Roman Catholic materials at St. John's Theological Seminary in Camarillo, California. Travel to conferences during the period the *RIS* was being compiled allowed visits to several significant seminary collections including the libraries of the Southern Baptist Theological Seminary in Louisville, Kentucky; the Graduate Theological Union in Berkeley, California; and the United Library of Garrett-Evangelical and Seabury-Western Theological Seminaries in Evanston, Illinois. Each library had unique material for inclusion in this text, and the seminary libraries greatly assisted the development of the *RIS* on specifically Christian topics.

Acknowledgments

During the years that the Institute for the Study of American Religion has been in Santa Barbara, we have received the unwavering support of the Library of the University of California—Santa Barbara. Joseph Boisse and his staff have aided our staff as we have worked on each of our projects. However, this project required special assistance from the staff of the Reference section, several of whom looked over the manuscript and made suggestions, and read parts of the text before it went to press. For their help we are most grateful.

Second, while compiling this collection, the efforts of many people went into the process of physically assembling the text and checking it for errors. We wish to acknowledge the effort and thank Isotta Poggi, Suzette Parrin Melton, and Elizabeth Pullen for their work on the manuscript. We also wish to thank Ninian Smart, Clark Wade Roof, and Philip Hammond for their looking over sections of the manuscript and making suggestions for improvements.

A Final Note

The authors welcome any suggestion concerning ways to improve this volume and make it a more useful tool, especially information concerning sources which were omitted from the text. We found new sources right up to the day we sent the volume off to the press, and are already creating a file to keep material for a new and improved version if such a effort is warranted. Please send any comments to the Institute for the Study of American Religion, Box 90709, Santa Barbara, California 93190-0709.

J. Gordon Melton
Michael A. Kőszegi
Santa Barbara, November 1991

AN INTRODUCTION TO NON-PRINT RESOURCES IN RELIGION

For most book oriented scholars, the process of dealing with non-print media has been accompanied by increasing levels of pain as new skills are learned and only slowly the potential of microphotography appreciated and the possibilities of the computer explored. Also, at an ever increasing pace, religious data is being stored in various non-print formats, and as they have been encountered, they have been listed by subject in the appropriate chapters throughout this work. Awareness of this new resource began for most as we encountered microfilms of newspapers and other periodicals. Along the way we have probably acquired a personal computer and depending upon our field acquired one or more of the several specialty computer programs developed for religious scholars. By chance we may have used oral history tapes or CD-ROM discs.

The first step in gaining access to the non-print storehouses is a simple mental step: begin to think in terms of looking for non-print sources. In most libraries that step is becoming easier as catalogues are transferred to computers and as one must encounter a video screen in the process of searching for books. Most libraries have CD-ROM readers and a set of discs with various indices and bibliographies and a bank of microfilm and microfiche readers. Below, we shall consider the various categories of non-print resources individually.

Microfilm/Microfiche

Over the past two decades the amount of religious material on microfilm and microfiche has grown in two areas. Among the earliest projects of the American Theological Library Association (ATLA) was the photography of old (nineteenth and early-twentieth century) rare but valuable religious texts and once again making them generally available. The second emphasis was in the microfilming of large archival collections on a single topic generally with the idea of distributing copies to major research libraries. The

Inter Documentation Company of Zug, Switzerland, has become the best known company in the production of such archival collections on microfiche.

University Microfilms, Inc., 300 North Zeeb Road, Ann Arbor, MI 48106 is another of the more important microphotography services, specializing in the publishing and distribution (on microfilm or in hard copy) of doctoral dissertations and master's theses. UMI publishes a separate catalogue in "Religion, Theology and Philosophy" for the years 1980-1988) and in "Religion and Theology" for 1985-1990 which facilitates locating and ordering specific works. TREN (Theological Research Exchange Network), P. O. Box 30183, Portland, OR 97230 provides microfiche copy of dissertations from over 50 schools, primarily conservative Evangelical Christian theological schools, not serviced by University Microfilms.

Discovering what is on microfilm is facilitated by *The Micropublishers Trade List Annual*, published by Chadwyck-Healey, Inc., 1101 King Street, Alexandria, VA 22314. Published on microfiche, the Annual carries the trade catalogue and information brochures of several hundred publishers including the following with specialties in religious materials:

The American Baptist Historical Society
American Theological Library Association
American Jewish Periodical Center
The Institute for the Advanced Studies of World Religions
Scholars Press
Southern Baptist Historical Library and Archives

Inter Documentation Company, whose materials cover the broad range of humanities from art to history to religion has some 15 sets of microfiche on church history, missology, and the Reformation. There are several additional sets on Islam and one important collection on the literature of Freemasonry.

Also helpful in locating materials is the *Guide to Microforms in Print*, which appears in three print volumes (authors, titles and subjects), listing all of the titles available on microfilm and microfiche. The subject volumes include religion as a major heading under which there are a number of subheadings. Materials on microfilm can also be recopied on paper if desired.

Computer Databases

David O. Moberg, a sociologist at Marquette University, pioneered an understanding of computer databases as a source for information useful to religious researchers. In 1970 he distributed a questionnaire to a number of religious agencies concerning their computer systems as they then existed and published the result in 1971 as the *International Directory of Religious Information Systems* (cited below as entry #28), a work badly in need of up-dating. He also led in the founding of ADRIS (Association for the Development of Religious Information Systems) whose newsletter has provided some up-dating of the *Directory* and is an important source of data on religious information systems.

During the 1980s, a number of on-line databases have been developed which individual subscribers can access from their personal computers once they are hooked up through the telephone system by way of a modem. Among the hundreds of such databases, which are listed in the *Directory of Online Databases* (Cuadra/Elsevier, 655 Avenue of the Americas, New York, NY 10010), ten fall under the subject religion. They are:

The ATLA Database (in cooperation with H. W. Wilson Company)
Bible (from Dialogue Information Services)
Catholic News Service
Christian Science Monitor
Credo (from the Centre de Recherches et de Documentation Bibliographique pour l'Antiquite Classique in France)
Francis: Historie et Sciences des Religions
Lutheran News Service
Origins: Catholic Documentary Service
RNS (Religious News Service) Daily News Reports
United Methodist Information

Consult the *Directory* for a brief description and of the various databases.

The ATLA Database contains hundreds of thousands of bibliographical citations and grows by the additions of thousands of new entries each year. The database supports *Religion Index One* (90) and *Religion Index Two* (64), two basic religious indexing services, which are available in a variety of formats, including print and CD-ROM. At various times the database has been tapped for bibliographies on various topics (see subject index under American Theological Library Association).

Among the first items to be placed on computer and made available to users both on floppy discs and through a call-in database was the text of various versions of the Bible and the related concordances. Dialogue Information Services and Thomas Nelson Publishers have made the text of the King James Version available through the database named Bible (see above). Among the growing number of companies offering Bible text software are: American Bible Society, 1865 Broadway, New York 10023 (Good News Version); Biblesoft, 22014 7th Avenue S, Seattle, WA 98198 (includes KJV, NIV, and ASV texts plus concordance); Bible Research Systems, 2013 Wells Branch Parkway, Austin, TX 78728 (KJV, NIV, RSV, NKJV Bible texts); Foundation Press Publications, P. O. Box 6439, Anaheim, CA 92816 (New American Standard bible text). There are a variety of software programs for Bible study, including a whole set of programs in biblical languages.

CD-ROM

CD-ROM (Compact Disc-Read Only Memory) are similar to the CDs which have largely replaced records for music today. CDs allow a significant amount of data to be stored in a compact format which is not subject to magnetic distortion and other disasters which can befall a floppy computer disc. It can be read by any personal computer with a hard drive, sufficient memory (640K), and an auxiliary CD drive unit.

To discover resources on CD-ROM consult *CD-ROMS in Print: An International Guide*, Meckler Publishing, 11 Ferry Lane West, Westport, CT 06880. Possibly the most important resources to appear on disc to date are the four indices from the ATLA Database, *Religion Index One* (90), *Religion Index Two* (64), *Research in Ministry* (1298) and *Index to Book Reviews in Religion* (83).

For Patristics scholars, a significant collection of the writings of the Christian authors of the first 1000 years of the church is offered by Chadwyck-Healey on CD-ROM under the title *Patrologia Latina*.

As with computer software, various biblical texts and related bible study aids are being placed on CD-ROM, though at a much slower pace since the CD-ROM market is still largely limited to libraries. The American Bible Society, 1865 Broadway, New York, NY 10023, has created the *ABS Reference Bible* which includes six complete translations of the English Bible, a Spanish and German text, and a translation of the Greek Septuagint, plus a variety of

Bible aids. which includes Dialogue Information Services and Thomas Nelson Publishers offer the complete King James Version of the Bible on CD-ROM. *The Bible Library*, published by Ellis Enterprises, offers 9 versions of the Bible, 31 concordances, and various study aids, and the FABS Electronic Bible System has 5 versions of the Bible and the related concordances. Check *CD-ROM in Print* for full details on ordering.

Oral History

The popualrity of lightweight cassette tape players and inexpensive cassette tape has undergirded the development of oral history projects and the emergence of oral history as a specialized field. And religious history has been almost a model arena in which to develop oral history collections. By the 1980s numerous oral history projects had been initiated and form collections of oral history material established. In response, Allen Smith of Simmons College in Boston, Massachusetts, established a clearing house for information on such collectons. That effort led to the compiling of the *Directory of Oral History Collections* (Phoenix, NY: Oryx Press, 1988). It includes religion as a subject and describes 22 collections scattered around the United States.

The Future

During the next generation, an increasing amount of reference material will be stored on various forms of non-print media. CD-ROM has shown itself an excellent media for indices, and micro-photography is being increasingly employed to save the content of old books. While books show no sign of being replaced in the educational process, it is quite obvious that the educated person must come to terms with these other forms of information storage. A new generation of scholars, who grew up computer literate will begin to expand creatively our ability to manipulate data and gain some command over an area of research, even nonquatifiable ones. Thus there is every reason to expect a steady stream of new resources on non-print media and monitoring it will become an imporatnt task for the religious studies community.

RELIGIOUS INFORMATION SOURCES: A WORLDWIDE GUIDE

I

RELIGION: GENERAL AND THEORETICAL CONSIDERATIONS

RELIGION: GENERAL SOURCES

Slowly, beginning in the nineteenth century, the field of comparative religion emerged to study the very different religious communities which the West encountered as the colonial empires spread to Africa, Asia, and the South Pacific. By the middle of the twentieth century, that field, as had every other in the theological schools, had changed, divided, and subdivided and it began to emerge as a new more self-conscious discipline: religious studies. A field still very much engaged in the process of self-definition and differentiation from the quest of the theological community, religious studies defines itself as the academic study of religion apart from the religious commitment so inherent in the theological quest. In practice, the border between theological studies and religious studies is very ill-defined and scholars who primarily identify themselves with "religious studies" and those who teach in theological schools pursue a parallel research agenda.

This first chapter concerns itself with the basic materials and tools produced by religious studies which summarize the finding of the last century, and with the organizations which have been founded to focus the work of the field. A careful scanning of this chapter should provide anyone with some idea of the basic information sources which attempt coverage of the field of religion. Highlighting the material in this chapter is *The Encyclopedia of Religion* (8). Mircea Eliade capped his fruitful career by compiling *The Encyclopedia of Religion*, destined to provide guidance for the entire field for the next generation, much as Schaff's *Encyclopedia* (21) did in previous decades.

Contemporary religious and theological studies is very much aided by the creation of a standard set of reference/index volumes, most notably *Religion Index One* (90) and the *Mosher Periodical Index* (87), which index the major religious periodicals, and *Religion Index Two* (62, 64), which indexes festschriften and other multi-author books.

As will be seen throughout this work, bibliographical control of religious literature has expanded during the last two decades to keep pace with the geometric expansion in the number of titles appearing annually. In regard to reference and tool books, special mention should be made of G. E. and Lyn Gorman's immense effort to compile a exhaustive bibliography of reference works in religion (43), most useful for its coverage of secular works with religious data and Christian sources.

The Nature of Religion: General Sources

These several textbooks deal with the basic question of "What Is Religion?" and survey both a variety of answers to that question and the host of proposed methodologies for shaping a response.

1. Capps, Walter H. *Ways of Understanding Religion.* New York: Macmillan Company, 1971. 399 pp.

2. Ramsey, Paul, ed. *Religion.* Englewood Cliffs, NJ: Prentice-Hall, 1965. 468 pp.

3. "The Santa Barbara Colloquy: Religion within the Limits of Reason Alone." Special issue of *Soundings: An Interdisciplinary Journal* 71, 2-3 (Summer/Fall 1988): 420 pp.

Encyclopedias and Dictionaries

Books in this section attempt to provide comprehensive coverage of the field of religion and as such they grade into the surveys of world religion to be found below in the next chapter.

4. Askmark, Ragnar, et al., eds. *Nordisk teologisk upplagsbok för kyrka och skola.* 3 vols. Lund, Sweden: Cleerup/Copenhagen, Denmark: Munksgaard, 1952-57.

5. Bertholet, Alfred. *Wörterbuch der Religionen.* Stuttgart: Alfred Kröner Verlag, 1952. 532 pp.

6. Bomberger, J. H. A., trans. *The Protestant Theological and Ecclesiastical Encyclopedia: Being a Condensed Translation of Herzog's Real Encyclopedia.* 2 vols. Philadelphia: Lindsay and Blakiston, 1958, 1860. See also: Herzog (13) and Schaff (21).

7. Douglas, J. D. *New Twentieth Century Encyclopedia of Religious Knowledge.* Grand Rapids, MI: Baker Book House, 1955. Rev. ed.: 1991. 864 pp.

8. Eliade, Mircea, ed. *The Encyclopedia of Religion.* 16 vols. New York: Macmillan Publishing Co., 1987.

9. *Enciclopedia delle Religioni.* 2 vols. Firenze, Italy: Vallecchi editore, 1970.

10. Ferm, Vergilius. *An Encyclopedia of Religion.* New York: Philosophical Library, 1945. 844 pp.

11. Galling, Kurt. *Die Religion in Geschichte und Gegenwart.* 1909-1913. Rev. ed.: 7 vols. Tübingen, Germany: Mohr, 1957-65.

12. Hastings, James (ed.). *Encyclopedia of Religion and Ethics.* 13 vols. New York: Charles Scribner's Sons, 1928.

13. Herzog, Johann Jacob. *Real-encyklopädie für Protestantische Theologie und Kirche.* 22 vols. Hamburg, Germany: R. Besser, 1854-68. 2nd ed.: 18 vol. Leipzig: J. C. Hinrichs, 1877-88. 3rd ed. 24 vols. Leipzig: J. C. Hinrichs, 1896-1913. *See also:* Bomberger (6), Schaff (21), Jackson (14, 24), and Loetscher (16).

14. Jackson, Samuel Macauley, ed. *The New Schaff-Herzog Encyclopedia of Religious Knowledge.* 13 vols. New York: Funk & Wagnalls, 1908-14. Rept.: 13 vols. Grand Rapids, MI: Baker Book House, 1949-50. Rept.: 1951-57. *See also:* Loetscher (16) and Jackson (24).

15. Kennedy, Richard. *International Dictionary of Religion.* New York: Crossroad, 1984. 256 pp.

16. Loetscher, Lefferts A., ed. *Twentieth Century Encyclopedia of Religious Knowledge: An Extension of the New Schaff-Herzog Encyclopedia of Religious Knowledge.* 2 vols. Grand Rapids, MI: Baker Book House, 1955. 1205 pp.

17. MacGregor, Geddes. *Dictionary of Religion and Philosophy.* New York: Paragon House, 1989. 696 pp.

18. Matthews, Boris, trans. *The Herder Symbol Dictionary: Symbols from Art, Archeology, Mythology, Literature, and Religion.* Wilmette, IL: Chiron Publications, 1986. 222 pp. Translation of *Herder Lexikon: Symbole.*

19. Matthews, Shailer, and Gerald Bierney Smith. *A Dictionary of Religion and Ethics.* New York: Macmillan Company, 1923. 513 pp. Rept.: Grand Rapids, MI: Baker Book House, 1960. 513 pp.

20. Meagher, Paul Kevin, Thomas C. O'Brien, and Consuelo Maria Aherne. *Encyclopedic Dictionary of Religion.* 3 vols. Washington, DC: Corpus Publications, 1979.

21. Schaff, Philip, ed. *A Religious Encyclopedia: or, Dictionary of Biblical, Historical, Doctrinal, and Practical Theology. Based on the Real-encyklopädie of Herzog.* 3 vols. New York: Funk & Wagnalls, 1882-83. 2nd ed.: 3 vols. 1882-84. 3rd ed., revised and enlarged: 3 vols. 1882-84. Rept. as: *New Schaff-Herzog Encyclopedia of Religious Knowledge.* 4 vols. New York: Funk & Wagnalls, 1891. With supplement: Jackson, S. M., ed. *Encyclopedia of Living Divines and Christian Workers of All Denominations in Europe and America. See also:* Herzog (13) and Jackson (14).

22. Schwertner, Siegfried. *Internationales Abkürzungsverzeichnis für Theologie und Grenzgebiete: Zeitschriften, Serien, Lexica, Quellenwerke mit bibliographischen Angaben.* [International Glossary of Abbreviations for Theology and Related Subjects]. Berlin, Germany: W. de Gruyter, 1974. 348 pp.

23. Warshaw, Thayer S. *Abingdon Glossary of Religious Terms.* Nashville, TN: Abingdon, 1978. 94 pp.

Biographical Volumes

24. Jackson, Samuel Macauley, ed. *Encyclopedia of Living Divines and Christian Workers of All Denominations in Europe and America; Being a Supplement to the Schaff-Herzog Encyclopedia of Religious Knowledge.* New York: Funk and Wagnalls, 1887. Rev. ed.: 1891. 296 pp. [Revised edition bound with volume 4 of the *New Schaff-Herzog Encyclopedia of Religious Knowledge.*] Rept.: 1894.

25. *Who's Who in Religion.* Chicago: Marquis Who's Who, 1975. 616 pp. Rev. ed.: 1977. 736 pp. Rev. ed.: 1985. 439 pp.

Directories

26. *Book Publishers in the Field of Religion.* RIC Supplements 50-52. Strasbourg, France: Cerdic-Publications, 1980. 125 pp.

27. *Directory of Religious Publishers.* Vol. 1- . Boston: Jarrow Press, 1974- . Annual.

28. Moberg, David O., ed. *International Directory of Religious Information Systems.* Milwaukee, WI: Marquette University, Department of Sociology and Anthropology, 1971. 88 pp.

Bibliographies

The bibliographies and guides to periodical literature immediately below are the basic working tools for religious research and studies. They provide the most general and practical access to the broad range of religious scholarship during the twentieth century. The various religious indices, along with the specialized indices on specific topics, cover the ongoing discussions of the vast array of religious topics.

In this regard, special mention should be made of the American Theological Library Association, which has during the several decades of its existence done yeoman service in providing bibliographic control of the ever-growing body of religious literature. Their contributions, including their sponsorship of microfilming, indexing and bibliographic projects, are cited throughout this volume.

29. *Alphabetical Arrangement of the Main Entries from the Shelf List.* Union Theological Seminary, New York City. 10 vols. Boston: G.K. Hall, 1960.

30. Barrows, John G. *A Bibliography of Bibliographies in Religion.* Ann Arbor, MI: Edward Brothers, 1955. 489 pp. This classic bibliographical work is based on Barrow's Ph.D. dissertation, Yale, 1930.

31. *Bibliographie zur altereuropäischen Religionsgeschichte.* 2 vols. Berlin, Germany: W. de Gruyter, 1967-74.

32. *Book Reviews of the Month: An Index to Reviews Appearing in Selected Theological Journals.* Vol. 1- . Ft. Worth, TX: Roberts Library, Southwestern Theological Seminary, 1962- . Monthly.

33. Boyde, George N. *Religion in Contemporary Fiction: Criticism from 1945 to the Present.* San Antonio, TX: Trinity University Press, 1973. 99 pp.

34. Cornish, Graham P. *A Brief Guide to Abstracting and Indexing Services Relevant to the Study of Religion.* Harrogate: Abstracting and Bibliographical Services, 1975.

35. Council on Graduate Studies in Religion. *Dissertation Title Index.* New York: Columbia University Press for the Council on Graduate Studies in Religion, 1952- . Annual. Originally entitled *Doctoral Dissertations in the Field of Religion.*

36. *Critical Review of Books in Religion.* Vol. 1- . Journal of The American Academy of Religion and the Journal of Biblical Literature, 1988- . Annual.

37. Desmarais, Norman. *Basic Resources for Studying Theology.* Baltimore, MD: St. Mary's Seminary and University, 1979. 93 pp.

38. Diehl, Katherine Smith. *Religions, Mythologies, Folklores: An Annotated Bibliography.* 1956. 2nd ed.: New York: Scarecrow Press, 1962. 573 pp.

39. *Doctoral Dissertations in the Field of Religion, 1889-1932.* American Church History Seminars, No. 1. Washington, DC: Catholic University of America, 1933.

40. *Doctoral Dissertations in the Field of Religion, 1940-1952.* New York: Columbia University Press, 1954. For the Council on Graduate Studies in Religion. Supplement to *Review of Religion* 18 (1954). 194 pp. *See also:* (26)

41. Freudenberger, Elsie. *Reference Works in the Field of Religion, 1977-1985: A Selective Bibliography.* Haverford, PA: Catholic Library Association, 1986. 65 pp.

42. Goodland, Roger. *A Bibliography of Sex Rites and Customs: An Annotated Record of Books, Arts, and Illustrations in All Languages.* London: George Routledge & Sons, 1931. 752 pp.

43. Gorman, G.E., and Lyn Gorman. *Theological and Religious Reference Materials.* 3 vols. Bibliographies and Indexes in Religious Studies Nos. 1,2, & 7. Westport, CT: Greenwood Press, 1984-1986.

44. Guru Nanak University Library. *Religion: A Select Bibliography.* Amritsar: Guru Nanak University Library, 1972. 257 pp.

45. Johnson, Alfred M., Jr., comp. *Bibliography of Semiological and Structural Studies of Religion.* Pittsburgh, PA: Pittsburgh Theological Seminary, 1979. 146 pp.

46. Jordan, Louis Henry. *Comparative Religion: Its Adjuncts and Allies.* London, etc.: Oxford University Press, 1915. 574 pp.

47. ———. *Comparative Religion: A Survey of Its Recent Literature. 2nd Section 1906-1909.* Edinburgh: Otto Schulze & Co., 1910. 72 pp.

48. Karpinski, Leszek M. *The Religious Life of Man: Guide to Basic Literature.* Metuchen, NJ: Scarecrow Press, 1978. 399 pp.

49. ———. *Religious Studies Without Tears Part I: Religions of Mankind.* Reference Publication No. 44. Vancouver: University of British Columbia Library, 1973. 57 pp.

50. ———. *Religious Studies Without Tears Part II: Primitive Religion, Religions of the Past.* Reference Publication No. 45. Vancouver: University of British Columbia Library, 1974. 179 pp.

51. ————. *Religious Studies Without Tears Part III: Judaism, Christianity, Gnosticism, Biblical Studies, Islamic Studies.* Reference Publication No. 46. Vancouver: University of British Columbia Library, 1974. 179 pp.

52. ————. *Religious Studies Without Tears Part IV: Asian Religions.* Reference Publication No. 47. Vancouver: University of British Columbia Library, 1975. 118 pp.

53. Kennedy, James R. *Library Research Guide to Religion and Theology: Illustrated Search Strategy and Sources.* Ann Arbor, MI: Pieran Press, 1974. 53 pp. 2nd ed.: 1984. 58 pp.

54. La Noue, George R., ed. *A Bibliography of Doctoral Dissertations Undertaken in American and Canadian Universities, 1940-1962 on Religion and Politics.* New York: National Council of Churches of Christ, 1963. 49 pp.

55. Library Association, County Libraries Group. *Readers' Guide to Books on Religion.* 2nd ed. Comp. by Robert Duckett. Readers' Guides, New Series No, 135. London: Library Association, 1974. 105 pp.

56. *List of Microfilms Available.* Rev. ed.: New Haven, CT: American Theological Library Association, 1971. 38 pp. Rev. ed.: Princeton, NJ: ATLA Board of Microtext, 1981.

57. Mitros, Joseph F. *Religions: A Select, Classified Bibliography.* Philosophical Questions Series 8. New York: Learned Publications/Louvain: Nauwelaerts, 1973. 435 pp.

58. *Monographs on Microfiche/Serials on Microfilm.* Evanston, IL: American Theological Library Association, 1991. 877 pp. This catalogue is a major product of the PREFIR program (Preservation Filming in Religion) begun in 1955.

59. National Library Service for the Blind and Physically Handicapped. *Religion: A Selected List of Books That Have Appeared in Talking Book Topics and Braille Book Review.* Washington, DC: Library of Congress, 1979. 68 pp.

60. ————. *Religion and Inspiration.* Washington, DC: Library of Congress, 1987. 87 pp.

61. O'Brien, Betty Alice, and Elmer John O'Brien, comps. *Bibliography of Festschriften in Religion Published Since 1960: A Preliminary Checklist.* Rev. ed. Dayton, OH: United Theological Seminary Library, 1973. 111 pp.

62. ————. *Religion Index Two: Festschriften 1960-69.* American Theological Library Association, 1980. 741 pp.

63. Pearl, Patricia. *Children's Religious Books: An Annotated Bibliography.* New York: Garland Publishing, 1988. 316 pp.

64. *Religion Index Two: Multi-Author Works.* 2 vol. G. Fay Dickerson and Ernest Rubinstein, eds. Chicago: American Theological Library Association, 1982.

65. *Religious and Inspirational Books & Series in Print 1987.* New York & London: R.R. Bowker, 1987. 1826 pp.

66. *Religious Books, 1876-1982.* 4 vols. New York: R.R. Bowker, 1983.

67. *Religious Books and Serials in Print.* New York: R.R. Bowker, 1978- . Irregular.

68. *Religious Reading: The Annual Guide.* Vol. 1- . Wilmington, NC: Consortium Books, 1973- . Annual.

69. *Religious Studies Review: A Quarterly Review of Publications in the Field of Religion and Related Disciplines.* Vol. 1- . 1975- . Macon, GA: Council of Societies for the Study of Religion. Quarterly.

70. Sayre, John L. *Tools for Theological Research.* Enid, OK: 1972. 39 pp. 8th ed.: Enid, OK: Seminary Press, 1989. 130 pp.

71. ———, and Roberta Hamburger. *An Index of Festschriften in Religion.* Enid, OK: Seminary Press, 1970. 121 pp. Supplement: *New Titles, 1971-73.* 1973. 136 pp.

72. *The Shelf List of the Union Theological Seminary Library in New York City, in Classification Order.* 10 vols. Boston: G. K. Hall, 1960.

73. Sonne, Niels H., ed. *A Bibliography of Post-Graduate Masters' Theses in Religion (Accepted by American Theological Seminaries).* Chicago: American Theological Library Association, 1951. 82 pp.

74. Trotti, John. *Aids to a Theological Library.* Missoula, MT: Scholars Press, for the American Theological Library Association, 1977. 69 pp.

75. *Union Catalog of the Graduate Theological Union Library.* 15 Vols. Berkeley, CA: Graduate Theological Union, 1972.

76. Walsh, Michael J., comp. *Religious Bibliographies in Serial Literature: A Guide.* Westport, CT: Greenwood Press, 1981. 216 pp.

77. Wilson, John F., and Thomas P. Slavens. *Research Guide to Religious Studies.* Chicago: American Library Association, 1982. 192 pp.

Guides to Periodical Literature

78. Cornish, Graham, ed. *Religious Periodicals Directory.* Santa Barbara, CA & Oxford: ABC-Clio, 1986. 330 pp.

79. Dawsey, James. *A Scholar's Guide to Academic Journals in Religion.* ATLA Bibliography Series No. 23. Metuchen, NJ & London: Scarecrow Press, 1988. 290 pp.

80. "Elenchus Bibliographicus." Appears as section of *Ephemerides Theologicae Lovanienses.* Vol. 1- . Leuven: Vitgeverij Peeters/Leuven University Press, 1924- . Irregular.

81. Fieg, Eugene C., Jr., comp. *Religion Journals and Serials: An Analytical Guide.* New York: Greenwood Press, 1988. 218 pp.

82. *Guide to Religious Periodical Literature.* Vol. 1- . Birmingham, England: Birmingham Public Libraries, 1975- . Bimonthly.

83. *Index to Book Reviews in Religion.* Vol. 1- Chicago: American Theological Library Association, 1986- . Bimonthly with annual accumulations.

84. *Index to Religious Periodical Literature: An Author and Subject Index to Periodical Literature Including an Author Index of Book Reviews.* 13 vols. Chicago, IL: American Theological Library Association, 1953-1977. In 1977 title changed to *Religion One.* See (90)

85. *International Bibliography of the History of Religions.* 23 vols. Leiden: E.J. Brill, for the International Association for the History of Religions. 1954-1979. Annual. Superseded by *Science of Religion* (94).

86. Kirkpatrick, L.H., ed. *A Study and Evaluation of Religious Periodical Indexing.* Syracuse, NY: ERIC Clearinghouse on Information Resources, 1978.

87. *Mosher Periodical Index.* Vol. 1- . Dallas, TX: Mosher Library, Dallas Theological Seminary, 1969- . Originally entitled: *Subject Index to Select Periodicals.*

88. Regazzi, John J., and Theodore C. Hines. *A Guide to Indexed Periodicals in Religion.* Metuchen, NJ: Scarecrow Press, 1975. 328 pp.

89. *Religious and Theological Abstracts.* Vol. 1- . Myerstown, PA: Religious & Theological Abstracts, Inc., 1958- .

90. *Religion Index One: Periodicals: A Subject Index to Periodical Literature Including an Author Index with Abstracts and a Book Review Index.* G. Fay Dickerson and John A. Peltz, eds. Chicago: American Theological Library Association, 1979-. Vols. 13-. Vols. 1-12 as *Index to Religious Periodical Literature.* Semiannual with annual cumulations.

91. *Religious Periodicals Index: A Quarterly Index of the Major Religious Periodicals in America.* Vol. 1- . New York: Jarrow Press, 1970- . Quarterly.

92. Richardson, Ernest Cushing, comp. & ed. *An Alphabetical Subject Index and Index Encyclopedia to Periodical Articles on Religion 1890-1899.* 2 vols. New York: Charles Scribner's Sons/London: G.E. Stechert & Co., 1907. 1168 pp.

93. ————. *Periodical Articles on Religion 1890-1899: Author Index.* New York: Charles Scribner's Sons/London: G.E. Stechert & Co., 1911. 876 pp.

94. *Science of Religion: Abstracts and Index of Recent Articles.* Vol. 1- . Amsterdam: Free University, Institute for the Study of Religion/Leeds: University of Leeds, Department of Theology and Religious Studies, 1976- . In 1980 *Science of Religion* absorbed and continued the *International Bibliography of the History of Religions.*

Atlases

95. al-Faruqi, Isma'il Ragial and David E. Sopher. *Historical Atlas of the Religions of the World.* New York: Macmillan Company, 1974. 346 pp.

96. Hawes, Gordon K. *Atlas of Man and Religion.* New York: Religious Education Press, 1970. 127 pp.

RELIGIOUS STUDIES

The emerging field of religious studies promotes the study of religious phenomena and, above and beyond its primary home in the faculties of colleges and universities, has spawned a number of research centers and professional societies that focus discussion of vital issues. Present as the field emerged was the discipline of "history of religions" which had a primary focus on world religions. In more recent decades separate fields of inquiry have assumed a prominent position in the field as religious scholars have interacted with philosophers, psychologists, sociologists and scientists.

Directories

97. *Graduate Studies in Religion.* Waterloo, ON: Published for the Council on Graduate Studies in Religion by the Council on the Study of Religion, 1982. 63 pp.

98. Mills, Watson E. *Council of Societies for the Study of Religion Directory of Departments and Programs of Religious Studies in North America.* 1989 ed. Macon, GA: CSSR, 1989. 464 pp. Periodically updated.

99. ———. *Council of Societies for the Study of Religion Directory of Faculty of Departments and Programs of Religious Studies in North America.* 1988 ed. Macon, GA: CSSR, 1988. 622 pp. Periodically updated.

Professional Associations

American Academy of Religion
c/o Scholars Press
P. O. Box 1608
Decatur, GA 30031-1608
The American Academy of Religion is the major professional organization for North

American scholars in the area of religion. It publishes a quarterly journal, *The Journal of the American Academy of Religion*, and two periodicals serving the membership, *Religious Studies News* and *OPENINGS: Job Opportunities for Scholars of Religion.* The archives of the AAR are located at Ira J. Taylor Library, Illif School of Theology, 2201 S. University Blvd., Denver, CO 80210.

American Society for the Study of Religion
c/o Department of Religious Studies
Rice University
Houston, TX 77001

Association for Religion and Intellectual Life
c/o Nancy M. Malone, O.S.U.
College of New Rochelle
New Rochelle, NY 10801
The Association sponsors *Cross Currents: Religion and the Intellectual Life.* Founded in 1950 by a group of Roman Catholics, it attempts to establish dialogue between religion and the contemporary world.

***La Communidad* of Hispanic American Scholars of Theology and Religion**
475 Riverside Drive, Ste. 832
New York, NY 10115-0008

Council of Societies for the Study of Religion
CSSR Executive Office
Mercer University
Macon, GA 31207
The Council publishes *Religious Studies Review* and the *Bulletin of the CSSR.*

Council on Graduate Studies in Religion
c/o Prof. J. Kenneth Kuntz, Sec./Treas.
School of Religion
University of Iowa
Iowa City, IA 52242

Council on Religion and International Affairs
170 East 64th Street
New York, NY 10021
The Council publishes *Disarmament News & International Views.*

Foundation for Religious and Educational Exchange, Inc.
Eastern Baptist Theological Seminary
Lancaster and Cuty Avenues
Philadelphia, PA 19151

International Association for the History of Religions
c/o ANZ Religious Publications
RFD No. 1, Box 171
Canterbury, NH 03224

International Religious Foundation
GPO Box 1311
New York, NY 10116
The Foundation is one of several organizations sponsored by the Unification Church, which promotes dialogue on religious issues of international relevance.

Korean Society for Religious Studies in North America
P. O. Box 8241
University Station
Grand Forks, ND 58202

Network for the Study of Implicit Religion
58 High Street
Winterbourne
Bristol BS17 IJQ, UK

North American Association for the Study of Religion
c/o Luther H. Martin
Department of Religion
University of Vermont
481 Main Street
Burlington, VT 05405

Research Group in the Sciences of Religion
Laval University
Cite universitaire
Quebec, PQ
Canada G1K 7P4
The Group supports research in the history, sociology and psychology of religion.

Centers and Research Facilities

Center for Religious Studies
University of Toronto
130 St. George Street
14th Floor, Room 14335
Toronto, ON M5S 1A1
The Center publishes *Toronto Studies in Religion.*

Center for the Study of Religion and American Culture
425 University Blvd., Room 344
Indianapolis, IN 46202-5140
The Center publishes *Religion and American Culture* and *News from the Center for the Study of Religion and American Culture.*

Center for the Study of Southern Culture and Religion
236 Williams Building
Florida State University
Tallahassee, FL 32306
The Center publishes the *Bulletin of the CSSCR*

Center for the Study of World Religions
Harvard University
42 Francis Avenue
Cambridge, MA 02138

Dharma Research Association
Centre for the Study of World Religions
Dharmaram College
Bangalore 560 029, India
The Centre publishes the *Journal of Dharma.*

Institute for Advanced Studies of World Religions
2150 Center Avenue
Fort Lee, NJ 07024
Cable: INASWOREL
or
Melville Memorial Library
State University of New York
Stony Brook, New York 11794
An independent center, the Institute houses a 72,000+ volume library and publishes a series of bibliographic monographs. The Center publishes *Asian Religious Studies Information*

Institute for the Advanced Study of Religion
University of Chicago
Swift Hall
1025 East 58th Street
Chicago, IL 60637

Institute for the Study of American Religion
Box 90709
Santa Barbara, CA 93190-0709

Institute of Religion
P. O. Box 20569
Houston, TX 77225

Instituut voor Godsdienstwetenschap
(Institute for the Study of Religion)
Vrije Universiteit
de Boelelaan 1105
1081 HV Amsterdam, the Netherlands
The Institute publishes the *Science of Religion Abstracts and Index of Recent Articles*, for the International Association for the History of Religions.

James A. Blaisdell Programs in World Religions and Cultures
Harper Hall 14
The Claremont Graduate School
Claremont, CA 91711

Louis Finkelstein Institute for Religious and Social Studies
Jewish Theological Seminary
3080 Broadway
New York, NY 10027
The Institute is described as an interfaith (Jewish/Christian) think tank focused upon religious issues seen to impact society and the larger religious community.

Nanzan Institute for Religion and Culture
18, yamazato-cho
Showa-ku
nagoya 466, Japan
The Institute publishes the quarterly, *Japanese Journal of Religious Studies.*

Riverdale Center for Religious Research
5801 Palisade Avenue
Bronx, NY 10471
Founded in 1970, the Center specializes in research on Earth-Human relationships.

PHILOSOPHY OF RELIGION

The interaction with philosophy has constituted an important part of theological endeavor over the centuries and theologians are expected to be somewhat conversant in philosophical concerns. The growth of large bodies of specialized knowledge in the twentieth century, however, has undergirded the development of "philosophy of religion" as a specialized sub-discipline within religious studies.

Encyclopedias and Dictionaries

100. Baldwin, James Mark, ed. *Dictionary of Philosophy and Psychology, Including Many of the Principal Conceptions of Ethics, Logic, Aesthetics, Philosophy of Religion, etc.*. New ed. 3 vols. in 4. New York: Macmillan, 1925. Rept.: Gloucester, MA: Peter Smith, 1949-1957.

101. Reese, W. L. *Dictionary of Philosophy and Religion: Eastern and Western Thought.* Atlantic Highlands, NJ: Humanities Press, 1980. 644 pp.

102. Wuellner, Berard. *A Dictionary of Scholastic Philosophy.* 2nd ed. Milwaukee, WI: Bruce Publishing Co., 1956. 138 pp. Rev. ed.: 1966. 339 pp.

Bibliographies

103. McLean, George F., ed. *An Annotated Bibliography of Philosophy in Catholic Thought 1900-1964.* Philosophy in the 20th Century: Catholic and Christian Vol. 1. New York: Frederick Unger Publishing Co., 1967. 371 pp.

104. ———. *A Bibliography of Christian Philosophy and Contemporary Issues.* New York: Frederick Unger Publishing Co., 1967. 312 pp.

105. Sandeen, Ernest R., and Frederick Hale. *American Religion and Philosophy: A Guide to Information Sources.* Detroit, MI: Gale Research Company, 1978. 377 pp.

106. Wainwright, William J. *Philosophy of Religion: An Annotated Bibliography of Twentieth-Century Writings in English.* New York: Garland Publishing, 1978. 776 pp.

Professional Associations and Research Centers

American Catholic Philosophical Society
c/o Department of Philosophy
Catholic University of America
Washington, DC 20064
The Society publishes a quarterly journal, *The New Scholasticism,* and an annual *Proceedings.*

Center for Philosophy of Religion
University of Notre Dame
330 Decio Hall
P. O. Box 1968
Notre Dame, IN 46556
The Center, founded in 1976, sponsors two conferences annually.

Evangelical Philosophical Society
c/o Dr. David K. Clark
Toccoa Falls College
Toccoa Falls, GA 30598

Institute for Philosophy and Religion
Boston University
745 Commonwealth Avenue, Room 523
Boston, MA 02215
The Institute, founded in 1970, sponsors an annual lecture series, the articles from which are published in the *Boston University Studies in Philosophy and Religion.*

International Society for the Study of Human Ideas on Ultimate Reality and Meaning
c/o Walter B. Gulick
Philosophy, Humanities & Religious Studies
Western Montana College
Billings, MT 59101

Jesuit Philosophical Association of the United States and Canada
c/o Rev. Harry J. Gensler
Loyola University
6525 N. Sheridan Road
Chicago, IL 60626

Society for Philosophy of Religion
c/o Frank R. Harrison III
Dept. of Philosophy of Religion
Peabody Hall
University of Georgia
Athens, GA 30602
The Society sponsors the *International Journal for Philosophy of Religion*.

Society for the Study of Human Ideas on Ultimate Reality and Meaning
Institute for Ultimate Reality and Meaning
c/o Dr. Tibor Horvath
Regis College
14 St. Mary Street
Toronto, ON M4Y 2R5

Society of Christian Philosophy
c/o Janine Marie Idziak
Box 936
Locas College
Dubuque, IA 52004

PSYCHOLOGY OF RELIGION

The interaction of psychology, especially its medical branch, psychiatry, with religion has been a major item on the scholarly agenda in the twentieth century. It has become somewhat critical because of a deep-seated animosity which exists between the two fields, partly the result of psychology's struggle to free itself from religion in order to become a mature discipline. While the two disciplines still frequently compete in their attempts to understand and explain human activity, many attempts have been made to bring the two fields into an agreeable relationship.

The theological discussion of psychology grows in large part out of the clinical situation and the religious concerns usually placed under the heading of pastoral counseling. At best, the line between the more academic discussion of the relation of psychology and religion and the application of psychology in pastoral situations is vague, but below some attempt has been made to separate them. This chapter is concerned with the more abstract discussion of the relation of psychology and religion. A later chapter on the Ministry includes a subchapter on Pastoral Counseling, which covers the more clinical appropriation of psychology by the religious community.

Biographical Volumes

107. Misiak, Henryk, and Virginia M. Staudt. *Catholics in Psychology: An Historical Survey.* New York: McGraw-Hill, 1954. 309 pp.

Directories

108. Klausner, Samuel Z. *Preliminary Annotated Bibliography and Directory of Workers in the Field of Religion and Psychiatry.* New York: Columbia University, Bureau of Applied Social Research, 1958. 250 pp.

Bibliographies

109. Alpert, Nancy L. *Religion and Psychology: A Medical Subject Analysis and Research Index with Bibliography.* Washington, DC: Abbe Publishers Association, 1985. 146 pp.

110. Beit-Hallahmi, Benjamin. *Psychoanalysis and Religion: A Bibliography.* Norwood, PA: Norwood Editions, 1978. 182 pp.

111. Capps, Donald, Louis Rambo, and Paul Ransohoff. *Psychology of Religion: A Guide to Information Sources.* Detroit: Gale Research Company, 1976. 352 pp.

112. Caputi, Natalino. *Unconscious: A Guide to Sources.* ATLA Bibliography Series No. 16. Metuchen, NJ: Scarecrow Press, 1985. 151 pp.

113. Cronbach, Abraham. "The Psychology of Religion: A Bibliographical Survey." *Psychological Bulletin* 25 (1926): 701-13.

114. ———. *Preliminary Bibliography of Religion and Psychiatry.* New York: Columbia University, Bureau of Applied Social Research, 1957. Supple. as: *Supplementary Bibliography of Religion and Psychiatry.* New York: Columbia University, Bureau of Applied Social Research, 1958.

115. Dalkey, Barbara Jeskalian. *Religion and Depth Psychology: A Selected Bibliography.* San Jose, CA: San Jose State University Library, 1977. 15 pp.

116. Hiltner, Seward. "A Selected Bibliography on Christian Faith and Health." *Pastoral Psychology* 12 (January 1962): 27-38.

117. Hurd, Albert E., ed. *Psychology and Religion: A Bibliography Selected from the ATLA Religion Data Base.* Evanston, IL: American Theological Library Association, 1986. Unpaged.

118. Lesh, Terry V. "Zen and Psychotherapy: A Partially Annotated Bibliography." *Journal of Humanistic Psychology* 10 (Spring 1970): 75-83.

119. Meissner, William W. *Annotated Bibliography in Religion and Psychology.* New York: Academy of Religion and Mental Health, 1961. 235 pp.

120. Menges, Robert J., and James E. Dittes. *Psychological Studies of Clergymen: Abstracts of Research.* New York: Thomas Nelson and Sons, 1965. 202 pp.

121. National Clearinghouse for Mental Health Information. *Bibliography on Religion and Mental Health, 1960-1964.* Public Health Service Publications No. 1599.

Washington, DC: Department of Health, Education and Welfare, Public Health Service, 1967. 106 pp.

122. Summerlin, Florence A. *Religion and Mental Health: A Bibliography.* Rockville, MD: National Institutes of Mental Health, 1980. 401 pp.

123. Van Dyke, Paul, II, and John Pierce-Jones. "The Psychology of Religion of Middle and Late Adolescence: A Review of Empirical Research, 1950-1960." *Religious Education* 58 (1963): 529-37.

124. Vande Kempe, Hendrika, and H. Newton Maloney. *Psychology and Religion: A Bibliography of Historical Bases for the Integration of Psychology and Theology.* Millwood, NY: Kraus International Publications, 1982.

125. ———. *Psychology and Theology in Western Thought, 1672-1965: A Historical and Annotated Bibliography.* Millwood, NY: Kraus International Publications, 1984. 367 pp.

Psychology of Religion Studies

American Catholic Psychological Association
c/o American Psychological Association
1200 17th Street, N.W.
Washington, DC 20036

National Guild of Catholic Psychiatrists
1211 Boulevard
Seaside Park, NJ 08752

Psychologists Interested in Religion
c/o American Psychological Association, Division 36
1200 Seventeenth Street, N.W
Washington, DC 20036
(202) 955-7600

SCIENCE AND RELIGION

The interplay between science and religion, especially the attacks of science upon some widely held religious beliefs, has had a determinative role in the development of the religious community in the twentieth century. That part of the community which has accepted the critique has moved on to a vital continuing dialogue with science as it continued its discoveries. Of continuing interest, however, is the segment which rejected the critique of science and has attempted to stand firm in its affirmation of special creation as opposed to the process of evolution as the means of humanity coming into existence. Interestingly enough, a significant part of the science-religion debate as the twentieth century closes still centers upon what many had thought was a dead issue.

Bibliographies

126. Brooks, Richard S. *The Interplay between Science and Religion in England, 1640-1720: A Bibliographical and Historical Guide.* Garrett-Evanston Bibliographic Lectures No. 10. Evanston, IL: Garrett-Evangelical Theological Seminary Library, 1975. 145 pp.

127. Eisen, Sydney, and Bernard V. Lightman. *Victorian Science and Religion: A Bibliography with Emphasis on Evolution, Belief, and Unbelief, Comprised of Works Published from c. 1900-1975.* Hamden, CT: Archon Books, 1984. 696 pp.

128. Maltby, A. *Religion and Science.* London: Library Association, 1965. 36 pp.

Guides to Periodical Literature

129. *Guide to Science and Religion in Periodical Literature.* Vol. 1- . Flint, MI: National Periodical Library, 1964- . Quarterly, with annual and triennial cumulations.

Professional Associations

American Scientific Affiliation
P.O. Box 668
Ipswich, MA 01938
Periodical(s): *Journal of the American Scientific Affiliation*

Association of Orthodox Jewish Scientists
1373 Coney Island Avenue
Brooklyn, NY 11219
The Association sponsors two conferences annually and publishes two periodicals, *Intercom* and *Halacha Bulletin.*

Study Centers and Research Facilities

Center for Advanced Study in Religion and Science
c/o Meadville/Lombard Theological School
5701 S. Woodlawn
Chicago, IL 60637
The Center is the co-sponsor of *Zygon: Journal of Religion and Science.*

Center for Faith and Science Exchange
93 Anson Road
Concord, MA 01742

Center for Theology and the Natural Sciences
c/o Graduate Theological Union
2465 LeConte Avenue
Berkeley, CA 94709

Conference on Science, Philosophy, and Religion
c/o Jewish Theological Seminary
3080 Broadway
New York, NY 10027

Institute for Science and Religion
2019 Delaware Avenue
Wilmington, DE 19806

Institute for Theological Encounter with Science and Technology
221 N. Grand Blvd.
St. Louis, MO 63103

Institute on Religion in an Age of Science
c/o Carol Gorski
CCRS/LSTC
1100 E. 55th Street
Chicago, IL 60615
The Institute was founded in 1954. It is the cosponsor of *Zygon: Journal of Religion and Science* and has its own *Newsletter*.

International Conference on the Unity of the Sciences (ICUS)
G. P. O. 1311
New York, NY 10116
Formed in the early 1970s by Rev. Sun Myung Moon, ICUS is possibly the most successful of the Unification Church's several efforts to engage the scholarly community issues it considers of priority concern. It publishes a newsletter, *ICUS Reports*, and annual proceedings of its fall conferences.

SOCIOLOGY AND RELIGION

Sociology, which emerged as a new academic discipline in the nineteenth century, now rivals psychology as a field with direct relevance to religious studies. Religious leaders quickly perceived its value and utilized sociology in attempts to undergird programs aimed at altering social patterns and to motivate a search for a more just society through the change of social structures. What was known as the social gospel, a search for the kingdom of God on earth, was made possible by the hope that through social change, human ills could be eradicated.

While the utopian optimism which accompanied the early blending of sociology and religion has faded, sociology has been able to prove its value to religious groups on the theoretical side by providing a perspective on the relation of religion and society, especially at the group level, and in more practical ways by providing vital information as denominations project plans for future growth.

Encyclopedias and Dictionaries

130. Kose, Alfred, ed., *Katholisches Soziallexikon.* Innsbruck, Austria: Tyrolia-Verlag, 1964. 1426 pp.

Bibliographies

131. Bauer, Gerhard. *Towards a Theology of Development: An Annotated Bibliography.* Geneva: Committee on Society, Development & Peace, 1970. 201 pp.

132. Berkowitz, Morris L., and J. Edward Johnson. *Social Scientific Studies of Religion: A Bibliography.* Pittsburgh, PA: University of Pittsburgh Press, 1967. 258 pp.

133. Blasi, Anthony J., and Michael W. Cuneo. *Issues in the Sociology of Religion: A Bibliography.* New York: Garland Publishing, 1986. 363 pp.

134. Brunkow, Robert de V., ed. *Religion and Society in North America: An Annotated Bibliography.* Santa Barbara, CA: ABC-Clio, 1983. 515 pp.

135. Carrier, Hervé, and Emile Pin. *Sociology of Christianity: International Bibliography, 1900-1961.* Studia Socialia 8. Rome: Presses de l'Université Grégorienne, 1964. 313 pp.

136. Carrier, Hervé, Emile Pin, and Alfred Fasola-Balogna. *Sociology of Christianity: Supplement, 1962-1966.* Studia Socialia 8. Rome: Presses de l'Université Grégorienne, 1968. 304 pp.

137. Demerath, Nicolas J., and Wade C. Roof. "Religion—Recent Strands in Research." *Annual Review of Sociology* 2 (1976): 19-33.

138. Homan, Roger, comp. *The Sociology of Religion: A Bibliographical Survey.* Bibliographies and Indexes in Religious Studies No. 9. New York: Greenwood Press, 1986. 309 pp.

139. Mauss, Armand L., and Jeffrey R. Franks. "Comprehensive Bibliography of Social Science Literature on the Mormons." *Review of Religious Research* 26, 1 (September 1984): 73-115.

140. Mitcham, Carl, and Jim Grote. "Bibliography of Theology and Technology." In *Theology and Technology.* Lanham, MD: University Press of America, 1984. pp. 325-502.

141. Silverman, William. *Bibliography of Measurement Techniques Used in the Social Scientific Study of Religion.* Psychological Documents 13, No. 2539. San Rafael, CA: Select Press, 1983.

142. ————. "Reference Books in the Sociology of Religion." *Review of Religious Research* 32, 1 (September 1990): 87-96.

143. *Social Compass: International Review of the Sociology of Religion.* Vol. 1- . Ottignies-Louvain-la-Neuve: Social Compass, 1953- . Quarterly.
Social Compass carries an annual bibliography of publications in the field.

144. *Sociology and Religion: A Bibliography from the ATLA Religion Data Base.* Chicago: American Theological Library Association, 1981. Rev. ed.: 1982. 251 pp. Rev. ed: 1988. 542 pp.

145. *Sociology of Religion and Theology.* 2 vols. Madrid: Editorial Cuadernos para el Dialogo, 1975. 474 pp.

146. Visvanathan, Susan. "Bibliography on Social Analysis of Indian Religions." *Social Compass* 33, 2-3 (1986): 285-97.

147. White, Anthony G. *Religion as an Urban Institution: A Selected Bibliography.* Monticello, IL: Council of Planning Librarians, Exchange Bibliography #450, 1973. 11 pp.

148. Wolcott, Roger T., and Dorita F. Bolger, comps. *Church and Social Action: A Critical Assessment and Bibliographical Survey.* Bibliographies and Indexes in Religious Studies No. 15. New York: Greenwood Press, 1990. 256 pp.

Guides to Periodical Literature

149. *Guide to Social Science and Religion in Periodical Literature.* Vol. 1- . Flint, MI: National Library of Religious Periodicals, 1964- . Quarterly with annual and triennial cumulations. Indexed by subject only. Formerly titled *Guide to Religious and Semi-Religious Periodicals.*

Professional Associations

Association for the Sociological Study of Jewry
Department of Sociology
Brooklyn College
Brooklyn, NY 11210

Association for the Sociology of Religion
Box U68A
University of Connecticut
Storrs, CT 06268
Formerly known as the **American Catholic Sociological Association**, the ASR publishes *Sociological Analysis* (q).

Christian Sociological Society
c/o Michael Leming
Department of Sociology
St. Olaf College
Northfield, MN 55057
Periodical(s): *Newsletter of the Christian Sociological Society*

Groupe de Sociologie des Religions
c/o Center National de la Rescherche Scientifique
59-61 rue Pouchet
75017 Paris, France
The Groupe publishes a quarterly journal, the *Archives de Sciences Socioles des Religions.*

International Conference of Sociology of Religion
(Conference Internationale de Sociologie des Religions)
c/o Roland J. Campiche
10, Torreaux
CH-103 Lausanne, Switzerland
The Conference publishes a quarterly *Bulletin.*

International Federation for Social and Socio-Religious Research
c/o Centre de recherches Socio-Religieuses
Université Catholique de Louvain
Louvain, Belgium
The Federation sponsors *Social Compass; International Review of the Sociology of Religion,* Sage Publications, 28 Banner Street, London EC1Y 8QE.

Religious Research Association, Inc.
c/o Catholic University of America
Marist Hall, Rm. 108
Washington, DC 20064
Periodical(s): *Review of Religious Research*

Society for the Scientific Study of Religion
c/o Department of Sociology and Anthropology
Stone Hall
Purdue University
West Lafayette, IN 47907
The Society publishes the *Journal for the Scientific Study of Religion* (q).

Study Centers and Research Facilities

Center for Social and Religious Research
Hartford Seminary
77 Sherman Street
Hartford, CT 06105

Center for the Study of Religion and Society
c/o Bryan Le Beau
Department of History
Creighton University
California at North Street
Omaha, NE 68178

Community for Religious Research and Education
St. Francis College
Religious Studies Department
Loretto, PA 15940

Cuyamungue Institute
Route 5, Box 358-A
Sante Fe, NM 87501
The Institute publishes the *Cuyamungue Institute Newsletter*

Institute for Interdisciplinary Research
2314 Broadway
New York, NY 10024
An independent organization, the Institute conducts research in the social sciences from a Judeo-Christian perspective.

Institute for the Study of Modern Jewish Life
City College of City University of New York
138th Street and Convent Avenue
New York, NY 10031
The Institute conducts social and scientific studies on contemporary Jewish life.

Leiffer Bureau of Social and Religious Research
Garrett-Evangelical Theological Seminary
2121 Sheridan Road
Evanston, IL 60201
The Bureau's research is concentrated in the area of interaction of the Christian church and society.

Louis Finkelstein Institute for Religious and Social Studies
Jewish Theological Seminary
3080 Broadway
New York, NY 10027

Princeton Religious Research Center
P. O. Box 628
Princeton, NJ 08542

Program for Research on Religion, Church, and Society
Center for the Study of Contemporary Society
University of Notre Dame
Notre Dame, IN 46556
The Program focuses study in sociology of religion and related fields.

Rockford Institute Center on Religion and Society
934 M. Main Street
Rockford, IL 67103

Woodstock Theological Center
c/o Georgetown University
Washington, DC 20057
The Center concentrates its research on contemporary political and social issues from the standpoint of Christian faith.

II

THE RELIGIONS OF THE WORLD

Part 1: General Sources

THE WORLD'S RELIGIONS: GENERAL SOURCES

The materials in this section cover the various religious traditions of the world, other than Christianity, which is treated separately in Section III. The coverage moves from the more comprehensive sources which treat all of the major religious traditions to those which concentrate on a set of religions from a particular geographical area, to those which are limited to coverage of a single tradition.

Encyclopedias

150. Bishop, Peter, and Michael Darton, eds. *The Encyclopedia of Living Faiths.* New York: Facts on File, 1988. 352 pp.

151. Blunt, John Henry. *Dictionary of Sects, Heresies, Ecclesiastical Parties, and Schools of Religious Thought.* London: Rivingtons, 1874. 648 pp. Rept.: Detroit, MI: Omnigraphics, 1990. 648 pp.

152. Brandon, Samuel George Frederick, ed. *A Dictionary of Comparative Religion.* New York: Charles Scribner's Sons/London: Weidenfeld and Nicolson, 1970.

153. Canney, Maurice A. *An Encyclopedia of Religions.* London: George Routledge & Sons, 1921. 397 pp. Rept. Detroit: Gale Research, 1970.

154. Crim, K. *Abingdon Dictionary of Living Religions.* Nashville, TN: Abingdon, 1981. Rept. as: *The Perennial Dictionary of World Religions.* New York: Harper & Row, 1989. 830 pp.

155. *Dictionary of World Religions.* New York: Harper & Row, 1989. 830 pp.

156. *Encyclopedia of World Religions.* London: Octopus Books, 1975. 252 pp.
The *Encyclopedia* is one of several volumes extracted from the *Man, Myth, and Magic* (2237) volumes.

157. Forlong, James George Roche. *Faiths of Man: A Cyclopaedia of Religions.* 3 vols. London: Bernard Quaritch, 1906. Rept. as: *Faiths of Man: Encyclopedia of Religions.* New Hyde Park, NY: University Books, 1964.

158. Friess, Horace L. *Non-Christian Religions, A to Z.* New York: Grosset & Dunlap, 1963. 278 pp. Derived from *Die Nichtchristlichen Religionen.* Frankfurt: Fischer Bucherei K. G., 1957.

159. Gardner, James. *Faiths of the World.* 2 vols. 1860. Rept.: Delhi, India: Manas Publications, 1986.

160. Gaskell, George Arthur. *A Dictionary of the Sacred Language of All Scriptures and Myths.* New York: McDevitt-Wilsons/London: George Allen & Unwin, 1923. 844 pp. Rept.: New York: Julian Press, 1978. 844 pp.

161. Gates, Brian Edward, and Mary Howard. *World Religions in Education.* Rev. ed. London: National Book League, 1977. 31 pp.

162. Hinnells, John R., ed. *The Penguin Dictionary of Religions.* London: Allen Lane, Penguin Books, 1984. 550 pp. Rept. as *The Facts on File Dictionary of Religions.* New York: Facts on File, 1984. 550 pp.

163. Ince, Richard. *A Dictionary of Religion and Religions including Theological and Ecclesiastical Terms.* London: Arthur Barke Ltd., 1935. 294 pp.

164. Jackson, Samuel McCauley, ed. *The New Schaff-Herzog Encyclopedia of Religious Knowledge, Embracing Biblical, Theological and Ecclesiastical Biography from the Earliest Times to the Present Day; Based on the Third Edition of the Realencyklodädie Founded by J.J. Herzog, and Edited by Albert Hauck.* 13 vols. New York: Funk & Wagnalls Co., 1908-1914. Rept.: 13 vols. Grand Rapids, MI: Baker Book House, 1949-1950.

165. Kauffman, Donald T. *The Dictionary of Religious Terms.* Old Tappan, NJ: Fleming H. Revell Company, 1967. 445 pp. Rept. as: *Baker's Pocket Dictionary of Religious Terms.* Grand Rapids, MI: Baker Book House, 1967. 445 pp.

166. Kennedy, Richard. *The Dictionary of Beliefs.* London: Ward Lock Educational, 1984. 256 pp. Rept. as *The International Dictionary of Religion.* New York: Crossroad, 1984. 256 pp.

167. Lurker, Manfred. *Dictionary of Gods and Goddesses, Devils and Demons.* London: Routledge and Kegan Paul, 1987. 451 pp.

168. Parrinder, Geoffrey. *Dictionary of Non-Christian Religions.* 2nd. ed.: Amersham, Bucks, UK: Hulton Educational Publications, 1971. 320 pp.

169. Pike, E. Royston. *Encyclopedia of Religion and Religions.* London: George Allen & Unwin, 1951. 406 pp.

170. Poupard, Paul, et al., eds. *Dictionnaire des Religions.* Paris: Presses Universitaires de France, 1984. 1838 pp.

171. Zaehner, Robert Charles, ed. *The Concise Encyclopaedia of Living Faiths.* New York: Hawthorne Books, 1959. Rept.: Boston, MA: Beacon Press, 1967. 2nd ed. London: Hutchinson, 1971. 436 pp.

172. Zettler, Howard G. *-Ologies and -Isms: A Thematic Dictionary.* Detroit, MI: Gale Research Company, 1978. 277 pp. 2nd ed.: 1981. 365 pp.

Bibliographies

173. Adams, Charles J., ed. *A Reader's Guide to the Great Religions.* New York: Free Press/London: Collier-Macmillan, 1965. 364 pp. 2nd ed. 1977. 521 pp.

174. Turner, Harold W. *Bibliography of New Religious Movements in Primal Societies.* 5 vols. Boston: G.K. Hall, 1977-1991.

Vol. I: Black Africa.
II: North America.
III: Oceania.
IV: Europe & Asia.
V: Latin America

175. *Unpublished Writings on World Religions.* Vol. 1- . Stony Brook, NY: State University of New York at Stony Brook, Institute for the Advanced Study of World Religions, 1977- . Semiannual.

THE RELIGIONS OF THE WORLD

Part 2: Eastern Religions

ASIAN RELIGION

Most sources on Asian religion deal primarily with Hindu or Buddhist traditions and can therefore be found in those sections. Here are listed those sources which deal either with the various religions of Asia or of a specific region of Asia.

General Sources

176. Rice, Edward. *Eastern Definitions.* Garden City, NY: Doubleday & Company, 1978. 433 pp.

Biographical Volumes

177. Beale, T. W. *An Oriental Biographical Dictionary.* Rev. ed. edited by Henry George Keene. London, 1894. 431 pp. Rept.: Delhi, India: Manohar Reprints, 1971. 431 pp.

178. Winternitz, Moriz. *Concise Dictionary of Eastern Religion, Being the Index to the Sacred Books of the East.* Oxford: Clarendon Press, 1910. 683 pp.

Bibliographies

179. *Asian Religious Studies Information.* Vol 1- . Stony Brook, NY/Fort Lee, NJ: Institute for the Advanced Study of Religion, 1983- . Semiannual. *Asian Religious Studies Information* was created in 1983 by the merger of *Buddhist Research Information* (1979-1983), *Sikh Religious Studies Information* (1979-1983), and *Hindu Text Information* (1981-1983).

180. James, E. O. *The Comparative Study of Religions of the East (Excluding Christianity and Judaism).* Reader's Guides, Third Series, No. 5. Cambridge: National Bookleague, 1959. 32 pp.

181. Smith, William M. "The Religions of Asia: a Bibliographical Essay." *Choice* 10, 5/6 (July/August 1973): 723-44.

Chinese Religion

Encyclopedias and Dictionaries

182. Werner, Edward T. C. *A Dictionary of Chinese Mythology.* New York: Julian Press, 1961. 627 pp.

183. Williams, C. A. S. *Encyclopedia of Chinese Symbolism and Art Motifs: An Alphabetical Compendium of Legends and Beliefs as Reflected in the Manners and Customs of the Chinese throughout Their History.* New York: Julian Press, 1960. 468 pp.

Bibliographies

184. Thompson, Laurence G. *Chinese Religion in Western Languages: A Comprehensive and Classified Bibliography of Publications in English, French, and German through 1970.* Encino & Belmont, CA: Dickenson Pub. Co., 1976. 190 pp. Rev. ed. through 1980: Tucson, AZ: University of Arizona Press, for the Association for Asian Studies, 1985. 302 pp.

185. Yu David C. *Guide to Chinese Religion.* Boston: G.K. Hall, 1985. 200 pp.

Japanese Religion

General

186. Bunce, William K. *Religions in Japan: Buddhism, Shinto, Christianity.* Rutland, VT and Tokyo: Charles E. Tuttle Co., 1955. 194 pp. Rept.: 1959.

187. Holzmen, Donald, et al. *Japanese Religion and Philosophy: A Guide to Japanese Reference and Research Materials.* Ann Arbor, MI: University of Michigan Press, for the Center for Japanese Studies, 1959. 102 pp.

188. *Japan's Religions. Directory.* No. 1- . Tokyo, n.p. 1957- .

189. Swyngedouw, Johannes. "A Brief Guide to English Language Materials on Japan's Religions." *Contemporary Religions in Japan* 11, 1/2 (March-June 1979): 80-97.

Atlases

190. *Religious Map of Japan.* Kyoto: Christian Center for the Study of Japanese Religions, 1959. 51 pp.

New Religions in Japan

Bibliographies

191. Earhart, H. Byron. *The New Religions of Japan: A Bibliography of Western Language Materials.* Tokyo: Sophia University, 1970. 496 pp.

192. Thomsen, Harry, comp. *Bibliography of the New Religions.* Kyoto: Christian Center for the Study of Japanese Religions, 1906. 37 pp.

BUDDHISM

Buddhism is the tradition founded in the 6th century B.C.E. by Siddhartha Gautama, who after an enlightenment experience became known as the Buddha ("the enlightened one"). Born a prince of the Shakya clan in South Nepal, India, he is sometimes referred to as Shakyamuni ("the sage of the Shakyas"). He renounced his aristocratic life and began a long quest for enlightenment, after which he spent the rest of his life teaching.

Although Buddhism enjoyed great popularity and became the state religion in the 3rd century B.C.E., it eventually virtually disappeared in India as Brahmanic Hinduism reasserted its predominance (though not without having assimilated many of the Buddhist ideas itself). While it faded from its homeland, however, Buddhism's missionary efforts reached far to the east, establishing Buddhism as a major religious force in China, Korea, Japan, and Southeast Asia.

Although several schools arose within Buddhism, the major division within the tradition occurred with the rise of the Mahayana ("The Great Vehicle") school at the beginning of the Common Era. Based on a freer and more elaborate interpretation of Buddhism, the Mahayanists referred to the more traditional schools as the Hinayana ("The Lesser Vehicle"), which held to a stricter interpretation. Mahayana became the more popular, developing many branches of its own, while the older schools diminished in numbers. Theravada, one of these older schools, has remained the most vital of these and its name is often used as a less derogatory synonym for Hinayana. Its influence today stretches from the island of Ceylon along the southern coast of Asia and down into Indochina. The rest of the Buddhist world follows some form of Mahayana. This includes, among other things, such varying forms as Tibetan Tantric Buddhism, various Pure Land schools, and Japanese Zen.

Encyclopedias and Dictionaries

193. Conze, Edward. *Materials for a Dictionary of the Prañaparamita Literature.* Tokyo: Suzuki Research Foundation, 1973. 447 pp.

194. *A Dictionary of Buddhism.* New York: Charles Scribner's Sons, 1972. 277 pp. Created by extracting entries on Buddhism from Brandon's *Dictionary of Comparative Religion* (152).

195. Eitel, Ernest J. *Handbook of Chinese Buddhism: Being a Sanskrit-Chinese Dictionary of Buddhist Terms, Words, and Expressions, with Vocabularies of Buddhist Terms in Pali, Singhalese, Siamese, Burmese, Tibetan, Mongolian, and Japanese.* 2nd ed. rev. and enlarged with a Chinese Index by K. Takakuwa. Amsterdam: Philo Press, 1970. 324 pp. Rept. of 1904 ed.

196. Gupte, R.S. *Iconography of the Hindus, Buddhists and Jains.* Bombay: D. B. Taraporevala Sons & Co., 1972. 201 pp.

197. Hackman, Heinrich Friedrich. *Erklärendes Wörterbuch zum Chinesischen Buddhismus: Chinesisch-Sanskrit-Deutsch.* 6 vols. Leiden: E. J. Brill, 1951-54.

198. Humphreys, Christmas. *A Popular Dictionary of Buddhism.* London: Arco Publications, 1962. 224 pp. 2nd. ed: London: Curzon Press/Totowa, NJ: Rowman and Littlefield, 1976. 223 pp. Supersedes March (202)

199. Inada, Kenneth K. *Guide to Buddhist Philosophy.* Boston: G.K. Hall, 1985. 226 pp.

200. Inagaki, Hisao. *A Dictionary of Japanese Buddhist Terms: Based on References in Japanese Literature.* Kyoto: Nagata Bunshodo, 1984. 473 pp.

201. Malalasekera, G. P., ed. *Encyclopaedia of Buddhism.* 4 vols. [Colombo]: The Government of Ceylon, 1961-79.

202. March, Arthur Charles. *A Brief Glossary of Buddhist Terms.* London: Buddhist Lodge, 1937. 99 pp. Superseded by Humphreys (198)

203. Morel, Hector V., and Jose Dali Morel. *Diccionario Budista.* Buenos Aires: Editorial Kier, 1989. 411 pp.

204. Nyanatiloka. *Buddhist Dictionary: Manual of Buddhist Terms and Doctrines.* Colombo: Frewin & Co., 1950. 189 pp.

205. Oort, H.A. Van. *The Iconography of Chinese Buddhism in Traditional China.* Iconography of Religions XII, 5, I. Vol. I: Han to Llio. Leiden: E.J. Brill, 1986. 30 pp. + 48 plates.

206. Soothill, William Edward, and Lewis Hodus. *A Dictionary of Chinese Buddhist Terms with Sanskrit and English Equivalents and a Sanskrit-Pali Index.* London:

Kegan Paul, 1937. 510 pp. Rept.: Taipei: Ch'eng-Wen Publishing Co., 1968. 510 pp.

207. Upsak, Chondrika Singh. *Dictionary of Early Buddhist Monastic Terms (Based on Pali Literature).* Varanasi: Bharati Prakasham, 1975. 245 pp.

208. Wood, Ernest. *Zen Dictionary.* London: P. Owen, 1963. 165 pp.

Directories

209. *Brief Introduction to Korean Buddhism.* Los Angeles: The Korean Buddhist Sangha Association of Western Territory in U.S.A., 1984. 38 pp. Includes a directory of both American centers and Korean headquarters.

210. *First Draft of an Address List of the World's Zen Centers and Institutions.* Kyoto: International Research Institute for Zen Buddhism, Hanazono College, [1990]. 9 pp.

211. *International Buddhist Directory.* London, UK: Wisdom Publications, 1985. 120 pp.

212. Roth, Martin and John Stevens. *Zen Guide.* New York: Weatherhill, 1985. 124 pp.

213. *World Buddhist Directory.* Colombo, Sri Lanka: The Buddhist Information Center, 1984. 198 pp.

Bibliographies

214. Bando, Shojun, et al. *A Bibliography of Japanese Buddhism.* Tokyo: The Cultural Interchange Institute for Buddhist Press, 1985. 180 pp.

215. Beautrix, Pierre. *Bibliographie du Bouddhisme.* Vol. 1- . Bruxelles, Belgium: Institute Belge des Haute Études Bouddhiques, 1970- .

216. ————. *Bibliographie du Bouddhisme Zen.* Bruxelles, Belgium: Institut Belge des Haute Études Bouddhiques. 1969. 114 pp.

217. ————. *Premier Supplement.* Bruxelles, Belgium: Institut Belge des Haute Études Bouddhiques, 1975. 119 pp.

218. *Buddhist Text Information.* 6 vols.New York: Institute for the Advanced Study of World Religions, 1974-1979. Superseded by *Buddhist Research Information* (219).

219. *Buddhist Research Information*. No. 1 (April 1979)-No. 10 (October 1983). Stony Brook, New York: Institute for the Advanced Study of World Religions, [1979-1983]. Semiannual. Merged with *Sikh Religious Studies Information* and *Hindu Text Information* to form *Asian Religious Studies Information* (179).

220. Collins, S. "Keeping Up with Recent Studies of Buddhism." *The Expository Times*, 97, 1 (October 1985): 3-8.

221. Conze, Edward. *Buddhist Scriptures: A Bibliography*. Garland Reference Library of the Humanities Vol. 113. New York & London: Garland, 1982. 161 pp.

222. Gard, Richard A. *A Select Bibliography for the Study of Buddhism in Burma in Western Languages*. Tokyo: International Institute for Advanced Buddhistic Studies, 1957. 40 pp.

223. ———. *A Select Bibliography for the Study of Buddhism in Ceylon in Western Languages*. 2nd ed., rev. and enl. Berkeley, CA: n.p., 1957. 97 pp.

224. ———. *A Select Bibliography for the Study of Buddhism in Thailand in Western Languages*. Bangkok: Mahāmakuta University Library, n.d. 17 pp.

225. Gemmyo, Ono, comp. *Bussho Kaisetsu Daijiten*. 12 vols. Tokyo: Daito Shuppansha, 1933-36. Rev. ed.: 14 vols. 1964-78. This work offers comprehensive coverage of Buddhist texts written in Japanese and Chinese.

226. Grönbold, Günter. *Der Buddhistische Kanon: eine Bibliographie*. Wisbaden: Harrassowitz, 1984. 70 pp.

227. Hamilton, Clarence Herbert. *Buddhism in India, Ceylon, China and Japan*. Chicago: University of Chicago Press, [c. 1931]. 107 pp.

228. Hanyama, Shinsho. *Bibliography on Buddhism*. Tokyo: Hokuseido Press, 1961. 869 pp.

229. Lancaster, Lewis R. *The Korean Buddhist Canon: A Descriptive Catalogue*. Berkeley, CA, etc.: University of California Press, 1979. 724 pp.

230. McDermot, Robert A. *Focus on Buddhism: A Guide to Audio-Visual Resources for Teaching Religion*. Chambersburg, PA: Anima Books, 1981. 165 pp.

231. Muraishi, Esho. "A Bibliography on Pure Land Buddhism Written in English." *Junshin gakuho* 2 (December 1983): 1-33.

232. Overseas Buddhist Studies Research Project. "Bibliography of Foreign-Language

Articles on Japanese Buddhism 1960 to 1987." *Annual Memoirs of the Otani University Shin Buddhist Comprehensive Research Institute* 6 (1988): 151-212.

233. Pfandt, Peter, comp. *Mahayana Texts Translated into Western Languages: A Bibliographical Guide.* Köln: E. J. Brill, 1983. 167 pp. Rev. ed. 1986. 208 pp.

234. Reynolds, Frank E. *Guide to Buddhist Religion.* Boston, MA: G.K. Hall, 1981. 415 pp.

235. Rhodes, Robert. "Bibliography of English-Language Works on Pure Land Buddhism 1960 to the Present." *Annual Memoirs of the Otani University Shin Buddhist Comprehensive Research Institute* 1 (1983): 1-28.

236. Satyaprakash. *Buddhism: A Select Bibliography.* Gurgaon, New Delhi, India: Indian Documentation Service, 1976. 172 pp.

237. Tanaka, Kenneth. "Bibliography of English-Language Works on Pure Land Buddhism Primarily 1983-1988." *The Pacific World* New Series, No. 5 (1989): 85-98.

238. Vessie, Patricia Armstrong. *Zen Buddhism: A Bibliography of Books and Articles in English, 1892-1975.* Ann Arbor, MI: University Microfilms International, 1976. 81 pp.

239. Wayman, A. "Buddhism." In C. L. Bleeker and G. Weingren. *Historia Religionum.* Leiden: E. J. Brill, 1969. pp. 372-464.

240. Yoo, Yushin. *Books on Buddhism: An Annotated Subject Guide.* Metuchen, NJ: Scarecrow Press, 1976. 251 pp.

Guides to Periodical Literature

241. *Bibliographie Bouddhique.* 32 vols. Paris: Librairie d'Amerique et d'Orient, 1930-1967.

242. Yoo, Yushin. *Buddhism: A Subject Index to Periodical Articles in English, 1728-1971.* Metuchen, NJ: Scarecrow Press, 1973. 162 pp.

Buddhism in North America

Directories

243. *The American Buddhist Directory.* New York, NY: The American Buddhist Movement, 1982. 94 pp.; 2nd ed.: 1985. 114 pp.

244. *Buddhist Organizations in America.* Hamilton, NY: Fund for the Study of the Great Kelipous, Colgate University, 1969. 9 pp.

245. *Directory of Buddhist Organizations in the Bay Area.* Berkeley, CA: Vesak Celebration Committee, 1984. 20 pp.

246. Morreale, Don, ed. *Buddhist America: Centers, Retreats, Practices.* Santa Fe, NM: John Muir Publications, 1988. 349 pp.

Buddhism in Europe

Directories

247. *The Buddhist Directory.* London: Buddhist Society, 1987. 75 pp. Includes a detailed list of Buddhist centers in the UK and Ireland, and a list of member organizations of the Buddhist Union of Europe.

Buddhist Studies

Many resources exist for Buddhist studies in the West, the most prominent being the **International Association of Buddhist Studies** in Berkeley, CA. The **Hsi-Lai Temple** in Hacienda Heights, CA, has established an important university for Buddhist studies in recent years. Other centers for Buddhist studies can be found across America and in Europe.

Buddhist Text Translation Society
City of 10,000 Buddhas
P.O. Box 217
Talmage, CA 95481
Associated with the Dharma Realm Buddhist University, the Society has been working since 1970 on the translation of the Tripitaka from its Chinese edition (Zhung Wen) into English.

American Institute for Buddhist Studies
61 Lincoln Avenue
Amherst, MA 80210

American Institute of Nichiren Buddhism
301 West 45th Street
New York, NY 10036

American Society of Buddhist Studies
214 Centre Street
New York, NY 10013

British Shingon Buddhist Association
Kongoryuji
London Road.
East Dereham, Norfolk NR19 1AS
United Kingdom
Houses a 15,000 volume collection in Buddhism including many texts in Oriental languages.

Buddhist Mission Library
Muzeum utca 5
H-1088 Budapest, Hungary
Houses a 4,000 volume collection on Buddhism.

College of Buddhist Studies
933 South New Hampshire Avenue
Los Angeles, CA 90006

Comunidad Budista Soto Zen - Biblioteca
Moro Zeit 11-6 A
E-46001 Valencia, Spain

Hsi-Lai University
3456 South Glenmark Drive
Hacienda Heights, CA 91745

Institute of Chinese Studies Library
1605 Elizabeth Street
Pasadena, CA 91104
A library specializing in Chinese studies used primarily serving Christian missionaries interested in evangelizing Chinese peoples.

Institute of Buddhist Studies Library
1900 Addison St.
Berkeley, CA 94704

International Association of Buddhist Studies
Institute of Buddhist Studies
1900 Addison Street
Berkeley, CA 94704
Associated with Buddhist Churches of America. Houses graduate program and 10,000+ volume library primarily in Japanese.

International Research Institute for Zen Buddhism
Hanzono College
8-1 Tsubonouchi-cho
Nishinokyo, Nakakyo-Ku
Kyoto 604, Japan
The Institute publishes an international directory of Zen centers, and a bi-lingual (Japanese/English) *Newsletter* which includes a running bibliography on Zen.

Koruda Institute for the Study of Buddhism & Human Values
c/o Religious Studies, 3014 FLB
University of Illinois
Urbana, IL 61801

Naropa Institute
2130 Arapahoe Avenue
Boulder, CO 80304
The Institute publishes the *Naropa Institute Journal of Psychology.*

Nyingma Institute
1815 Highland Place
Berkeley, CA 94704
The Nyingma Institute has been working with Dharma Publishing to produce translations of the Tibetan Buddhist Canon.

Society for Buddhist Christian Studies
c/o Sharon Peeble Burch
Graduate Theological Union
2400 Ridge Road
Berkeley, CA 94709

HINDUISM AND RELATED INDIAN RELIGIONS

Hinduism is a collective term developed by Western scholars to refer to the indigenous religious traditions of India. It does not refer to a single religion with a particular founder, canon, and belief system; rather, it includes a bewildering variety of traditions each with their own beliefs and practices. Many common elements are shared by these traditions, however, such as notions of reincarnation, karma, and various forms of yoga.

Hindus generally understand there to be a variety of ways to attain spiritual progress (yogas), including bhakti (devotion), jnana (knowledge), karma (work), and raja ("royal") yoga which emphasizes meditative practices.

Hinduism first attracted the attention of the West with the formation of the Asiatic Society of Bengal in the eighteenth century, whose founder, Sir William Jones, began translating Sanskrit literature into English. The nineteenth century saw significant portions of the Hindu holy books translated by Max Müller and others. While Hindu ideas thereby came to influence Western thought (especially in Theosophical circles), it was not until the immigration of large numbers of Indians to the West that Hinduism made its presence felt as a religion.

The traditions imported to the West by these immigrants are various, including Vaishnavism (the worship of Vishnu), Saivism (the worship of Shiva), and others. In addition, the Vaishnavite Krishna movement (ISKCON) and many yogic traditions have found a large number of Western adherents. While there is not a large number of academic centers for Hindu studies in the West, this will no doubt change with the acceleration of Indian immigration. Perhaps the best source about contemporary Hinduism is the periodical *Hinduism Today.*

General Studies

248. *Hinduism Today,* 1819 Second Street, Conrad, CA 94519
This is a monthly tabloid newspaper covering Hindu and related issues.

Encyclopedias and Dictionaries

249. Dowson, John. *A Classical Dictionary of Hindu Mythology and Religion, Geography, History, and Literature*. 1879. Rev. ed.: New Delhi: Oriental Books Reprint Corporation, 1973. 411 pp.

250. Gupte, R.S. *Iconography of the Hindus, Buddhists and Jains*. Bombay: D.B. Taraporevala Sons & Co., 1972. 201 pp.

251. Macdonnell, Arthur Anthony, and Arthur B. Keith. *Vedic Index of Names and Subjects*. 2 vols. London: Murray, 1912. Rept.: Delhi: Motilal Banarsidass, 1967.

252. Mani, Vettam. *Puranic Encyclopaedia: A Comprehensive Dictionary with Special Reference to the Epic and Puranic Literature*. Delhi: Motilal Banarsidass, 1975. 922 pp.

253. Sivananda Saraswati, Swami. *Yoga Vedanta Dictionary*. Delhi: Motilal Banarsidass, 1973. 190 pp.

254. Stutley, Margaret. *An Illustrated Dictionary of Hindu Iconography*. London & Boston: Routledge & Kegan Paul, 1985. 175 pp.

255. Stutley, Margaret, and James Stutley. *Harper's Dictionary of Hinduism: Its Mythology, Folklore, Philosophy, Literature and History*. New York: Harper & Row, 1977. 372 pp. Published in England as *A Dictionary of Hinduism: Its Mythology, Folklore, and Development 1500 B.C.-A.D. 1500*. London and Henley, UK: Routledge & Kegan Paul, 1977. 372 pp.

256. Subrahmanian, N.S. *Encyclopaedia of the Upanisads*. London: Oriental University Press, 1986. 564 pp.

257. Walker, Benjamin. *The Hindu World: An Encyclopedic Survey of Hinduism*. 2 vols. New York & Washington: Frederick A. Praeger/London: Allen & Unwin, 1968.

258. Wood, Ernest. *Vedanta Dictionary*. London: Owen, 1964. 225 pp.

Directories

259. *Vaishnava Directory and Resource Guide*. San Diego, CA: Vaishnava Directory & Resource Guide, 1992. Forthcoming.

Bibliographies

260. Ali, Syed Mohammed, and H.S. Sharma, eds. *Hinduism: A Select Bibliography.* Gurgaon, India: Indian Documentation Service, 1984. 352 pp.

261. Dandekar, Ramchandra Narayan. *Vedic Bibliography.* 3 vols. Bombay: Karnatak Publishing House/Poona: University of Poona, 1946-1973.

262. Dell, David J. *Guide to Hindu Religion.* Boston: G.K. Hall, 1981. 461 pp.

263. Farquhar, John N. *An Outline of the Religious Literature of India.* 1920. Rept.: Delhi: Motilal Banarsidass, 1967. 451 pp.

264. Henn, Katherine. *Rabindranath Tagore: A Bibliography.* ATLA Bibliography Series No. 13. Metuchen, NJ: 1985. 351 pp.

265. Holland, Barron. *Popular Hinduism and Hindu Mythology: An Annotated Bibliography.* Westport, CT: Greenwood Press, 1979. 394 pp.

266. Kanellakos, Demitri P., and Jerome S. Lukas. *The Psychobiology of Transcendental Meditation: A Literature Review.* Menlo Park, CA: Stanford Research Institute, 1973. 103 pp.

267. Kanitkar, Helen. "Bibliography: Hindus and Hinduism in Great Britain." In *Hinduism in Great Britain.* London: Tavistock Publications, 1987. pp. 252-283.

268. Kapoor, Jagdish Chander. *Bhagavad-Gītā: An International Bibliography of 1785-1979 Imprints.* Garland Reference Library of the Humanities, Vol. 306. New York: Garland Publishing, 1983. 371 pp.

269. Natu, Bal. *Avatar Meher Baba Bibliography 1928 to February 25, 1978: Works By and About Meher Baba in English and Other European Languages.* Edited by J. Flagg Kriss. New Delhi: The Editor, 1978. 82 pp.

270. Padhi, Bibhu, and Minakshi Padhi. *Indian Philosophy and Religion: A Reader's Guide.* Jefferson, NC: McFarland, 1990. 430 pp.

271. Renou, Louis. *Bibliographie Védique.* Paris Adrien-Maison-Neuve, 1932. 339 pp.

Yoga

Encyclopedias and Dictionaries

272. Day, Harvey. *Yoga Illustrated Dictionary.* New York: Barnes & Noble, 1971.

273. Wood, Ernest. *Yoga Dictionary.* New York: Philosophical Library, 1956.

Bibliographies

274. Jarrell, Howard R. *International Yoga Bibliography, 1950 to 1980.* Metuchen, NJ: Scarecrow Press, 1981. 221 pp.

275. Weiman, Mark. *Yoga: A Bibliography.* Berkeley, CA: The Movable Foundation Workshop Press, 1980. 135 pp.

Hindu Studies

California Institute of Integral Studies
765 Ashbury
San Francisco, CA 97117
Houses 26,000 volume library on Hinduism, yoga and related subjects.

Society for Tantric Studies
c/o James H. Sanford
Dept. of Religious Studies
University of North Carolina at Chapel Hill
Chapel Hill, NC 27514

OTHER INDIAN FAITHS

Jainism

Jainism was founded in the 6th century B.C.E. by Vardhamana Mahavira, a contemporary of Gautama Buddha. Like the Buddha, Mahavira was born to the ruling caste but renounced his position to seek spiritual enlightenment. His teachings grew out of the Brahmanic Hinduism of his day but disputed Vedic authority in preference of logic and experience.

One of the most important concepts in Jainism is that of ahimsa, or non-violence. While present in other Hindu traditions, the Jaina concept of ahimsa is extended to even the tiniest living beings, some Jains going so far as to wear masks to keep from inhaling flies. Similarly, some Jains take the ascetic ideas of Jainism to mean rejection of any form of ownership, including clothes. Not all Jains, however, follow such a strict interpretation of their teachings. The main community of Jains is in Gujarat, India, though a small Jain community has now been established in the West.

Bibliographies

276. Guérinot, A. *Essai de Bibliographie Jaina: Répertoire Analytique et Méthodique des Travaux Relatifs au Jainisme avec Planches hors Texte.* Paris: Ernest Leroux, 1906. 568 pp.

277. Jain, Chhotelal. *Jaina Bibliography.* 1945. 2nd. ed.: 3 vols. Edited by Satya Rangan Banerjee. Rept.: New Delhi, India: Vir Sewa Mandir, 1982- .

Sikhism/Sant Mat

Sikhism began as a reform movement in India around 1500 C.E. Founder Guru Nanak synthesized elements of Hinduism such as karma and reincarnation with the Islamic idea of monotheism. Nanak was succeeded as the leader of the Sikh community by nine other Gurus, the tenth of which initiated two major reforms—militarizing the Sikhs for their defense by forming the Khalsa (the Community of the Pure), and declaring that he was the last human Guru. After him, the *Adi Granth* (the Sikh scriptures) became the Guru.

Sikhism came to the West in small numbers at the beginning of the twentieth century, when some Sikhs immigrated to Canada and then the United States. The ban on Asian immigration halted this inflow, which was resumed when the ban was repealed in 1965. Since then, the Sikh community in America has not only grown by immigration but by conversion as well, due mainly to the efforts of Yogi Bhajan's organization, Sikh Dharma in the West.

Encyclopedias and Dictionaries

278. Singha, H.S. *Junior Encyclopedia of Sikhism.* New Delhi: Vikas Pub. House, 1985. 181 pp.

Bibliographies

279. Barrier, N. Gerald. *The Sikhs and Their Literature: A Guide to Tracts, Books, and Periodicals, 1849-1919.* Delhi: Manohar Book Service, 1970. 153 pp.

280. Lane, David. *The Radhasoami Tradition: An Annotated Bibliography.* Sects and Cults in America Series Vol. 13. New York: Garland Publishing, 1992. c. 250 pp.

281. Rai, Priya Muhar. *Sikhism and the Sikhs: An Annotated Bibliography.* Bibliographies and Indexes in Religious Studies No. 13. New York: Greenwood Press, 1989. 257 pp.

282. Singh, Ganda. *A Select Bibliography of the Sikhs and Sikhism.* Amritsar, Punjab: Sikh Itihas Research Board, 1965. 432 pp.

Biographies

283. Singh, Ranbir. *Glimpses of the Divine Masters: Guru Nanak-Guru Gobind Singh, 1469-1708.* New Delhi: International Traders Corp., [1965]. 498 pp.

SHINTO

Shinto is the state religion of Japan, literally meaning "the way of the gods." It evolved from indigenous folk traditions and became organized in the sixth century C.E., spurred by the arrival of Buddhism to Japan.

Shinto reveres the Kami, or life force, seeing Kami in natural phenomena such as rivers, mountains, storms, etc., the chief Kami being that of the sun, Amaterasu. The emperors of Japan are thought to be descended from the Kami and therefore objects of reverence, although since the end of World War II the divine status of the emperor has been considerably de-emphasized. The character of Shinto is such that, while it has traveled to the West with Japanese immigrants, it has not nor is it interested in spreading beyond the Japanese community.

Encyclopedias and Dictionaries

284. *Basic Terms of Shinto.* Compiled by the Shinto Committee for the IXth International Congress for the History of Religions. Tokyo: Jinja Honcho, Kokugakun University, 1958. 510 pp.

Bibliographies

285. Herbert, Jean. *Bibliographie du Shinto et des Sectes Shintoistes.* Leiden: E. J. Brill, 1968. 73 pp.

286. Kato, Genchi, Karl Reitz, and Wilhelm Schiffer. *A Bibliography of Shinto in Western Languages, from the Oldest Times till 1952.* Tokyo: Meiji Jingu Shamusho, 1953. 58 pp.

287. Schwade, Arcadio. *Shintō—Bibliography in Western Languages: Bibliography on Shinto and Related Sects, Intellectual Schools and Movements Influenced by Shintoism.* Leiden: E.J. Brill, 1986. 124 pp.

TAOISM

Taoism is the indigenous organized religion of China, and, along with Confucianism and Buddhism, forms part of the complex make-up of Chinese religion. Its primary philosophical text is the Tao-te Ching, written by Lao Tzou. It is unknown whether Lao Tzou ("the old one") was an actual person or merely a pseudonym.

The central concept of Taoism is the ineffable Tao, or Way, around which developed a tradition of mysticism. Later Taoists studied alchemy in hopes to attain immortality. At the popular level, Taoism has come to include elaborate theatrical rituals and charms.

Like other Asian religions, Taoism has travelled to the West with its immigrants as well as gaining some Western adherents. Little data is available on this, however, due to the lack of organization.

Bibliographies

288. Pas, Julian. *A Select Bibliography of Taoism.* IASWR Bibliographical Monographs No. 1. Stony Brook, NY: Institute for Advanced Studies of World Religions, 1988. 52 pp.

289. Soyié, Michael, and F. Litsch. "Bibliographie du Taoisme: Etude dans les Langes Occidentales." *Dokyo Kenkyu* 3 (1968): 1-72.

THE RELIGIONS OF THE WORLD

Part 3: Africa and the Middle East

AFRICAN RELIGIONS

In recent years, more attention has begun to be focused on the indigenous religious traditions of Africa, as indicated by the American Academy of Religion forming a section on African Religions. There is still a paucity of resources, however, though hopefully this situation is not likely to last.

Bibliographies

290. Mitchell, Robert Cameron, and Harold W. Turner. *A Comprehensive Bibliography of Modern African Religious Movements.* Evanston, IL: Northwestern University Press, 1966. 132 pp.

291. Ofori, Patrick E. *Black African Traditional Religions and Philosophy: A Select Bibliographic Survey of the Sources from the Earliest Times to 1974.* Nendel, Liechtenstein: KTO Press, 1975. 421 pp.

292. Pigault, Gérard, and Damien Rwegara. *Marriages in Sub-Saharan Africa: International Bibliography 1945-1975 Indexed by Computer.* RIC Supplements 23-26. Strasbourg, France: Cerdic-Publications, 1975.

293. Turner, Harold W. *Bibliography of New Religious Movements in Primal Societies Volume I: Black Africa.* Boston: G.K. Hall, 1977. 277 pp. *See also:* (173).

African Studies

Melville J. Herskovits Library of African Studies
Northwestern University Library
Evanston, IL 60208-2300

RELIGIONS OF THE ANCIENT NEAR EAST

There were a variety of religious communities which existed in the ancient Near East and died out as Christianity rose to power. These have become the subject of intense scholarly interest because of their relationship to Judaism and Christianity. The discovery of the Dead Sea Scrolls and other caches of manuscripts have greatly stimulated the interest in these old religions.

The Dead Sea Community

294. Burchard, Christoph. *Bibliographie zu den Handschriften vom Toten Meer.* 2 vols. Berlin: Alfred Töpelmann, 1957-65.

295. Fitzmyer, Joseph A. *The Dead Sea Scrolls: Major Publications and Tools for Study.* Society of Biblical Literature Sources for Biblical Study No. 8. Missoula, MT: Scholars Press, 1975, 1977. 171 pp.

296. Jongeling, Bastiaan. *A Classified Bibliography of the Finds in the Desert of Judah; 1958-1969.* Vol. VII of the Studies in the Texts of the Desert of Judah. Leiden: E. J. Brill, 1971. 140 pp.

297. LaSor, William Sanford. *Bibliography of the Dead Sea Scrolls, 1948-1957.* Fuller Theological Seminary Bibliographical Series No. 2. Pasadena, CA: Fuller Theological Seminary Library, 1958. 92 pp.

Pseudepigrapha/Apocryphal Literature

Bibliographies

298. Charlesworth, James H. *The New Testament Apocrypha and Pseudepigrapha.* ATLA Bibliography Series No. 17. Metuchen, NJ: Scarecrow Press, 1987. 468 pp.

299. ————, and P. Dykers. *The Pseudepigrapha and Modern Research.* Septuagint and Cognate Studies No. 7. Missoula, MT: Scholars Press for the Society of Biblical Literature, 1976. 245 pp.

300. Scholer, David M. *Nag Hammadi Bibliography 1948-1969.* Leiden: E.J. Brill, 1971. 201 pp.

Manicheanism

301. Klinkheit, Hans-Joachim, comp. *Bibliography of Manichean Materials.* Stony Brook, NY: Institute for Advanced Studies of World Religions, 1980. 10 pp.

Samaritans

302. Crown, Alan David. *A Bibliography of the Samaritans.* ATLA Bibliography Series No. 10. Metuchen, NJ: Scarecrow Press, 1984. 212 pp.

303. Mayer, L.A. *A Bibliography of the Samaritans.* Ed. by D. Broadribb. Supplements to Abr-Nahrain, vol. 1. Leiden: E.J. Brill, 1964. 49 pp.

304. Weiss, Raphael. *Select Bibliography on the Samaritans: The Samaritans and the Samaritan Text of the Torah.* 2nd ed. Jerusalem: Academon, [1970].

Other

305. Pallis, Svend Aage. *Mandean Bibliography 1560-1930.* London: 1933. Rept.: Amsterdam: Philo Press, 1974. 240 pp.

Research/Resource Centers

American Schools of Oriental Research
4243 Spruce Street
Philadelphia, PA 19104
The American Schools of Oriental Research is a consortium of institutions united for research and study of the ancient Near East. It publishes several periodicals including the *Bulletin of the American Schools of Oriental Research*, the *Journal of Cuneiform Studies*, the *ASOR Newsletter*, and the *Biblical Archeologist.*

Institute for Antiquity and Christianity
Claremont Graduate School
831 N. Dartmouth Avenue
Claremont, CA 91711-6178

BAHA'I FAITH

Originating in Persia in the mid-nineteenth century, the Baha'i faith is founded on the teachings of Siyyid Ali Muhammad of Shiraz (1819-1850), better known as the Bab ("the Gate"), and his follower Mirza Husayn-Ali (1817-1892), who renamed himself Baha'u'llah ("the Glory of God"). Proclaiming himself the Mahdi whose coming was foretold by the Bab, he suffered persecution at the hands of the Muslims during his lifetime but continued to teach and write what became the scriptures of the Baha'i.

Baha'i teaching came to emphasize the unity of humanity and the essential oneness of all religions. It was brought to America at the end of the nineteenth century and has slowly grown until the present. Baha'i has just recently come to the interest of the academic community, and Baha'i studies is now rapidly growing field.

Encyclopedias and Dictionaries

306. Sail, Marzieh. *Baha'i Glossary: Persian and Arabic Words in the Baha'i Writings.* Wilmette, IL: Baha'i Publishing Trust, 1955. 56 pp.

Bibliographies

307. Bjorling, Joel. *The Baha'i Faith: A Historical Bibliography.* Sects & Cults in America Series Vol. 6. New York: Garland, 1985. 179 pp.

308. Braun, Eunice. *A Reader's Guide to the Development of Baha'i Literature in English.* Oxford: George Ronald, 1986. 164 pp.

309. Collins, William P. *Bibliography of English-Language Works on the Babi and Baha'i Faiths, 1845-1985.* Wilmette, IL: Baha'i Publishing Trust, 1991. 550 pp.

310. Heggie, J.S., comp. *An Index of Quotations from the Baha'i Sacred Writings.* Oxford: George Ronald, 1983. 811 pp.

Archival Depositories

American Baha'i Faith Archives and Library
536 Sheridan Road
Wilmette, IL 60091

Baha'i Faith Library & Archives
5209 N. University
Peoria, IL 61614

Baha'i World Centre Library
16 Golomb Ave.
P.O. Box 155
31001 Haifa, Israel

ISLAM

In the seventh century C.E., Muhammad, an Arab of the Quraish clan, received revelations which were written down as the Qur'an. These revelations proclaimed the oneness of God and the need to submit to His divine will. Islam literally means "submission" to this divine will. Muhammad claimed to be the last in a long line of prophets sent by God, prophets who included Abraham, Moses and Jesus. The Jews, it was asserted, had corrupted the words God revealed to them, as did the Christians thereafter. The Qur'an was the clear, uncorrupted message which God had given humanity in a final, perfect form.

Islam spread rapidly throughout the Arab and Persian world, eventually stretching from the straits of Gibraltar to the islands of Indonesia. Along the way, many schools of thought arose within Islam. The primary division among these schools is that between the Shi'a Muslims, who insist that the succession of the leadership of the Muslim community passed down through the family of the Prophet, and the Sunni Muslims, who rejected this idea. The Sunni form the majority of Muslims, while Shi'ite parties, throughout history, have often formed among politically dispossessed minorities in the Muslim world. This division, however, does not prevent Shi'ites and Sunnis from acknowledging each other as co-religionists.

Islam has come to the West in some numbers, although its presence has been remarkably little documented until recently. The Islamic presence in America began as primarily immigrant, but Islam has come to attract a large number of converts among the Afro-American population. While some of these Black Muslim groups are seen as heterodox by the world Muslim community, others have gained acceptance as orthodox. In addition, Sufism (Islamic mysticism) has exerted a strong influence on some Western metaphysical/occult groups.

Islamic studies has grown to include several major centers in the West, predominant among which is the Institute of Islamic Studies at McGill University in Montreal and the American Institute for Islamic Studies in Denver, Colorado.

Encyclopedias and Dictionaries

311. ul-Amine, Hasan. *Shorter Islamic Shi'ite Encyclopedia.* Beirut, Lebanon: n.p., 1969.

312. Bosworth, Clifford E. *The Islamic Dynasties: A Chronological Handbook.* Edinburgh: University Press, 1967. 245 pp.

313. Al-Faruqi, Isma'il R. *Toward Islamic English.* Islamization of Knowledge Series No. 3. Herndon, VA: International Institute of Islamic Thought, 1988, c. 1986. 64 pp.

314. Gibb, H. A. R., and J. H. Kramers. *Shorter Encyclopedia of Islam.* Ithaca, NY: Cornell University Press, c. 1953. 671 pp.

315. Glassé, Cyril. *The Concise Encyclopedia of Islam.* San Francisco: Harper & Row, 1989. 472 pp.

316. Houtsma, M. Th., et al. *The Encyclopaedia of Islam.* 4 Vols. Leiden: E.J. Brill, 1913-34. *Supplement.* London: Luzac & Co., 1938. 267+15 pp. New ed. 5 vols. Ed. by H. A. R. Gibb. Leiden: E.J. Brill, 1954-83.

317. Hughes, Thomas Patrick. *A Dictionary of Islam, Being a Cyclopaedia of the Doctrines, Rites, Ceremonies, and Customs, Together with the Technical and Theological Terms, of the Muhammedan Religion.* Clifton, NJ: Reference Book Publishers, 1965. 750 pp.

318. Lane-Poole, S. *The Mohammedan Dynasties.* Westminster: A Constable, 1894. 361 pp. Rept.: Paris: P. Guenther, 1925. Rept.: New York: F. Unger, 1965. Rept.: Beirut: Khaayts, 1966. Rept.: New Delhi: Lotus Publishers, 1986.

319. Mir, Mustansir. *Dictionary of Qur'anic Terms and Concepts.* Garland Reference Library of the Humanities Vol. 693. New York & London: Garland, 1987. 244 pp.

320. Wensinck, A. J. *A Handbook of Early Muhammedan Tradition, Alphabetically Arranged.* Leiden: E.J. Brill, 1960. 268 pp.

321. ———, and J. H. Kramers. *Handwörterbuch des Islam.* Leiden: Brill, 1941. 833 pp.

Biographical Volumes

322. Hitti, Philip Khuri. *Makers of Arab History.* New York: St. Martin's Press, [1968]. 268 pp.

323. Ibn Khallikan. *Biographical Dictionary.* Trans. by Mac Guckin de Slane. 4 vols. New York: Johnson Reprints, 1961.

Bibliographies

324. Anees, Munawar Ahmad, and Alia N. Athar. *Guide to Sira and Hadith Literature in Western Languages.* London & New York: Mansell, 1986. 371 pp.

325. Behn, Wolfgang. *Islamic Book Review Index.* Vol. 1- . Berlin: Adıyok, 1982- .

326. ————. *Index Islamicus, 1665-1905: A Bibliography of Articles on Islamic Subjects in Periodicals and Other Collective Publications.* Millersville, PA: Adiyok, c. 1989. 869 pp.

327. "Bibliographie: l'Islam Contemporain en Europe Occidentale." *Archives de Sciences Sociales des Religions,* 1989, 68/2 (Octobre-Décembre) 151-165.

328. Ede, David. *Guide to Islam.* Boston: G.K. Hall, 1983. 261 pp.

329. Fiegenbaum, J. W. "A Bibliography of the Islamic Tradition." *Choice* 9, 10 (1972): 1268-74.

330. Gabrieli, Giuseppe. *Manuale di Bibliografia Mussulmana. Parte I. Bibliografia Generale.* Roma: Tipografia dell'Unione Ed., 1916. 491 pp.

331. Geddes, C. L. *An Analytical Guide to the Bibliographies on Islam, Muhammad and the Qur'an.* Bibliographic Series No. 3. Denver, CO: American Institute of Islamic Studies, 1973. 102 pp.

332. ————. *Books in English on Islam, Muhammad, and the Qur'an: A Selected and Annotated Bibliography.* Bibliographic Series No. 5. Denver, CO: American Institute of Islamic Studies, 1976. 68 pp.

333. ————. *Guide to Reference Books for Islamic Studies.* Bibliographic Series No. 9. Denver, CO: American Institute for Islamic Studies, 1985. 429 pp.

334. Grimwood-Jones, Diana. *Middle East and Islam: A Bibliographical Introduction.* Rev. ed. Zug, Switzerland: InterDocumentation Co., c. 1979. 429 pp. *See also:* (336)

335. Hampson, Ruth M. *Islam in South Africa: A Bibliography.* Cape Town, South Africa: University of Cape Town School of Librarianship, 1964. 55 pp.

336. Hopwood, Derek, and D. Grimwood-Jones. *Middle East and Islam: a Bibliographical Introduction.* Zug, Switzerland: Inter-Documentation Co., 1972. 368 pp. *See also*: (334)

337. Hussain, Asaf. *Islamic Movements in Egypt, Pakistan, and Iran: An Annotated Bibliography.* London: Mansell, 1983. 168 pp.

338. *Islam in Paperback.* Bibliographic Series No. 1. Denver, CO: American Institute of Islamic Studies, 1969. 58 pp.

339. Ivanow, W. *A Guide to Ismaili Literature.* London: Royal Asiatic Society, 1933. Rev. ed. as: Ismaili Literature: A Bibliographical Survey. Teheran: Ismaili Society, 1963. 245 pp.

340. Khan, Muhammad Akrain, comp. *Islamic Economics: Annotated Sources in English and Urdu.* Leicester: The Islamic Foundation, 1983. 221 pp.

341. Ofori, Patrick E. *Islam in Africa South of the Sahara: A Select Bibliographic Guide.* New York: KTO Press, 1977. 223 pp.

342. Paetow, Louis John. *A Guide to the Study of Medieval History.* Rev. ed. New York: Crofts, 1931. 643 pp. This volume includes an important chapter on "Muslim Culture in the West."

343. Pfanmüller, Gustav. *Handbuch der Islam-Literatur.* Berlin: W. De Gruyter, 1923. 436 pp.

344. Sauvaget, Jean. *Introduction to the History of the Muslim East: A Bibliographic Guide.* Based on the 2nd ed. as recast by Claude Cohen. Berkeley & Los Angeles: University of California Press, 1965. 252 pp. Rept.: Westport, CT: Greenwood Press, 1982. 252 pp.

345. *Select Bibliography on Arab Islamic Civilization and Its Contributions to Human Progress.* Kuwait: University, 1972. 152 pp.

346. Shinar, Pessah. *Essai de Bibliographie Sélective et Annotée sur l'Islam Maghrébin Contemporain: Maroc, Algérie, Tunisie, Libye (1830-1978).* Paris: Éd. du Centre National de la Recherche Scientifique, 1983. 506 pp.

347. Siddiqi, Muhammad Nejatullah. *Contemporary Literature on Islamic Economics: A Select Classified Bibliography of Works in English, Arabic and Urdu up to 1975.* Jeddah: International Centre for Research on Islamic Economics, King Abdul Aziz University; Leicester: Islamic Foundation, 1978. 69 pp.

348. Siddiqui, Iqtidar Husain. *Modern Writings on Islam and Muslims in India.* Aligarh, India: International Book Traders, 1974. 112 pp.

349. Slugett, Peter. *Theses on Islam, the Middle East and North-West Africa, 1880-1978: Accepted by Universities in the United Kingdom and Ireland.* London: Mansell, 1983. 147 pp.

350. Sumardi, Muljanto. *Islamic Education in Indonesia: A Bibliography.* Singapore: Institute of Southeast Asian Studies, 1983. 133 pp.

351. Tabataba'i, Hossein Modarressi. *An Introduction to Shi'a Law: A Bibliographical Study.* London: Ithaca Press, 1984. 258 pp.

352. Tajdin, Nigib, comp. & ed. *A Bibliography of Ismailism.* Delmar, NY: Caravan Books, 1985. 180 pp.

353. Wismer, Don. *The Islamic Jesus: An Annotated Bibliography of Sources and English and French.* New York & London: Garland, 1977. 305 pp.

354. Zoghby, Samir M. *Islam in Sub-Saharan Africa: A Partially Annotated Guide.* Washington, DC: Library of Congress, 1978. 318 pp.

Guides to Periodical Literature

355. Pearson, J.D., comp. *Index Islamicus 1906-1955: A Catalogue of Articles on Islamic Subjects in Periodicals and Other Collective Publications.* Cambridge: W. Heffer & Sons, 1958. 897 pp. Rept. London: Mansell, 1972. 897 pp. *Supplements*:
1956-1960. Cambridge: W. Heffer & Sons, 1962.
1961-1965. Cambridge: W. Heffer & Sons, 1967. 342 pp.
1966-1970. London: Mansell, 1972. 384 pp.
1971-1975. London: Mansell, 1977. 429 pp.
1976-1980. London: Mansell, 1983.

356. *Revue des Etudes Islamiques.* Vol. 1- . Paris: 1927- . Carries an annual bibliography, "Abstracta Islamica."

357. *The Quarterly Index Islamicus.* Vol. 1- . London: Mansell, Jan. 1977- . Cumulated annually and quinquennially by supplements to *Index Islamicus.*

Atlases

358. al-Faruqi, Isma'il, and Lois Lamya'ad Faruqi. *The Cultural Atlas of Islam.* New York: Macmillan, 1986. 512 pp.

359. Hazard, Harry W. *Atlas of Islamic History.* 3rd ed.: Princeton, NJ: Princeton University Press, 1954. 49 pp.

360. Roolvink, R., et al., comps. *Historical Atlas of the Muslim Peoples.* Cambridge, MA: Harvard University Press, 1957. 40 pp.

361. Weekes, Richard V., ed. *Muslim Peoples: A World Ethnographic Survey.* 2 vols. Westport, CT: Greenwood Press, 1978. 2nd ed.: 1984.

Islam in North America

General Sources

362. Abugiedeiri, el Tagani A. *A Survey of North American Muslims.* Indianapolis, IN: Islamic Teaching Center, 1977. 30 pp.

Bibliographies

363. Haddad, Yvonne Y. "Muslims in America: A Select Bibliography." *The Muslim World* 76 (1986): 93-122.

364. Nyang, Sulayman S. "Islam in the United States: Review of Sources." *The Search: Journal for Arab and Islamic Studies* 1 (1980): 164-82. Rept.: *Journal Institute of Muslim Minority Affairs* 2, 1 (Winter 1980): 189-199.

365. Williams, Daniel T., and Carolyn L. Redden. *The Black Muslims in the United States: A Selected Bibliography.* N.p.: Tuskeegee Institute, 1964. 19 pp. + 2 p. supplement.

Sufism

366. Driscoll, J. Walter. *Gurdjieff: An Annotated Bibliography.* New York: Garland, 1985. 363 pp.

Islamic Studies

American Institute for Islamic Affairs
School of International Service
The American University
4900 Massachusetts Avenue, N.W.
Washington, DC 20016

American Institute of Islamic Studies
P. O. Box 10398
Denver, CO 80210
The Institute, founded in 1965, supports the Muslim Bibliographic Center and publishes a Bibliographic Series.

American Research Center in Egypt
50 Washington Square South
New York University
New York, NY 10012
Supports a program in New York and Cairo, Egypt, focused upon Ancient and Islamic civilization.

Center for Arab-Islamic Studies
P. O. Box 543
Brattleboro, VT 05301

Duncan Black MacDonald Center for the Study of Islam and Christian Muslim Relations
Hartford Seminary
77 Sherman Street
Hartford, CT 06105
Publishes the quarterly, *The Muslim World.*

Federation of Islamic Associations in the United States and Canada Library
25351 5 Mile Rd.
Redford, MI 48259

Institut Francais d'Etudes Arabes de Damas Bibliotheque
B.P. 344
Damascus, Syrian Arab Republic
Houses a 50,000 volume multi-language collection in Islamic and Arabic studies.

Institute for Islamic Judaic Studies
c/o Center for Judaic studies
University of Denver

University Park
Denver, CO 80208
The Institute researches the interaction of Muslim and Jewish cultures both historically and in contemporary settings.

Institute of Islamic Studies
McGill University
3485 McTavish Street, Room 319
Montreal, PQ H3A 1Y1
Supports an expansive research program which includes work in Persian/Iranian studies at a branch in Teheran. The Institute is also affiliated with the Aga Khan Foundation in London which specializes in studies of the Ismaili Shi'a Muslim tradition. It is supported by a 120,000 volume Islamic collection in the McGill Library.

Institute for Islamic-Judaic Studies
University of Denver
Denver, CO 80208

Instituto de Estudios Islamicos, Biblioteca General
Calle Rey de bahamonde 121
Vista Alegre, Surco
Lima 33, Peru

Islamic Computing Centre Library
73 St. Thomas's Rd.
London N4 2QJ, England
Produces the Al-Hadith Databases and the Al-Quran Database, as well as JANET electronic mail service.

Organization of the Islamic Conference
Research Center for Islamic History, Art, and Culture
IRCICA Library
Barbaros Bulvari
Yildiz Sarayi
Besiktas 80700
Istanbul, Turkey

JUDAISM

Judaism, the religion of the Jewish people, is also the parent religion of both Christianity and Islam. Centered on the concepts of one God and the special covenant relationship between God and the people Israel, Judaism remains numerically small but still very important in the religious and historical life of the world.

Jews have had a presence in America since the beginning of European settlement, the early immigrants being Sephardic (of Spanish/Portuguese descent). The Jewish community remained quite small, however, until the mass immigration of Ashkenazic (Eastern European) Jews in the late nineteenth century. America has provided fertile soil for the growth of the diverse movements within Judaism, and today this spectrum includes Orthodox, Conservative, Reform and Reconstructionist schools. In addition, the ultra-orthodox Hasidic movement has grown rapidly in recent years.

As can be seen by the size of the next section, Jewish Studies is a very active field with a vast number of books published and many libraries and centers across the world. One of the difficulties in sorting through this field is the lack of a sharp distinction between the religious and the secular history of Jews. We have tried to focus on resources of a more religious nature, excluding categories which deal primarily with Jewish ethnicity rather than religion. We have not included, for example, a section on Zionism as it is involved mainly with Jewish ethnic and political identity. On the other hand, we have included such topics as anti-Semitism and Holocaust studies, which have greater implications for the study of religion. Also included are many area studies dealing with Judaism in various countries. Especially numerous in this regard are the sources on Judaism and the Jewish community in the Soviet Union.

Of the many centers and archival depositories dealing with Jewish studies, two institutions deserve particular note. The American Jewish Historical Society, located in Brandeis University, maintains the largest collection of American Hebraica in the world. Hebrew Union College hosts the American Jewish Archives, the American Jewish Periodical Center, the Center for the Study of the American Jewish Experience, and the Jewish Institute of Religion.

General Sources

Jewish Information Bureau
250 W. 57th Street
New York, NY 10019
(212) 582-5318
A clearinghouse for inquiries on matters relating to the Jewish community.

367. *Jewish Yearbook.* Vol 1- . London: "Jewish Chronicle," 1896- . Annual.

Encyclopedias and Dictionaries

368. Adler, Cyrus. *Jewish Encyclopedia.* 12 vols. New York: Funk & Wagnalls, 1901-1906. Rept.: New York: Ktav Publishing House, 1964.

369. Ausubel, Nathan. *The Book of Jewish Knowledge: An Encyclopedia of Judaism and the Jewish People, Covering All Elements of Jewish Life from Biblical Times to the Present.* New York: Crown, 1964. 560 pp.

370. Bader, Gershom. *The Encyclopedia of Talmudic Sages.* Trans. by Solomon Katz. London: Jason Aronson, 1988. 876 pp.

371. Birnbaum, Phillip. *A Book of Jewish Concepts.* New York: Hebrew Publishing Co., 1964. 719 pp. Rev. ed.: New York: Hebrew Pub. Co., 1975. 722 pp.

372. Bridger, David, ed. *The New Jewish Encyclopedia.* New York: Behrman House, 1962. 541 pp.

373. Chavel, Charles B. *Encyclopedia of Torah Thoughts.* New York: Shilo Publishing House, 1980. 719 pp.

374. Cohen, Harry Alan. *A Basic Jewish Encyclopedia: Jewish Teachings and Practices Listed and Interpreted in the Order of Their Importance Today.* Hartford, CT: Hartmore House, 1965. 205 pp.

375. Cohen, Simon, comp. *The Universal Jewish Encyclopedia: A Reading Guide and Index.* New York: The Universal Jewish Encyclopedia, 1948. 78 pp.

376. DeHaas, Jacob. *The Encyclopedia of Jewish Knowledge.* New York: Behrman's Jewish House, 1934. 686 pp. Rept. 1938, 1944.

377. *Encyclopaedia Judaica: Das Judentum in Geschichte und Gegenwart.* 10 vols. Berlin: Verlag Eshkol, 1928-34.

378. *Encyclopaedia Judaica.* 16 vols. New York: Macmillan Company, 1972.

379. *Encyclopaedia Judaica, Decennial Book, 1973-82.* Jerusalem, Encyclopaedia Judaica, 1982. 684 pp.

380. *Encyclopaedia Judaica Yearbook.* Vol. 1- . Jerusalem: Encyclopaedia Judaica, 1973- .

381. *Encyclopedia Talmudica: A Digest of Halachic Literature and Jewish Law from the Tannaitic Period to the Present Time, Alphabetically Arranged.* 3 vols. Jerusalem: Talmudic Encyclopedia Institute, 1969.

382. Herlitz, Georg, and Bruno Kirschner. *Jüdisches Lexicon; Ein Enzyklopädisches Handbuch des jüdischen Wissens.* 4 vols. Berlin, Jüdischer Verlag, 1927-30.

383. Isaacson, Ben. *Dictionary of the Jewish Religion.* Ed. by David Gross. Englewood, NJ: SBS Publishing Co., 1979. 196 pp.

384. Isaacson, Ben, and Deborah Wigoder. *The International Jewish Encyclopedia.* Englewood Cliffs, NJ: Prentice-Hall; Jerusalem: Masada Press, 1973. 366 pp.

385. Jacobs, Joseph. *The Jewish Encyclopedia: A Guide to Its Contents, an Aid to Its Use.* New York: Funk & Wagnalls Co., 1910. 162 pp. Rept. by Ktav, 1964.

386. Kaganoff, Benzion C. *A Dictionary of Jewish Names and Their History.* New York: Schocken Books, 1977. 250 pp.

387. Kasher, Menahem Mendel. *Encyclopedia of Biblical Interpretation: A Millennial Anthology.* Trans. under the editorship of Harry Freedman. 8 vols. New York: American Biblical Encyclopedia Society, 1953-1970.

388. Landman, Isaac, ed. *The Universal Jewish Encyclopedia: An Authoritative and Popular Presentation of Jews and Judaism Since the Earliest Times.* 10 vols. New York: The Universal Jewish Encyclopedia, Inc., 1939-1940.

389. Neuman (Noy), Dov. *Motif-Index of Talmudic-Midrashic Literature.* Bloomington: Ph.D. Dissertation, Indiana University 1954. 861 pp.

390. Nulman, Mary. *Concise Encyclopedia of Jewish Music.* New York: McGraw-Hill, 1975. 276 pp.

391. Oppenheimer, John F., ed. *Lexicon des Judentums.* Gütersloh, Germany: Bertelsmann, 1967. 928 Col.

392. Patai, Raphael, ed. *Encyclopedia of Zionism and Israel.* 2 vols. New York: Herzl Press, 1971.

393. Roth, Cecil, ed. *The Standard Jewish Encyclopedia.* Garden City, NY: Doubleday, 1959. Rev. ed. 1960. 989 pp. Rev. ed. 1966, 989 pp. 4th ed.: Ed. by Cecil Roth and Geoffrey Wigoder. *The New Standard Jewish Encyclopedia.* 1970. 5th ed.: Ed. by Geoffrey Wigoder. Garden City, NY: Doubleday, 1977. 2028 col.

394. Roth, Cecil, and Geoffrey Wigoder, eds. *Encyclopaedia Judaica.* 16 Vols. Jerusalem: Keter Publishing House/New York: The Macmillan Company, 1971. Annual supplements.

395. Runes, Dagobert D. *Concise Dictionary of Judaism.* New York: Greenwood Press, 1966. 124 pp.

396. Schonfield, Hugh J. *A Popular Dictionary of Judaism.* London: Arco Publications, 1962. 153 pp.

397. Shulman, Albert M. *Gateway to Judaism: Encyclopedia Home Reference.* 2 vols. South Brunswick, NJ: Thomas Yoseloff, 1971. 1056 pp.

398. Singer, Isidore, ed. *The Jewish Encyclopedia: A Descriptive Record of the History, Religion, Literature, and Customs of the Jewish People from the Earliest Times to the Present Day.* 12 vols. New York & London: Funk & Wagnalls, 1907. Rept. New York: KTAV Publishing House, 1964.

399. Winfeld, E., ed. *Enciclopedia Judaic Castellana.* 10 vols. Mexico: Editorial Enciclopedia Judaica Castellana, 1945-1951.

400. Werblowsky, R. J. Zwi, and Geoffrey Wigoder. *The Encyclopedia of the Jewish Religion.* New York: Holt, Rinehart and Winston, 1965. 415 pp. Rept. Tel Aviv: Masada Press, 1967. Rev. ed. New York: Adama Books, 1986. 415 pp.

401. Wigoder, Geoffrey. *The Encyclopedia of Judaism.* New York: Macmillan Company, 1989. 768 pp.

402. ———. *Everyman's Judaica: An Encyclopedia Dictionary.* London: W.H. Allen/Jerusalem: Keter Publishing House, 1975. 673 pp.

403. Witty, Rachel J. *A Vocabulary of Jewish Tradition: A Transliterated Glossary.* Calgary, Alberta, Canada: Letter Perfect, 1985. 153 pp.

Biographical Volumes

404. Comay, Joan. *Who's Who in Jewish History: After the Period of the Old Testament.* New York: D. McKay Co./London: Weidenfeld and Nicolson, 1974. 448 pp.

405. Karpman, I. J. Carmin, ed. *Who's Who in World Jewry: A Biographical Dictionary of Outstanding Jews.* New York: Pitman Publishing Corp., Inc., 1972. Rev. ed.: Tel-Aviv, Israel: Olive Books of Israel, 1978.

406. Kolatch, Alfred J. *Who's Who in the Talmud.* New York: Jonathan David, 1964. 315 pp.

407. Rottenberg, Dan. *Finding Our Fathers: A Guidebook to Jewish Genealogy.* New York: Random House, 1977. 401 pp.

408. Winiger, Solomon. *Grosse jüdische National-Biographie mit mehr als 12,000 Lebensbeschreibungen namhafter jüdischer Männer und Frauen aller Zeiten und Länder. Ein Nachschlagewerk für das jüdische Volk und dessen Freunde.* 7 vols. Cernauti: Arta, 1925-37.

409. Zubatsky, David S., and Irwin M. Berent. *Jewish Autobiographies and Biographies: An International Bibliography of Books and Dissertations in English.* New York: Garland Publishing, 1989. 370 pp.

410. ————. *Jewish Genealogy: A Sourcebook of Families and Genealogies.* 2 vols. New York: Garland Publishing, 1989-90. 452 pp.

Directories

411. Cohen, Iva. *Jewish Organizations: A Worldwide Directory.* New York: Conference of Jewish Communal Service, 1970. 48 pp. 2nd ed.: 1975.

412. *Zionist Year Book. Since 1950: The Complete Guide to the Zionist World.* London: Zionist Federation of Great Britain and Ireland, 1987. 240 pp.

Bibliographies-Catalogues of Jewish Collections

413. Freimann, Aron. *Union Catalog of Hebrew Manuscripts and Their Location.* 2 vols. New York: American Academy for Jewish Research, 1964-73. Rept.: New York: Kraus Reprint, 1979.

414. Glatzer, Mordechai. *Hebrew Manuscripts in the Houghton Library of the Harvard College Library: A Catalogue.* Ed. by Charles Berlin and Rodney Gove Dennis. Cambridge, MA: Harvard University Library, 1975. 68pp.

415. Harvard University Library. *Catalogue of Hebrew Books.* 6 vols. Cambridge, MA: Harvard University Press, 1968-72. *Supplement.* 3 vols.

416. ———. *Judaica: Classification Schedule, Classified Listing by Call Number, Chronological Listing, Author and Title Listing.* Widener Library Shelflist No. 39. Cambridge, MA: Harvard University Library, 1971. 302 pp.

417. ———. *Dictionary Catalog of the Klau Library, Cincinnati.* 32 vols. Boston: G.K. Hall & Co., 1964.

418. *Manuscript Catalog of the American Jewish Archives, Cincinnati.* 4 vols. Boston: G.K. Hall & Co., 1971. *First Supplement.* Boston: G.K. Hall & Co., 1978.

419. Margoliouth, George, and Jacob Leveen. *Catalogue of the Hebrew and Samaritan Manuscripts in the British Museum.* 4 vols. London: Trustees of the British Museum, 1965.

420. New York Public Library. Reference Department. *Dictionary Catalogue of the Jewish Collection.* 14 vols. Boston: G.K. Hall & Co., 1960. *First Supplement.* 8 vols. Boston: G.K. Hall & Co., 1975.

421. New York Public Library. Research Libraries. *Hebrew-character Title Catalog of the Jewish Collection.* 4 vols. Boston: G. K. Hall, 1981.

Bibliographies-General

422. *Atid Bibliography: A Resource for the Questioning Jew.* New York: United Synagogue of America, Dept. of Youth Activities, 1977. 153 pp.

423. Benjacob, Isaac. *Ozar Ha-Sepharim (Bcherschatz). Bibliographie der Gesammten Hebraeischen Literatur mit Einschluss der Handschriften (bis 1863).* Wilna: Benjacob, 1880. 678 pp.

424. Berlin, Charles, ed. *Index to Festschriften in Jewish Studies.* Cambridge, MA: Harvard College Library/New York: Ktav Publishing House, 1971. 319 pp.

425. *Bibliographia Judaica.* Vol. 1- . Cincinnati, OH: Hebrew Union College, Jewish Institute of Religion, 1969- . Irregular.

426. *Bibliographical Essays in Medieval Jewish Studies.* New York: Anti-Defamation League of B'nai B'rith, 1976. 392 pp.

427. Breslauer, S. Daniel. *Contemporary Jewish Ethics: A Bibliographical Survey.* Westport, CT: Greenwood Press, 1985. 213 pp.

428. Brisman, Shimeon. *A History and Guide to Judaic Bibliography.* Cincinnati: Hebrew Union College Press/New York: Ktav Publishing House, 1977. 325 pp.

429. ———. *Jewish Research Literature.* Vol. 1- . Bibliographica Judaica, Nos. 7- . Cincinnati: Hebrew Union College Press/New York: Ktav Publishing House, 1977- .

430. Cohn, Margot, and Rafael Buber. *Martin Buber: A Bibliography of His Writings, 1897-1978.* Munich: K.G. Saur; Jerusalem: Hebrew University, 1980. 160 pp.

431. Cutter, Charles, and Micha Falk Oppenheim. *Jewish Reference Sources: a Selective Annotated Bibliographic Guide.* Garland Reference Library of Social Science, vol. 126. New York: Garland Publishing, 1982. 180 pp.

432. *Doctoral Dissertations and Master's Theses Accepted by American Institutions for Higher Learning.* 6 vols. New York: Yivo Institute for Jewish Research, 1966-1974. Later as *American Doctoral Dissertations and Master's Theses on Jewish Subjects.*

433. Edelheit, Abraham J., and Herschel Edelheit. *The Jewish World in Modern Times: A Selected, Annotated Bibliography.* Boulder, CO: Westview Press/London: Mansell, 1988. 569 pp.

434. Eichstädt, Volkmar. *Bibliographie zur Geschichte der Judenfrage. Bd.1, 1750-1848.* Hamburg: Hanseatische Verlagsanstalt, 1938. 267 pp.

435. Eppler, Elizabeth E., comp. & ed. *International Bibliography of Jewish Affairs, 1966-1967: A Select Annotated List of Books and Articles Published in the Diaspora.* New York: Holmes & Meir, 1976. 401 pp.

436. ———. *International Bibliography of Jewish Affairs, 1976-1977: A Selectively Annotated List of Books and Articles Published in the Diaspora.* Boulder, CO: Westview Press for the Institute of Jewish Affairs, in association with the World Jewish Congress, 1983. 42 pp.

437. Frank, Ruth S., and William Willheim. *A Reader's Guide to Judaism.* San Francisco: Harper & Row, 1986. 320 pp.

438. Freiberg, Bernhard. *Bet Ekad Sepharim: Bibliographical Lexicon of the Whole Hebrew and Jewish-German Literature, Inclusive of the Arab, Greek, French-Provençal, Italian, Latin, Persian, Samaritan, Spanish-Portuguese and Tartarian Works, Printed in the Years 1474-1950 with Hebrew Letters.* 4 vols. 2nd ed.: Tel Aviv: n.p., 1951-56.

439. Griffiths, David B. *A Critical Bibliography of Writings on Judaism.* 2 vols. Lewiston, NY: Edwin Mellen Press, 1988.

440. Grossfeld, Bernard. *A Bibliography of Targum Literature.* Cincinnati: Hebrew Union College Press; New York: Ktav Publishing House, 1972. 131 pp.

441. Heskes, Irene. *The Resource Book of Jewish Music: A Bibliographical and Topical Guide to the Book and Journal Literature and Program Materials.* Westport, CT: Greenwood Press, 1985. 302 pp.

442. *Immanuel.* No. 1- . Jerusalem: Ecumenical Theological Research Fraternity in Israel, 1972- . Semi-annual.

443. *Jewish Public Library Bulletin/Bibliothèque Publique Juive Bulletin.* Vol. 1- . Montreal: Jewish Public Library, 1971- . Monthly.

444. Jongeling, B. *A Classified Bibliography of the Finds in the Desert of Judah, 1958-1969.* Leiden: E.J. Brill, 1971. 140 pp.

445. Kaplan, Jonathan, ed. *International Bibliography of Jewish History & Thought.* München: K.G. Saur/Jerusalem: Magnes Press, Hebrew University, 1984. 483 pp.

446. ———. *2000 Books and More: An Annotated and Selected Bibliography of Jewish History and Thought.* Jerusalem: Magnes Press, Hebrew University, 1983. 483 pp.

447. *Katalog der Judaica und Hebraica.* Vol. 1. Frankfurt am Main: M. Lehrberger, 1932. 646 pp.

448. Kohn, Gary J., comp. *The Jewish Experience: A Guide to Manuscript Sources in the Library of Congress.* Cincinnati, OH: American Jewish Archives, 1986. 166 pp.

449. Korsch, Boris. *Soviet Publications on Judaism, Zionism, and the State of Israel, 1984-1988: An Annotated Bibliography.* New York: Garland Publishing, 1989. 176 pp.

450. Lubetski, Edith. *Writings on Jewish History: A Selected Annotated Bibliography.* New York: Publications Service of the American Jewish Committee, 1970. 31 pp.

451. Lubetski, Edith, and Meir Lubetski. *Building a Judaica Library Collection: A Resource Guide.* Littleton, CO: Library Unlimited, 1983. 185 pp.

452. Marcus, Jacob Rader, and Albert Bilgray. *Index of Jewish Festschriften.* Cincinnati: Hebrew Union College, 1937. 154 pp. Rept.: New York: Kraus, 1970.

453. Marcus, Ralph. *A Selected Bibliography (1920-1945) of the Jews in the Hellenistic-Roman Period.* New York: [American Academy for Jewish Research], 1947. 181 pp.

454. Mayer, L. A. *Bibliography of Jewish Art.* Ed. by Otto Kurz. Jerusalem: Magnes Press, Hebrew University, 1967. 374 pp.

455. Mor, Menahem, and Uriel Rappaport. *Bibliography of Works on Jewish History in the Hellenistic and Roman Periods 1976-1980.* Jerusalem: Zalman Shazar Center, 1982. 95 pp.

456. Purvis, James D. *Jerusalem, the Holy City: A Bibliography.* ATLA Bibliography Series No. 20. 1988. 499 pp.

457. Rothenberg, Joshua, comp. *Judaica Reference Materials: A Selective Annotated Bibliography.* Preliminary ed. Waltham, MA: Brandeis University Library, 1971. 87 pp.

458. Schlesinger, Benjamin. *The Jewish Family: A Survey and Annotated Bibliography.* Toronto: University of Toronto Press, 1971. 175 pp.

459. ———. *Jewish Family Issues: A Resource Guide.* New York: Garland Publishing, 1987. 168 pp.

460. Schmelzer, Menahem Hayyim, ed. *Bibliographical Studies and Notes Describing Rare Books and Manuscripts in the Library of the Jewish Theological Seminary of America.* New York: Ktav Publishing House, 1977. 591 pp.

461. Sendrey, Alfred, comp. *Bibliography of Jewish Music.* New York: Columbia University Press, 1951. 404 pp.

462. Shermis, Michael. *Jewish-Christian Relations: An Annotated Bibliography and Resource Guide.* Bloomington: Indiana University Press, 1988. 291 pp.

463. Shunami, Shlomo. *Bibliography of Jewish Bibliographies.* 2nd ed. Jerusalem: Magnes Press, 1965. Rept. New York: Ktav Publishing House/Jerusalem: Magnes Press, 1969. 992 pp. *Supplement to Second Edition.* Jerusalem: Magnes Press, 1975. 464 pp.

464. *The Study of Judaism: Bibliographical Essays.* 2 vols. New York: Anti-Defamation League of B'nai B'rith, 1972-1976.

465. *Teaching about Jews and Judaism.* New York: Anti-Defamation League of B'nai B'rith, 1974. 14 pp.

466. Weisser, Albert, comp. *Bibliography of Publications and Other Resources on Jewish Music.* New York: National Jewish Music Council, 1969. 117 pp.

467. Yassif, Eli. *Jewish Folklore: An Annotated Bibliography.* New York and London: Garland, 1986. 341 pp.

Bibliographies-Various Countries

468. Bihl, Wolfdieter. *Bibliographie der Dissertationen über Judentum und jüdische Persönlichkeiten, die 1872-1962 an österreichischen Hochschulen (Wien, Granz, Innsbruck) approbiert wurden.* Wien: Notring der Wissenschaftlichen Verbände Österreichs, 1965. 51 pp.

469. Blumenkranz, Bernhard, and Monique Lévy. *Bibliographie des Juifs en France.* Toulose: The Author, 1974. 349 pp.

470. Braham, Randolph L. *The Hungarian Jewish Catastrophe: A Selected and Annotated Bibliography.* 2nd ed. New York: Columbia University Press, 1984. 501 pp.

471. ———. *Jews in the Communist World: A Bibliography 1945-1960.* New York: Twayne Publishers, 1961. 569 pp.

472. Braham, Randolph L., and Mordecai M. Hauer. *Jews in the Communist World: A Bibliography 1945-1962.* New York: Pro Arte Publishing, 1963. 125 pp.

473. Cohen, Ytshak Yosef, and M. Piekarz. *Jewish Publications in the Soviet Union, 1917-1960.* Jerusalem: Historical Society of Israel, 1961. 502 pp.

474. Fluk, Louise R. *Jews in the Soviet Union: An Annotated Bibliography.* New York: American Jewish Committee, 1975. 44 pp.

475. Hundert, Gershon David, and Gershon C. Bacon. *The Jews in Poland and Russia: Bibliographical Essays.* Bloomington, IN: Indiana University Press, 1986. 230 pp.

476. Kisch, Guido. *Judaistische Bibliographie. Ein Verzeichnis der in Deutschland und der Schweiz von 1956-1970 erschienenen Dissertationen und Habilitationsschriften.* Basel and Stuttgart: Helbing & Lichtenhahn, 1972. 104 pp.

477. Kisch, Guido, and Kurt Roepke. *Schriften zur Geschichte der Juden, eine Bibliographie der in Deutschland und der Schweiz 1922-1955 erschienenen Dissertationen.* Tubingen: Mohr, 1959. 49 pp.

478. Lehmann, Ruth P. *Anglo-Jewish Bibliography: 1937-1970.* London: Jewish Historical Society of England, 1973. 364 pp.

479. ———. *Nova Bibliotheca Anglo-Judaica: A Bibliographical Guide to Anglo-Jewish History 1937-1960.* London: Jewish Historical Society of England, 1961. 232 pp.

480. Lerski, George J., and Halina T. Lerski, comps. *Jewish-Polish Coexistence, 1772-1939: A Topical Bibliography.* New York: Greenwood Press, 1986. 230 pp.

481. Milano, Attilio. *Bibliotheca Historica Italo-Judaica.* Firenze, Italy: Sansoni, 1954. 209 pp.

482. Pinkus, B., and Greenbaum, A. A. *Russian Publications on Jews and Judaism in the Soviet Union, 1917-1967: A Bibliography.* Jerusalem: Society for Research on Jewish Communities, 1970. 273 pp.

483. Romano, Giorgio. *Bibliografia Italo-Hebraica (1848-1977).* Firenze: Olschki, 1979. 208 pp.

484. Rosenberg, Louise Renée. *Jews in the Soviet Union: An Annotated Bibliography 1967-1971.* New York: American Jewish Committee, 1971. 59 pp.

485. Roth, Cecil. *Magna Bibliotheca Anglo-Judaica: A Bibliographical Guide to Anglo-Jewish History.* New ed. London: Jewish Historical Society of England, 1937. 464 pp.

486. Sable, Martin H. *Latin American Jewry: A Research Guide.* Cincinnati: Hebrew Union College Press/New York: Ktav Publishing House, 1978. 633 pp.

487. Singerman, Robert. *The Jews in Spain and Portugal: A Bibliography.* New York & London: Garland Publishing Co., 1975. 364 pp.

488. Szajkowski, Zosa. *Franco-Judaica: An Analytical Bibliography of Books, Pamphlets, Decrees, Briefs, and Other Printed Documents Pertaining to the Jews in France, 1500-1788.* New York: American Academy for Jewish Research, 1962. 160 pp.

489. Wolff, R. Ilse. *German Jewry: Its History, Life and Culture.* Wiener Library, Cat. ser., no.3. London: Vallentine, Mitchell 1958. 279 pp. Rept.: Westport, CT: Greenwood Pr., 1975.

Guides to Periodical Literature

490. Fraenkel, Josef, ed. *The Jewish Press of the World.* 5th ed. London: Cultural Department of the World Jewish Congress, 1961. 104 pp. First published in 1953.

491. *Guide to Judaica Serials in Microfilm in the Harvard College Library.* Research Materials Available in Microfilm in the Harvard University Library Guide No. 1. Cambridge, MA: Harvard University Library, 1981. 32 pp.

492. Hupper, William G. *An Index to English Periodical Literature on the Old Testament and Ancient Near Eastern Studies.* Vol. 1- . 1987- .

493. *Index of Articles on Jewish Studies.* Vol. 1- . Jerusalem: The Jewish National and University Library, 1969- . Annual.

494. *Index to Jewish Periodicals: An Author and Subject Index to Selected American and Anglo-Jewish Journals of General and Scholarly Interest.* Vol. 1- . Cleveland, OH: College of Jewish Studies Press, 1963- . Semi-annual with annual cumulations.

495. *The Joseph Jacobs Directory of the Jewish Press in America.* New York: Joseph Jacobs Organization, Inc., 1970. 140 pp.

496. *Judaica Serials and Ephemera Microfilmed Under the Strengthening Research Library Resources Program, Title II-C of the Higher Education Act of 1965.* Vol. 1- . Cambridge, MA: Harvard University Library, 1979- .

497. Marcus, Jacob R., ed. *An Index to Scientific Articles on American Jewish History.* Cincinnati, OH: American Jewish Archives/New York: Ktav, 1971. 240 pp.

498. Schwab, Moïse. *Index of Articles Relative to Jewish History and Literature Published in Periodicals from 1665 to 1900.* Augmented ed. New York: Ktav Publishing House, 1971. 539 pp. Rept. of *Répetoire des Articles Relatifs a l'histoire et a la Littérature Juives, parus dan les Périodiques de 1665 a 1900.* Paris, 1914-9123.

499. Singerman, Robert, comp. *Jewish Serials of the World: A Research Bibliography of Secondary Sources.* New York: Greenwood Press, 1986. 377 pp.

Atlases

500. de Lange, Nicolas. *Atlas of the Jewish World.* New York: Facts on File, 1984. 240 pp.

501. Gilbert, Martin. *Jewish History Atlas.* New York: Macmillan Company, 1969. 112 pp. Rev. ed.: London: Weidenfeld and Nicolson, 1976. Rev. ed.: New York: Macmillan, 1977. Rev. ed.: London: Weidenfield and Nicolson, 1985. 124 pp.

Judaism in North America

Encyclopedias

502. Gottesman, Eli, comp. *Canadian Jewish Reference Book and Directory,* 1963. Montreal: Jewish Institute of Higher Research, Central Rabbinical Seminary of Canada, 1963. 415 pp.

503. Pinsker, Sanford, and Jack Fischel, eds. *Encyclopedia of Jewish-American History and Culture.* New York: Garland Publishing, 1990. 600 pp.

504. Rosen, Oded. *The Encyclopedia of Jewish Institutions: United States and Canada.* Tel Aviv, Israel: Mosadot Publications, 1983. 501 pp.

Biographical Volumes

505. Herman, Edward, comp. *Jewish Americans and Their Backgrounds: Sources of Information.* Chicago: American Library Association, Office for Library Service to the Disadvantaged, 1976. 28 pp.

506. Lakeville Press. *American Jewish Biographies.* New York: Facts on File, 1982. 493 pp.

507. Nadell, Pamela S. *Conservative Judaism in America: A Biographical Dictionary and Sourcebook.* New York: Greenwood Press, 1988. 409 pp.

508. Rosenbloom, Joseph R. *A Biographical Dictionary of Early American Jews: Colonial Times through 1800.* Lexington: University of Kentucky Press, 1960. 175 pp.

509. *Who's Who in American Jewry: A Biographical Dictionary of Living Jews of the United States and Canada.* 3 vols. New York: National News Associations, 1927-1938.

Directories

510. *American Jewish Organizations Directory.* New York: Frenkel Mailing Service. Updated periodically. Formerly: *American Synagogue Directory.*

511. Israelowitz, Oscar. *Guide to Jewish Canada & U.S.A.* Volume I. *Eastern Provinces.* Brooklyn, NY: Israelowitz Publishing, 1990. 326 pp.

512. ———. *Guide to Jewish U.S.A.* Volume II. *The South.* Brooklyn, NY: Israelowitz Publishing, 1988. 175 pp.

513. Mason, Philip. *Directory of Jewish Archival Institutions.* Detroit, MI: National Foundation for Jewish Culture, 1975. 76 pp.

514. *American Jewish Yearbook.* Vol. 1- . New York: The American Jewish Committee/Philadelphia: The Jewish Publication Society, 1899- . Published annually.

515. Tillem, Ivan L., ed. *The Jewish Directory and Almanac.* New York: Pacific Press, 1984. 518 + 167 pp. Rev. ed. as: *The 1986 Jewish Directory and Almanac.* 1986. 748 pp. Rev. ed. as: *The 1987-88 Jewish Almanac.* 1987. 516 + 166 pp.

Bibliographies

516. Bloch, Joshua. *Of Making Many Books: An Annotated List of Books Issued by the Jewish Publication Society of America, 1890-1952.* Philadelphia: Jewish Publication Society of America, 1953. 329 pp.

517. Brickman, William W. *The Jewish Community in America: An Annotated and Classified Bibliographical Guide.* New York: Burt Franklin, 1977. 396 pp.

518. Cogan, Sara G. *Pioneer Jews of the California Mother Lode, 1849-1880.* Berkeley, CA: Western Jewish History Center, Judah L. Magnes Memorial Museum, 1968. 54 pp.

519. Davies, Raymond Arthur. *Printed Jewish Canadiana, 1685-1900.* Montreal: The Author, 1955. 57 pp.

520. Glanz, Rudolf. *The German Jew in America: An Annotated Bibliography.* Cincinnati, OH: Hebrew Union College Press/New York: Ktav Publishing House, 1969. 192 pp.

521. Gurok, Jeffrey S. *American Jewish History: A Bibliographical Guide.* New York: Anti-Defamation League of B'nai B'rith, 1983. 195 pp.

522. Karkhanis, Sharad. *Jewish Heritage in America: An Annotated Bibliography.* New York: Garland Publishing, 1988. 434 pp.

523. Korros, Alexandra Shecket, and Jonathan D. Sarna. *American Synagogue History: A Bibliography and State of the Field Survey.* New York: Marcus Weiner Publishing, 1988. 247 pp.

524. Levine, Allan E. *An American Jewish Bibliography.* 32 vols. Dictionary Catalog of the Klau Library, Cincinnati. Boston: G. K. Hall, 1964.

525. ————. *An American Jewish Bibliography.* Cincinnati, OH: American Jewish Archives, 1959. 100 pp.

526. Marcus, Jacob Rader. *An Index to Scientific Articles on American Jewish History.* Cincinnati, OH: American Jewish Archives, 1971. 240 pp.

527. Rafael, Ruth Kelson. *Western Jewish History Center: Guide to Archival and Oral History Collections.* Berkeley, CA: Western Jewish History Center, Judah L. Magnes Museum, 1987. 207 pp.

528. Rischin, Moses. *An Inventory of American Jewish History.* Cambridge, MA: Harvard University Press, 1954. 66 pp.

529. Rosenbach, A. S. W. *An American Jewish Bibliography, Being a List of Books and Pamphlets by Jews or Relating to Them Printed in the United States from the Establishment of the Press in the Colonies until 1850.* N.p.: American Jewish Historical Society, 1926. 486 pp.

530. Singerman, Robert. *Judaica Americana: A Bibliography of Publications to 1900.* 2 vols. New York: Greenwood Press, 1990.

531. Stern, Norton B. *California Jewish History: A Descriptive Bibliography.* Glendale, CA: Arthur H. Clark Co. 1967. 175 pp.

532. William E. Wiener Oral History Library. *Catalogue of Memoirs.* New York: American Jewish Committee, 1978. 145 pp.

Guides to Periodical Literature

The American Jewish Periodical Center, at Hebrew Union College, 3101 Clifton Avenue, Cincinnati, OH 45220, maintains a microfilm collection of all Jewish periodicals published in America prior to 1925 and of a selected list of periodicals published since. In 1957 it published *Jewish Periodicals and Newspapers on Microfilm* and has since released several supplements.

533. *Index to Jewish Periodicals.* Vol.1- , June 1963- . Cleveland, 1963- . Issued Bi-annually.

534. *Jewish Periodicals and Newspapers on Microfilm.* Cincinnati: American Jewish Periodical Center, 1957. Supplements.

Anti-Semitism

Bibliographies

535. Cohen, Susan M., ed. *Antisemitism: An Annotated Bibliography.* 2 vols. Sponsored by the Vidal Sassoon International Center for the Study of Antisemitism. New York: Garland Publishing, 1989.

536. Liebman, Seymour B. *The Inquisitors and the Jews in the New World: Summaries of Procesos: 1500-1810: and Bibliographical Guide.* Coral Gables, FL: University of Miami Press, 1975. 224 pp.

537. Singerman, Robert. *Antisemitic Propaganda: An Annotated Bibliography and Research Guide.* New York: Garland Publishing, 1982. 448 pp.

The Holocaust

Bibliographies

538. Braham, Randolph L. *The Hungarian Jewish Catastrophe: A Selected and Annotated Bibliography.* New York: Social Science Monographs and Institute for Holocaust Studies, 1984. 501 pp.

539. Cargas, Harry James. *The Holocaust: An Annotated Bibliography.* Haerford, PA: Catholic Library Association, 1977. 86 pp. 2nd ed.: Chicago & London: American Library Association, 1985. 196 pp.

540. Edelheit, Abraham J., and Herschel Edelheit. *Bibliography on Holocaust Literature.* Boulder & London: Westview Press, 1986. 842 pp.

541. ———. *Bibliography on Holocaust Literature: Supplement.* Boulder, CO: Westview Press, 1986. 684 pp.

542. Eitinger, Leo, and Robert Krell. *The Psychological Effects of Concentration Camps and Related Persecutions on Survivors of the Holocaust: A Research Bibliography.* Vancouver: University of British Columbia Press, 1985. 168 pp.

543. Fisher, Russell G. "The History of the Holocaust: A Selective Annotated Bibliography of Books and Films in English." *Bulletin of Bibliography* 43, 1 (March 1986): 38-43.

544. Friedlander, Henry, and Sybil Milton, eds. *Archives of the Holocaust.* 18 vols. New York: Garland Publishing, 1989-90.

545. Goldstein, Marianne. *Books on the Holocaust: Non-Fiction Titles Held by Selected Libraries in Western New York.* Buffalo, NY: Collection Development, Lockwood Memorial Library, State University of New York at Buffalo, 1985. 117 pp.

546. Laska, Vera. *Nazism, Resistance & Holocaust in World War II: A Bibliography.* Metuchen, NJ: Scarecrow Press, 1985. 183 pp.

547. Mendelsohn, John, and Donald S. Detwiler, eds. *The Holocaust: Selected Documents in 18 Volumes.* New York: Garland Publishing, 1982.

548. Robinson, Jacob. *The Holocaust and After: Sources and Literature in English.* Jerusalem: Israel Universities Press, 1973. 353 pp.

549. Skirball, Sheba F. *Films of the Holocaust: An Annotated Filmography of Collections in Israel.* Garland Filmographies Vol. 2. New York: Garland Publishing, 1990. 350 pp.

550. Szonyi, David M. *The Holocaust: An Annotated Bibliography and Resource Guide.* New York: Ktav for National Jewish Resource Center, 1985. 386 pp.

551. Wyman, David S., ed. *America and the Holocaust.* 13 vols. New York: Garland Publishing, 1990. Facsimile series of the documentation for the editor's book, *The Abandonment of the Jews.*

552. Yad Washem Martyrs' and Heroes Memorial Authority, Jerusalem, and Yivo Institute for Jewish Research. *Joint Documentary Projects. Bibliographical Series.* 14 vols. New York: Yivo Institute, 1960-74.

Jewish Studies

Annenberg Research Institute
420 Walnut St.
Philadelphia, PA 19106
The Institute houses a library on Jewish studies.

Association for the Sociological Study of Jewry
Department of Sociology
Brooklyn College
Brooklyn, NY 11210
The Association sponsors conferences, promotes research, and publishes a journal, *Contemporary Jewry*, and the *ASSJ Newsletter*.

Association of Jewish Studies
Widener Library
Harvard University
Cambridge, MA 02138
Promotes Jewish studies through sponsoring conferences, assisting in teacher placement, and publication of two periodicals, *AJS Review* and a *Newsletter*.

Berman Center for Jewish Studies
321 Maginnes 9
Lehigh University
Bethlehem, PA 18015

Center for Contemporary Judaica
304 East 49th Street
New York, NY 10017

Center for Israel and Jewish Studies
Columbia University
Broadway and West 116th Street
New York, NY 10027

The Center for Jewish Community Studies
c/o Daniel J. Elazar
555 Gladfelter Hall
Temple University
Philadelphia, PA 19122

Center for Jewish Studies
City University of New York
c/o Graduate School and University Center

33 West 42nd Street
New York, NY 10036
Located in the heart of one of the largest Jewish communities in the world, the Center conducts an expansive program which includes four major subsidiary units: the Mazur Institute for Advanced Study in Judaica, the Institute for Sephardic Studies, the Institute for Jewish Community Life, and the Emeric and Illana Institute for Holocaust Studies.

Center for Jewish Studies
Harvard University
6 Divinity Avenue, Room 210
Cambridge, MA 02138
Publishes two series of books in Jewish Studies.

Center for Judaic Studies
Boston University
745 Commonwealth Avenue, Room 615
Boston, MA 02215
Supports visiting scholars, research, and the Judaica program at Boston University.

Center for Judaic Studies
University of Denver
University Park
Denver, CO 80208
The Center conducts a broad research program and supports a subsidiary unit, the Maimonides Society, the Institute for Islamic-Judaic Study, and the Holocaust Awareness Institute.

Center for the Study of the American Jewish Experience
Jewish Institute of Religion
Hebrew Union College
3101 Clifton Avenue
Cincinnati, OH 45220
Supports interdisciplinary research on American Judaism and publishes bibliographies, monographs, and a reprint series, the Master Works of Modern Jewish Writing.

Department of Jewish Studies
McGill University
3511 Peel Street, Room 102
Montreal, PQ H3A 1W7
Conducts a research program on Eastern European Jewry.

Henry Fischel Institute for Research in Talmud and Jewish Law
5 Hapisga St.
P.O. Box 16002
Jerusalem, Israel
The Institute's library contains over 40,000 volumes.

Institute for Advanced Talmudic Studies
515 Coldstream Avenue
Toronto, M6B 2K7
An independent center, the Institute supports an extensive research program in Talmudic studies, Jewish law, and Jewish philosophy. It also publishes *Halmayon*.

Institute on American Jewish-Israeli Relations
American Jewish Committee
165 East 56th Street
New York, NY 10022

Joseph Cardinal Bernardin Center for the Study of Eastern European Jewry
Spertus College of Judaica
618 S. Michigan Avenue
Chicago, IL 60605

Judah L. Magnes Memorial Museum
2911 Russell Street
Berkeley, CA 94709
The Museum houses a Rare Book collection and the Western Jewish History Center.

Judaica and Near Eastern Research Program
Annenberg Research Institute
420 Walnut Street
Philadelphia, PA 19106
Supports post-graduate research in Jewish studies. It is supported by the 150,000+ volume Judaica collection of the Annenberg Institute.

Max Weinreich Center for Advanced Jewish Studies
1048 Fifth Avenue
New York, NY 10028

National Jewish Information Service for the Propagation of Judaism
3761 Decade Street
Las Vegas, NV 89121
Dedicated to the propagation of Judaism to people not ethnically Jewish, the center supports research on conversions to Judaism historically.

Research Center of Kabbalah
200 Park Ave.
Suite 303E
New York, NY 10017

Research Foundation for Jewish Immigration
570 Seventh Ave.
New York, NY 10018

Research Institute of Religious Jewry
471 W. End Avenue
New York, NY 10024

Schocken Institute for Jewish Research
6 Balfour St.
92192 Jerusalem, Israel
The library of the Institute includes a manuscript collection.

Soviet Jewry Research Bureau
10 E. 40th Street, Ste. 907
New York, NY 10016

Tauber Institute for the Study of European Judaism
Located at Brandeis University, the Institute publishes the Tauber Institute Series.

Archival Depositories

Collections of Jewish materials can be found at the several Jewish seminaries in North America. There is a **Council of Archives and Research Libraries in Jewish Studies**, 222 East 42nd Street, Ste. 1512, New York, NY 10168, that provide some guidance and coordination between the various centers. A lengthy guide to the significant archives in Cincinnati has been published as:

553. Clasper, James W., and M. Carolyn Dellenbach. *Guide to the Holdings of the American Jewish Archives.* Cincinnati, OH: American Jewish Archives, 1979. 211 pp.

Other works describing archival collections include:

554. Mason, Philip. *Directory of Jewish Archival Institutions.* Detroit, MI: National Federation for Jewish Culture/Wayne State University Press, 1975. 76 pp.

555. Rabinowicz, Harry M. *The Jewish Literary Treasures of England and America.* New York: Thomas Yoseloff, 1962. 166 pp.

556. ———. *Treasures of Judaica.* South Brunswick, NJ: Thomas Yoseloff, 1971. 240 pp.

The major archival depositories of American Jewish material include:

American Jewish Archives
3101 Clifton Avenue
Cincinnati, OH 45220
Located on the campus of Hebrew Union College, the American Jewish Archives are the main depository of Reform Jewish materials. It publishes the quarterly *American Jewish Archives.* Also on campus are the American Jewish Periodical Center and the Manuscript Library of the Jewish Institute of Religion, which contains over 300,000 items in Jewish studies and related fields.

American Jewish Historical Society
2 Thornton Road
Waltham, MA 02154
Located on the campus of Brandeis University, the Society's collection contains over 4 million items on all aspects of American Jewish life. The Society publishes two periodicals, *American Jewish History* and *Heritage.*

Bay Area Council on Soviet Jewry Archives
106 Baden
San Francisco, CA 94131

Frances-Henry Library
3077 University Ave.
Los Angeles, CA 90007
The Frances-Henry Library is part of the Hebrew Union College's Jewish Institute of Religion. It contains over 85,000 books, as well as collections of rare Hebraica, periodicals, phonograph records, and dissertations.

Historical Society of Israel
[Hevre ha Historit ha Israelit]
22 Rashba St.
P.O. Box 4179
91041 Jerusalem, Israel

Jewish Theological Seminary of America
Library
3080 Broadway
New York, NY 10027
Included in the library collection are the archives of the American Jewish Historical Center and the files of the Jewish Information Bureau.

Leo Baeck Institute
29 East 73rd Street
New York, NY 10021
The Institute collection is centered on the history of German-speaking Jewry of central Europe from the eighteenth century through the time of the Holocaust.

Mordecai M. Kaplan Library
Reconstructionist Rabbinical College
Church Road & Greenwood Ave.
Wyncote, PA 19095

National Jewish Information Service for the Propagation of Judaism - Research Library and Archives
3761 Decade St.
Las Vegas, NV 89121
Includes a collection on conversion to Judaism in history and literature and publishes an annual periodical for its members entitled *Voice of Judaism.*

Yeshiva University
500 W. 185th Street
New York, NY 10033
The oldest Jewish university in America has a graduate school and a seminary and a vast collection of Jewish literature to undergird its research programs.

Yivo Institute for Jewish Research
1048 Fifth Avenue
New York, NY 10028
The Institute is the primary center for research on Eastern European Jewish life both in Europe and North America. It publishes the *Yivo Annual of Jewish Social Studies* among its several periodicals.

Canadian Jewish Congress: The archives for Canadian Jewry are centered in three locations. The National archives are at the national headquarters, 1590 Ave. Docteur Penfield, Montreal H3G 1C5. Regional archives can be found at the Jewish Historical Society of Western Canada, 402-365 Hargrave Street, Winnipeg, MB R3b 2K3 and at the Toronto Jewish Congress, Ontario Regional Archives, 4600 Bathurst St., Willowdale, ON M2R 3V2. The National Archives publishes a newsletter.

Holocaust Studies

Holocaust centers can now be found in most large Jewish communities in the United States, however, the focus of Holocaust studies centers upon the following organizations and centers:

Anne Frank Institute of Philadelphia for Interfaith Holocaust Education
P. O. Box 40119
Lafayette Building, Ste. 608
5th and Chestnut Streets
Philadelphia, PA 19106-5119
Sponsors research, conferences, and publications. Publishes a newsletter.

Center for Holocaust Studies, Documentation and Research
1610 Avenue J
Brooklyn, NY 11230
As its name implies, the center supports research on anti-Semitism, especially during the World War II era, and continues the ongoing process of documenting the Holocaust. It also publishes a *Newsletter*.

Emeric and Ilana Csengeri Institute for Holocaust Studies
City University of New York
33 West 42nd Street, Room 1450
New York, NY 10036
A unit of the University's Center for Jewish Studies

Fred Roberts Crawford Witness to the Holocaust Project
Emory University
Atlanta, GA 30322
Under the guidance of the University's Department of Religion, the Project specializes in collecting the records of those who participated in the liberation of the concentration camps.

Holocaust Awareness Institute
c/o Center for Judaic Studies
University of Denver
University Park
Denver, CO 80208
Functioning as a unit of the Center for Judaic Studies at the University, the Institute collects and archives oral histories of Holocaust survivors.

Holocaust Survivors Memorial Foundation
350 Fifth Avenue, Ste. 3508
New York, NY 10118

Interfaith Council on the Holocaust
125 S. 9th Street
Philadelphia, PA 19107

International Center for Holocaust Studies
823 United Nations Plaza
New York, NY 10017
Houses a 3,000 volume library on the Holocaust.

Philadelphia Coordinating Council on the Holocaust
260 S. 15th Street, Ste. 500
Philadelphia, PA 19102
An interfaith effort of Christians and Jews to document and reflect upon the meaning of the Holocaust.

Simon Wiesenthal Center
9760 West Pico Blvd.
Los Angeles, CA 90035
The Center is on the campus of the Los Angeles campus of Yeshiva University.

Yad Vashem, The Holocaust Martyrs' and Heroes' Remembrance Authority
Har Hazikaron
P. O. Box 3477
Jerusalem, Israel
Yad Vashem sponsors *Holocaust and Genocide Studies: An International Journal* (semiannual).

Black Jews

American Association for Ethiopian Jews
2789 Oak Street
Highland Park, IL 60035
The Association attempts to generate support within the American Jewish community for the Falashas, the Jews of Ethiopia. It publishes a Newsletter and distributes a variety of literature.

The **American Religions Collection** of the University of California-Santa Barbara has a large collection of black Jewish material.

ZOROASTRIANISM

Zoroastrianism was a powerful religious force in the ancient world, becoming the official religion of the Persian Empire up until its conquest by the armies of Islam. Founded by Zoroaster (or Zarathustra) around the seventh century B.C.E., it came to express a duotheistic theology of the good Ahura Mazda and the evil Ahriman. According to this system, the world was the battlefield between these two forces. In the end, the forces of good would win and the forces of evil would be plunged into the abyss. Zoroastrian eschatology clearly played a role in the other major religions to emerge from the ancient Near East.

Despite its influence, however, the religion itself has suffered over the years and today retains but a small community of believers. Much of its scriptures, the Avesta, were destroyed first by Alexander the Great in the fourth century B.C.E. and then by the Muslims in the seventh century C.E. The Zoroastrian community in Persia was all but wiped out by the Muslims. Some fled these persecutions to India, where they are today known as the Parsis. Recent immigration has also created a Parsi community in North America.

Bibliographies

557. Boyce, Mary, ed. *Textual Sources for the Study of Zoroastrianism.* Totowa, NJ: Barnes & Noble/Manchester, UK: Manchester University Press, 1984. 166 pp.

558. Oxtoby, Willard Gurdon. *Ancient Iran and Zoroastrianism in Festschriften: an Index.* Waterloo, ON: Council on the Study of Religion, Waterloo University/Shairaz, Iran: Asia Institute of Pahlavi University, 1973. 207 pp.

Research/Resource Centers

Center for Zoroastrian Research
801 E. Tenth Street
Bloomington, IN 47401

THE RELIGIONS OF THE WORLD

Part 4: The Americas, Europe and Oceania

RELIGION IN LATIN AMERICA AND THE CARIBBEAN

Latin America and the Caribbean have developed a unique religious character due to the blending of Christian missionary efforts, native religious traditions, and the traditions of the African slaves brought over in great numbers during the colonial period. Scholarship on these areas has just recently begun in earnest, however. The short list below will no doubt grow considerably in future editions.

Sources which deal solely with Christianity and Christian missions in these regions can be found in the chapters on Christianity.

Bibliography

559. Chevannes, Barry. "The Literature of Rastafari." *Social and Economic Studies* 26, 2 (June 1977): 239-62.

560. ————. "A Preliminary Rastafari Bibliography." *Caribbean Quarterly* 24, 3/4 (September/December 1978): 56-58.

561. Owens, Joseph V. "Literature on the Rastafari, 1955-1974: A Review." *Savacoa* 11/12 (September 1975): 86-105, 113.

562. Simpson, George Eaton. "Religious Organizations in Jamaica." *Social and Economic Studies* 5, 4 (December 1956): 334-405.

563. Turner, W. Harold. *Bibliography of New Religious Movements in Primal Societies. Vol. 5. Latin America.* Boston, MA: G. K. Hall, 1991. 233 pp. *See also:* (174).

RELIGION IN NORTH AMERICA

Studying "religion" in North America rather than "Christianity" in North America is a relatively new idea; overwhelmingly texts on the United States and Canada have been limited to consideration of Christianity, with some passing menition of Judaism. In this section are listed those sources on religion in North America and the various regions thereof. Also, particular issues impacting on the religious culture of North America are included, such as church-state relationships. Sources dealing primarily with Christianity in North America are listed separately in a later chapter.

Encyclopedias and Dictionaries

564. Hill, Samuel S., ed. *Encyclopedia of Religion in the South.* N.p.: Mercer University Press, 1984. 878 pp.

565. Lippy, Charles H., and Peter W. Williams. *Encyclopedia of the American Religious Experience: Studies of Traditions and Movements.* 3 vols. New York: Charles Scribner's Sons, 1988.

566. Melton, J. Gordon. *Encyclopedia of American Religions.* 2 vols. Wilmington, NC: Consortium, 1979. *Supplement.* Detroit, MI: Gale Research Company, 1985. 177 pp. 2nd ed.: Detroit, MI: Gale Research Company, 1987. 899 pp. *Supplement.* 1987. 157 pp. 3rd ed.: Detroit, MI: Gale Research Company, 1989. 1100 pp. Rept.: 3 vols. New York: Triumph Books, 1991.

567. ————. *Encyclopedia of American Religions: Religious Creeds.* Detroit, MI: Gale Research Company, 1988. 838 pp. Rept.: 3 vols. New York: Triumph Books, 1991.

Biographical Volumes

568. Bowden, Henry Warner. *Dictionary of American Religious Biography.* Westport, CT: Greenwood Press, 1977. 572 pp.

569. Lippy, Charles H., ed. *Twentieth Century Shapers of American Popular Religion.* New York: Greenwood Press, 1989. 494 pp.

570. Melton, J. Gordon. *Biographical Dictionary of American Cult and Sect Leaders.* New York: Garland Publishing, 1986. 354 pp.

571. ———. *Religious Leaders of America.* Detroit, MI: Gale Research Company, 1991. 604 pp.

572. Schwarz, Julius Caesar, ed. *Who's Who in the Clergy.* 1936. Rev. as *Religious Leaders in America.* New York: J.C. Schwarz, 1941.

Directories

573. *The Directory of Religious Organizations in the United States.* Falls Church, VA: McGrath, 1982. 518 pp.

574. Geisendorfer, James V., ed. *Directory of Religious Organizations in the United States of America.* Wilmington, NC: McGrath Publishing Co., 1977. 553 pp

575. Geisendorfer, James V. *Religion in America: A Directory.* Leiden: E. J. Brill, 1983, 175 pp. Rev. ed as: *A Directory of Religious and Parareligious Bodies and Organizations in the United States.* Lewiston, NY: Edwin Mellen Press, 1989. 427 pp.

576. Melton, J. Gordon, with James V. Geisendorfer. *A Directory of Religious Bodies in the United States.* New York: Garland Publishing, 1977. 305 pp. Rev. ed. as: *Religious Bodies in the United States: A Directory.* New York: Garland Publishing, 1990. 313 pp.

Bibliographies

577. Brunkow, Robert de V., ed. *Religion and Society in North America: An Annotated Bibliography.* Santa Barbara, CA: American Bibliographic Society/Clio Press, 1983. 515 pp.

578. Burr, Nelson R. *A Critical Bibliography of Religion in America.* 2 vols. Volume IV, Parts 1 & 2 of *Religion in American Life.* Princeton, NJ: Princeton University Press, 1961.

579. ———, comp. *Religion in American Life.* New York: Meredith, 1971. 171 pp.

580. Crysdale, Stewart, and Jean-Paul Montminy. *Religion in Canada: Annotated Inventory of Scientific Studies of Religion (1945-1972).* Histoire et Sociologie de la Culture 8. Downsview, Ont.: York University; Québec, P.Q.: Les Presses de l'Université Laval, 1974. 189 pp.

581. Fraker, Anne T., ed. *Religion and American Life: Resources.* Urbana & Chicago: University of Illinois Press, 1989. 236 pp.

582. Gaustad, Edwin S. *American Religious History.* Washington, DC: Service Center for Teachers of History, 1966. 27 pp.

583. Lippy, Charles. *Bibliography of Religion in the South.* Macon, GA: Mercer University Press, 1985. 498 pp.

584. Lo, Clarence Y. H. "Countermovements and Conservative Movements in the Contemporary United States." *Annual Review of Sociology* 8 (1982): 107-34.

585. Menendez, Albert J. *Religion and the U.S. Presidency: A Bibliography.* New York: Garland Publishing, 1986. 160 pp.

586. ———. *Religious Conflict in America: A Bibliography.* New York & London: Garland, 1985. 130 pp.

587. ———. *School Prayer and Other Religious Issues in American Public Education: A Bibliography.* New York: Garland Publishing, 1985. 168 pp.

588. Ralston, Helen. "Strands of Research of Religious Movements in Canada." *Studies in Religion* 17 (1988): 157-77.

589. Shulman, Albert M. *The Religious Heritage of America.* San Diego: A.S. Barnes, 1981. 527 pp.

590. Wilson, John F. *Church and State in America: A Bibliographical Guide. The Colonial and Early National Periods.* 2 vols. Westport, CT: Greenwood Press, 1986.

Research Centers

Center for the Study of American Religion
Princeton University
613 Seventy-nine Hall
Princeton, NJ 08544-1006
The Center was founded in 1991 and has projected a program of research and conferences.

Institute for the Study of American Religion
Box 90709
Santa Barbara, CA 93190-0709
Founded in 1969, the Institute carries on an extensive program of research and publication and sponsors occasional conferences.

NATIVE AMERICAN RELIGION

The consideration of Native American religious life from the perspective of religious studies has been neglected, though the 1980's have seen the emergence of Native American religious traditions as a specialized area within Native American studies in general. There is an immediate need for basic reference tools only a few of which have been compiled and published.

Among scholars, the topic given the most attention, for a number of very good and a few not so worthy reasons, is the peyote movement and the Native American Church. Two other nineteenth-century pan-Indian movements revolving around the ghost dance and the sun dance have also attracted a degree of schoalrly interest.

Bibliographies

591. La Barre, Weston. "Twenty Years of Peyote Studies." *Current Anthropology* 1 (1960): 45-60.

592. Turner, W. Harold. *Bibliography of New Religious Movements in Primal Societies. Vol. 2. North America.* Boston, MA: G. K. Hall, 1978. 286 pp. *See also:* (174)

RELIGION IN EUROPE

Through the twentieth century Europe has led the West in the development of a pluralistic religious environment, yet has been much slower to document the significant religious changes overtaking the continent. The items listed below attempt to document the broad range of religious groups in Europe and its several countries, including the older Christian churches, the newer evangelical sectarian groups and the so-called new religious movements. Volumes dealing primarily with just the new religious movements are cited in a later chapter (see page 129).

Similar to studies of religion in North America, most literature on religion in Europe deals with the presence of Christianity. Those sources are to be found in later chapters as the sources cited immediately below relate more to the pluralistic religious topography of modern Europe.

Encyclopedias and Dictionaries

593. Bosch, J. *Iglesias, sectas y nuevos cultos.* Madrid, Spain: Bruño, 1981.

594. Denaux, A. *Godsdienstsekten in Vlaanderen.* Leuven, Belgium: DF, 1982.

595. Eggenberger, Oswald. *Die Kirchen, Sondergruppen und religiösen Vereinigungen.* Zurich: Theologischer Verlag, 1986. 337 pp.

596. Grundler, J. *Lexikon der Christlichen Kirchen und Sekten.* Vol.I-II. Vienna, Austria: Herder, 1961.

597. Hoekstra, E. G., and M. H. Ipenburg. *Wegwijs in gelovig Nederland: Een alfabetische beschrijving van Nederlandse kerken en religieuze groeperingen.* Den Haag: CIP-Gegevens Konninklijke Bibliotheek, n.d. 279 pp.

598. Hutten, Kurt. *Seher Grubler Enthusiasten.* Rev. ed.: Stuttgart: Quell Verlag, rev. edition, 1989. 896 pp.

599. Mayer, Jean-François. *Les Sectes et Vous.* Paris and Fribourg: Éditions Saint-Paul, 1989. 99 pp.

600. *Religieuze Bewegingen in Nederland.* Amsterdam: VU Uitgeverij, 1989. 134 pp.

601. Schmidtchen, Gerhard. *Sekten und Psycho Kultur. Reichweite und Attraktivität von Jugendreligionen in der Bundesrepublik Deutschland.* Freiburg, Basel, Wien: Herder, 1987. 124 pp.

Bibliographies

602. Turner, W. Harold. *Bibliography of New Religious Movements in Primal Societies. Vol. 4. Europe and Asia.* Boston, MA: G. K. Hall, 1991. 279 pp. See also: (174)

ATHEISM/HUMANISM/FREETHOUGHT

Frequently negelected in works on religion, atheism and other non-theistic appraoches to life form an extremely important, if small, element of the religious environment since their emergence in force in the nineteenth century. Atheists, Humanists, Rationalists, and Freethinkers have fought the power of the institutional church in Western society and their literature was dominated by arguments against Christian thesim. They have effectively challenged pre-modern supernaturalistic worldviews though they have had less success in coping with the wide range of new theologies which have made adjustments for the more traditional atheist arguments.

While attempting to create a positive philosophy, most notably as humanism, the real life of atheism has been based upon its opposition to Christianity. It has hence been unable to develop many strong institutional expressions and little cultural life. Its most important role has been the posing of a radical alternative to traditional Christianity. The revival of Evangelcial Protestantism, creationism, and new forms of supernaturalism in the late twentieth century has provided a new generation of targets for non-theistic attacks.

International

Encyclopedias and Dictionaries

603. McCabe, Joseph. *A Rationalist Encyclopaedia: A Book of Reference on Religion, Ethics and Science.* 1948. 2nd ed.: London: Watts, 1950. 633 pp.

604. Odell, Robin, and Tom Barfield, comps. *A Humanist Glossary.* London: Pemberton, 1967. 24 pp.

605. Stein, Gordon. *The Encyclopedia of Unbelief.* 2 vols. Buffalo, NY: Prometheus Books, 1985.

Bibliographies

606. *Catalogue of the Library of the Rationalist Press Association.* London: Watts & Co., 1937.

607. Stein, Gordon. *Atheism: A World Bibliography.* New York: Garland Publishing, 1990. c. 300 pp.

608. ———. *Freethought in the United Kingdom and the Commonwealth: A Descriptive Bibliography.* Westport, CT: Greenwood Press, 1981. 193 pp.

Biographical Volumes

609. Bennett, De Robigne Mortimer. *The World's Sages, Infidels and Thinkers.* New York: The Author, 1876. 1075 pp.

610. McCabe, Joseph, comp. *A Biographical Dictionary of Modern Rationalists.* London: Watts & Co., 1920. 934 pp. Rev. ed. as: *A Biographical Dictionary of Ancient, Medieval and Modern Freethinkers.* Girard, KS: Haldeman-Julius Publications, 1945. 96 pp.

611. Wheeler, Joseph Mazzini. *A Biographical Dictionary of Freethinkers of All Ages and Nations.* London: Progressive Publishing Co., 1889. 355 pp.

North America

Bibliographies

612. Brown, Marshall G., and Gordon Stein. *Freethought in the United States: A Descriptive Bibliography.* Westport, CT: Greenwood Press, 1978. 146 pp.

613. ———. *Robert G. Ingersoll: A Checklist.* Kent, OH: Kent State University Press, 1969. 128 pp.

Archival Depositories

A list of freethought collections in U.S. libraries is published in the second appendix of Brown and Stein (612). The more important of these include the **Library of Congress** (freethought periodicals, Ingersoll's papers), **Harvard University** (includes the papers of Francis Ellingwood Abbot), the **New York City Public**

Library (includes perhaps the largest collection of bound freethought pamphlets), **Union Theological Seminary** in New York City (the McAlpin Collection on British Deism), the **American Philosophical Society** (probably the best collection on Thomas Paine), and the **University of Wisconsin** (especially strong in British materials). Other collections include:

Charles E. Stevens American Atheist Library and Archives, Inc.
Box 14505
Austin, TX 78761
This is the library and archives of American Atheists, Inc.

Fellowship of Religious Humanism Archives
Box 278
Yellow Springs, OH 45387

NEW RELIGIOUS MOVEMENTS IN THE WEST

In the 1960s, scholars first confronted a host of unconventional expressions of religion among Western young adults along the West Coast of the United States. The same phenomena was soon discovered to exist across North America and Europe. Originally believed to be a part of the counter-culture movement, it has since shown itself as the harbinger of a significant cultural shift in the West toward the establishment of a very pluralistic religious culture in which religious hegemony is shared by many diverse forms of Christianity, many newer forms of Western religions (from Mormonism to the Occult), and the whole array of the world's religions.

Moving from the more derogatory label "cult," scholars began to use the terms "new religions" or "NRMs," and while noting the inadequacy of the terms, have been unable as yet to find a more descriptive one. The opposition to the emergence of the new religions and the resulting controversy has, however, led to the production of a vast literature. Those items cited below are useful in guiding one through the controversy.

International Perspectives

Directories

614. *A Pilgrim's Guide to Planet Earth.* San Raphael, CA: Spiritual Community Publications, 1981. 320 pp.

Bibliographies

615. Beckford, James A., and James T. Richardson. "A Bibliography of Social Scientific Studies of New Religion Movements." *Social Compass* 30 (1983): 111-35.

616. Blood, L. O. *Comprehensive Bibliography on the Cult Phenomenon.* Weston, MA: American Family Foundation, 1984. 111 pp.

617. Donahue, Michael J. *New Religious Movements: A Bibliography.* Washington, DC: American Psychological Association, 1984. 49 pp.

618. Foucart, E. *Répertoire Bibliographique. Sectes et Mouvements Réligieux marginaux de l'Occident contemporain.* Quebec, Canada: Etudes et Documents en Sciences de la Religion, 1982.

619. Hexham, Irving. A Bibliographical Guide to Cults, Sects, and New Religious Movements." *Update: A Quarterly Journal on New Religious Movements* Part 1. 7. 4 (1983): 40-46. Part 2. 8, 1 (1984): 36-48.

620. Lusk, Mildred K., comp. *Cults in the United States: Selected Bibliography of Sources in the Texas Tech University Library.* Lubbock, TX: Texas Tech University Library, 1982. 42 pp.

621. *The New Religions: An Annotated Introductory Bibliography.* Berkeley, CA: Program for the Study of New Religious Movements in America, Graduate Theological Union, 1978. 10 pp. Rev. ed. as: Hackett, David G. *The New Religions. An Annotated Introductory Bibliography.* Berkeley, CA: Center for the Study of New Religious Movements, 1981. 38 pp.

622. Robbins, Thomas, comp. *Civil Liberties, "Brainwashing" and "Cults": A Select Annotated Bibliography.* 2nd ed. Berkeley, CA: NRM Publications, 1981. 48 pp.

623. ———. "New Religious Movements, Brainwashing, and Deprogramming—The View from the Law Journals: A Review Essay and Survey." *Religious Studies Review* 11 (1985): 361-70.

624. ———. Sociological Studies of New Religious Movements: A Selective Review." *Religious Studies Review* 9 (9183): 233-39.

625. ———, and Dick Anthony. "The Sociology of Contemporary Religious Movements." *Annual Review of Sociology* 5 (1979): 75-89.

626. ———, Dick Anthony, and James T. Richardson. "Theory and Research in Today's 'New Religions'." *Sociological Analysis* 39 (1978): 95-112.

627. Roszak, Betty, comp. *A Select Filmography on New Religious Movements.* Berkeley, CA: NRM Publications, 1979.

628. Saliba, John A. *Psychiatry and the Cults: An Annotated Bibliography.* New York: Garland Publishing, 1987. 601 pp.

629. ———. *Social Science and the Cults: An Annotated Bibliography.* New York: Garland Publishing, 1990. 694 pp.

630. *Selected Bibliography on New Religious Movements in Western Countries.* Rome, Italy: International Documentation and Communication Center, 1979.

North America

631. Choquette, Diane, comp. *New Religious Movements in the United States and Canada: A Critical Assessment and Annotated Bibliography.* Bibliographies and Indexes in Religious Studies No. 5. Westport, CT: Greenwood Press, 1985. 235 pp.

632. Melton, J. Gordon. *Biographical Dictionary of Cult and Sect Leaders.* New York: Garland Publishing, 1986. 354 pp.

633. ———. *Encyclopedic Handbook of Cults in America.* New York: Garland Publishing, 1986. 272 pp.

Europe

Encyclopedias and Dictionaries

634. Del Re, Michele. *Culti Emergenti e Diritto Penale.* Camerino, Italy: University Press, 1982. 467 pp.

635. Eggenberger, Oswald, et al. *New Age aus christlicher Sicht.* Freibourg: Paulusverlag/Zurich: Theologischer Verlag, 1988. 175 pp.

636. Ferrari, Sivio. *Diritti dell'Uomo e Libertà dei Gruppi Religiosi. Problemi giuridici dei nuovi movimenti religiosi.* Padova, Italy: Cedam, 1989. 268 pp.

637. Filoramo, Giovanni. *I Nuovi Movimenti Religiosi. Metamorfosi del Sacro.* Bari, Italy: Laterza, 1986, 192 pp.

638. Haack, Friedrich-Wilhelm. *Jugend Religionen: Ursachen-Trends-Reaktionen.* Munchen: Wilhelm Heyne Verlag, 1981. 528 pp.

639. Hernando, J. G. *Pluralismo Religioso, II, Sectas y Religiones No Cristianas.* Madrid, Spain: Sociedad de Educacion Atenas: Centro Ecumenico "Missioneras de la Unidad, 1983.

640. Introvigne, Massimo. *Le Nuove Religioni.* Milano: Sugar Co., 1989. 429 pp.

641. ————. *Le Sette Cristiane. Dai Testimoni di Geova al Reverendo Moon.* Milano, Italy: Mondadori, 1989. 190 pp.

642. Keller, Carl E., et al. *Jesus Ausserhalb der Kirche. Das Jesusverständnis in neuen religiösen Bewegungen.* Freiburg, Switzerland: Paulusverlag, 1989. 159 pp.

643. Terrin, A. N. *Nuove Religioni. Alla Ricerca della Terra Promessa.* Brescia, Italy: Morcelliana, 1985.

644. Vernette, J. *Au Pays du Nouveau-sacré. Voyage à l'intérieur de la jeune génération.* Paris, France: Du Centurion, 1981.

645. ————. *Sectes et réveil religieux.* Paris, France: Salvator, 1976.

Counter Cult Efforts

646. Pement, Eric, ed. *The 1987 Directory of Cult Research Organizations.* Chicago: Cornerstone Press, 1987. 63 pp. Rev. ed. as: *The 1988 Directory of Cult Research Organizations.* Chicago: Cornerstone Publications, 1988. 66 pp.

647. Shupe, Anson D., David G. Bromley, and Donna L. Oliver. *The Anti-Cult Movement in America: A Bibliography and Historical Survey.* New York: Garland Publishing, 1984. 169 pp.

648. Tolbert, Keith Edward. *ARC Cult Literature Index 1987, Module 4.* Trenton, MI: Apologetic Research Coalition, 1988. 183 pp.

New Religions Studies

Centre d'Information sur les Nouvelles Religions
8010, rue Saint Denis
Montreal, PQ
H2R 2G1 Canada
The primary Canadian research facility, CINR maintains a data base, publishes a variety of books, and conducts a regular series of public programs.

Centre for New Religious Movements
Shelly Oaks Colleges
Birmingham B29 6LQ, UK

Centre for New Religious Movements
c/o Dr. Peter Clarke
King's College London
Strand, London WC2R 2LS
England
The Centre publishes *Religion Today: A Journal of Contemporary Religions.*

CESNUR
(Center for Studies of New Religions)
c/o Dr. Massimo Introvigne
Via Bertola, 86
10122 Torino, Italy

Flora Lamson Hewlett Library
Graduate Theological Union
2400 Ridge Road
Berkeley, CA 94709
The Graduate Theological Union hosted the short-lived Center for the Study of New Religions, and retained the Center's collection.

INFORM
c/o Dr. Eileen Barker
The Lionel Robbins Building
10 Portugal Street
London WC2A 2HD
England
Funded by the British government, INFORM conducts research, maintains a data base, and provides information to the public.

Institute for the Study of American Religion
P. O. Box 90709
Santa Barbara, CA 93190
In 1985, ISAR deposited its 30,000 volume collection of primary source materials on New Religions in the Library of the University of California-Santa Barbara. Today it is the Library's **American Religions Collection**. The Institute actively supports the continued growth of the Collection, which adds several thousand volumes each year. In addition the Collection includes some 30 filing cabinets of pamphlets, newspaper clippings and other ephemera. It has also been designated the Western depository for the Communal Studies Association. The Institute also continues an active publication program annually producing reference books about both new religions and the larger Western religious scene and occasionally sponsoring conferences.

New Religion—Individual Churches

Scientology

649. Hubbard, L. Ron. *Dianetics and Scientology Technical Dictionary.* Los Angeles: Publications Organization, 1975.

650. Littler, June D. *The Church of Scientology: A Bibliography.* Sects & Cults in America Series vol. 16. New York: Garland, 1990. c.400 pp.

Unification Church

651. Mickler, Michael L. *The Unification Church in America: A Bibliography and Research Guide.* Sects & Cults in America Series Vol. 9. New York & London: Garland, 1987. 240 pp.

RELIGION IN OCEANIA

Oceania is a collective term for the islands of the South Pacific, and includes, for purposes of this volume the Philippines, Australia and New Zealand. The traditional religions and religious movements of Oceania have been left primarily to anthropologists and attention from religious studies is only beginning to manifest. Oceania has been the target of Christian missions, and the additional literature on Christianty's presence in the islands is covered in a later chapter.

Bibliographies

652. La Barre, Weston. "Materials for a History of Studies of Crisis Cults: A Bibliographical Essay." *Current Anthropology* 12 (1971): 3-44.

653. Turner, W. Harold. *Bibliography of New Religious Movements in Primal Societies. Vol. 3. Oceania.* Boston, MA: G. K. Hall, 1990. 450 pp.

III

ISSUES IN COMPARATIVE RELIGION

Part 1: Forming the Religious Life

COMMUNAL/UTOPIAN STUDIES

The communal impulse has been a part of the religious life from ancient times. It was instilled in Christianity at its beginning and experienced a new resurgence in the centuries after the Reformation. Since the early nineteenth century, religious communalism has steadily grown in the West as an alternative lifestyle embodying various religious virtues. That communal impulse gave birth to the communally organized Christian orders. Today there are not only Christian communes and social experiments, but significant Jewish, Hindu, Buddhist and New Age intentional communities. The Communal Studies Association emerged in the 1970s to provide a focus for study of historical communes and discussion of present-day communal life.

Directories

As a whole, twentieth century communalists have not been separationists and have tried to establish networks with other communities of like mind. Hence they have placed a high priority on the production of directories and the budgeting of resources to create them.

654. *A Directory of Christian Communities & Groups* [in Britain]. Birmingham, UK: Community Resource Center, 1980. 101 pp.

655. *The Guide.* Washington, DC: Mid Atlantic Rainbow Outreach, 1985-1986. 48 pp.

656. *The 1990/91 Directory of Intentional Communities: A Guide to Cooperative Living.* Evansville, IN: Fellowship for Intentional Community/Stelle, IL: Communities Publications Cooperative, 1990. 310 pp. *Update.* Evansville, IN: Fellowship of Intentional Communities, 1991. 17 pp.

657. *The Rainbow Nation Cooperative Community Guide.* McCall, ID: The Rainbow Nation. V, 1982. 94 pp. VI, 1982-82. 44 pp. VII, 1983-84. 30 pp. VII, 1984-85. 32 pp.

Bibliographies

658. Adams, Raymond. *Booklist of American Communities: A Collection of Books in the Library of Raymond Adams.* Chapel Hill, NC: University of North Carolina English Department, 1935. 2 pp.

659. Bassett, T. D. Seymour, comp. "Bibliography: Descriptive and Critical." In Donald Drew Egbert and Stow Parsons, eds. *Socialism and American Life.* 2 vols. Princeton, NJ: Princeton University Press, 1952. Bassett's bibliography comprises volume 2 of this significant study.

660. Bauer, Patricia M., ed. *Cooperative Colonies in California: A Bibliography Collected from Printed and Manuscript Material Located in the Bancroft Library and Doe Memorial Library.* Berkeley, CA: n.p., n.d. 26 pp.

661. Conover, Patrick. *The Alternative Culture and Contemporary Communes, Revised: A Partly Annotated Bibliography.* Monticello, IL: Council of Planning Librarians, Exchange Bibliography #952, 1976.

662. Dare, Philip N. *American Communes to 1860: A Bibliography.* Sects & Cults in America Series Vol. 12. New York: Garland Publishing, 1989. 224 pp.

663. Fogarty, Robert S. "Communal History in America." *Choice* 20 (June 1973): 578-90. Rept: *American Studies: An International Newsletter* 12 (Winter 1973): 2-31.

664. Gollin, G. Lindt. "Religious Communitarianism in America: A Review of Recent Research." *Archives Internationales de Sociologie de la Cooperation et du Development* 28 (1970): 125 pp.

665. Jones, Helen Dudenbostel, comp. *Communal Settlements in the United States: A Selected List of References.* Washington, DC: Library of Congress, 1909, 1947. Unpaged.

666. Mariampolski, Hyman. "Communes and Utopias, Past and Present: A Bibliography of Post 1945 Studies." *Bulletin of Bibliography* 36 (July-September 1979): 119-27, 143.

667. Melton, J. Gordon, and Robin Martin. *A Bibliography of American Communalism.* Evanston, IL: Institute for the Study of American Religion, 1984. 23 pp.

668. Miller, Timothy. *American Communes, 1860-1960: A Bibliography.* Sects & Cults in America Series Vol. 14. New York: Garland Publishing, 1990. 583 pp.

669. Negley, Glen. *Utopian Literature: A Supplementary Listing of Works Influential in Utopian Thought.* Lawrence, KS: The Regents Press of Kansas, 1977. 228 pp.

670. Owings, Loren C. *The American Communitarian Tradition, 1693-1940: A Guide to the Sources in the Library of the University of California at Davis.* Davis, CA: University of California Library, 1971. 88 pp.

671. Pigault, Gérard. *Christian Communities.* Strasbourg, France: Cerdic-Publications, 1974. 40 pp. Rev. ed. as: *Christian Communities: International Bibliography 1975-1982.* RIC Supplements 72-73. Strasbourg, France: Cerdic-Publications, 1982. 160 pp.

672. Sargent, Lyman Tower. *British and American Utopian Literature, 1516-1975: An Annotated Bibliography.* Boston: G. K. Hall & Co., 1979. 324 pp.

Shakers

Shaker studies provide a special interest for communal scholars. The elaborate culture produced by this very successful nineteenth-century communal system had stimulated a vital stream of research and speculation.

673. McKinstry, E. Richard, comp. *The Edward Deming Andrews Memorial Shaker Collection.* New York: Garland Publishing, 1987. 412 pp.

674. MacLean, J.P. *A Bibliography of Shaker Literature.* 1905. Rept. New York: Burt Franklin, 1971. 71 pp.

675. Meader, Robert F. W., comp. *Catalogue of the Emma B. King Library of the Shaker Museum.* Old Chatham, NY: Shaker Museum Foundation, 1970. 62 pp.

676. Richmond, Mary L. *Shaker Literature: A Bibliography.* 2 vols. Hannock, MA: Shaker Community, 1977. The most comprehensive work on Shaker-related materials. Dare (662) updates Richmond with material published from 1977-88.

677. Winter, Esther C., comp. *Shaker Literature in the Rare Book Room of the Buffalo and Erie County Public Library.* Buffalo, NY: Buffalo and Erie County Public Library, 1967. 43 pp.

Communal Studies/Archive Depositories

Besides Miller (668) and Dare (662) cited above, information on archival collections can be found in:

678. Selth, Jefferson. *Alternative Life Styles: A Guide to Research Collections of International Communities, Nudism, and Sexual Freedom.* Westport CT; Greenwood Press, 1985. 133 pp.

679. Sweetland, James H. "Federal Sources for the Study of Collective Communities," *Government Publications Review* 7A (1980): 129-38.

680. Weimer, Mark F. "William A. Hinds American Communities Collection." *Communal Societies* 7 (1987): 85-103.

Some of the more important locations of collections, along with organizations devoted to the study of communal life, are cited below:

American Jewish Archives
Hebrew Union College
3101 Clifton Avenue
Cincinnati, OH 45220
The Archives holds the largest collection of material related to Jewish communal living, with a special focus on the late-nineteenth century experiments.

Americans for Progressive Israel
27 W. 20th St.
New York, NY 10011
The organization supplies information on the Kibbutzim in Israel. It publishes a periodical, *Israel Horizons.*

Center for Icarian Studies
University Libraries
Western Illinois University
Macomb, IL 61455
A research and archival center concerned with those communities which grew out of the thought of Etienne Cabet (1788-1895).

Centre for the Study of Cooperatives
c/o Diefenbaker Centre
University of Saskatchewan
Saskatoon, SK S7N 0W0
Canada

Communal Studies Association
c/o Center for Communal Studies
86000 University Blvd.
Evansville, IN 47712
The major professional association engaged in study and research on communal life. It publishes the annual journal *Communal Studies*, holds a national conference annually in October, and supports the communal collection and archive at the Center for Communal Studies. The Pacific Coast Chapter holds an annual meeting in May. CSA has designated the American Religions Collection at the University of California-Santa Barbara as its archival depository for the western United States.

Community Service, Inc.
Yellow Springs, OH
The files of Community Service, a support organization for people living or wishing to live communally, contains unique material gathered over its many years of interaction with communes. At some point, the files are to be transferred to nearby Antioch College.

Cooperative Library
University Center for Cooperatives
University of Wisconsin
Lowell Hall, Room 526
610 Lexington Street
Madison, WI 53703
A library and archive which focuses research on all aspects of cooperative living worldwide.

Federation of Egalitarian Communities
c/o East Wind Community
Box DC-9
Tecumseh, MO 65760

Federation of Kibbutz Movements
Kibbutz Studies Center
c/o Yad Tabenkin, Research and Documentation Center
for the United Kibbutz Movement
Pamat Efal 52960, Israel
The Federation sponsors the quarterly *Kibbutz Trends* (a merger of *Kibbutz Trends* and *Kibbutz Studies*.

Fellowship for Intentional Community
c/o Center for Communal Studies
8600 University Blvd.
Evansville, IN 47712

International Communal Studies Association
c/o Yaacov Oved
Yad Tabenkin Institute
Raat Efal 52 960
Israel

International Communes Network
Communidad-ICN
Box 15128, S-10465
Stockholm, Sweden
The Network publishes a quarterly bulletin and a list of participating communities.

Society for Utopian Studies
c/o Lawrence Hough
Department of Political Science
EC University
Greenville, NC 27858

Shaker Studies

Emma B. King Library
Shaker Museum Foundation
Old Chatham, NY 12136

The Shaker Library
United Society of Believers
R. R. #1, Box 640
Poland Springs, ME 04274

South Union Shaker Museum Library
Shakertown at South Union
Hwy 68-80
Russelville, KY 42276

CONVERSION

The growth of religious pluralism in the West, the accompanying mobility of individuals moving from one religious community to another, and the heightened threat felt by some nonconversionist groups has joined the older interest in the dynamics of revivalism to stimulate scholarship on the nature of religious conversion. The literature is diverse and disagreements intense.

Bibliographies

681. Franck, Loren, Monty L. Lynn, Mark Mendenhall, and Gary R. Oddous. *Seven Years of Religious Conversion: A Selected Annotated Bibliography.* Washington, DC: American Psychological Association, 1982. 6 pp.

682. Rambo, Lewis R. "Current Research on Religious Conversion," *Religious Studies Review* 8, 2 (April 1982): 146-59.

683. Snow, David A., and Richard Machalek. "The Sociology of Conversion." *Annual Review of Sociology* 10 (1984): 167-90.

684. Wallis, Roy. "What's New in the New Religions?: A Review of Recent Books." *Zetetic Scholar* 6 (1980): 155-69.

CREATION/EVOLUTION

While most felt the issue of creation versus evolution had died in the 1930s, it remained alive within Evangelical Christian circles. It has arisen anew as Evangelicalism has regrouped and liberal Protestantism declined in popular support. Much of the debate has grown around what is termed "scientific creationism," the attempt of some scholars of the hard sciences to argue for a recently created earth. It also has involved new ways of accepting majority opinions about the age of the earth while criticizing various aspects of evolutionary theory, especially on some of its social implications. While most scholars are reluctant to reopen the debates, proponents of various forms of creationism have forced the issue, primarily around challenges to public school curricula.

Encyclopedias and Directories

685. Milner, Richard. *Encyclopedia of Evolution: Humanity's Search for Its Origin.* New York: Facts on File, 1990. 500 pp.

Bibliographies

686. Fox, Sidney. "Creationism and Evolutionary Protobiogenesis." In Montagu, Ashley. *Science and Creationism.* New York: Oxford University Press, 1984. 434 pp.

Creationist Studies

Creation Research Society
P. O. Box 14016
Terre Haute, IN
The Society publishes the *Creation Research Society Quarterly.*

Creation Science Research Center
P. O. Box 23195
San Diego, CA 92123

Creation Social Sciences and Humanities Society
1429 N. Holyoke
Wichita, KS 67208

Institute for Creation Research
P. O. Box 2667
El Cajun, CA 92021

HEALING

Beginning in Spiritualism, revivalist-oriented Protestantism, and Christian Science, spiritual healing began a climb to a position of new prominence within the larger religious world. Its course differs in different countries. In England, Spiritualists took the lead. In North America Christian Science raised the issue in a decisive manner. In both Europe and North America, conservative Protestants within the Holiness and Pentecostal movement did the most to integrate healing within the mainline church. Throughout the twentieth century, the focus on spiritual healing within liberal Protestantism has come in waves, beginning with the Emmanuel Movement.

While Christians were appropriating a spiritual healing emphasis, a whole new approach to healing developed within the New Age metaphysical movement, fueled by insights from the East. It was called the Holistic Health movement and was developed in part by physicians hoping to find an alternative to the variety of painful and less than effective treatments used within the medical establishment, and in part by individuals seeking health out of a very different spiritual-metaphysical world view. As the movement emerged, it championed methods to assist the body with natural and non-invasive means to strengthen itself and cast off disease naturally, rather than approaches in which disease is fought with drugs or surgery. In many ways, the holistic health practitioners are, like other doctors, being forced to function in a secular setting. At the same time, they function as carriers of a new alternative religious vision.

General Sources

Bibliographies

687. Melton, J. Gordon. *A Reader's Guide to the Church's Ministry of Healing.* Evanston, IL: Academy of Religion and Psychical Research, 1973. 78 pp. Rev. ed.: Independence MO: Academy of Religion and Psychical Research, 1977. 102 pp. Written just as the Holistic Health Movement was beginning, this volume provides a bibliographic survey of the whole field of nonconventional healing from divine healing in the church to psychic surgery and Oriental medicine.

Christian Science

Biographical Volumes

688. *Pioneers of Christian Science.* Brookline, MA: Longyear Historical Society, 1972. Unpaged.

Bibliographies

689. Orcutt, William Dana. *Mary Baker Eddy and Her Books.* Boston: Christian Science Publishing Society, 1950. 198 pp.

Archives/Research Centers

There are two primary archival collections representative of Christian Science. The largest is the **Library and Archives of the First Church of Christ, Scientist** located in the headquarters building at 175 Huntington Avenue, Boston, MA 02115. It contains a set of church publications, extensive files, and materials on dissident movements. A lesser known but important collection is the nearby **Longyear Historical Society & Museum**, 120 Seaver Street, Brookline, MA 02146, whose collection is almost as large as that at the headquarters in Boston. The church has been increasingly open to outsiders using the collection, but potential users should apply directly to each for authorized access to the collections.

It should also be noted that smaller but significant collections of Christian Science literature can be found in the **Bridwell Library** at Southern Methodist University, Dallas, Texas, and in the **American Religions Collection** at the library of the University of California-Santa Barbara. The Bridwell collection was donated by Arthur Corey, a former Christian Science practitioner who left the Church of Christ, Scientist and wrote several books critical of it. Its library contained a complete set of all of the editions of Mary Baker Eddy's *Science and Health with Key to the Scriptures* and the *Church Manual.* The collection at Santa Barbara, built around the library of a long-time practitioner, Robert A. Burns, is especially strong in the independent Christian Science movement.

Independent Christian Science

Over the years many practitioners have left Christian Science yet continued to function as Christian Science healers. Some like Joel Goldsmith have attained a high profile. Most have worked very quietly and are little heralded. Over the years, the independents have been served by the **Rare Book Company**, Box 957, Freehold, NJ 07728. During the 1980s a new assertive spirit was noticed by independents who have established a national network. **The Bookmark**, P. O. Box 60184, Pasadena, CA 91106, has nurtured the network and serves as a second publishing distribution center.

New Thought

Encyclopedias and Dictionaries

690. Flowers, Sarah. *Metaphysical Thesaurus of Positive and Negative Words.* Los Angeles: The Author, 1942. 75 pp. Rev. ed as: *Metaphysical Thesaurus and Metaphysical Dictionary.* Los Angeles: The Author, 1946. 88 pp.

691. Holmes, Ernest. *New Thought Terms and Their Meanings.* New York: Dodd, Mead and Co., 1942. 167 pp.

Biographical Volumes

692. Beebe, Tom. *Who's Who in New Thought.* Lakemont, GA: CSA Publishers, 1977. 318 pp.

Directories

A directory of New Thought centers has frequently been carried as a feature in New Thought magazines. From the nineteenth century periodicals, one can look at issues of *Harmony* (1888-1906) and for the early twentieth century, *Master Mind* (1911-1927). In more recent years, *New Thought*, the periodical of the International New Thought Alliance, has carried a directory of member churches. A list of Religious Science churches and practitioners can be found in *Science of Mind* (United Church of Religious Science) and *Creative Thought* (Religious Science International). The Association of Unity Churches publishes an annual directory of member churches and ministers.

Bibliographies

693. *A Bibliography of New Thought Literature from 1875 to the Present: With Specific Reference to the Main Repositories Where the Materials May Be Found.* [Unity Village, MO]: Privately Published, n.d. 90 pp.

694. Braden, Charles. *Spirits in Rebellion.* Dallas, TX: Southern Methodist University Press, 1963. 571 pp. This standard text on New Thought also contains an extensive bibliography.

695. du Chant, Dell, and J. Gordon Melton. *The New Thought Movement: A Bibliographical Survey.* New York: Garland Publishing Co., forthcoming. An exhaustive survey of New Thought literature to be published in the Garland Series of Bibliographies of Cult and Sect Movements.

Archival Collections

The largest collection of published New Thought literature is now to be found in the **American Religions Collection** of the library of the University of California-Santa Barbara. However, running close seconds are the **Archives of the International New Thought Alliance** and of the **Unity School of Christianity**. The former, located at INTA headquarters, 5003 E. Broadway Road, Mesa, Arizona 85206, moved from the Bridwell Library at Southern Methodist University to Unity Village and finally to a permanent home in Arizona in 1989. It includes the records of the INTA and a large collection of New Thought literature. The Unity Library at the headquarters of the Unity School of Christianity, Unity Village, MO 64065, was developed to service the students at the Unity School. It is supplemented by the Unity Archives, housed in a separate room adjacent to the library, which contains the letters and papers of Charles and Myrtle Fillmore, Unity founders, and a complete set of publications of both the Unity School of Christianity and the associated Association of Unity Churches.

Lesser collections, but each containing unique items not found elsewhere, are at the headquarters of the **United Church of Religious Science** and **Divine Science Federation International**. The UCRS library and the separately housed church archives are located at the church's headquarters, 3251 W. 6th Street, Los Angeles, CA 90075. They contain a comprehensive collection of the writings of Religious Science founder Ernest Holmes and his brother Fenwicke Holmes as well as a collection of church publications including a complete run of *Science of Mind* magazine.

The archives of the Divine Science Federation International, 1819 E. 14th Street, Denver, CO 80218, contains a complete run of *Harmony*, the original periodical of the Movement (1888-1906), as well as the twentieth century periodicals and monograph publications.

Christian Healing

General Sources

696. Dwyer, Walter W. *The Churches' Handbook for Spiritual Healing.* New York: Ascension Press, 1958. Rev. ed.: 1962. 102 pp.

697. ———. *Spiritual Healing in the United States and Great Britain.* New York: The Author, 1955. 40 pp.

Bibliographies

698. Chase, Elise. *Healing Faith: A Bibliography of Christian Self-Help Books.* Westport, CT: Greenwood Press, 1985. 199 pp.

699. Raudszus, Juanita. *Divine Healing: A Bibliography.* Tulsa: Oral Roberts University Library, 1973. 29 pp.

The Holistic Health Movement

General Sources

700. Kalson, Carol, and Stan Kalson, eds. *Learn by Doing Holistic H.E.L.P. Handbook.* Phoenix, AZ: International Holistic Center, 1979. 59pp. 4th rev. ed.: Ed. by Stanley Steven Kalson. 1981. 96 pp. Rev. ed. as: *Holistic H.E.L.P. Handbook: Guide to Healthy Living.* 1990. 128 pp.

701. Kaslof, Leslie J. *Wholistic Dimensions in Healing: A Resource Guide.* Garden City, NY: Doubleday & Company, 1978. 295 pp. Includes directory.

702. Ross, Marlena. *Practices for Holistic Living: A Resources Guide.* Los Angeles: The Author, 1983. 197 pp. Includes bibliography and directory.

703. Thyme, Lauren O. *Alternative for Everyone: A Guide to Non-Traditional Health Care.* Fullerton, CA: Thyme Publishers, 1988. 335 pp. Includes directory.

Encyclopedias and Dictionaries

704. Ankerberg, John, and John Weldon. *Can You Trust Your Doctor?* Brentwood, TN: Wolgemuth & Hyatt, publishers, 1991. 446 pp.

705. Day, Harvey. *Enyclopedia of Natural Health and Healing.* Santa Barbara, CA: Woodbridge Press Publishing Company, 1979. 206 pp.

706. Hill, Ann, ed. *Encyclopedia of Unconventional Medicine.* New York: Crown Publishers, 1979. 240 pp.

707. Hulke, Malcolm, ed. *The Encyclopedia of Alternative Medicine and Self Help.* New York: Schocken Books, 1979. 240 pp.

708. Inglis, Brian, and Ruth West. *The Alternative Health Guide.* New York: Alfred A. Knopf, 1983. 352 pp.

709. Miller, Don Ethan. *Bodymind.* Englewood Cliffs: NJ: Prentice-Hall, 1974. 213 pp.

710. Peterson, Severin. *A Catalog of the Ways People Grow.* New York: Ballantine Books, 1971. 368 pp.

711. *Practices for Holistic Living: A Resource Guide.* Los Angeles: The Author, 1983. 197 pp.

712. Walker, Benjamin. *Encyclopedia of Metaphysical Medicine.* London: Routledge and Kegan Paul, 1978. 323 pp.

Directories

713. Brady, Kate, and Mike Considine. *Holistic London: The London Guide to Mind, Body and Spirit.* London: Brainwave, 1990. 314pp. *See:* (2431)

714. Butts, Dan, et al., eds. *New Age Service Directory for Southeastern Michigan.* Detroit, MI: New Age Service Directory, 1982. 52pp. Rev. ed. as: *Michigan Holistic Health Directory: A Guide to Professional Health Services, Centers and Resources.* Ferndale, MI: Michigan Holistic Health Association, 1983. 76pp. Rev. ed. as: *Directory of Alternative Resourcs for Michigan.* Southfield, MI: phenomeNEWS/ Warren, MI: MECCA, 1988. 84 pp.

715. Coleman, Beverly, and Elaine Morales. *Health Find: 1987 Holistic Therapies Directory, Chicago Area.* Morton Grove, IL: The Authors, 1986. 56 pp.

716. Cronk, Loren Kennett. *Annual Directory of Vegetarian Restaurants.* Angwin, CA: Daystar Publishing Company, 1980. 2nd ed.: 1981. 309 pp.

717. *The Health and Wellness Resource Directory.* Denver, CO: Colorado Holistic Health Network, 1983-84. 181 pp.

718. *Holistic Health Directory: Serving Santa Barbara, Ojai, Ventura/Oxnard, Thousand Oaks, San Luis Obispo.* Santa Barbara, CA: Kimberly Press, Inc., 1984. 55pp.

719. James, Susan, ed. *Insight Northwest Holistic Resource Yearbook/Directory.* Seattle, WA: Insight Northwest, 1985. 50pp. Rev. ed. as: *Holistic Resources Directory.* 1986. 58 pp. Rev. ed.: 1988/89. 262pp

720. Kalson, Stan. *International H.E.L.P. Directory: Resources for Healthy Living.* Phoenix, AZ: International Holistic Center, 1991. 20 pp.

721. Kulvinskas, Victoras. *The New Age Directory: Holistic Health Guide.* Woodstock Valley, CT: Omangod Press, [1979] 156pp. Rev. ed.: 1981. 229 pp.

722. Linde, Sherley, and Donald J. Carrow, eds. *The Directory of Holistic Medicine and Alternative Care Services in the U.S.* Phoenix, AZ: Health Plus publishers, 1985. 262 pp.

723. *Nutrition-Minded Doctors in the U. S. and Canada.* Buena Park, CA: Alacer Corp., 1980. 45 pp.

724. Rudee, Martine, and Jonathan Blease. *Traveler's Guide to Healing Centers and Retreats in North America.* Santa Fe, NM: John Muir Publications, 1989. 217 pp.

725. *Santa Barbara Holistic Directory: A Resource Guide for Healthy Living.* Santa Barbara, CA: Lasting Impressions Publ., 1982. 64 pp.

726. Weiss, David I., John R. Boynton, and Marcia Guntzel. *Directory of Holistic Practitioners for the Greater Boston Area.* Brookline, MA: David I. Weiss Publishing, 1987. 106 pp.

Bibliographies

727. Dyer, Judith C. *Vegetarianism: An Annotated Bibliography.* Metuchen, NJ: Scarecrow Press, 1982. 280 pp.

728. Popenoe, Cris. *Wellness.* Washington, DC: Yes!, Inc., 1977. 443 pp.

729. West, Ruth, and Joanna E. Trevelyan. *Alternative Medicine: A Bibliography of Books in English.* London: Mansell Publishing Ltd., 1985. 210 pp.

MYSTICISM AND SPIRITUALITY

Mysticism, the quest for spiritual union with the divine or first-hand knowledge of ultimate reality, has been a part of virtually all religious traditions throughout history. As such, mysticism serves as an imporatnt foundation for arguments of the essential unity of religion. Closely related to mysticism is the life of spirituality, which is often built around mystical experiences.

This section lists resources for the study of mystical/religious experience and spiritual practice. Several of these works deal with mysticism within particular religious traditions or with the career of particular well-known mystics. Since the various mystical teachings often cross the traditional boundaries of their parent religions and exhibit cross-cultural similarities, they have been brought together here in their own category.

Encyclopedias and Dictionaries

730. Cary-Elwes, Columbia. *Experiences with God: A Dictionary of Spirituality and Prayer.* London: Sheed and Ward, 1986. 222 pp.

731. De Fiores, Stefano, and Tullio Goffi, eds. *Dictionnaire de la Vie Spirituelle.* Paris: Editions du Cerf, 1983. 1246 pp.

732. Drury, Nevill. *Dictionary of Mysticism and the Occult.* San Francisco: Harper & Row, 1985. 281 pp.

733. *Encyclopédie de la Mystique Juive.* Paris: Berg International, 1977. 1528 Col.

734. Ferguson, John. *An Illustrated Encyclopedia of Mysticism and the Mystery Religions.* New York: Seabury Press; London: Thames and Hudson, 1977. 227 pp.

735. Gaynor, Frank. *Dictionary of Mysticism.* New York: Philosophical Library, 1963. 210 pp.

736. Viller, Marcel, et al., eds. *Dictionnaire de Spiritualite.* Vol. 1- . Paris: Gabriel Beauchesne et ses Fils, 1937- .

737. Wakefield, Gordon S. *Dictionary of Christian Spirituality.* London: SCM, 1983. 400 pp. Rept. as: *Westminster Dictionary of Christian Spirituality.* Philadelphia: Westminster Press, 1983. 400 pp.

Bibliographies

Ongoing dialogue on mysticism is facilitated by several periodicals. *Mystics Quarterly*, c/o Publications Order Department, University of Iowa, Graphics Services Building, Iowa City, IA 52242, includes occasional bibliographical articles on selected subjects, a running bibliographical column, "Publications and Reviews," which notes recent publications in the field, a research column, "Research in Progress," and a chatty survey of conferences at which papers on mysticism have been given.

738. Alper, Harvey P. "A Working Bibliography for the Study of Mantras." In Alper, Harvey P., ed. *Understanding Mantras.* Albany: State University of New York Press, 1988. pp. 327-443.

739. *Bibliographia Internationalis Spiritualitatis.* Vol. 1- . Roma: Pontifico Instituto de Spiritualita, Edizioni dei Oadri Carmelitani Scalzi, 1966- . Annual.

740. Bowman, Mary Ann, comp. *Western Mysticism: A Guide to Basic Works.* Chicago: American Library Association, 1978. 113 pp.

741. Breit, Marquita E. *Thomas Merton: A Bibliography.* ATLA Bibliography Series No. 2. Metuchen, NJ: Scarecrow Press, 1974. 180 pp.

742. ———, and Robert E. Daggy, comps. *Thomas Merton: A Comprehensive Bibliography, New Edition.* New York: Garland Publishing, 1986. 710 pp.

743. Dagens, Jean. *Bibliographie Chronologique de la Littérature de Spiritualité et de ses Sources, 1501-1610.* Paris: Desclée, 1953. 208 pp.

744. Dell'Isola, Frank. *Thomas Merton: A Bibliography.* Rev. and expanded ed. Serif series: Bibliographies and Checklists No. 31. Kent, OH: Kent State University Press, 1975. 220 pp.

745. Dols, Jean Michel Emile. *Bibliographie de Modern Devotie.* 2 vols. Nijmegen: Centrale Drukkerij, 1936, 1941.

746. Greene, Dana. "Bibliography of Works About and By Evelyn Underhill." *Bulletin of Bibliography* 45, 2 (1988): 92-107.

747. Gregory, Carol F. R. "For Further Reading [on Spirituality]." *Caribbean Journal of Religious Studies* Special Issue (1884): 70-76.

748. *Index Illuminatis: The Most Worthwhile Books on Christian Mysticism and Medieval Philosophy and of Devotional and Inspirational Character.* New York: Confraternity of the Mystical Life, n.d. 14 pp.

749. Jarrell, Howard R. *International Meditation Bibliography, 1950-1982.* ATLA Bibliography Series No. 12. Metuchen, NJ: Scarecrow Press, 1984. 444 pp.

750. Jolliffe, P. S. *A Checklist of Middle English Prose Writings of Spiritual Guidance.* Toronto: Pontifical Institute of Medieval Studies, 1974. 253 pp.

751. Lagorio, Valerie Marie, and Ritamary Bradley. *The 14th-Century English Mystics.* New York: Garland Publishing, 1981. 197 pp.

752. *Reel Guide to the Kaballah and Mysticism Collection, Reels 1-65, from the Library of the Jewish Theological Seminary of America.* Ann Arbor, MI: University Microfilms, 1977. 62 pp.

753. Sawyer, Michael E. *A Bibliographical Index of Five English Mystics: Richard Rolle, Julian of Norwich, the Author of the Cloud of Unknowing, Walter Hilton, Margery Kempe.* Bibliographia Tripotamopolitana No. 10. Pittsburgh, PA: Clifford E. Barbour Library, Pittsburgh Theological Seminary, 1978. 126 pp.

754. Shapiro, Deane H., and Roger N. Walsh, eds. *Meditation: Classic and Contemporary Approaches.* Hawthorne, NY: Aldine, 1984. 722 pp.

755. Sharma, Umesh, and John Arndt. *Mysticism--A Select Bibliography.* Waterloo, ON: Waterloo Lutheran University, 1973. 109 pp.

756. Spector, Sheila A. *Jewish Mysticism: An Annotated Bibliography on the Kabbalah in English.* New York: Garland Publishing, 1984. 399 pp.

757. *Tzaddikim: A Catalogue of Chassidic, Kabbalistic and Selected Judaic Books.* Oakland, CA: Judaic Book Service, 1973- . Semi-annual.

Research Centers/Professional Associations

Center for Contemporary Spirituality
Theology Department
Fordham University
Bronx, NY 10458

Institute for Formative Spirituality
Duquesne University
Pittsburgh, PA 15282
The Institute publishes *Envoy: Journal of Formative Reading.*

International Thomas Merton Society
c/o Christine M. Bochen
Nazareth College
425 East Ave.
Rochester, NY 14618-3790

Rufus Jones Collection
Haverford College
Haverford, PA 19041
Rufus Jones was by-far the most famous Quaker scholar/mystic of the twentieth century.

Schocken Institute for Jewish Research
6 Balfour Street
Jerusalem, Israel
Research program includes a specialization in Jewish mysticism. The Institute is formally connected with the Jewish Theological Seminary in America.

Thomas Merton Studies Center
Bellarmine College
Newburg Road
Louisville, KY 40205

WOMEN AND RELIGION
(including Feminist Spirituality)

Women's studies has become a vital and growing field in academia, and as the role of religious institutions in the oppression of females has been examined, women's religious studies has become an increasingly important part of the field. Women's religious studies has also been stimulated by the drive for ordination and official recognition of women in positions of leadership in the major religious bodies.

Sources cited below center upon three broad areas of research. First of all, there are several sources on the historical role of women in various traditions. Secondly, with many religious groups struggling to define new roles for women, there is a growing body of material on the ordination of women in traditionally male-dominated clergies. Finally, there has been an emergence of feminist-influenced theologies which have sought to integrate on a spiritual level what traditional feminism has worked for on a social and political level.

General Sources

758. Swidler, Arlene, and Walter E. Conn. *Mainstreaming Feminist Research for Teaching Religious Studies.* Lanham, MD: University Press of America, 1985. 83 pp. A broad survey of feminist studies and methods of integrating it into a theological and/or religious studies curriculum. Includes significant reflections on readily available source materials.

Encyclopedias and Dictionaries

759. Hammack, Mary L. *A Dictionary of Women in Church History.* Chicago: Moody Press, 1984. 167 pp.

760. Walker, Barbara G. *The Women's Encyclopedia of Myths and Secrets.* San Francisco: Harper & Row, 1983. 1124 pp.

Biographical Materials

761. Claghorn, Gene. *Women Composers and Hymnists: A Concise Biographical Dictionary.* Metuchen, NJ: Scarecrow Press, 1984. 272 pp.

762. Hanson, E. R. *Our Women Workers: Biographical Sketches of Women Eminent in the Universalist Church.* Boston, MA: Universalist Publishing House, 1882.

763. Hitchings, Catherine F. "Universalist and Unitarian Women Ministers." *The Journal of the Universalist Historical Society* 10 (1975): 3-165.

764. Parbury, Kathleen. *Women of Grace: A Biographical Dictionary of British Saints, Martyrs, and Reformers.* Stockfield, UK: Oriel Press, 1984. 199 pp.

Bibliographies

765. Bass, Dorothy C., and Sandra Hughes Boyd. *Women in American Religious History: An Annotated Bibliography and Guide to Sources.* Boston: G. K. Hall, 1986. 155 pp.

766. "Bibliography [on women in the Latin American, Asian, and African church]." *IDOC Bulletin* new series #10 (1982): 22-25.

767. Carson, Ann. *Feminist Spirituality and the Feminine Divine: An Annotated Bibliography.* Freedom, CA: Crossing Press, 1986. 139 pp.

768. Epp, Maureen. "A Selected Bibliography of English-language Writings on the History of Anabaptist/Mennonite Women." *Conrad Grebel Review* 8 (Fall 1990): 321-23.

769. Ganghofer, Odilie. *The Woman in the Church: International Bibliography 1973-June 1975 Indexed by Computer.* RIC Supplement 21. Strasbourg, France: Cerdic-Publications, 1975. 45 pp.

770. Kastner, G. Ronald. "Selected Bibliography [on women writers in the early church]." In Patricia Wilson-Kastner. *A Lost Tradition: Women Writers of the Early Church.* Lanham, MD: University Press of America, 1981. pp. 173-78.

771. Kendall, Patricia A. *Women and the Priesthood: A Selected and Annotated Bibliography.* Philadelphia: Commission to Promote the Cause of and to Plan for the Ordination of Women to the Priesthood, Epis. Diocese of Pennsylvania, 1976. 57 pp.

772. Lindboe, Inger Marie. "Recent Literature: Development and Prospective in New Testament Research on Women." *Studies Theologica* 43 (1989): 153-63.

773. Morgan, John H. *The Ordination of Women: A Comprehensive Bibliography, 1960-1976.* Wichita, KS: Institute of Ministry and the Elderly, 1977. 41 pp.

774. Raud, Inger Marie. *Women and Judaism.* New York: Garland Publishing, 1988. 232 pp.

775. *A Resource Guide for Women in Seminary.* Chicago: Ecumenical Women's Centers, 1976. 36 pp.

776. Roszak, Betty. *Feminist Spirituality.* Berkeley, CA: Program for the Study of New Religious Movements in America, 1979. 4 pp. Rev. ed as: Choquette, Diane, comp. *The Goddess Walks Among Us: Feminist Spirituality in Thought and Action.* Berkeley, CA: NRM Publications, 1981.

777. Szasz, Ferenc M. "An Annotated Bibliography of Women in American Religious History: The Christian Tradition, 1607-1900." *Iliff Review* 40 (Fall 1983): 41-59.

778. Webster, Ellen Low. "An Annotated Bibliography on the Church and Women in the Third World." In John C. Webster and Ellen Low Webster. *The Church and Women in the Third World.* Philadelphia, PA: Westminster Press, 1985. pp. 137-47.

779. Young, Katherine K., and Arvind Sharma. *Images of the Feminine—Mythic, Philosophic and Human—In the Buddhist, Hindu, and Islamic Traditions: A Bibliography of Women in India.* Chico, CA: New Horizons Press, 1974. 36 pp.

Archival Depositories

780. Thomas, Evangeline, CSJ. *Women Religious History Sources: A Guide to Repositories in the United States.* New York: R. R. Bowker Company, 1983. 329 pp. A thorough examination of Catholic and Episcopal religious orders for women and their archival holdings. It also includes a table listing of all the orders (with pertinent data such as date of formation, place of formation and location of present headquarters) and a table of all the women who have either founded orders in America or served as a mother superior.

Professional Associations

American Women's Clergy Association
214 P St., N.W.
Washington, DC 20001

Coalition of Woman and Religion
4729 15th Ave., N.E.
Seattle, WA 98100
The Coalition publishes *The Flame* on a quarterly basis.

International Association of Women Ministers
c/o Rev. Carol S. Brown
579 Main St.
Stroudsburg, PA 18360
The Association publishes a quarterly periodical, *Woman's Pulpit.*

Research Centers

Center for Woman and Religion
Graduate Theological Union
2400 Ridge Road
Berkeley, CA 94709
The Center publishes an annual *Journal of Women and Religion.*

Women's Studies in Religion Program
Harvard University
c/o Harvard Divinity School
45 Francis Avenue
Cambridge, MA 02138

ISSUES IN COMPARATIVE RELIGION

Part 2: The Interaction of Religious Communities

INTERFAITH DIALOGUE

Since the 1893 World's Parliament of Religions, interfaith dialogue has presented itself as a major option for guiding the relationships between major religious communities. In spite of its promise, it has remained one of the most difficult courses of action to follow. In our increasingly interconnected world, many have addressed the problem of living together and the realities of a religiously pluralistic environment by stressing the need for inter-religious dialogue. While the secondary literature on this has not grown much of late, there are a good number of organizations dedicated to the study of interfaith relations, especially Jewish-Christian relations.

Directories

781. Braybrook, Marcus. *Inter-faith Organizations, 1893-1979: An Historical Directory.* New York and Toronto: Edwin Mellen Press, 1980. 213 pp.

782. Clark, Francis. *Interfaith Directory.* New York: International Religious Foundation, 1987. 178 pp.

Bibliographies

783. Celnik, Max, and Isaac Celnik, comps. *Bibliography on Judaism and Jewish-Christian Relations: A Selected, Annotated Listing of Works on Jewish Faith and Life, and the Jewish-Christian Encounter.* New York: Anti-Defamation League of B'nai B'rith, [1965]. 68 pp.

784. *Children of One Father: An Annotated Bibliography of Pamphlets and Reports on Jewish-Christian Relations.* New York: American Jewish Committee, 1966. 23 pp.

785. Facelina, Raymond. *Christianism and Religions: International Bibliography 1972-June 1974 Indexed by Computer.* RIC Supplement 13. Strasbourg, France: Cerdic-Publications, 1974. 57 pp.

786. Hackett, David G. *The Christian-Buddhist Encounter: A Select Bibliography.* Berkeley, CA: Graduate Theological Union, Center for the Study of New Religious Movements, 1979. 16 pp.

Research/Resource Centers

The organizations listed in this section engage in religious dialogue and promote cooperation among people of different religious traditions.

Council for a Parliament of World Religions
5423 South Hyde Park Boulevard
Chicago, IL 60615

World Faiths Center for Religious Experience and Study
Box 4165
Overland Park, KS 66204
The Center publishes *The CRES Release*

Jewish Christian Relationships

Center for Jewish Christian Learning
P. O. Box 5010
College of St. Thomas
2115 Summit Avenue
St. Paul, MN 55105

Center for Jewish-Christian Studies
General Theological Seminary
175 9th Avenue
New York, NY 10011
The center publishes a quarterly newsletter, *Dialogue.*

Center for Jewish-Christian Studies and Relations
Chicago Theological Seminary
5757 S. University
Chicago, IL 60637

Institute for Jewish-Christian Relations
c/o American Jewish Congress
15 East 84th Street
New York, NY 10028

Institute of Judeo-Christian Studies
Seton Hall University
South Orange, NJ 07079
The Institute supports research and conferences on Jewish-Christian relations.

Paula K. Lazarus Library of Intergroup Relations
National Conference of Christians and Jews
71 Fifth Avenue
New York, NY 10003
The Library houses a collection of some 2,000 items on intergroup (primarily Christian-Jewish) relations. However, the NCCJ archives are housed at the Social Welfare History Archives at the Wilson Library, University of Minnesota, Minneapolis, MN 55455.

IV

CHRISTIANITY

CHRISTIANITY: GENERAL SOURCES

Christianity has been the dominant religion in Europe for many centuries and has since the sixteenth century become the dominant religion in North and South America. From its base in the West, throughout the nineteenth and twentieth centuries Christianity pushed itself into every corner of the globe and now has a significant if minority following in most countries of the world. Worldwide it is the major religious tradition with the largest following.

In this first chapter of Christian sources are listed those books and materials which attempt to cover the whole of the tradition temporally and spatially. Of particular note is Barrett's *World Christian Encyclopedia* (787), the most comprehensive and information-filled book on modern Christianity. Barrett's volume is unique in its assemblage of information and also because it attempts what few in contemporary times attempt: comprehensive coverage of such a vast field as the Christian Church internationally and interdenominationally. As can be seen by perusing the chapters below, most newer reference tools limit themselves to a single country, time period, or denominational family.

Encyclopedias and Dictionaries

787. Barrett, David B. *World Christian Encyclopedia: A Comparative Survey of Churches and Religions in the Modern World, A.D. 1900-2000.* Oxford: Oxford University Press, 1982. 1010 pp.

788. Blunt, John Henry, ed. *Dictionary of Sects, Heresies, Ecclesiastical Parties and Schools of Religious Thought.* London: Rivingtons, 1874. Rept. Detroit: Gale Research, 1974. 647 pp.

789. Buchberger, Michael. *Lexikon für Theologie und Kirche.* 10 vols. Freiburg: Herder, 1957-65.

790. Bumpus, John Skelton. *A Dictionary of Ecclesiastical Terms, Being a History and Explanation of Certain Terms Used in Architecture, Ecclesiology, Music, Ritual,*

Cathedral Construction, etc. London: T.W. Laurie, 1910. Rept. Detroit: Gale Research, 1969. 323 pp.

791. *The Clergyman's Fact Book.* Vol. 1- . New York: M. Evans, 1963/64- .

792. Cross, F. L., ed. *The Oxford Dictionary of the Christian Church.* Oxford: Oxford University Press, 1957. 698 pp. 2nd ed.: by Cross, F. L. and E. A. Livingston. 1974. 1520 pp.

793. Dewey, Dellon Marcus. *Handbook of Church Terms: Being a Pocket Dictionary, or Brief Explanations of Words in Common Use Relating to the Order, Worship, Architecture, Vestments of the Church Designed for the General Reader As Well As for Instruction in Bible Classes.* 3rd ed. New York: E. P. Dutton and Co., 1880. 56 pp.

794. Douglas, James Dixon. *The Concise Dictionary of the Christian Tradition: Doctrine, Liturgy, History.* Grand Rapids, MI: Zondervan Publishing House, 1989. 419 pp.

795. ————., ed. *The New International Dictionary of the Christian Church.* 2nd ed. Grand Rapids, MI: Zondervan Publishing House/Exeter: Paternoster Press, 1978. 1074 pp.

796. Eckel, Frederick. *A Concise Dictionary of Ecclesiastical Terms.* Boston: Whittemore Associates, 1960. 64 pp.

797. Ferm, Vergilius. *Concise Dictionary of Religion: A Lexicon of Protestant Interpretation.* New York: Philosophical Library, 1951. Rept.: New York: Philosophical Library, [1964?]. 283 pp.

798. Franchetti, Nicolo. *A Churchman's Pocket Dictionary.* Toronto: Anglican Church of Canada, Board of Religious Education, 1959.

799. Gentz, William H. *The Dictionary of Bible & Religion.* Nashville: Abingdon, 1986. 1147 pp.

800. Gouker, Loice, comp. *Dictionary of Church Terms and Symbols.* Norwalk, CT: C.R. Gibson Co., 1964. 69 pp.

801. Hendricks, J. Sherrell, Gene E. Sease, Eric Lane Titus, and James Bryan Wiggins. *Christian Word Book.* Nashville: Abingdon Press, 1968. 320 pp.

802. Hook, Walter Farquhar. *Church Dictionary.* London: J. Murray, 1859. 807 pp.

803. Jackson, Samuel Macauley. *Concise Dictionary of Religious Knowledge and Gazetteer.* New York: Christian Literature Company, 1891. 996+34 pp.

804. Kerr, James S., and Charles Lutz. *A Christian's Dictionary: 1600 Names, Words and Phrases.* Philadelphia: Fortress Press, 1969. 178 pp.

805. Livingston, Elizabeth A. *The Concise Oxford Dictionary of the Christian Church.* Oxford: Oxford University Press, 1977. 570 pp.

806. Malloch, James M., comp. *A Practical Church Dictionary.* New York: Morehouse-Barlow, 1964. 520 pp.

807. McClintock, John, and James Strong. *Cyclopedia of Biblical, Theological, and Ecclesiastical Literature.* 12 vols. New York: Harper & Brothers, 1867-1887. Rept.: 12 vols. Grand Rapids, MI: Baker Book House, 1968-1970. Rept.: 10 vols. New York: Arno Press, 1969.

808. Moore, Arthur. *A Pocket Dictionary of the Christian Church.* London: Mowbray, 1985. 87 pp.

809. Palmer, Edwin H. *The Encyclopedia of Christianity.* 4 vols. Marshalltown, DE: National Foundation for Christian Education, 1964-72. Editor for vol. 2, Gary R. Cohen. Editor for vol. 3, Philip E. Hughes.

810. Purvis, J. S. *Dictionary of Ecclesiastical Terms.* London: Thomas Nelson & Sons, 1962. 204 pp.

811. Shannon, Ellen C. *A Layman's Guide to Christian Terms.* South Brunswick, N.J.: A. S. Barnes, 1969. 347 pp.

812. Sydnor, William. *More Than Words: A Dictionary of the Christian Faith Offering Definitions and Insight to Preachers, Teachers, and Other Church Leaders.* San Francisco: Harper & Row, 1990. 152 pp.

813. Thein, John. *Ecclesiastical Dictionary.* New York: Benziger Bros., 1900. 749 pp.

814. Ward, Carol. *The Christian Sourcebook.* New York: Ballantine Books, 1989. 460 pp.

815. White, Richard Clark. *The Vocabulary of the Church: A Pronunciation Guide.* New York: Macmillan Company, 1960. 178 pp.

Directories

816. *Associated Church Press Directory.* Geneva, IL: The Associated Church Press, 1947- . Annual.

817. Beaver, R. Pierce. *The Native American Christian Community: A Directory of Indian, Aleut, and Eskimo Churches.* Monrovia, CA: MARC, 1979. 395 pp.

818. *Directory of Christian Councils.* 1971. Rev. ed.: Geneva, Switzerland: World Council of Churches, 1985. 244 pp.

819. *Directory of Christian Work Opportunities: U.S. and International Edition.* Seattle, WA: Intercristo, 1977- . Semiannual.

820. *Directory of Sabbath-Observing Groups.* Fairview, OK: Bible Sabbath Association, 1957. Rev. ed.: 1957. Rev. ed.: 1961. Rev. ed.: 1969. 37 pp. Rev. ed.: 1974. 258 pp. Rev. ed.: 1980. 147 pp. Rev. ed.: 1986. 231 pp.

821. Gainsbrugh, Jonathan, and Jeanette Gainsbrugh. *The Christian Resource Directory.* Old Tappan, NJ: Fleming H. Revell Company, 1986, 1988. 731 pp.

822. Rodda, Dorothy, and John Harvey, comps. *Directory of Church Libraries.* Drexel Library School Series No. 22. Philadelphia: Drexel Press, 1967. 83 pp.

823. Van der Bent, Ans J. *Handbook: Member Churches, World Council of Churches.* Geneva, Switzerland: World Council of Churches, 1982. 281 pp. Rev. ed.: 1985. 289 pp.

824. *World Christian Handbook.* Ed. by Kenneth G. Grubb and E. J. Bingle. London: World Dominion Press, 1949. 405 pp. Rev. ed.: Ed. by H. Wakelin Coxill and Kenneth Grubb. London: World Dominion Press, 1962. 400 pp. Rev. ed.: Ed. by H. Wakelin Coxill, Kenneth Grubb, and Kathleen A. Knapp. London: Lutterworth Press, 1968. 400 pp. Superseded by Barrett, *World Christian Encyclopedia* (787)

Biographical Volumes

825. Barker, William P. *Who's Who in Church History.* Old Tappan, NJ: Fleming H. Revell Company, 1969. 319 pp. Superseded by Moyer (829)

826. Carter, N. F. *The Native Ministry of New Hampshire.* Concord, NH: Rumford Printing Co., 1906. 1017 pp.

827. Castle, Tony. *Lives of Famous Christians.* Servant Publications, 1988. 306 pp.

828. Jackson, Samuel Macauley, ed. *Encyclopedia of Living Divines and Christian Workers of All Denominations in Europe and America, Being a Supplement to the Schaff-Herzog Encyclopedia of Religious Knowledge.* New York: Funk & Wagnalls, 1887. 171 pp. Rev. ed: 1891. 296 pp. Rev. ed.: 1894.

829. Moyer, Elgin Sylvester. *The Wycliffe Biographical Dictionary of the Church.* Chicago: Moody Press, 1982. 449 pp. Supersedes Barker (825)

830. Russo-Alesi, Anthony Ignatius. *Martyrology Pronouncing Dictionary; It Contains the Pronunciation of Over 5000 Names of Martyrs, Confessors, Virgins, Emperors, Cities and Places Occurring in the Roman Martyrology with a Daily Calendar and a List of the Patron Saints.* New York: Edward O'Toole Co., 1939. 177 pp. Rept.: Detroit, MI: Gale Research Company, 1973. 177 pp.

831. Schwarz, J.C. *Who's Who in the Clergy.* New York: The Author, 1936. 1224 pp. Rev. ed as: *Religious Leaders in America.* 1942. 1147 pp.

832. Smith, William, and Henry Wace, eds. *A Dictionary of Christian Biography, Literature, Sects and Doctrines, Being a Continuation of The Dictionary of the Bible.* 4 vols. London: John Murray, 1877-87. Rept.: New York: AMS Press, 1967.

833. Wace, Henry, and William C. Piercy. *A Dictionary of Christian Biography and Literature to the End of the Sixth Century A.D., with an Account of the Principal Sects and Heresies.* Boston: Little, Brown and Co./London: John Murray, 1911. 1028 pp.

834. *Who's Who in Religion.* Chicago: Marquis Who's Who, 1975. 616 pp. Rev. ed.: 177. 736 pp. Rev. ed.: 1985. 439 pp.

Bibliographies

835. *Archives of Religious and Ecclesiastical Bodies and Organizations Other Than the Church of England.* Reprints No. 3. London: British Records Association, 1936. 22 pp.

836. Batson, Beatrice. *A Reader's Guide to Religious Literature.* Chicago: Moody Press, 1968. 188 pp.

837. *Bibliographisches Beiblatt: Die Theologische Literatur das Jahres 1922-1942.* Leipzig: Hinrichs, 1922-1943. Irregular

838. *Catalogue of Doctoral Dissertations, 1944-1960.* Compiled by O'Brien, Elmer John. Princeton, NJ: Princeton Theological Seminary, 1962. 119 pp.

839. *Christianity in Books: A Guide to Current Literature.* London: National Book League, 1964. 141 pp.

840. *Current Christian Books.* Volume 1- . Colorado Springs, CO: CBA Service Corporation. 1975- . Updated annually.

841. *Current Theological Bibliography II: BTIMARC Files to November 1971.* Cambridge, MA: Boston Theological Institute, 1971. 103 pp.

842. Dulles, Avery, and Patrick Granfield. *The Church: A Bibliography.* Wilmington, DE: M. Glazier, 1985. 166 pp.

843. Foust, Roscoe T. *Books for the Church Library.* Prepared for the Church Library Department of the Christian Herald. New York: Christian Herald, 1964. 57 pp.

844. Gorman, G. E., and Lyn Gorman. *Theological and Religious Reference Materials.* 3 vols. Bibliographies and Indexes in Religious Studies Nos. 1, 2, & 7. Westport, CT: Greenwood Press, 1984-1986.

845. Gottwald, Norman K., ed. "Theological Bibliographies: Essential Books for a Minister's Library." *Andover Newton Quarterly* 4, 1 (September 1963): 1-138; Supplement as "1964-1966 Supplement to Theological Bibliographies: Essential Books for a Minister's Library." *Andover Newton Quarterly* 6, 4 (March 1966): 70-84. Supplement also printed as a separate pamphlet.

846. Le Leannec, Bernard, and Jean Schlick. *Authority in the Church: International Bibliography 1972-1975 Indexed by Computer.* RIC Supplement 27. Strasbourg, France: Cerdic-Publications, 1976. 38 pp.

847. Malcom, Howard. *Theological Index: References to the Principal Works in Every Department of Religious Literature.* Boston: Gould & Lincoln/London: Trübner & Co., 1868. 489 pp.

848. Merchant, Harish D., ed. *Encounter with Books: A Guide to Christian Reading.* Downers Grove, IL: Inter-Varsity Press, 1970. 262 pp.

849. Messner, Francis, and Jean Schlick. *Participation in the Church: International Bibliography 1968-June 1975 Indexed by Computer.* RIC Supplement 19. Strasbourg, France: Cerdic-Publications, 1975. 52 pp.

850. Midwestern Baptist Theological Seminary, Faculty of the. *A Selected Bibliography for Theological Students.* Kansas City, MO: Midwestern Baptist Theological Seminary, 1964. 61 pp.

851. Miethe, Terry L., and Vernon J. Bourke. *Thomistic Bibliography, 1940-1978.* Westport, CT: Greenwood Press, 1980. 318 pp.

852. Morris, Raymond Philip. *A Theological Book List.* Oxford: Basil Blackwell and Mott, 1960. 242 pp. Rept.: Middletown, CT: Greeno, Hadden and Co., 1971.

853. *Penance and Reconciliation: International Bibliography 1975-1983.* RIC Supplements 86-87. Strasbourg, France: Cerdic-Publications, 1984. 144 pp.

854. Peterson, Kenneth G. *An Introductory Bibliography for Theological Students.* Berkeley, CA: Pacific Lutheran Theological Seminary, 1964. 31 pp.

855. Principe, Walter Henry, and Ronald E. Diener. *Bibliographies and Bulletins in Theology.* Toronto: Pontifical Institute of Medieval Studies, 1967. 44 pp.

856. Samuelson, Sue. *Christmas: An Annotated Bibliography of Analytical Scholarship.* Garland Folklore Bibliographies Vol. 4. New York: Garland Publishing, 1982. 130 pp.

857. Sayre, John Leslie, Jr., ed. *Recommended Reference Books and Commentaries for a Minister's Library.* 3rd ed. Enid, OK: Seminary Press, 1978. 27 pp.

858. ———, and Roberta Hamburger, comps. *An Index of Festschriften in the Graduate Seminary Library of Phillips University.* Enid, OK: Haymaker Press, 1970. 121 pp.

859. ———, and Roberta Hamburger, comps. *An Index of Festschriften in the Graduate Seminary Library of Phillps University: New Titles, 1971-1973.* Enid, OK: Seminary Press, 1973.

860. SCM Press Editorial Department, comp. *Religion and Theology 6: A Select Book Guide.* London: SCM Press, 1981.

861. Sonne, Niels Henry, ed. *A Bibliography of Post-Graduate Masters' Theses in Religion.* Prepared by the Committee on a Master List of Research Studies in Religion. Chicago: American Theological Library Association, 1951. 82 pp.

862. Strange, Douglas C. *The Nascent Marxist-Christian Dialogue: 1961-1976: A Bibliography.* Bibliographical Series No. 5 (1968). N.p.: AIMS, 1968. 27 pp.

863. *Theologische Literaturzeitung.* Vol.1- . Leipzig, Germany: Hinrichs, 1876- . Biweekly.

864. *Theologischer Jahresbericht, 1881-1913.* 33 vols. Tübingen: Mohr, 1882-1916.

865. Trotti, John B., ed. *Christian Faith amidst Religious Pluralism: An Introductory Bibliography.* Richmond, VA: Union Theological Seminary in Virginia, Library, 1980.

866. Van der Bent, Ans J. *The Christian-Marxist Dialogue: An Annotated Bibliography, 1959-1969.* Geneva: World Council of Churches, 1969.

867. Zimmerman, Marie, et al. *RIC (Répertoire Bibliographique des Institutions Chrétiennes/Bibliographical Repertory of Christian Institutions).* Vol. 1- . Strasbourg, France: Cerdic-Publications, 1967- .

Guides to Periodical Literature

868. *Book Reviews of the Month: An Index to Reviews Appearing in Selected Theological Journals.* Vol. 1- . Fort Worth, TX: Southwestern Baptist Theological Seminary, Fleming Library, 1964- . Monthly

869. *B.T.I. Union List of Periodicals: Preliminary Checking Edition, March 1974.* Boston, MA: Boston Theological Institute, 1974. 409 pp.

870. Chicago Area Theological Library Association. *Union List of Serials.* Chicago: CATLA, 1974. 673 pp.

871. *Christian Periodical Index: An Index to Subjects, Authors and Book Reviews.* Vol. 1- . West Seneca, NY: Christian Libraries Fellowship, 1959- . Quarterly with annual, triennial, and quincennial cumulations.

872. Montgomery, John Warwick, ed. *A Union List of Serial Publications in Chicago-Area Protestant Theological Libraries, Containing All Periodicals Currently Received and Many Non-Current Serials in the Libraries of Bethany Biblical Seminary [et al.].* Compiled by the staff of the University of Chicago Divinity and Philosophy Library. Chicago: n.p., 1960. Unpaged.

873. *Religious and Theological Abstracts.* Vol. 1- . Myerstown, PA: Religious and Theological Abstracts, 1958- . Quarterly.

874. *Religious Book Review Index.* Vol. 1- . Calcutta, India: K.K. Roy, 1970- . Bimonthly.

875. Reese, Ed. *The 1979 CIS Guide to Christian Periodicals.* Wheaton, IL: Christian Information Service, 1979. 151 pp.

Atlases

876. Chadwick, Henry, and G. R. Evans. *Atlas of the Christian Church.* London: Macmillan, 1987. 240 pp. Rept: Oxford: Phaidon, 1990. 240 pp.

Christian Studies

Association for the Advancement of Christian Scholarship
229 College Street
Toronto, ON M5T 1R4
Canada
The Association publishes a periodical: *Perspective.*

Association of Christian Engineers and Scientists
479 Rose Avenue
Vernonia, OR 97064

Center for the Study of Christian Values in Literature
Brigham Young University
Jesse Knight Humanities Building
Provo, UT 84602

Centre de Recherches et de Documentation des Institutions
Christian Institutions Research and Documentation Center
2, rue Goethe-Palais Universitaire
F-67000 Strasbourg, France

Christian Sociological Society
c/o Dr. Michael Leming
Department of Sociology
St. Olaf College
Northfield, MN 55057

Christianity Today Institute
465 Gundersen Drive
Carol Stream, IL 60188
The Institute is affiliated with the Evangelical magazine *Christianity Today.*

Foundation for Religious and Educational Exchange, Inc.
Eastern Baptist Seminary
Lancaster and City Avenues
Philadelphia, PA 19151

Glenmary Research Center
750 Piedmont Avenue, NE
Atlanta, GA 30308

Institute for Christian Studies
Barrington College
Barrington, RI 02806

Institute for Christian Studies Library
c/o University Church of Christ
1909 University Avenue
Austin, TX 78705
The Institute publishes the quarterly *ICS Report* and the semiannual *Christian Studies: Faculty Bulletin for the Institute for Christian Studies.*

Institute for the Study of Christianity and Marxism
Wheaton College
Wheaton, IL 60187

Institute of Christian Organizational Management
Barrington College
Barrington, RI 02806

International Christian Studies Association
Institute for Interdisciplinary Studies
2828 Third St., Ste 11
Santa Monica, CA 90405
The Association publishes the *Journal of Interdisciplinary Studies* twice annually.

V

CHRISTIANITY:

ISSUES IN CHRISTIAN STUDIES

CHRISTIANITY AND THE ARTS

Christianity's interaction with the arts has over the centuries been as intense as it has been varied. Significant Christian art works can be found as paintings, architecture, sculpture, and drama. If one area could be lifted out as most important, it would possibly be music. In the twentieth century, along with the more traditional arts, radio and television broadcasting have added a significant new dimension to the churches' use of the artistic community. Below, sources on music, which form the largest set of resource materials on Christianity and the arts, have been given a separate listing.

Encyclopedias and Dictionaries

877. Appleton, LeRoy H., and Stephen Bridges. *Symbolism in Liturgical Art.* New York: Charles Scribner's Sons, 1959. 120 pp.

878. Bernen, Satia, and Robert Bernen. *Myth and Religion in European Painting, 1270-1700: The Stories as the Artists Knew Them.* New York: George Braziller/ London: Constable, 1973. 280 pp.

879. Cirlot, Juan Eduardo. *A Dictionary of Symbols.* Trans. from the Spanish by Jack Sage. 1962. 2nd ed.: London: Routledge and Kegan Paul, 1971. 419 pp.

880. Clement (Waters), Clara Erskine. *Saints in Art.* Boston: L.C. Page & Co., 1899. 428 pp.

881. Drake, Maurice, and Wilfred Drake. *Saints and Their Emblems.* Philadelphia: J. B. Lippincott/London: T.W. Laurie, 1916. Rept.: Detroit, MI: Gale Research Co., 1971. 235 pp.

882. Gillerman, Dorothy, ed. *Gothic Sculpture in American Collections. Volume 1: The New England Museums.* New York: Garland Publishing, 1989. 434 pp. First of a projected three-volume series.

883. Gouker, Loice, comp. *Dictionary of Church Terms and Symbols.* Norwalk, CA: C. R. Gibson Company, 1964. 69 pp.

884. Husenbeth, Frederick Charles. *Emblems of the Saints by Which They Are Distinguished in Works of Art.* 3rd ed. by Augustus Jessop. Norwich, England: A.H. Goose and Co., for the Norfolk and Norwich Archaeological Society, 1882. 426 pp.

885. Metford, J. C. J. *Dictionary of Christian Lore & Legend.* London: Thames & Hudson, 1983. 272 pp.

886. Sill, Gertrude Grace. *A Handbook of Symbols in Christian Art.* 2 vols. Trans. by Janet Seligman. Greenwich, CT: New York Graphic Society, 1971. Translation of 2nd German ed. of *Ikonographie der christlichen Kunst.* Gerd Mohn, Gütersloh: Gütersloher Verlagshaus, 1966, 1969.

887. Stafford, Thomas Albert. *Christian Symbolism in the Evangelical Churches with Definitions of Church Terms and Usages.* New York: Abingdon Press, 1942. 176 pp.

888. Tabor, Margaret E. *The Saints in Art, with Their Attributes and Symbols Alphabetically Arranged.* London: Methuen & Co., 1908. Rept. Detroit, MI: Gale Research Company, 1969. 208 pp.

Bibliographies

889. Cornish, Graham P., comp. *Inter-Action between Modern Drama and the Church: A Selective Bibliography.* Theological and Religious Bibliographies Vol. 3. Harrogate, North Yorkshire: G.P. Cornish, 1981.

890. *Conservation of Churches and Their Treasures: A Bibliography.* London: Council for the Care of Churches, 1970.

891. Hill, George H., and Lenwood Davis. *Religious Broadcasting 1920-1983: A Selectively Annotated Bibliography.* New York: Garland Publishing, 1984. 243 pp.

892. Ohlgren, Thomas H., et al. *Insular and Anglo-Saxon Illuminated Manuscripts: An Iconographic Catalogue c. A.D. 625 to 1100.* New York: Garland Publishing, 1986. 480 pp.

893. Parshall, Linda B., and Peter W. Parshall. *Art and the Reformation: An Annotated Bibliography.* Boston: G. K. Hall, 1986. 282 pp.

894. Roberts, Helene E. *Iconographic Index to Old Testament Subjects Represented in Photographs and Slides of Paintings in the Visual Collections, Fine Arts Library,*

Harvard University. New York: Garland Publishing, 1990. 224 pp.

895. Woodruff, Helen. *Index of Christian Art, Princeton University.* Princeton, NJ: Department of Art and Archaeology, Princeton University, 1963.

Music

General Sources

896. Higginson, J. Vincent. *Handbook for American Catholic Hymnals.* New York: Hymn Society of America, 1976. 334 pp.

Encyclopedias and Dictionaries

897. Britt, Matthew, ed. *A Dictionary of the Psalter, Containing the Vocabulary of the Psalms, Hymns, Canticles and Miscellaneous Prayers of the Breviary Psalter.* New York: Benziger Brothers, 1923. 299pp. Rept.: New York: Benziger Bros., 1928. 299 pp.

898. Carroll, Joseph Robert. *Compendium of Liturgical Music Terms.* Toledo, OH: Gregorian Institute of America, 1964. 86 pp.

899. Davidson, James Robert. *A Dictionary of Protestant Church Music.* Metuchen, NJ: Scarecrow Press, 1975. 349 pp.

900. Dreves, Guido Maria, and Clemens Blume. *Analecta Hymnica Medii Aevi.* 55 vols. Leipzig: Reisland, 1886-1922. Rept: New York: Johnson Reprint Corp., 1961.

901. Ellinwood, Leonard. *Dictionary of American Hymnology: First Line Index.* New York: University Music Editions, 1984. 179 microfilm reels.

902. Hughes, Anselm. *Liturgical Terms for Music Students: A Dictionary.* Boston, MA: McLaughlin and Reilly, 1940. 40 pp. Rept.: St. Clair Shores, MI: Scholarly Press, 1972. 40 pp.

903. Julian, John, ed. *A Dictionary of Hymnology, Setting Forth the Origin and History of Christian Hymns of All Ages and Nations.* 1892. Rev. ed.: London: John Murray, 1907. 131 pp. Rept.: 2 vols. New York: Dover Publications, 1957.

904. McCuchan, Robert Guy. *Hymn Tune Names: Their Sources and Significance.* Nashville: Abingdon Press, 1957. 206 pp.

905. Stubbings, George Wilfred. *A Dictionary of Church Music.* London: Epworth Press, 1949. 129 pp. Rept.: New York: Philosophical Library, 1950. 127 pp.

Biographical Volumes

906. Hatfield, Edwin F. *Poets of the Church: A Series of Biographical Sketches of Hymn-Writers with Notes on Their Hymns.* New York: Anson D. F. Randolph & Co., 1884. 719 pp. Rept.: Detroit: Gale Research Co., 1978. 719 pp.

907. Thomson, Ronald William. *Who's Who of Hymn Writers.* London: Epworth Press, 1967. 104 pp.

908. Tillett, Wilbur F., and Charles S. Nutter. *The Hymns and Hymn Writers of the Church: An Annotated Edition of The Methodist Hymnal.* Nashville, TN: Smith & Lamar, 1911. 567 pp.

Bibliographies and Indices

909. Anderson, Frank J., comp. *Hymns and Hymnody.* Wofford College Library Special Colls. Checklists No. 1. Spartanburg, SC: Wofford Library Press, 1970. 25 pp.

910. Bishop, Selma L., comp. & ed. *Watts's Hymns and Spiritual Songs (1707): A Publishing History and a Bibliography.* Ann Arbor, MI: Pierian Press, 1974. 479 pp.

911. Blume, Clemens. *Repertorium Repertorii: Kritischer Wegweiser durch U. Chevalier's Repertorium Hymnologicum. Alphabetisches Register Falscher, Mangelhafter oder Irreleitender Hymnenanfänge und Nachweise mit Erörterung über Plan und Methode des Repertoriums.* Leipzig: O. R. Reisland, 1901. 315 pp. Supplement to Chevalier (916).

912. Brooke, William Thomas. *Bibliotheca Hymnologica.* London: Charles Higham, 1890. 107 pp. Rept.: London: C. Higham, 1981. 107 pp.

913. Bryden, John Rennie, and David G. Hughes, comps. *An Index of Gregorian Chant.* 2 vols. Cambridge, MA: Harvard University Press, 1969.

914. Burnsworth, Charles C. *Choral Music for Women's Voices: An Annotated Bibliography of Recommended Works.* Metuchen, NJ: Scarecrow Press, 1968. 180 pp.

915. Buszin, Walter, et al. *A Bibliography of Music and the Church.* New York: National Council of Churches of Christ, 1958.

916. Chevalier, Cyr Ulisse Joseph. *Repertorium Hymnologicum. Catalogue des Chants, Hymnes, Proses, Séquences, Tropes en Usage dans l'église Latine depuis les Origines Jusqu'à nos Jours.* 6 vols. Louvain, Bruxelles: Soc. des Bollandistes, 1892-1920. *See*: Blume (911).

917. Clark, Keith C. *A Short Bibliography for the Study of Hymns.* Papers of the Hymn Society of America No. 25. New York: Hymn Society of America, 1964. Rev. as: *A Selective Bibliography for the Study of Hymns.* Papers of the Hymn Society of America No. 33. Springfield, OH: Hymn Society of America, 1980. 42 pp.

918. *Complete Pepper Guide to the Sacred Music of All Publishers.* Philadelphia: J. Pepper, n.d.

919. Daniel, Ralph T., and Peter Le Huray, comps. *The Sources of English Church Music, 1549-1660.* Early English Church Music Supplementary Vol. 1. London: Stainer and Bell, 1972.

920. Dearmer, Percy. *A Subject Index of Hymns in "The English Hymnal" and "Songs of Praise".* London: Oxford University Press, 1926. 104 pp.

921. Diehl, K. S. *Hymns and Tunes: An Index.* New York: Scarecrow, 1966. 1185 pp.

922. Ellinwood, Leonard. *Bibliography of American Hymnals.* New York: University Music Editions, 1983. 27 microfiches.

923. Episcopal Church. Joint Commission on Church Music. *Service Music and Anthems for the Nonprofessional Choir.* Greenwich, CT: Seabury Press, 1955. 56 pp. Rev. ed.: New York: H.W. Gray Co., 1963. 54 pp.

924. Espina, Noni. *Vocal Solos for Christian Churches: A Descriptive Reference of Solo Music for the Church Year, Including a Bibliographical Supplement of Choral Works.* 3rd ed. Metuchen, NJ: Scarecrow Press, 1984. 256 pp.

925. Frere, Walter Howard. *Bibliotheca Musico-Liturgica: A Descriptive Handlist of the Musical and Latin-Liturgical Manuscripts of the Middle Ages Preserved in the Libraries of Great Britain and Ireland.* 2 vols. London: Bernard Quaritch for the Plainsong and Medieval Music Society. Rept.: Hildeshaim: George Olms, 1967.

926. Gombosi Marilyn, comp. *Catalog of the Johannes Herbst Collection.* Chapel Hill, NC: University of North Carolina Press, 1970. 255 pp. A catalog of Moravian music.

927. *Guide to Music for the Church Year.* 1962. 4th ed. Minneapolis, MN: Augsburg Publishing House, 1975. 144 pp.

928. Hartley, Kenneth R. *Bibliography of Theses and Dissertations in Sacred Music.* Detroit Studies in Music Bibliography No. 9. Detroit, MI: Information Coordinators, 1966. 127 pp.

929. Hughes, Andrew. *Medieval Music: The Sixth Liberal Art.* Rev. ed. Toronto: University of Toronto Press, 1980. 360 pp.

930. Laster, James. *Catalogue of Choral Music Arranged in Biblical Order.* Metuchen, NJ: Scarecrow Press, 1983. 269 pp.

931. ———. *Catalogue of Vocal Solos and Duets Arranged in Biblical Order.* Metuchen, NJ: Scarecrow Press, 1984. 212 pp.

932. Leaver, Robin A., comp. *English Hymns and Hymn Books: Catalogue of an Exhibition Held at the Bodleian Library, Oxford.* Oxford: Bodleian Library, 1981. 34 pp.

933. ———. *Hymn Book Survey, 1962-1980.* Grove Worship Series No. 71. Bramcore, Nottinghamshire: Grove Books, 198. 24 pp.

934. ———. *Hymns with the New Lectionary.* Bramcote, Nottinghamshire: Grove Books, 1980.

935. ———. *A Thematic Guide to the Anglican Hymn Book.* London: Church Book Room Press, 1975. 65 pp.

936. Lutheran Church in America. Commission on Worship. *Index of Free Accompaniments for Hymn Tunes of the "Service Book and Hymnal".* New York: Lutheran Church in America, 1965.

937. Mearns, James. *Early Latin Hymnaries: An Index of Hymns and Hymnaries Before 1100, with an Appendix from Later Sources.* Cambridge, England: Cambridge University Press, 1913. 107 pp.

938. Metcalf, Frank Johnson, comp. *American Psalmody; or, Titles of Books Containing Tunes Printed in America from 1721 to 1820.* New York: Heartmann, 1917. 54 pp. Rept.: New York: Da Capo Press, 1968. 54 pp.

939. Meyer-Baer, Kathi. *Liturgical Music Incunabula: A Descriptive Catalogue.* London: Bibliographical Society, 1962. 63 pp.

940. Moore, Edgar J. *A Guide to Music in Worship: A Comprehensive, Current Index of Sacred Solos in Print.* Great Neck, NY: Channel Press, 1959. 86 pp.

941. Parks, Edna D. *Early English Hymns: An Index.* Metuchen, NJ: Scarecrow Press, 1972. 168 pp.

942. Perry, David W. *Hymns and Tunes Indexed; by First Lines, Tune Names, and Metres.* Croydon, England: Hymn Society of Great Britain and Ireland and Royal School of Music, 1980. 306 pp.

943. Rau, Albert George, and Hans Theodore David, comps. *Catalogue of Music by American Moravians, 1742-1842, from the Archive of the Moravian Church of Bethlehem, Pa.* Bethlehem, PA: Moravian Seminary and College for Women, 1938. Rept.: New York: AMS Press, 1970. 118 pp.

944. Revitt, Paul Joseph, comp. *The George Pullen Jackson Collection of Southern Hymnody: A Bibliography.* UCLA Library Occasional Papers No. 13. Los Angeles: University of California Library, 1964. 25 pp.

945. Rhodes University. James Rodger Hymnological Collection. *Catalogue.* Grahamstown, So. Africa: Rhodes University Library, 1966. 21 pp.

946. Richardson, Alice Marion. *Index to Stories of Hymns: An Analytical Catalog of Twelve Much-Used Books.* Yardley, PA: F. S. Cook, 1929. 76 pp. Rept.: New York: AMS Press, 1975. 76 pp.

947. Robertson, Festus G., Jr. *Church Music for Adults.* Nashville, TN: Convention Press, 1969. 101 pp.

948. Rogal, Samuel J. *Guide to Hymns and Tunes of American Methodism.* New York: Greenwood Press, 1986. 318 pp.

949. Rogers, Kirby. *English and Scottish Psalms and Hymn Tunes: An Index.* MLA Index Series No. 8. Ann Arbor, MI: Music Library Association, 1967. 531 pp.

950. Routley, Erik. *An English-Speaking Hymnal Guide.* Collegeville, MN: Liturgical Press, 1979. 125 pp.

951. Royal School of Church Music. *Church Music Recommended by the Musical Advisory Board.* Rev. ed. Croyden: Royal School of Church Music, 1967. 23 pp.

952. ———. *A Selected List of Church Music Recordings.* Croyden: Royal School of Church Music, 1967. 12 pp.

953. Shaw, John Mackay. *The Poetry of Sacred Song: A Catalogue.* Tallahassee, FL: Friends of the Library, Florida State University, 1972. 18 pp.

954. Spencer, Donald Amos, comp. *Hymn and Scripture Selection Guide: A Cross Reference of Scripture and Hymns with over 12000 References for 380 Hymns and Gospel Songs.* Valley Forge, PA: Judson Press, 1977. 176 pp.

955. Steere, Dwight. *Music for the Protestant Church Choir: A Descriptive and Classified List of Worship Material.* Richmond, VA: John Knox Press, 1955. 229 pp.

956. Studwell, William E. *Christmas Carols: A Reference Guide.* Garland Folklore Bibliographies Vol. 4. New York: Garland Publishing, 1985. 278 pp.

957. Verret, Mary Camilla. *A Preliminary Survey of Roman Catholic Hymnals Published in the United States of America.* Washington, DC: Catholic University of America Press, 1964. 165 pp.

958. Voigt, Louis, and Ellen Jane Porter. *Hymnbook Collections of North America.* New York: Hymn Society of America, 1980. 32 pp.

959. Warrington, James. *Short Titles of Books, Relating to or Illustrating the History and Practice of Psalmody in the United States, 1620-1820.* Philadelphia: Privately printed, 1878. Rept.: Bibliographia Tripotamopolitana No. 1. Pittsburgh, PA: Pittsburgh Theological Seminary, Clifford E. Barbour Library, 1970. 96 pp. Rept.: Burt Franklin Bibliography and Reprint Series Vol. 438. New York: Burt Franklin, 1971. 96 pp.

960. Wilkes, Roger. *English Cathedrals and Collegiate Churches and Chapels: Their Music, Musicians and Musical Establishments; A Select Bibliography.* London: Friends of Cathedral Music, 1968. 12 pp.

961. Yeats-Edwards, Paul. *English Church Music: A Bibliography.* London: White Lion Publishers, 1975. 217 pp.

Directories

962. Center for Contemporary Celebration. *Directory of Artists and Religious Communities.* West Lafayette, IN: The Center, [1975]. 145 pp.

963. *Christian Booking Directory.* 5th ed. Ojai, CA: Christian Booking Directory, 1990. 56 pp. Periodically updated. Formerly known as the *Christian Booking and Program Directory.* It is a sister publication of the *Christian Activities Calendar*, a bi-monthly magazine and guide to Christian programming around the United States.

964. *Concert Artists Directory.* Ojai, CA: Regularly updated.

965. *Christian Music Directories: Printed Music.* San Jose, CA: Resources Publications, updated regularly. Formerly known as *The Music Locater.* There are supplemental *Update* issues released between cumulative volumes.

966. *Christian Music Directories: Recorded Music.* San Jose, CA: Resources Publications, updated regularly.

967. Littauer, Fred. *National Directory of Christian Artists.* 1986 ed. Eugene, OR: Harvest House Publishers, c. 1985. 264 pp.

968. *National Directory of Christian Artists.* San Bernadino, CA: Praise Ministry Associates. 1985. 264 pp.

969. *The Rainbow Road.* Mesquite, TX: Rainbow Road Maps. Guide to Christian radio stations nationally.

970. Stevens, Marjorie, ed. *The Directory of Religious Broadcasting.* Morristown, NJ: National Religious Broadcasters, issued annually.

Professional Associations

Association of Christian Television Stations
c/o Dr. Lester Sumrall
Box 50250
Indianapolis, IN 46250

Church Music Association of America
548 LaFond Avenue
St. Paul, MN 55103

Church Musicians' National Referral Service
P. O. Box 36
Huntington, WV 25706

Council for the Care of Churches
83 London Wall
London EC2M 5NA
United Kingdom
The Council is concerned with the preservation of English churches and cathedrals.

Hymn Society of America
Texas Christian University
Fort Worth, TX 76129

The Society supports a library, a quarterly magazine, *The Hymn*, and a computer project, the *Dictionary of American Hymnology*. Part of the library is housed at Union Theological Seminary in New York City.

Interfaith Forum of Religion, Art, and Architecture
1913 Architects Building
Philadelphia, PA 19103

National Association of Christians in the Arts
Box 2995
Boston, MA 02101

National Council for Art in Jewish Life
15 84th Street
New York, NY 10028

National Religious Broadcasters
CN 1926
Morristown, NJ 07960

St. John of Damascus Association of Orthodox Iconographers, Iconologists, and Architects
2907 Oakwood Lane
Torrance, CA 90505

Research/Resource Centers

American Music Research Center
Dominican College
San Rafael, CA 94901
The Center houses a collection of "California Mission" (1769-1840), gospel, and Shaker music.

Ecumenical Music & Liturgy Resources Library
8000 Hickory Lane
P. O. Box 30221
Lincoln, NE 68503-0221

Index of Christian Art Project
Department of Art and Archeology
Princeton University
Princeton, NJ 08544-1018

THE BIBLE

The Bible, the sacred book of Christianity, is the most thoroughly researched, indexed, and analyzed book in the world, and Bible-related research from linguistics studies to archeological digs are proceeding continuously. Regularly, new Bible encyclopedias appear with the latest information, and over the twentieth century specialized books such as dictionaries, indices, and surveys have added to the storehouse of information. The quality of Bible reference books from the major publishers is high, each usually backed by a team of biblical scholars, and are to be distinguished more by their relative depth from the concise one-volume works to the comprehensive and detailed multi-volume works. Different books will also find an audience because of their identification with a particular Christian community, most notably the Roman Catholic, liberal Protestant, or Evangelical, though in fact the differences between them are relatively marginal.

The growth of biblical research in the twentieth century, greatly spurred by reactions to the historical-critical approach to the Bible that developed in nineteenth-century Germany, has also meant that most biblical scholars have had to specialize, the primary distinction being between those who study the Jewish Scriptures (the Old Testament) and those who study the Greek Scriptures (the New Testament). Bibliographical tools also vary from the very detailed international listing of the *Elenchus Bibliographicus Biblicus*, *Old Testament Abstracts*, and *New Testament Abstracts*, to the guides assisting the new Bible student to enter what can be an overwhelming field.

Some mention is necessary of the limitations of the list below. The intent of sourcebooks relative to the Bible has been to list those sources aimed at highlighting our historical understanding of the Bible's life and times, its linguistic and textual origins, and the environment in which it was written, rather than those works primarily aimed at an exposition and advocacy of the religious message of the Bible. In practice, of course, such a distinction tends to become vague and most difficult to apply, especially in the area of biblical theology. However, in a broad sense, it had led to the decision to exclude, for example, the numerous translations of the Bible into English or other Western languages. Nor does it list the various concordances which have been created as word indexes to the more popular translations. Also not included are the many Bible commentaries. These, more than any other reference volumes on the Bible, are reflective of the various religious communities into which Christians are divided and are aimed more at religious instruction than the historical study of the Bible, aimed more at pastors and church members than the scholarly community.

Among the subjects we have included is the rather large field of Bible collecting which has both a popular and a scholarly side to it. Finally, at another level of interest similar to that of Bible collecting, biblical research includes the development of some self-conscious interest in the study of modern study about the Bible, i.e., the historiography of nineteenth- and twentieth-century biblical studies. Books reflective of that interest are scattered throughout this chapter but are most evident in the study of the books about Jesus. See the texts by Birney (1210), Kissinger (1215) and Wismer (1221).

Biblical Studies

Encyclopedias and Dictionaries

971. Achtemeier, Paul J., gen. ed. *Harper's Bible Dictionary.* San Francisco: Harper & Row, 1985. 1178 pp.

972. Alexander, George M. *The Handbook of Biblical Personalities.* Greenwich, CT: Seabury Press, 1962. 299 pp.

973. Alexander, Patricia, ed. *Eerdmans' Concise Bible Encyclopedia.* Grand Rapids, MI: William B. Eerdmans Publishing Co., 1981. 384 pp.

974. ———. *Eerdmans' Family Encyclopedia of the Bible.* Grand Rapids, MI: William B. Eerdmans Publishing Co., 1978. 328 pp. Rev. ed. as: *The Lion Encyclopedia of the Bible.* Batavia, IL: Lion Publishing Co., 1986. 352 pp.

975. Allmen, J.-J. von, ed. *A Companion to the Bible.* New York: Oxford University Press, 1958. 479 pp. Originally published as *Vocabulaire Biblique*, Neuchatel & Paris: Delachaux & Niestlé, 1954. Trans. from 2nd French ed., 1956, by P. J. Allcock, et al.

976. Anderson, David A. *All the Trees and Woody Plants of the Bible.* Waco, TX: Word Books, 1979. 294 pp.

977. Arnold, A. Stuart. *ABC of Bible Lands.* Nashville, TN: Broadman Press, 1977.

978. Blaiklock, Edward Musgrave, ed. *Bible Characters and Doctrines.* 16 vols. Grand Rapids, MI: William B. Eerdmans Publishing Co., 1972-1975.

979. Bogaert, Pierre-Maurice, et al., eds. *Dictionnaire Encyclopedique de la Bible.* Brepols, 1987. 1363 pp. Prepared under the direction of the Centre Informatique et Bible Abbaye de Maredsous.

980. Bridges, Ronald, and Luther A. Weigle. *The Bible Word Book: Concerning Obsolete or Archaic Words in the King James Version of the Bible.* New York: Thomas Nelson & Sons, 1960. 422 pp.

981. Bromiley, Geoffrey W., et al., eds. *The International Standard Bible Encyclopedia.* 4 vols. Grand Rapids, MI: William B. Eerdmans Publishing Co., 1979-88. Revision of (1029).

982. Bruce, Frederick Fyvie, et al., eds. *The Illustrated Bible Dictionary.* 3 vols. Wheaton, IL: Tyndale House Publishers/Leicester: Inter-Varsity Press, 1980. Rev. and expanded from (988).

983. Bryant, T. Alton. *The New Compact Bible Dictionary.* Special Crusade ed. Minneapolis: Billy Graham Evangelistic Assoc., 1967. 621 pp. + maps.

984. Buttrick, George, ed. *The Interpreters' Dictionary of the Bible: An Illustrated Encyclopedia.* 4 vols. New York: Abingdon, 1962. *See also*: Crim (993)

985. Calmet, Antoine Augustin. *Calmet's Great Dictionary of the Holy Bible: Historical Critical, Geographical, and Etymological.* London: C. Taylor, 1897-1801. Rev. ed. as: *Calmet's Dictionary of the Holy Bible.* London: W. Stafford for C. Taylor, 1800-01. Rev. Ed.: 5 vols. Charleston, MA: Samuel Etheridge, 1812-1817. 9th ed.: Rev. by Edward Robinson. Boston, MA: Crocker and Brewster, 1852. 1003 pp.

986. Cansdale, George Soper. *All the Animals of the Bible Lands.* Grand Rapids, MI: Zondervan Publishing House/Exeter: Paternoster Press, 1970. 272 pp.

987. Charley, Julian. *50 Key Words: The Bible.* Richmond, VA: John Knox Press, 1971. 69 pp.

988. Cheyne, T. K., and J. Sutherland Black. *Encyclopedia Biblica: A Critical Dictionary of the Literary, Political and Religious History, the Archeology, Geography and Natural History of the Bible.* 4 vols. London: Adam & Charles Black, 1899-1906. Rept. 1 vol. New York: Macmillan Company, 1914. Includes maps & illustrations.

989. Coggins, R. J., and J. L. Houlden. *Dictionary of Biblical Interpretation.* London: SCM Press/Philadelphia: Trinity Press International, 1990. 751 pp.

990. *Combined Biblical Dictionary and Concordance for the New American Bible.* Charlotte, NC: C.D. Stampley Enterprises, 1971. 252 pp.

991. Cornfeld, Gaalyahu, ed. *Pictorial Biblical Encyclopedia: A Visual Guide to the Old and New Testaments.* New York: Macmillan/London: Collier-Macmillan, 1964. 713 pp.

992. Corswant, Willy. *A Dictionary of Life in Bible Times.* Trans. by Arthur Heathcote. New York: Oxford University Press/London: Hodder & Stoughton, 1960. 308 pp.

993. Crim, Keith R., ed. *The Interpreter's Dictionary of the Bible: Supplementary Volume.* Nashville, TN: Abingdon Press, 1976. 998 pp. *See:* (984)

994. Daigle, Richard J., and Frederick R. Lapides. *The Mentor Dictionary of Mythology and the Bible.* New York: New American Library, 1973.

995. Davis, John D. *Dictionary of the Bible.* Philadelphia: Westminster Press, 1898. Rev. eds., 1903, 1911, 1924. Rept. as: *Davis Dictionary of the Bible.* Grand Rapids, MI: Baker Book House, 1972. Rev. by Henry Snyder Gehman as: *The Westminster Dictionary of the Bible.* Philadelphia: Westminster Press, 1944. 658 pp.

996. Dheilly, Joseph. *Dictionnaire Biblique.* Tournai: Desclée, 1964. 1260 pp.

997. Douglas, J. D., et al., eds. *The New Bible Dictionary.* Grand Rapids, MI: William B. Eerdmans Pub. Co., 1962. 1375 pp. 2nd. ed: Leicester, UK: Inter-Varsity Press/Wheaton, IL: Tyndale House Publishers, 1982. 1326 pp. Rev. ed. as: *The New International Dictionary of the Bible.* Grand Rapids, MI: William B. Eerdmans Publishing Company, 1987. 1162 pp.

998. Dow, James Leslie. *Collins Gem Dictionary of the Bible.* London: William Collins Sons and Co., 1964. 639 pp.

999. Easton, Matthew George. *Illustrated Bible Dictionary and Treasury of Biblical History, Biography, Geography, Doctrine and Literature with Numerous Illustrations and Important Chronological Tables and Maps.* 3rd ed. London: Thomas Nelson and Sons, 1897. Reprint. as *Baker's Illustrated Bible Dictionary* (Grand Rapids, MI: Baker Book House, 1977.

1000. Fairbairn, Patrick, ed. *The Imperial Bible-Dictionary: Historical, Biographical, Geographical, & Doctrinal, Including the Natural History, Antiquities, Manners, Customs, and Religious Rites and Ceremonies Mentioned in the Scriptures, and an Account of the Several Books of the Old and New Testaments.* 6 vols. London, etc.: Blackie & Son, 1890. Rept.: Grand Rapids, MI: Zondervan Publishing House, 1957.

1001. Fausset, A. R. *Bible Encyclopedia and Dictionary: Critical and Expository.* Grand Rapids, MI: Zondervan Publishing House, n.d. 753 pp.

1002. Fulghum, Walter Benjamin. *A Dictionary of Biblical Allusions in English Literature.* New York: Holt, Rinehart and Winston, 1965. 291 pp.

1003. Gardner, James. *The Christian Cyclopedia or Repertory of Biblical and Theological Literature.* Enlarged ed.: London: Blackie & Son, 1874. 984 pp.

1004. Gehman, Henry Snyder. *The New Westminster Dictionary of the Bible.* Philadelphia: Westminster Press, 1970. 1027 pp.

1005. Grant, Frederick Clifton, and Harold Henry Rowley. *Dictionary of the Bible.* Rev. ed. New York: Charles Scribner's Sons, 1963.

1006. Graydon, H., D. E. Jenkins and E. C. D. Stanford. *Bible Meanings: A Short Theological Word-Book of the Bible.* London: Oxford University Press, 1963.

1007. Hartman, Louis F. *Encyclopedic Dictionary of the Bible.* New York, etc.: McGraw-Hill, 1963. 2633 pp. Trans. and adapted from A. van den Born's *Bijbels Woordenboek*, 2nd rev. ed., 1954-57.

1008. Hastings, James, ed. *Dictionary of the Bible.* 5 vols. New York: Charles Scribner's Sons/Edinburgh: T. & T. Clark, 1898-1904. Rev. ed.: Edited by Frederick C. Grant and H. H. Rowley. New York: Charles Scribner's Sons, 1963. 1059 pp.

1009. Horn, S. H., ed. *Seventh-Day Adventist Bible Dictionary.* Washington, DC: Review and Herald Publishing Co., 1961. 1199 pp.

1010. *Illustrated Dictionary and Concordance of the Bible.* New York: Macmillan/Collier, 1986. 1070 pp.

1011. Jacobus, Melancthon W., et al., eds. *A Standard Bible Dictionary.* New York: Funk & Wagnalls, 1909. 2nd ed.: 1926. 3rd rev. ed. as: *A New Standard Bible Dictionary: Designed as a Comprehensive Help to the Study of the Scriptures, their Languages, Literary Problems, History, Biography, Manners and Customs, and their Religious Teachings.* New York & London: Funk & Wagnalls, 1936. 965 pp. Rept.: New York: Funk & Wagnalls, 1950. Also published as *Funk and Wagnalls New Standard Bible Dictionary.* 3rd rev. ed.: Garden City, NY: Garden City Books, 1936.

1012. Kalt, Edmund. *Biblisches Reallexicon.* 2 Vols. Paderbon: Ferdinand Schöningh, 1931.

1013. Kasher, Menachem. *Encyclopedia of Biblical Interpretation: A Millennial Anthology.* Vol. 1- . New York: American Bible Encyclopedia Society, 1953- .

1014. Kitto, John. *Cyclopaedia of Biblical Literature.* 1840? 3rd ed.: 3 vols. Edinburgh: Adam and Charles Black, 1862-1866; Philadelphia: J.B. Lippincott Co., 1866. Rev. ed.: 1893.

1015. Lockyer, Herbert. *All the Trades and Occupations of the Bible.* Grand Rapids, MI: Zondervan, 1969. 327 pp.

1016. ———, et al., eds. *Nelson's Illustrated Bible Dictionary.* Nashville, TN: Thomas Nelson Publishers, 1986. 1128 pp.

1017. Lueker, Erwin Louis. *The Concordia Bible Dictionary.* St. Louis, MO: Concordia Publishing House, 1963. 146 pp.

1018. McKenzie, John L. *Dictionary of the Bible.* Milwaukee, WI: Bruce Publishing Co., 1965. Rept.: New York: Macmillan Company, 1967. 959 pp.

1019. Marijnen, P.A., ed. *The Encyclopedia of the Bible.* Trans. by D.R. Welsh with emendations by Claire Jones. Englewood Cliffs, NJ: Prentice-Hall, 1965. 248 pp. Originally published as: *Elsevier's Encyclopedie van de Bijbel.*

1020. Miller, Madeline S., and J. Lane Miller. *An Encyclopedia of Bible Life.* New York & Evanston: Harper & Row, 1944. 493 pp. Rev. ed. as: *Harper's Encyclopedia of Bible Life.* San Francisco: Harper & Row, 1978. 423 pp.

1021. ———. *Harper's Bible Dictionary.* New York: Harper & Brothers, 1952. 3rd ed.: 1955. 8th ed.: New York: Harper & Row, 1973. 850 pp. British ed. as: *Black's Bible Dictionary.* London: A. and C. Black, 1954. 850 pp.

1022. Mills, Watson E., gen. ed. *Mercer Dictionary of the Bible.* Macon, GA: Mercer University Press, 1990. 1051 pp.

1023. Mitchell, Antoinette. *Bible Places...Historic and Geographic Highlights.* Norwalk, CT: C. R. Gibson Company, 1964. 71 pp.

1024. Moldenke, H. N., and A. L. Moldenke. *Plants of the Bible.* Waltham, MA: Chronica Botanica Company, 1952. 328 pp. Rept.: New York: Dover Press, 1986. 328 pp.

1025. Møller-Christensen, Vilhelm, and Karl Eduard Jordt Jorgensen. *Encyclopedia of Bible Creatures.* Ed. by M. Theodore Heinecken and trans. by Arne Unhjem. Philadelphia: Fortress Press, 1965. 302 pp.

1026. Myers, Allen G., ed. *The Eerdmans Bible Dictionary.* Grand Rapids, MI: William B. Eerdmans Publishing Company, 1987. 1094 pp. A translation and updated revision of W. H. Gispen, et al., eds. *Bijbelse Encyclopedie.* Kampen, Netherlands: J. H. Kok, 1975.

1027. Neill, Stephen Charles, et al., eds. *The Modern Reader's Dictionary of the Bible.* New York: Association Press, 1966. Published in England as *Concise Dictionary of the Bible.* 2 vols. London: Lutterworth Press, 1966.

1028. Odelain, O., and R. Séguineau. *Dictionary of Proper Names and Places in the Bible.* Garden City, NY: Doubleday & Company, 1981. 479 pp. Trans. and adapted by Matthew J. O'Connell. Originally published in French as *Dictionnaire des Noms Propres de la Bible.* Paris: Les Editions du Cerf et Desclée De Brouwer, 1978.

1029. Orr, James, et al. *The International Standard Bible Encyclopedia.* 1915. Rev. ed.: 5 vols. Chicago: Howard-Severance Co., 1929. Superseded by (981).

1030. Osterloh, Edo, and Hans Engelland. *Biblisch-theologisches Handwörterbuch zur Lutherbibel und zu neueren Übersetzungen.* Göttingen, Germany: Vandenhoeck & Ruprecht, 1959. 752 pp.

1031. Payne, J. Barton. *Encyclopedia of Biblical Prophecy: The Complete Guide to Scriptural Predictions and Their Fulfillment.* New York: Harper & Row, 1973. Rept.: Grand Rapids, MI: Baker Book House, 1980.

1032. Pfeiffer, Charles Franklin, et al., eds. *The Wycliffe Bible Encyclopedia.* 2 vols. Chicago: Moody Press, 1975.

1033. Potts, Cyrus Alvin, comp. *Dictionary of Bible Proper Names: Every Proper Name in the Old and New Testaments Arranged in Alphabetical Order; Syllabified and Accented: Vowel Sounds Diacritically Marked; Definitions Given in Latin and English.* New York: Abingdon Press, [c. 1922]. 288 pp.

1034. Richards, Lawrence O., ed. *The Revell Bible Dictionary.* Old Tappan, NJ: Fleming H. Revell Company, 1990. 1156 pp.

1035. Rowley, Harold Henry. *A Dictionary of Bible Place Names.* Old Tappan, NJ: Fleming H. Revell/London: Oliphants, 1970. 173 pp.

1036. ———. *Dictionary of Bible Themes.* London: Thomas Nelson and Sons, 1968.

1037. Smith, Barbara. *Young People's Bible Dictionary for Use with the Revised Standard Version of the Bible.* Philadelphia: Westminster Press, c. 1965. 161 pp. Rept. as: *Westminster Concise Bible Dictionary.* Philadelphia: Westminster Press, [1981].

1038. Smith, William. *A Dictionary of the Bible, Comprising Its Antiquities, Biography, Geography and Natural History.* 3 vols. London: John Murray, 1860-1863. Rev. ed. as: *A Dictionary of the Bible, Comprising Its Antiquities, Biography, Geography, Natural History and Literature with the Latest Researches and References to the Revised Version of the New Testament.* Rev. by Francis Nathan Peloubet and M.A. Peloubet. Philadelphia: J.C. Winston Co., 1948. 818 pp. Rept: Grand Rapids, MI: Zondervan Publishing House, 1948. Rev. ed. as: *The New Smith's Bible Dictionary.* Rev. by Revel G. Lemmons et al. Garden City, NY: Doubleday & Company, 1966.

1039. Soulen, Richard N. *Handbook of Biblical Criticism.* 1976. 2nd ed.: Atlanta: John Knox Press, 1981. 239 pp.

1040. Steinmuller, John E., and Kathryn Sullivan, eds. *Catholic Biblical Encyclopedia: Old and New Testaments.* 2 vols. New York: Joseph F. Wagner, 1956.

1041. Sundemo, Herbert. *Revell's Dictionary of Bible Times.* Trans. by Brigitta Sharpe. Old Tappan, NJ: Fleming H. Revell Co., 1979.

1042. Tenney, Merrill Chapin, ed. *The Zondervan Pictorial Bible Dictionary.* Grand Rapids, MI: Zondervan Publishing House/London: Marshall, Morgan and Scott, 1963. Rept. Grand Rapids, MI: Zondervan Publishing House, 1969. 927 pp.

1043. ———. *The Zondervan Pictorial Encyclopedia of the Bible.* 5 vols. Grand Rapids, MI: Zondervan Publishing House, 1975.

1044. Thompson, David Walker. *A Dictionary of Famous Bible Places.* Nashville, TN: Abingdon Press, 1974.

1045. Unger, Merrill Frederick. *Unger's Bible Dictionary.* 3rd ed. Chicago: Moody Press, [c. 1966]. 1192 pp.

1046. ———, and William White, Jr., eds. *Nelson's Expository Dictionary of the Old Testament.* Nashville, TN: Thomas Nelson and Sons, c. 1984. 524 pp. Rev. ed.: 1985. 775 pp.

1047. United Bible Societies Committee on Translation. *Fauna and Flora of the Bible.* Helps for Translators Vol. 11. London: United Bible Societies, 1972.

1048. Van Duersen, Arie. *Illustrated Dictionary of Bible Manners and Customs.* New York: Philosophical Library, 1967. 138 pp.

1049. Vigouroux, Fulcran Grégoire, and Louis Pirot. *Dictionnaire de la Bible, Contenant tous les noms de personnes, de lieux, de plantes, d'animaux mentionnés dans les Saintes Écritures, les questions théologiques, archéologiques....* 5 vols. and supple. Paris: Letouzey, 1907-83. Included in *Encyclopédie des Sciences Religieuses.*

1050. Vine, W. E., and F. F. Bruce, ed. *Vine's Expository Dictionary of the Old and New Testament Words.* Old Tappan, NJ: Fleming H. Revell Company, 1981.

1051. Walker, William O., ed. *Harper's Bible Pronunciation Guide.* San Francisco: Harper & Row, 1989. 170 pp.

1052. Wright, Charles Henry Hamilton. *The Bible Reader's Encyclopaedia and Concordance, Based on "The Bible Reader's Manual"; under One Alphabetical Arrangement.* Rev. by William Maccallum Clow. London: Collins Clear-type Press, 1962. 407 pp.

1053. ———. *Bible Reader's Manual.* London: William Collin's Sons and Co.; New York: International Bible Agency, 1892. 192 pp.

1054. Zohary, Michael. *Plants of the Bible.* Cambridge: Cambridge Univ. Press, 1982. 223 pp.

Biographical Volumes

1055. Barker, William Pierson. *Everyone in the Bible.* Westwood, NJ: F. H. Revell Co., 1966/London: Oliphants, 1967. 370 pp.

1056. Barr, George. *Who's Who in the Bible.* Middle Village, NY: Jonathan David, [1975].

1057. Calvocoress, Peter. *Who's Who in the Bible.* New York: Viking, 1987. 269 pp.

1058. Coggins, Richard, comp. *Who's Who in the Bible.* New York: Barnes and Noble/London: B.T. Batsford, 1981. 232 pp.

1059. Cully, Iris V., and Kendig Brubaker Cully. *From Aaron to Zerubbabel.* New York: Hawthorn Books, 1976. 149 pp.

1060. Davies, Gwynne Henton, and A. B. Davies. *Who's Who in the Bible, Including the Apocrypha.* London: English Universities Press, 1970. 227 pp.

1061. Deen, Edith. *All of the Women of the Bible.* New York: Harper, 1955. 410 pp.

1062. Lockyer, Herbert. *All the Men of the Bible.* Grand Rapids, MI: Zondervan Publishing House, 1958. 381 pp.

1063. Mead, Frank Spencer. *250 Bible Biographies: Thumb Nail Sketches of the Men and Women of the Bible.* New York: Harper and Brothers, 1934. Rept. as: *Who's Who in the Bible: 250 Bible Biographies.* New York: Harper and Row, 1966.

1064. Rowley, Harold Henry. *Dictionary of Bible Personal Names.* New York: Basic Books/London: Thomas Nelson and Sons, 1968. 168 pp.

1065. Thompson, David Walter. *A Bible Who's Who.* Nashville, TN: Abingdon Press, 1974.

1066. *Who's Who in the Bible.* New York: Bonanza, 1980. 448 pp. Combined edition of Joan Comay, *Who's Who in the Old Testament* (1157) and Robert Brownrigg, *Who's Who in the New Testament* (1177).

1067. Wright, John Stafford. *Dictionary of Bible People.* London: Scripture Union, 1978. Also published as: *Revell's Dictionary of Bible People.* Old Tappan, NJ: Fleming H. Revell Company, 1978. 239 pp.

Bibliographies

The bibliographies on the Bible range from selective bibliographies of introductory material for students and pastors to exhaustive bibliographies for scholars. The *Elenchus Bibliographicus Biblicus* indexes ongoing research on an international basis.

1068. *Bibliography of Bible Study: For Theological Students.* Princeton Theological Seminary, 1948. 85 pp. 2nd ed.: 1960. 107 pp.

1069. Brown, Gerald M. *Michigan Coptic Texts.* Barcelona: Papyrologica Castroctaviana, 1979. 77 pp.

1070. Campbell, Richard H., and Michael R. Pitts. *The Bible on Film: A Checklist, 1897-1980.* Metuchen, NJ: Scarecrow Press, 1981. 224 pp.

1071. Cully, Iris V., and Kendig Brubaker Cully. *A Guide to Biblical Resources.* Wilton, CT: Morehouse-Barlow, 1981. 153 pp.

1072. Danker, Frederick W. *Multipurpose Tools for Bible Study.* 1960. 3rd ed.: St. Louis, MO: Concordia Publishing House, 1966. 295 pp. Rept.: 1970. 295 pp.

1073. Davis, M. C. *Hebrew Bible Manuscripts in the Cambridge Genizah Collections.* 2 vols. Cambridge: Cambridge University Press, 1978, 1980.

1074. *Directory of Bible Resources: A Comprehensive Guide to Tools for Bible Study.* Nashville: Thomas Nelson Publishers, 1983. 240 pp.

1075. *École Biblique et Archéologique Française. Bibliotèque.* Catalog of the Library of the French Biblical and Archeological School. 13 vols. Jerusalem, Israel/Boston: G. K. Hall, 1975.

1076. Favilene, M. R., comp. *Historical Catalogue of the Manuscripts of Bible House Library.* Ed. by Alan F. Jesson. London: British and Foreign Bible Soc., 1982. 252 pp.

1077. Glanzman, George S., and Joseph A. Fitzmyer. *An Introductory Bibliography for the Study of Scripture.* Westminster, MD: Newman Press, 1961. 135 pp. Rev. ed.: Rome: Biblical Institute Press, 1981. 154 pp.

1078. Gottcent, John H. *The Bible as Literature: A Select Bibliography.* Boston: G.K. Hall, 1979. 170 pp.

1079. *Internationale Zeitschriftenschau für Bibelwissenschaft und Grenzgebiete (International Review of Biblical Studies).* Vol. 1- . Stuttgart, Germany: Verlag Katholisches Bibelwerk, 1952- . Issued annually.

1080. Jongeling, Bastiaan. *A Classified Bibliography of the Finds in the Desert of Judah.* Studies on the Texts of the Desert of Judah Vol. 8. Leiden: E.J. Brill, 1971. 1140 pp.

1081. Kammerer, Winifred, comp. *A Coptic Bibliography.* University of Michigan General Library Publications No. 7. Ann Arbor, MI: University of Michigan Press, 1950. 205 pp.

1082. Kelly, Balmer Hancock, and Donald G. Miller, eds. *Tools for Bible Study.* Richmond, VA: John Knox Press, 1956. 159 pp.

1083. Khan, Geoffrey. *Karaite Bible Manuscripts from the Cairo Genizah.* Cambridge: Cambridge University Press, 1990. 186 pp.

1084. Langevin, Paul-Émile. *Biblical Bibliography.* 3 vols. Québec: Presses l'Université Laval, 1972-85.

1085. Marrow, Stanley B. *Basic Tools for Biblical Exegesis: A Student's Manual.* Rome: Biblical Institute Press, 1976. 91 pp. Rept.: 1978 with addenda and corrigenda.

1086. Metzger, Bruce, ed. *A Bibliography of Bible Study for Theological Students.* Princeton Seminary Pamphlets No. 1. Princeton, NJ: Princeton Theological Seminary, 1948. 85 pp.

1087. *Quarterly Check-List of Biblical Studies: An International Index of Current Books, Monographs, Brochures & Separates.* Vol. 1- . Darien, CT: American Bibliographic Service, 1958- . Quarterly.

1088. Rounds, Dorothy, comp. *Articles on Antiquity in Festschriften: The Ancient Near East: The Old Testament; Greece; Rome; Roman Law; Byzantium; An Index.* Cambridge, MA: Harvard University Press, 1962. 560 pp.

1089. Rowley, H. H. *Eleven Years of Bible Bibliography: The Book Lists of the Society for Old Testament Study, 1946-1956.* Indian Hills, CO: Falcon's Wing Press, 1957. 804 pp. Supplemented annually.

1090. Smith, Wilbur Moorehead. *A List of Bibliographies of Theological and Biblical Literature Published in Great Britain and America, 1595-1931, with Critical, Biographical and Bibliographical Notes.* Coatesville, PA: The Author, 1931. 62 pp.

1091. Spurgeon, Charles Haddon. *Commenting and Commentaries: Lectures Addressed to the Students of the Pastor's College, Metropolitan Tabernacle; with a List of the Best Biblical Commentaries and Expositions.* New York: Sheldon and Co., 1876. Rev. ed.: Grand Rapids, MI: Kregel Publications, 1954. Rept.: London: Banner of Truth Trust, 1969.

1092. Stegmüller, Friedrich. *Repertorium Biblicum Medii Aevi.* 7 vols. Madrid, Spain: Consejo Superior de Investigaciones Científicas, Inst. Francisco Suárez, 1940.

1093. Warshaw, Thayer S., and Betty Lou Miller, eds. *Bible-Related Curriculum Material: A Bibliography.* Nashville, TN: Abingdon Press, [1976]. 168 pp.

Guides to Periodical Literature

1094. *Elenchus Bibliographicus Biblicus.* Vol. 1- . Rome: Editrice Pontifico Instituto Biblico, 1920- . A comprehensive index of biblical writings. Since 1986 it has been published as a separate publication.

1095. Wahl, Thomas Peter. *Saint John's University Index to Biblical Journals.* Collegeville, MN: St. John's University Press, 1971. 184 pp.

Atlases

1096. Aharoni, Yohanan, and Michael Avi-Yonah. *The Macmillan Bible Atlas.* Rev. ed.: New York: Macmillan Company; London: Collier-Macmillan, 1977. 184 pp.

1097. Baly, Denis, and A.D. Tushingham. *Atlas of the Biblical World.* New York: World Publishing Co., 1971. 208 pp.

1098. *Bible Lands and the Cradle of Western Civilization.* Washington, DC: National Geographic Society, 1946. 18 pp.

1099. *Bible Lands and the Cradle of Western Civilization: Index.* Washington, DC: National Geographic Society, 1946.

1100. Bimson, J. J., et al., eds. *New Bible Atlas.* Leicester, UK: Inter-Varsity Press/Wheaton, IL: Tyndale House Press, 1985. 128 pp.

1101. *Dowley Bible Atlas.* Jackson, MI: Dowley Bible Atlas Co., 1972. 330 pp.

1102. Frank, Harry Thomas, ed. *Hammond's Atlas of the Bible Lands.* New ed.: Maplewood, NJ: Hammond, c. 1977. 48 pp. Rev. ed. as: *Atlas of Bible Lands.* 1948. 48 pp.

1103. Gardner, Joseph Lawrence. *Reader's Digest Atlas of the Bible: An Illustrated Guide to the Holy Land.* Pleasantville, NY: Reader's Digest Assoc., 1982. 256 pp.

1104. Grollenberg, Lucas Hendricus Antonius. *Atlas of the Bible.* Trans. from the 2nd Dutch ed. of *Atlas van de Bijbel.* 1956. 165 pp. 2nd ed.: New York: Thomas Nelson and Sons, 1963/London: Thomas Nelson and Sons, 1966.

1105. ———. *The Shorter Atlas of the Bible.* Trans. by Mary F. Hedlund. London: Thomas Nelson and Sons, 1959/New York: Thomas Nelson and Sons, 1961.

1106. Hurlbut, Jesse Lyman. *A Bible Atlas: A Manual of Biblical Geography and History.* New York: Rand McNally & Co., 1884. Rev. ed.: 1887. 158 pp. Rev. ed.: 1928. 168 pp. Hurlbut now appears as somewhat of a curiosity from the turn-of-the-century. In fact he was a very popular educator who stood at the fountainhead of the adult education movement. A widely read religious writer, his atlas went through numerous editions and documents the state of then-current knowledge.

1107. Kraeling, Emil Gottlieb Heinrich, ed. *The Rand McNally Bible Atlas.* 3rd ed.: Chicago: Rand McNally and Co., 1966. 487 pp.

1108. ———. *Rand McNally Historical Atlas of the Bible.* Chicago: Rand McNally and Co., 1959. Rept.: London: Vane, 1960. 88 pp.

1109. *Lands of the Bible Today with Descriptive Notes.* Washington, DC: National Geographic Society, 1976.

1110. *Lands of the Bible Today with Descriptive Notes Index.* Washington, DC: National Geographic Society, 1976.

1111. May, Herbert Gordon, and G. N. S. Hunt, eds. *Oxford Bible Atlas.* 2nd ed. New York/Oxford University Press, 1974. 3rd ed.: Ed. by John Day. 1984. 144 pp.

1112. Negenman, John H. *New Atlas of the Bible.* Ed. by Harold H. Rowley. London: Collins, 1969. 208 pp.

1113. Pfeiffer, Charles Franklin, ed. *Baker's Bible Atlas.* Rev. ed. Grand Rapids, MI: Baker Book House, 1961. Rept.: 1973. 333 pp.

1114. ———. *The Bible Atlas.* Nashville, TN: Broadman Press, 1975.

1115. Rasmussen, Carl G. *Zondervan NIV Atlas of the Bible.* Grand Rapids, MI: Zondervan Publishing House, 1989. 256 pp.

1116. Rogerson, John. *Atlas of the Bible.* New York: Facts on File Publishers, 1985. 237 pp.

1117. Smith, George Adam. *Atlas of the Historical Geography of the Holy Land.* London: Hodder and Stoughton, 1915. 60 pp.

1118. Wright, George Ernest, and Floyd Vivian Filson, eds. *The Westminster Historical Atlas of the Bible.* 1945. 5th rev. ed.: Philadelphia: Westminster Press, 1956. 130 pp. Rept: London: SCM Press, 1957.

Archeology

Encyclopedias and Dictionaries

1119. Avi-Yonah, Michael, ed. *Encyclopedia of Archaeological Excavations in the Holy Land.* 4 vols. Englewood Cliffs, NJ: Prentice-Hall, 1975-78/London: Oxford University Press, 1976-78.

1120. Blaiklock, Edward M., and R. K. Harrison, eds. *The New International Dictionary of Biblical Archeology.* Grand Rapids, MI: Regency Reference Lib., Zondervan, 1983. 485 pp.

1121. Corswant, Willy. *Dictionnaire d'Archéologie Biblique. Revu et Illustré par Edouard Urech.* Neuchâtel, Paris: Delachaux et Niestlé, 1956. 324 pp.

1122. Negev, Abraham, ed. *Archeological Encyclopedia of the Holy Land.* New York: Putnam, 1972. 354 pp.

1123. Pfeiffer, Charles Franklin, ed. *The Biblical World: A Dictionary of Biblical Archaeology.* Grand Rapids, MI: Baker Book House/New York: Bonanza Books, 1966. 612 pp.

Biblical Theology

1124. Bauer, Johannes B., ed. *Sacramentum Verbi: An Encyclopedia of Biblical Theology.* 3 vols. New York: Herder & Herder, 1970. Translation of 3rd ed. of *Bibeltheologisches Wörterbuch.* Graz: Verlag Styria, 1967. Also published as *Bauer Encyclopedia of Biblical Theology.* 3 vols. London: Sheed and Ward, 1970. Rept. New York: Crossroad Press, 1981.

1125. Léon-Dufour, Xavier, ed. *Dictionary of Biblical Theology.* Trans. under the direction of P. Joseph Cahill. 2nd ed. New York: Seabury Press/London: Geoffrey Chapman, 1973. Originally published as *Vocabulaire de Théologie Biblique.* 2e éd. Paris: Editions du Cerf, 1970.

1126. Richardson, Alan, ed. *A Theological Word Book of the Bible.* London: SCM Press, 1957/New York: Macmillan Company, 1960.

Biblical Theology-Old Testament

1127. Botterweck, G. Johannes, and Helmer Ringgren, eds. *Theological Dictionary of the Old Testament.* Trans. by John T. Willis. 1974 Rev. ed.: 6 vols. Grand Rapids, MI: William B. Eerdmans Publishing Company, 1977.

1128. Harris, R. Laird. *Theological Wordbook of the Old Testament.* 2 vols. Chicago: Moody Press, 1980.

1129. Jenni, Ernst. *Theologisches Handwörterbuch zum Alten Testament...unter Mitarbeit von Claus Westermann.* 2 vols. München: C. Kaiser, 1971-76.

Biblical Theology-New Testament

1130. Brown, Colin, ed. *The New International Dictionary of New Testament Theology.* 3 vols. Grand Rapids, MI: Zondervan Publishing House/Exeter: Paternoster Press, 1975-1978.

1131. Kittel, Gerhard, ed. *Theological Dictionary of the New Testament.* 10 vols. Grand Rapids, MI: Zondervan Publishing House, 1975-78. 1365 pp.

1132. Kittel, Gerhard, and Gerhard Friedrich, eds. *Theological Dictionary of the New Testament Abridged in One Volume.* Translated and abridged by Geoffrey W. Bromiley. Grand Rapids, MI: William B. Eerdmans Publishing Company, 1985.

1133. Townsley, David, and Russell Bjork. *Scripture Index to the New International Dictionary of New Testament Theology.* Grand Rapids, MI: Zondervan Publishing House, 1985. 320 pp.

The Bible in Translations: Versions

During the last century the number of translations of the Bible or the New Testament into English has greatly increased. Even more spectacular has been the number of translations made into all the languages of the world, few peoples being left without at least a portion of the Bible in their native tongue. At the same time, Bible collecting has arisen as a popular hobby. Some collections center upon older and rarer editions, others emphasize editions in the many different languages, and others the variety of modern English translations, some of the more interesting ones being produced by small religious groups who embody their particular sectarian ideas in the new translations. The **International Society of Bible Collectors** (1260 Orchard Lane, Lansdale, PA 19446) serves Bible collectors with its quarterly periodical, *Bible Collectors World* (formerly *The Bible Collector*).

The largest single publicly accessible collection seems to be that of the **American Bible Society**, 1865 Broadway, New York, NY 10023, who, along with the **Wycliffe Bible Translators**, have been the most active in translating the Bible into the different foreign languages. The work of Bible translation accounts for, in large part, the remarkable spread of Christianity among so many of the world's peoples during the last century.

Bibliographies

1134. American Bible Society. *Scriptures of the World: A Compilation of 1603 Languages in Which at Least One Book of the Bible Has Been Published.* Stuttgart: United Bible Societies, 1976. 106 pp.

1135. *The Bible: 100 Landmarks from the Elizabeth Perkins Prothro Collection.* Dallas: Bridwell Library, 1990.

1136. Chambers, Bettye Thomas. *Bibliography of French Bibles: Fifteenth- and Sixteenth-century French-language Editions of the Scriptures.* Geneva, Switzerland: Droz, 1983. 548 pp.

1137. Coldham, Geraldine E. *A Bibliography of Scriptures in African Languages.* 2 vols. London: British and Foreign Bible Society, 1966.

1138. ———. *Supplement (1964-1974) to "A Bibliography of Scriptures in African Languages."* London: British and Foreign Bible Society, 1975. 198 pp.

1139. Cotton, Henry. *A List of Editions of the Bible and Parts Thereof in English, from the Year MDV to MDCCCXX.* Oxford: Clarendon Press, 1821. 168 pp.

1140. Darlow, T. H., and H.F. Moule, comps. *Historical Catalogue of the Printed Editions of Holy Scriptures in the Library of the British and Foreign Bible Society.* 2 vols. in 4. London: Bible House, 1903-1911. Rept.: 2 vols. in 4. New York: Kraus Reprints, 1968.

1141. Elliott, Melvin E. *The Language of the King James Bible: A Glossary Explaining its Words and Expressions.* Garden City, NY: Doubleday & Co., 1967. 227 pp.

1142. *General Catalog of Printed Books.* 3 vols. London: British Museum, Department of Printed Books, 1965.

1143. Herbert, A. S. *Historical Catalogue of Printed Editions of the English Bible 1525-1961; Rev. and exp. from the ed. of T. H. Darlow and H. F. Moule, 1903.* London: British and Foreign Bible Society/New York: American Bible Society, 1968. 549 pp.

1144. Hester, Goldia, comp. & ed. *Guide to Bibles in Print.* Austin, TX: Richard Gordon and Associates, 1966- . Annual.

1145. Hills, Margaret T., ed. *The English Bible in America: A Bibliography of Editions of the Bible and the New Testament Published in America 1777-1957.* New York: American Bible Society and the New York Public Library, 1961. 477 pp.

1146. Nida, Eugene Albert, ed. *The Book of a Thousand Tongues.* Rev. ed. London: United Bible Societies, 1972. 536 pp.

1147. O'Callaghan, Edmund Bailey. *A List of Editions of the Holy Scriptures and Parts Thereof Printed in America Previous to 1860.* Albany, NY: Munsell & Rowland, 1861. 415 pp. Rept.: Detroit: Gale Research, 1966. 415 pp.

1148. Pope, Hugh. *English Versions of the Bible.* Rev. by Sebastian Bullough. St. Louis, MO: Herder, 1952. 787 pp. Rept.: Westport, CT: Greenwood Press, 1972. 787 pp.

1149. Prime, George Wendell. *Fifteenth Century Bibles: A Study in Bibliography.* New York: A. D. F. Randolph and Company, 1888. Rept.: Kennebunkport, ME: Milford House, n.d.

1150. Rumball-Petre, Edwin A. *America's First Bibles, with a Census of 555 Extant Bibles.* Portland, ME: Southworth Athoensen Press, 1940. 184 pp.

1151. ———. *Rare Bibles: An Introduction for Collectors and a Descriptive Checklist.* New York: Philip C. Duschnes, 1938. 6 pp. Rev. ed.: 1954. 53 pp. Rept.: 1963.

1152. Shea, John Dawson Gilmary. *A Bibliographical Account of Catholic Bibles, Testaments and Other Portions of Scripture Translated from the Latin Vulgate and Printed in the United States.* New York: Cramoisy Press, 1859. Rept.: New York: Gordon Press, 1980. 48 pp.

1153. Wares, Alan C., comp. *Bibliography of the Wycliffe Bible Translators.* Santa Ana, CA: Wycliffe Bible Translators, 1970. 84 pp.

1154. Wright, John. *Early Bibles of America.* New York: T. Whittaker, 1892. 171 pp.

1155. ———. *Historic Bibles in America.* New York: T. Whittaker, 1905. 222 pp.

Resource Centers

The Library of the **American Bible Society**, 1865 Broadway, New York, NY 10023, has a collection of 50,000 copies of the Bible and its various parts, in over 1,800 languages. It has a large collection of Bible reference books and the archives of several prominent Bible societies.

Old Testament Studies

Encyclopedias and Dictionaries

1156. Harris, R. Laird. *Theological Wordbook of the Old Testament.* 2 vols. Chicago: Moody Press, 1980.

Biographical Volumes

1157. Comay, Joan. *Who's Who in the Old Testament, Together with the Apocrypha.* New York: Holt, Rinehart and Winston/London: Weidenfeld and Nicolson, 1971. 448 pp. Rev. ed: London: Hodder and Stoughton, 1982. 421 pp. See: (1066)

Bibliographies

1158. Ackroyd, Peter R. *Bible Bibliography 1967-1973 Old Testament: The Book Lists of the Society for Old Testament Study, 1967-1973.* Oxford: Basil Blackwell, 1974. 505 pp.

1159. Anderson, G. W., ed. *A Decade of Bible Bibliography: The Book Lists of the Society for Old Testament Study, 1957-1966.* Oxford: Blackwell, 1967. 706 pp.

1160. Barker, Kenneth L., and Bruce K. Waltke. *Bibliography for Old Testament Exegesis and Exposition.* 3rd ed.: Dallas, TX: Dallas Theological Seminary, 1975. 66 pp.

1161. Brock, Sebastian P., Charles T. Fritsch, and Sidney Jellicoe, comps. *A Classified Bibliography of the Septuagint.* Leiden: E. J. Brill, 1973. 217 pp.

1162. Buss, Martin J. *Old Testament Dissertations 1928-1958.* Rept.: Ann Arbor, MI: University Microfilms, 1964. 57 pp.

1163. Childs, Brevard Springs. *Old Testament Books for Pastor and Teacher.* Philadelphia: Westminster Press, 1977. 120 pp.

1164. Dirksen, P. B. *An Annotated Bibliography of Peshitta of the Old Testament.* Leiden: E.J. Brill, 1989. 119 pp.

1165. Goldingay, John. *Old Testament Commentary Survey.* Madison, WI: Theological Students' Fellowship, 1977. 37 pp.

1166. Leiden University Peshitta Institute, ed. *List of Old Testament Peshitta Manuscripts (Preliminary Issue).* Leiden: E.J. Brill, 1961. 114 pp.

1167. *Old Testament Abstracts.* Vol. 1- . Washington, DC: Catholic University of America, 1978- . Triannual.

1168. Rowley, H. H., ed. *Eleven Years of Bible Bibliography: The Book Lists of the Society of Old Testament Study, 1946-1956.* Indian Hills, CO: Falcon's Wing Press, 1957. 804 pp.

Guides to Periodical Literature

1169. Hupper, William G. *An Index to English Periodical Literature on the Old Testament and Ancient Near Eastern Studies.* V. 1- . Metuchen, NJ: Scarecrow Press, 1987- . Three volumes have been published so far.

1170. *Near East/Biblical Periodical Index.* Vol. 1- . Aurora, IL: NEBPI Press, 1981- . Irregular.

1171. *OT/ANE Permucite Index: An Exhaustive Interdisciplinary Indexing System for Old Testament Studies/Ancient Near East Studies.* Vol. 1- . Stellenbosch: Infodex, 1978- . Triannual with annual cumulations.

New Testament Studies

Encyclopedias and Dictionaries

1172. Balz, Horst, and Gehard Schneider. *Exegetical Dictionary of the New Testament.* Grand Rapids, MI: William B. Eerdmans Publishing Compamy, 1990. 463 pp.

1173. Earle, Ralph. *Word Meanings in the New Testament.* Vol. 1- . Grand Rapids, MI: Baker Book House, 1974- .

1174. Hastings, James, ed. *Dictionary of the Apostolic Church.* 2 vols. Edinburgh: T. & T. Clark/New York: Charles Scribner's Sons, 1915.

1175. Léon-Dufour, Xavier, ed. *Dictionary of the New Testament.* New York: Harper & Row, 1980. 458 pp.

1176. Partridge, Eric. *A New Testament Word Book: A Glossary.* London: G. Routledge and Sons, 1940. Rept. Freeport, NY: Books for Libraries Press, 1970. 448 pp.

Biographical Volumes

1177. Brownrigg, Ronald. *Who's Who in the New Testament.* New York: Holt, Rinehart and Winston/London: Weidenfeld and Nicolson, 1971. *See*: (1066)

Bibliographies

1178. Akaishi, Tadashi, ed. *Bibliography of New Testament Literature (1900-1950).* San Anselmo, CA: San Francisco Theological Seminary, 1953. 312 pp.

1179. Belle, Gilbert Van, comp. *Johannine Bibliography 1966-1985: A Cumulative Bibliography on the Fourth Gospel.* Biblioteca Ephemeridum Theologicarum Lovaniensium 82. Louvain, Belgium: Louvain University Press, 1988. 563 pp.

1180. Bowman, John Wick, et al. *Bibliography of New Testament Literature, 1900-1950.* San Anselmo, CA: San Francisco Theological Seminary, 1953. 312 pp.

1181. Doty, William. *The Discipline and Literature of the New Testament Form Criticism.* Evanston, IL: Garrett Theological Seminary Library, 1967.

1182. Elliott, J. K. *A Bibliography of Greek New Testament Manuscripts.* Cambridge: Cambridge University Press, 1989. 210 pp.

1183. Forestell, J. T. *Targumic Traditions and the New Testament: An Annotated Bibliography with a New Testament Index.* SBL Aramaic Studies No. 4. Chico, CA: Scholars Press, 1979. 137 pp.

1184. France, R. T. *A Bibliographical Guide to New Testament Research.* 1968. 3rd ed.: Sheffield, England: JSOT Press, 1979. 56 pp. Rept.: 1983.

1185. Hadidian, Dikran Y., ed. *A Periodical and Monographic Index to the Literature on the Gospels and Acts Based on the Files of the École Biblique in Jerusalem.* Bibliographia Tripotamopolitana No. 111. Pittsburgh, PA: Clifford E. Barbour Library, Pittsburgh Theological Seminary, 1971. 330 pp.

1186. Humphrey, Hugh M. *A Bibliography for the Gospel of Mark 1954-1980.* Studies in the Bible and Early Christianity Vol. 1. New York & Toronto: Edwin Mellen Press, 1981. 163 pp.

1187. Hurd, John Collidge, Jr., comp. *A Bibliography of New Testament Bibliographies.* New York: Seabury Press, 1966. 75 pp.

1188. Lyons, William Nelson, ed. *New Testament Literature in 1940.* Chicago: New Testament Club of the University of Chicago, 1941.

1189. ————. *New Testament Literature in 1941.* Chicago: New Testament Club of the University of Chicago, 1942.

1190. ———, and Merrill M. Parvis. *New Testament Literature: An Annotated Bibliography [1943-1945].* Chicago: University of Chicago Press, 1948.

1191. Martin, Ralph P. *New Testament Books for Pastor and Teacher.* Philadelphia: Westminster Press, 1984. 152 pp.

1192. Mattill, A. J., Jr., and Mary Bedford Mattill, comps. *A Classified Bibliography of Literature on the Acts of the Apostles.* Leiden: E.J. Brill, 1966. 513 pp.

1193. ———. *A Classified Bibliography of Literature on the Acts of the Apostles.* New Testament Tools and Studies Vol. 7. Leiden: E. J. Brill, 1966. 513 pp.

1194. Metzger, Bruce, ed. *Annotated Bibliography of the Textual Criticism of the New Testament 1914-1939.* Copenhagen: Ejnar Munksgaard, 1955. 133 pp.

1195. ———. *Index of Articles on the New Testament and the Early Church Published in Festschriften.* Journal of Biblical Literature Monograph Series Vol. 5. Philadelphia: Society of Biblical Literature, 1951. *Supplementary Volume.* 1955. 20 pp.

1196. Millard, Alan Ralph, Graham N. Stanton, and R. T. France, comps. *A Bibliographical Guide to New Testament Research.* Cambridge: Tyndale Fellowship for Biblical Research, 1974. 45 pp. 3rd. ed.: Sheffield, England: JSOT Press, 1979. 56 pp. Rept.: 1983.

1197. Mills, Watson E. *An Index of Reviews of New Testament Books between 1900-1950.* Perspectives in Religious Studies, Special Studies Series No. 2. Dancille, VA: Association of Baptist Professors of Religion, 1977. 69 pp.

1198. *New Testament Abstracts.* Vol. 1- . Waterloo, Ont: Council on the Study of Religion, 1956- . Triannual.

1199. *New Testament Literature: An Annotated Bibliography.* Vol. I. Chicago: University of Chicago Press, 1948. Volume I covers the years 1940-1945. Volume II never appeared.

1200. Nickels, Peter. *Targum and the New Testament: A Bibliography together with a New Testament Index.* Rome: Pontifical Bible Institute, 1967. 88 pp.

1201. Parvis, Merrill M. *New Testament Literature in 1942.* Chicago: New Testament Club of the University of Chicago, 1943. 107 pp.

1202. Rowlingson, Donald T. *The History of New Testament Research and Interpretation: A Bibliographical Outline.* Rev. ed. Boston, MA: Boston University Book Store, 1963. 45 pp.

1203. Scholer, David M. *A Basic Bibliographic Guide for New Testament Exegesis.* South Hamilton, MA: Gordon-Conwell Bookcentre, 1971. 2nd ed.: Grand Rapids, MI: William B. Eerdmans, 1973. 94 pp.

1204. Thiselton, Anthony C. *New Testament Commentary Survey.* Rev. by Don A. Carson. Madison, WI: Theological Students' Fellowship, 1977. 3rd ed.: Ed. by Don A. Carson. Grand Rapids, MI: Baker Book House, 1988. 79 pp.

1205. Wagner, Günter, ed. *An Exegetical Bibliography of the New Testament.* Macon, GA: Mercer University Press, 1987. 350 pp.

Guides to Periodical Literature

1206. Metzger, Bruce. *Index to Periodical Literature on the Apostle Paul.* New Testament Tools and Studies Vol. 1. Grand Rapids, MI: William B. Eerdmans Publishing Co./Leiden: E.J. Brill, 1960. 183 pp.

Jesus and the Gospel Narratives

Encyclopedias and Dictionaries

1207. Hastings, James, ed. *Dictionary of Christ and the Gospels.* 2 vols. New York: Charles Scribner's Sons; Edinburgh: T. & T. Clark, 1909.

Bibliographies

1208. Aure, David E. *Jesus and the Synoptic Gospels: A Bibliographic Study Guide.* Chicago: InterVarsity Press, 1981.

1209. Ayres, Samuel Gardiner. *Jesus Christ Our Lord: An English Bibliography of Christology, Comprising over Five Thousand Titles Annotated and Classified.* New York: A.C. Armstrong and Son, 1906. 502 pp.

1210. Birney, Alice L. *The Literary Lives of Jesus: An International Bibliography.* New York: Garland Publishing, 1989. 208 pp.

1211. Case, Adelaide Teague. *As Modern Writers See Jesus: A Descriptive Bibliography of Books about Jesus.* Boston: Pilgrim Press, 1927. 128 pp.

1212. Dorneich, Monica. *Vaterunser Bibliographie.* Freiburg im Breisgau: Herder, 1982. 240 pp.

1213. Freitag, Ruth S. *The Star of Bethlehem: A List of References.* Washington, DC: Library of Congress, 1979. 44 pp.

1214. Garland, David E. *One Hundred Years of Study on the Passion Narratives.* NABPR Bibliographic Series No. 3. Macon, GA: Mercer Univ. Press, 1989. 174 pp.

1215. Kissinger, Warren S. *The Lives of Jesus: A Bibliography.* New York: Garland Publishing, 1985. 240 pp.

1216. ————. *The Parables of Jesus: A History of Interpretation and Bibliography.* ATLA Bibliography Series No. 4. Metuchen, NJ: Scarecrow Press, 1979. 463 pp.

1217. ————. *The Sermon on the Mount: A History of Interpretation and Bibliography.* ATLA Bibliography Series No. 3. Metuchen, NJ: Scarecrow Press, 1975. 309 pp.

1218. Longstaff, Thomas Richmond Willis, and Page A. Thomas, comps. & eds. *The Synoptic Problem: A Bibliography, 1716-1988.* New Gospel Studies 4. Macon, GA: Mercer University Press, 1988. 235 pp.

1219. Malatesta, Edward, comp. *Saint John's Gospel 1920-1965: A Cumulative and Classified Bibliography of Books and Periodical Literature on the Fourth Gospel.* Analecta Biblica 32. Rome: Pontifical Bible Institute, 1967. 205 pp.

1220. Segroeck, Frans, comp. *The Gospel of Luke: A Cumulative Bibliography 1973-1988.* Biblioteca Ephemeridum Theologicarum Lovaniensium 88. Louvain, Belgium: Louvain University Press, 1989. 243 pp.

1221. Wismer, Don. *The Islamic Jesus: An Annotated Bibliography of Sources in English and French.* New York: Garland Publishing, 1977. 305 pp.

Guides to Periodical Literature

1222. Metzger, Bruce, ed. *Index to Periodical Literature on Christ and the Gospels.* New Testament Tools and Studies Vol. 6. Grand Rapids, MI: William B. Eerdmans Publishing Company, 1966. 602 pp.

Biblical Studies

Directories

1223. *Who's Who in Biblical Studies and Archeology.* Washington, DC: Biblical Archeology Society, 1986-87. 272 pp.

Professional Associations

Biblical Archeology Society
3000 Connecticut Avenue, S.W., Ste. 300
Washington, DC 20008

Catholic Biblical Association
c/o John P. Meier
Catholic University of America
Washington, DC 20064
The CBA sponsors the publication of *New Testament Abstracts.*

Chicago Society of Biblical Literature
Saint Xavier College
Chicago, IL 60655
The Society publishes *Biblical Research* (annual).

International Association of Biblicists and Orientalists
(Internacia Asocia de Biblistoj Kaj Orientalistoj)
Piazza Duomo 4
1-48100 Ravenna, Italy
The Association publishes the *Biblia Revuo.*

International Foundation for Biblical Studies
423 First National Bank Building
Peoria, IL 61602

International Organization for Septuagint and Cognate Studies
c/o Leonard J. Greenspoon
Department of Philosophy and Religion
Clemson University
Clemson, SC 29634-1508
The Organization publishes an annual *Bulletin.*

National Association of Biblical Instructors to Foster Religion in Education
Superseded by the American Academy of Religion

Society of Biblical Literature
1544 Clairmont Road, Ste. 204
Decatur, GA 30033-4635
or
c/o Scholars Press
P. O. Box 15288
Atlanta, GA 30333
The Society is the major organization giving a focus to biblical studies in North America. It publishes several periodicals, the *Journal of Biblical Literature*; a newsletter; *Semeia*, a monograph series; and, in cooperation with the **American Academy of Religion**, *Religious Studies News*, *Openings*, and the annual *Critical Reviews in Religion*.

Studiorum Novi Testamenti Societas
c/o Dr. C. M. Tuckett
Faculty of Theology
University of Manchester
Manchester M13 9PL, UK
The Society sponsors the publication of *New Testament Studies*, published by Cambridge University Press.

Research Centers

Hebrew University Bible Project
Magnes Press
Jerusalem, Israel
Publishes *Textus*.

Institute for Biblical Research
c/o Dr. Edwin Yamaguchi
History Department
Miami University
Oxford, OH 45056

Institute for Biblical Research
c/o Dr. Gerald Hawthorne
Wheaton College
Wheaton, IL 60187

Interdisciplinary Biblical Research Institute
c/o Tobert C. Newman
P. O. Box 423
Hatfield, PA 19440

International Center for Biblical Studies
P. O. Box 758
Metamora, IN 61548

International Organization for the Study of the Old Testament
(Organisation Internationale pour l'Etude de l'Ancien Testament)
c/o Prof. D. A. Emerton
St. John's College
Cambridge CB2 1TP
United Kingdom
The Organization publishes *Vetus Testamentum* (q).

Society for New Testament Study
c/o Faculty of Theology
University of Manchester
Manchester M13 9PL
United Kingdom

ECUMENISM

The modern ecumenical movement emerged in the nineteenth century among Protestants who were reacting to the increasing divisions of Western Christianity. Its organizational high points were in the 1908 formation of the National Council of Churches in the United States and, on an international level, the formation of the World Council of Churches following World War II. In the years since World War II, the Eastern Orthodox have become very active in the conciliar phase of ecumenism and, in the wake of Vatican II, the Roman Catholic Church has expressed renewed interest in dialogue with the major Protestant churches.

While the ecumenical movement brought many Christians together, Christianity continued to expand through the century. Hundreds of new denominations came into existence, and ecumenical organizations of those more conservative churches, who felt unable to cooperate with liberal Protestant denominations, were formed. In the United States the National Association of Evangelicals and the American Council of Christian Churches represent Evangelical Protestants and Separatist Fundamentalists, respectively. These same groups are represented on the international scene by the World Evangelical Fellowship and the International Council of Christian Churches.

The overwhelming majority of the literature presented below comes from the liberal Protestant/Orthodox phase of the ecumenical movement. It is among these churches that both an ecumenical theology to undergird the search for Christian unity and an understanding of the church as responsible for social structures has arisen that has motivated ecumenical dialogue and mutual action on a wide variety of international issues. Among conservative Protestants, ecumenical efforts have tended to be more limited to a search for doctrinal uniformity.

Encyclopedias and Dictionaries

1224. Basdekis, Athanasios, et al. *Ökumene Lexicon: Kirchen, Religionen, Bewegungen.* Frankfurt am Main: Lembeck Kneth, 1983. 1326 pp.

1225. *Ecumenical Terminology.* Geneva: World Council of Churches, 1975. 564 pp.

1226. Losskey, Nicolas, et al., eds. *Dictionary of the Ecumenical Movement.* Geneva: World Council of Churches/Grand Rapids, MI: William B. Eerdmans Publishing Company, 1991. 1196 pp.

1227. Van der Bent, Ans J. *Six Hundred Ecumenical Consultations, 1948-1982.* Genevé, Switzerland: World Council of Churches, 1983. 246 pp.

Directories

The largest ecumenical network globally has been established by the World Council of Churches. The several directories defining it are cited as items (818) and (823) above.

1228. Deemer, Philip, ed. *Ecumenical Directory of Retreat and Conference Centers.* San Francisco: Jarrow Press, 1974. 3rd ed.: 1984. Periodically updated.

1229. *Ecumenism Around the World: A Directory of Ecumenical Institutes, Centers, and Organizations.* Rome: Friars of the Atonement, 1971. 2nd ed.: [1975]. 169 pp.

1230. *Yearbook of American and Canadian Churches.* Nashville, TN: Abingdon Press, issued annually. Includes a directory of Christian ecumenical organizations in North America.

Bibliographies and Indices

1231. *Bibliography of Church Union in Canada.* Toronto: American Theological Library Association, 1959. 16 pp.

1232. *Bibliography on Catholic-Protestant Understanding.* [Stoughton, MA: Packard Manse, 1960]. 19 pp.

1233. Boffa, P., A. J. Van der Bent, C. Homberger, and R. de Pourtales. *Index: Reports and Statements.* Genevé: World Council of Churches, 1968. 119 pp.

1234. ———. *Index to the World Council of Churches Official Statements and Reports, 1948-1978.* Genevé: World Council of Churches, 1978. 104 pp.

1235. Brandreth, Henry Renaud Turner. *Unity and Reunion: A Bibliography.* 2nd ed. London: Adams and Charles Black, 1948. 158 pp.

1236. *Classified Catalog of the Ecumenical Movement.* 2 vols. Boston: G.K. Hall and Co., 1981. *Supplement.* Vol. 1- . 1981- .

1237. Crow, Paul A. *The Ecumenical Movement in Bibliographical Outline.* New York: National Council of Churches of Christ in the U.S.A., Dept. of Faith and Order, 1965. 80 pp.

1238. DeGroot, Alfred Thomas. *Check List Faith & Order Commission Official, Numbered Publications Series I, 1910-1948; Series II, 1948 to Date (1962).* Geneva, Switzerland: Faith and Order Commission, World Council of Churches, 1963. No pagination.

1239. ———. *An Index to the Doctrines, Persons, Events, etc. of the Faith and Order Commission, World Council of Churches; Given in the English Language Editions, Official, Numbered Publications, 1910-1948; and Check List, Faith and Order Commission Official, Numbered Publications: Series I, 1910-1948: Series II, 1948-1970.* 3rd ed.: Geneva: World Council of Churches, 1970. 258 pp.

1240. *Doctoral Dissertations on Ecumenical Themes: A Guide for Teachers and Students.* Geneva: World Council of Churches, 1977. 70 pp.

1241. *Ecumenical Book Shelf.* 5 vols. New York: World Council of Churches, 1950-1969.

1242. *Internationale Ökumenische Bibliographie/International Ecumenical Bibliography (IOB).* Vol. 1- . Mainz: Matthias-Grünewald-Verlag/München: Chr. Kaiser Verlag, 1962- .

1243. Lambeth Palace Library. *Christian Unity: The Anglican Initiative; Catalogue of an Exhibition of Books and Manuscripts Held in the Library of Lambeth Palace.* London: SPCK, 1966. 23 pp.

1244. Landis, Benson Young. *Doctoral Dissertations Relevant to Ecumenics.* New York: World Council of Churches, [1965].(a) National Council of Churches of Christ in the U.S.A. *Triennial Report.* New York: NCC, 1946- . Triennial.

1245. Lescrauwaet, Josephus Franciscus. *Critical Bibliography of Ecumenical Literature.* Bibliographia ad Usum Seminariorum Vol. 7. Nijmegen: Bestel Centrale V.S.K.B., 1965. 93 pp.

1246. *Oecumene 2: International Bibliography 1977 Indexed by Computer.* RIC Supplements 43-44. Strasbourg, France: Cerdic-Publications, 1978. 144 pp.

1247. *Oecumene 3: International Bibliography 1978-1980.* RIC Supplements 53-56. Strasbourg, France: Cerdic-Publications, 1980. 292 pp.

1248. *Oecumene 4: International Bibliography 1980-1983.* RIC Supplements 80-836. Strasbourg, France: Cerdic-Publications, 1983. 320 pp.

1249. Puglisi, James J. *A Bibliography of Interchurch and Interconfessional Theological Dialogues.* Roma: Centro Pro Unione, 1984. 260 pp.

1250. ———. *A Workbook of Bibliographies for the Study of Interchurch Dialogues.* Roma: Centro Pro Unione, 1978.

1251. Senaud, Auguste. *Christian Unity, a Bibliography: Selected Titles Concerning International Relations between Churches and International Christian Movements (from a Larger Bibliography).* Geneva: World's Committee of YMCAs, 1937. 173 pp.

1252. Suftin, Edward J., and Maurice Lavanoux. *A Selected, Annotated Bibliography on Ecumenical and Related Matters.* Haverford, PA: Catholic Library Association, 1967. 56 pp.

1253. Van der Bent, Ans Joachim. *The Whole Oikoumene: A Collection of Bibliographies of the Works of Phillip A. Potter.* Geneva: World Council of Churches, 1980.

1254. Zimmerman, Marie. *Oecumene 1: International Bibliography 1975-1976 Indexed by Computer.* RIC Supplements 31-34. Strasbourg, France: Cerdic-Publications, 1977. 268 pp.

Resources/Research Centers

Canadian Centre for Ecumenism (Centre Canadien d'Oecumenisme)
2065 Sherbrooke St. W.
Montreal, PQ
Canada H3H 1G6
The Centre houses a library and publishes a quarterly journal, *Ecumenism/Oecumenisme.*

Charis, The Ecumenical Center for Church and Community
c/o Phillip E. Pedersen, Director
Concordia College
Moorhead, MN 56560
Charis publishes *Charis Perspective*

Ecumenical Library
475 Riverside Drive, Room 900
New York, NY 10115
The Ecumenical Library was created in 1905 at the same time the National Council of Churches was formed. It is located in the Interchurch Center in New York City.

Ecumenical Library
World Council of Churches
150, route de Ferney
B.P. 2100
CH-1211 Genevé 2, Switzerland

Graymoor Ecumenical Institute
Garrison, NY 10524
The Institute publishes *Ecumenical Trends*

Institute for Ecumenical and Cultural Research
Collegeville, MN 56321

Institute for Ecumenical Research
8 rue Gutave-Klotz
67000 Strasbourg, France

North American Academy of Ecumenists
c/o Prof. J. Robert Wright
General Theological Seminary
175 9th Avenue
New York, NY 10011
The Academy sponsors the *Journal of Ecumenical Studies* and *Ecumenical Trends.*

ETHICS AND THE SOCIAL APPLICATION OF CHRISTIANITY

Traditionally, ethics concerns itself with the nature of good and evil and the appropriate behavior to maximize good and minimize evil. Christian ethics asks of the nature of good and evil in the light of the posited revelation of God in creation and in Jesus Christ and then asks, "How shall we act?" A variety of different answers to the basic ethical question have been offered by church ethicists who have in turn offered variant advice concerning the nature of appropriate ethical behavior. The literature in this chapter surveys those often very different options and introduces the contemporary debates.

Few issues have so split the contemporary church as have the disagreement over its proper role as an ethical agent in the secular social order. The issue was molded by the rise of sociology and the possibility that a more perfect society could be created by changing social structures. This possibility undergirded what became known as the social gospel, the vision of the kingdom or God on earth generated by restructuring a just social order that would end the continuing problems of war, poverty, and crime. For the social gospel, the vision of the kingdom of God bore more than a passing resemblance to a socialist society.

Those who accepted the social gospel tended to believe that the church should focus its attention on building a just social order. Those opposed to the social gospel called for a church primarily oriented upon evangelism and turning the hearts of individuals from evil. For the latter the church appropriately sets moral standards and calls members to observe those standards. The most important social issues tend to be those which relate to personal behavior, especially life cycle and sexuality issues. These two essentially opposing views of the church still inform the more important current ethical debates and can be seen in the document collections made by Melton and others (Manning, Piediscalzi, Ward) on such issues as abortion, homosexuality, and capital punishment.

Encyclopedias and Dictionaries

1255. Compagnoni, Francesco, Siannino Piana, and Salvatore Privitera, eds. *Nuovo Dizionario di Teologia Morale.* Milano: Edizioni Paoline, 1990. 1551 pp.

1256. *Dictionary of Moral Theology.* Compiled under the direction of Francesco Cardinal Roberti. London: Burns & Oates, 1962. 1352 pp.

1257. Henry, Carl Ferdinand Howard, ed. *Baker's Dictionary of Christian Ethics.* Grand Rapids, MI: Baker Book House, 1973. 726 pp.

1258. Hörmann, Karl, ed. *Lexicon der Christichen Moral.* Wien, Österreich: Tyrolia Verlag, 1968. 1414 pp. Rev. ed.: 1976. 1718 pp.

1259. Hoffé, Otfried, ed. *Dictionnaire de Morale.* Paris: Editions du Cerf/Fribourg: Editions Universitaires, 1983. 242 pp.

1260. Macquarrie, John, ed. *A Dictionary of Christian Ethics.* Philadelphia: Westminster Press/London: SCM Press, 1967. Revised ed.: James F. Childress and John Macquarrie. *The Westminister Dictionary of Christian Ethics.* Philadelphia: Westminster Press, 1967. 678 pp.

1261. Stoeckle, Bernhard, ed. *Wörterbuch Ethik in 84 Artikeln mit Literaturenbaben.* Freiburg, Germany: Herderbücherei, 1975. 284 pp. English ed. as: *The Concise Dictionary of Christian Ethics.* New York: Seabury Press, 1979. 285 pp.

Bibliographies

1262. Brunkow, Robert De V., ed. *Religion and Society in North America: An Annotated Bibliography.* Santa Barbara, CA: ABC-Clio, 1983. 515 pp.

1263. Church of England. National Assembly. Joint Board of Studies. *Current Problems in the Understanding of Personal Responsibility: A Bibliography Selected from the Fields of Psychology, Sociology, Ethics and Theology.* London: Church Information Office, 1960.

1264. Fecher, Vincent John, comp. *Religion and Aging: An Annotated Bibliography.* San Antonio, TX: Trinity University Press, 1982. 119 pp.

1265. Gustafson, R. K. *The Literature of Christian Ethics, 1932-1956.* Richmond, VA: M.A. Thesis, Union Theological Seminary in Virginia, 1957.

1266. *Human Rights: International Bibliography 1975-1981.* RIC Supplement 69. Strasbourg, France: Cerdic-Publications, 1982. 104 pp.

1267. Klejment, Anne, and Alice Klejment. *Dorothy Day and the Catholic Worker: A Bibliography and Index.* New York & London: Garland Publishing, 1986. 412 pp.

1268. Müller, Karl, and Marie Zimmerman. *Mixed Marriage: International Bibliography 1960-June 1974 Indexed by Computer.* RIC Supplement 11. Strasbourg, France: Cerdic-Publications, 1974. 71 pp.

1269. Pigault, Gérard. *Development and Justice: International Bibliography 1972-1973 Indexed by Computer.* RIC Supplement 12. Strasbourg, France: Cerdic-Publications, 1974. 41 pp.

Directories

1270. Zagano, Phyllis. *Religion and Public Affairs: A Directory of Organizations and People.* Rockford, IL: Rockford Institute, 1987. 203 pp.

Abortion

General Sources

1271. Melton, J. Gordon, and Gary L. Ward, eds. *The Churches Speak on Abortion: Official Statements for Religious Bodies and Ecumenical Organizations.* Detroit, MI: Gale Research Company, 1989. 199 pp.

Bibliographies

1272. Guérin, Daniel. *Abortion: International Bibliography 1973-June 1975 Indexed by Computer.* RIC Supplement 20. Strasbourg: Cerdic-Publications, 1975. 51 pp.

Capital Punishment

General Sources

1273. Melton, J. Gordon, ed. *The Churches Speak on Capital Punishment: Official Statements from Religious Bodies and Ecumenical Statements.* Detroit, MI: Gale Research Company, 1989. 165 pp.

Church and State

General Sources

1274. Panoch, James V., and David L. Barr. *Religion Goes to School: A Practical Handbook for Teachers.* New York: Harper and Row, 1968. 183 pp.

Bibliographies

1275. Buzzard, Lynn Robert. *Law and Theology: An Annotated Bibliography.* Oak Park, IL: Christian Legal Society, 1979. 55 pp.

1276. *Church and State: International Bibliography 1978-1980.* RIC Supplements 59-60. Strasbourg, France: Cerdic-Publications, 1980. 156 pp. *Supplement* for 1980-1983. 1983. 198 pp.

1277. Drouin, Edmond Gabriel. *The School Question: A Bibliography on Church-State Relationships in American Education, 1940-1960.* Washington, DC: Catholic University of America Press, 1963. 261 pp.

1278. Gianni, Andrea. *Religious Liberty: International Bibliography 1918-1978.* RIC Supplements 47-49. Strasbourg, France: Cerdic-Publications, 1980. 134 pp.

1279. Le Leannec, Bernard. *Church and State: International Bibliography 1972-1977 Indexed by Computer.* RIC Supplements 35-38. Strasbourg, France: Cerdic-Publications, 1978. 214 pp.

1280. ———. *Religious Liberty: International Bibliography 1968-1975 Indexed by Computer.* RIC Supplement 28. Strasbourg, France: Cerdic-Publications, 1976. 39 pp.

1281. Menendez, Albert J. *Church-State Relations: An Annotated Bibliography.* Garland Reference Library of Social Science Vol. 24. New York: Garland Publishing, 1976. 126 pp.

1282. Metz, René, and Jean Schlick. *Church and State: International Bibliography 1972 Indexed by Computer.* RIC Supplement 2. Strasbourg, France: Cerdic-Publications, 1973. 37 pp.

1283. ———. *Politics and Faith: International Bibliography 1972-June 1973 Indexed by Computer.* RIC Supplement 7. Strasbourg, France: Cerdic-Publications, 1973. 43 pp.

Euthanasia

General Sources

1284. LaRue, Gerald A. *Euthanasia and Religion: A Survey of Attitudes of the World's Religions to the Right-to-Die.* Los Angeles: Hemlock Society, 1985. 155 pp.

1285. Melton, J. Gordon, and Christel Manning, eds. *The Churches Speak on Euthanasia: Official Statements from Religious Bodies and Ecumenical Organizations.* Detroit, MI: Gale Research Company, 1991.

Peace and War

Directories

1286. *LA Peace Directory: Greater Los Angeles and Orange County Social Change Groups and Information.* Los Angeles: LA Peace Directory, 1989-90. Unpaged. Updated periodically.

Bibliographies

1287. Brock, Peter. *The Military Question in the Early Church: A Selected Bibliography of a Century's Scholarship.* Toronto: The Author, 1988. 15 pp.

1288. Hiebel, Jean-Luc. *Armed Forces and Churches: International Bibliography 1970-1972 Indexed by Computer.* RIC Supplement 3. Strasbourg, France: Cerdic-Publications, 1973. 42 pp.

1289. ———. *War, Peace and Violence: International Bibliography 1973-1974 Indexed by Computer.* RIC Supplement 18. Strasbourg, France: Cerdic-Publications, 1975. 53 pp.

1290. *War, Peace and Violence: International Bibliography 1975-1981.* RIC Supplements 67-68. Strasbourg, France: Cerdic-Publications, 1982. 146 pp.

1291. *War, Peace and Violence: International Bibliography 1983-1984.* RIC Supplements 101-102. Strasbourg, France: Cerdic-Publications, 1985. 120 pp.

Pornography

General Sources

1292. Melton, J. Gordon, and Gary L. Ward, eds. *The Churches Speak on Pornography: Official Statements from Religious Bodies and Ecumenical Organizations.* Detroit, MI: Gale Research Company, 1989. 267 pp.

Sexuality

General Sources

1293. Melton, J. Gordon, ed. *The Churches Speak on AIDS: Official Statements from Religious Bodies and Ecumenical Organizations.* Detroit, MI: Gale Research Company, 1989. 263 pp.

1294. ———. *The Churches Speak on Homosexuality: Official Statements from Religious Bodies and Ecumenical Organizations.* Detroit, MI: Gale Research Company, 1991. 278 pp.

1295. ———, and Nicholas Piediscalzi, eds. *Sex and Family Life: Official Statements from Religious Bodies and Ecumenical Organizations.* Detroit, MI: Gale Research Company, 1991. 203 pp.

Directories

1296. Malinowshy, H. Robert. *International Directory of Gay and Lesbian Periodicals.* Phoenix, AZ: Oryx Press, 1987. 226 pp.

Bibliographies

1297. Horner, Thom. *Homosexuality and the Judeo-Christian Tradition: An Annotated Bibliography.* ATLA Bibliography Series No. 5. Metuchen, NJ: Scarecrow Press, 1981. 131 pp.

Research/Resource Centers

Institute of Gay Spirituality and Theology
c/o Malcolm Boyd
1227 4th Street
Santa Monica, CA 90401

Ethical Studies

Religion and Ethics Institute
Box 644
Evanston, IL 60204

Religion and Ethics Network
c/o Patricia Washburn
Earlham School of Religion
Richmond, IN 47347

The Society of Christian Ethics
c/o John Cartwright
Boston University
745 Commonwealth Ave.
Boston, MA 02215

Society of Christian Ethics
c/o Terence R. Anderson, Exe. Sec.
Vancouver School of Theology
6000 Iona Drive
Vancouver, BC
Canada V6T 1E7

THE MINISTRY

Religion moves from its more abstract consideration to its more concrete expression in the church's ministry to its members and the world through local congregations, clergy, and educational endeavors. The materials in this chapter introduce several related areas, though as a whole this area of religions has been least receptive to information processing and the resulting production of the variety of source materials in other areas of religious studies. Religious education (both the training of church members and the development of institutions of higher learning) and pastoral psychology have emerged as two specialized areas of church life within which professionals have gathered and produced a recognizable body of information.

Pastoral counseling has emerged as a diverse field split by theological differences and disagreements over the role of the religious counselor, the level of training required for certification, and the depth of the religious appropriation of secular psychological insights.

The Ministry

Bibliographies

1298. *Research in Ministry: An Index to Doctor of Ministry Reports and Theses Submitted by Reporting ATS Schools.* . Vol. 1- . Chicago: American Theological Library Association, 1981- .

Bibliographies—the Ministerial Library

The bibliographies listed below were designed to assist pastors to sift through the massive amount of material being published today and build an adequate personal resource center on a very limited budget. A similar set of bibliographies have been produced covering just books on the Bible and they can be found listed in that chapter. The term "theological" as used in the title has the more inclusive meaning of those subjects covered in a seminary curriculum, rather than the narrower meaning of "theology" as intellectual thought on religious questions.

1299. Barber, Cyril J. *The Minister's Library.* Grand Rapids, MI: Baker Book House, 1974. 430 pp. Rev. 1985. 510 pp. Supplement. 1986/86. Supplement. 1986/87. 171 pp.

1300. *A Basic Bibliography for Ministers, Selected and Annotated by the Faculty.* 2nd ed. New York: Union Theological Seminary, 1960. 139 pp.

1301. *Bibliography for Pastors and Theological Students.* Fort Worth, TX: Southwestern Baptist Theological Seminary, c. 1960. 140 pp.

1302. Bollier, John A. *The Literature of Theology: A Guide for Students and Pastors.* Philadelphia, PA: Westminster Press, 1979. 208 pp.

1303. Cleaver, William. *A List of Books Recommended to the Younger Clergy and Other Students of Divinity within the Diocese of Chester.* 3rd ed. Oxford: J. Cooke and J. Parker, 1808. Rept.: New York: Scholarly Press, 1977.

1304. *Essential Books for a Pastor's Library.* 5th ed. Richmond, VA: Union Theological Seminary, 1976.

1305. Katt, Arthur. *Practical Theology: Bibliography for Graduate Studies in the Cincinnati Bible Seminary.* Cincinnati, OH: Cincinnati Bible Seminary, 1969.

1306. Morris, Raymond. *A Theological Book List.* Oxford and Naperville, IL: Theological Education Fund of the International Missionary Council, 1960. 242 pp. Rept.: Middletown, CT: Greeno, Hadden and Co., 1971.

1307. Peterson, Kenneth G. *An Introductory Bibliography for Theological Students.* Berkeley, CA: Pacific Lutheran Theological Seminary, 1964. 31 pp.

1308. Pinnock, Clark H. *A Selective Bibliography for the Study of Christian Theology.* Madison, WI: Theological Students' Fellowship, [1974?]. 12 pp.

1309. Princeton Theological Seminary. *A Bibliography of Practical Theology.* Princeton Seminary Pamphlets No. 3. Princeton, NJ: Theological Book Agency, 1949. 71 pp.

1310. ———. *A Bibliography of Systematic Theology for Theological Students.* Princeton Seminary Pamphlets No. 2. Princeton, NJ: Princeton Theological Seminary Library, 1949. 44 pp.

1311. Riss, Paul, et al. *A Guide to Christian Thought for the Lutheran Scholar: Annotated Bibliography.* New York: n.p., 1962. 30pp.

1312. *A Selected Bibliography for Theological Students.* 2nd ed. Kansas City, MO: Midwestern Baptist Theological Seminary, 1964.

1313. *Theological Bibliographies: Essential Books for a Minister's Library.* Newton Centre, MA: Andover Newton Theological School, 1964. 138 pp. *Supplement,* 1964-66.

1314. Trotti, John, ed. *Aids to a Theological Library.* Library Aids Vol. 1. Rev. ed. Missoula, MT: Scholars Press, for the American Theological Library Association, 1977. 69 pp.

Professional Associations

Academy of Parish Clergy
13500 Shaker Blvd., Ste. 10
Cleveland, OH 44120
The Academy publishes a quarterly, *Sharing the Practice.*

Center for Professional Development in Ministry
Lancaster Theological Seminary
555 West James Street
Lancaster, PA 17603
(717) 393-7451

Christian Education

The materials in this section relate to the church's activity in training children and youth and in the growing field of adult education.

Encyclopedias and Dictionaries

1315. Cully, Iris V., and Kendig Brubaker Cully, ed. *Harper's Encyclopedia of Religious Education.* San Francisco, CA: Harper & Row, 1990. 716 pp.

1316. Cully, Kendig Brubaker, ed. *The Westminster Dictionary of Christian Education.* Philadelphia: Westminster Press, 1963. 812 pp.

1317. Gable, Lee J., ed. *Encyclopedia for Church Group Leaders.* New York: Association Press, 1959. 633 pp.

1318. McNeill, George S., ed. *Sunday School Encyclopedia.* Wheaton, IL: National Sunday School Association, 1965.

1319. Sutcliffe, John M., ed. *A Dictionary of Religious Education.* London: SCM Press, 1984. 376 pp.

Bibliographies

1320. *Annual Review of Research in Religious Education.* Schenectady, NY: Union College, Character Research Project, 1980- . Annual.

1321. *Bibliography for the Use of Teachers of Religious Knowledge.* 5th ed. London: Institute of Christian Education At Home and Overseas, 1959.

1322. Carey, Marie Aimée. *A Bibliography of Christian Formation in the Family.* Glen Rock, NJ: Paulist Press, 1964. 175 pp.

1323. *Catechetics and Education: International Bibliography 1979-1983.* RIC Supplements 88-90. Strasbourg, France: Cerdic-Publications, n.d. 239 pp.

1324. Cronin, Lawrence J., comp. *Resources for Religious Instruction of Retarded People.* Boston, MA: Archdiocese of Boston, Office of Religious Education, 1974.

1325. Dalglish, William A., ed. *Media for Christian Formation: A Guide to Audio-Visual Resources.* Dayton, OH: G.A. Pflaum, 1969. 393 pp.

1326. ———. *Media Three; for Christian Formation: A Guide to Audio-Visual Resources.* Dayton, OH: G.A. Pflaum/Standard, 1973. 372 pp.

1327. ———. *Media Two; Media for Christian Formation: A Guide to Audio-Visual Resources.* Dayton, OH: G.A. Pflaum, 1970. 502 pp.

1328. Little, Lawrence Calvin. *Abstracts of Selected Doctoral Dissertations on Adult Religious Education.* Pittsburgh, PA: Department of Religious Education, University of Pittsburgh, 1966. 322 pp.

1329. ———. *A Bibliography of American Doctoral Dissertations in Religious Education, 1885-1959.* Pittsburgh, PA: Department of Religious Education, University of Pittsburgh, 1962. 215 pp.

1330. ———. *Bibliography of Doctoral Dissertations in Character and Religious Education.* Pittsburgh, PA: Department of Religious Education, University of Pittsburgh, 1960. 273 pp.

1331. ———. *Religion and Public Education: A Bibliography.* 2nd ed.: Pittsburgh, PA: University of Pittsburgh Book Center, 1967. 3rd ed.: 1968. 214 pp.

1332. ———. *Research in Personality, Character and Religious Education: A Bibliography of Doctoral Dissertations 1885-1959.* Pittsburgh, PA: University of Pittsburgh Press, 1962. 215 pp.

1333. Parker, Franklin. *Catholic Education: A Partial List of 189 American Doctoral Dissertations.* Austin, TX: n.p., 1961. 15 pp.

1334. Pitts, V. Peter. *Concept Development and the Development of the God Concept in the Child: A Bibliography.* Schenectady, NY: Character Research Press, 1977. 62 pp.

1335. *Resource Guide for Adult Religious Education.* Rev. ed. Kansas City, MO: National Catholic Reporter Publishing Co., 1975. 208 pp.

1336. Schmauk, Theodore E. *Religious Education and Child Psychology: An Annotated Bibliography of the Literature.* Philadelphia: United Lutheran Publication House, 1920. 90 pp.

1337. Sokolosky, Barbara A. *American Sunday School Union Papers, 1817-1915: A Guide to the Microfilm Edition.* Sanford, NC: Microfilming Corporation of America, 1980. 154 pp.

1338. White, A. Sandri. *Guide to Religious Education.* Allenhurst, NJ: Aurea Publications, 1979. 85 pp.

1339. Wilt, Matthew Richard, ed. *Books for Religious Education: An Annotated Bibliography.* Haverford, PA: Catholic Library Association, 1976.

1340. Wyckoff, D. Campbell. *Bibliography of Christian Education for Presbyterian College Libraries, 1960; Submitted by the Joint Committee of Nine for Us in the Program for the Preparation of Certified Church Educators (Assistants in Christian Education).* Philadelphia: United Presbyterian Church in the U.S.A., 1960. Rev. ed. as: *Bibliography in Christian Education for Seminary and College Libraries.* Philadelphia: Board of Christian Education, United Presbyterian Church in the U.S.A., 1966-69.

Guides to Periodical Literature

1341. Corrigan, John T., ed. *Periodicals for Religious Education Resource Centers and Parish Libraries: A Guide to Magazines, Newspapers, and Newsletters.* Haverford, PA: Catholic Library Association, 1976.

Christian Education Resource Centers

Ada M. Kidder Memorial Library
Houghton College - Buffalo Extension Campus
910 Union Road
West Seneca, NY 14224
Library has a special collection on Christian education.

Association of Professors and Researchers in Religious Education
c/o Clarisse C. Croteau-Chonka
1300 W. Thorndale Ave.
Chicago, IL 60660

Christian Educators Association International
P. O. Box 50025
Pasadena, CA 91115
The Association publishes *Christian Educators International Vision*, a bi-monthly.

International Association for Studies in Religious Education
(Centre International d'Etude de la Formation Religieuse)
184-186 rue Washington
B-1050 Brussels
The Association publishes the quarterly *Lumen Vitae, International Review of Religious Education.*

Religious Education Association
409 Prospect Street
New Haven, CT 06511
The Association publishes two quarterlies, *REACH (Religious Education Association Clearing House)* and *Religious Education.*

Higher Education

Directories

1342. *Directory of Christian Colleges in Asia, Africa, the Middle East, the Pacific, Latin America, and the Caribbean.* New York: Missionary Research Library, 1961. 38 pp.

1343. *Directory of Protestant Theological Seminaries and Bible Schools in Asia, Africa, the Middle East, Latin America, the Caribbean, and Pacific Area.* New York: Missionary Research Library, 1961.

1344. *Directory of Theological Schools in Africa, Asia, the Caribbean, Latin America, and the So. Pacific.* 6th ed. London: Theological Educational Fund, 1968. 55 pp.

1345. Ruoss, George Martin. *A World Directory of Theological Libraries.* Metuchen, NJ: Scarecrow Press, 1968. 220 pp.

Bibliographies

1346. Day, Heather F. *Protestant Theological Education in America.* ATLA Bibliography Series No. 15. Metuchen, NJ: Scarecrow Press, 1985. 523 pp.

1347. Hunt, Thomas C., and James C. Carper. *Religious Colleges and Universities in America: A Selected Bibliography.* New York: Garland Publishing, 1988. 380 pp.

1348. ———. *Religious Seminaries in America: A Selected Bibliography.* New York: Garland Publishing, 1989. 244 pp.

1349. Hunt, Thomas C., James C. Carper, and Charles R. Kniker. *Religious Schools in America: A Selected Bibliography.* New York: Garland Publishing, 1986. 391 pp.

Professional Associations

American Association of Bible Colleges
130-F North College
P. O. Box 1523
Fayetteville, AR 72702

American Theological Library Association
1020 Church Street, 3rd Floor
Evanston, IL 60201

Association for Theological Education in South East Asia
4 Mount Sophia
Singapore 0922, Singapore

Association of Theological Schools in the United States and Canada
10 Summit Park Drive
Pittsburgh, PA 15275-1103

Homiletics

Encyclopedias and Dictionaries

1350. Herrera Oria, Angel, ed. *The Preacher's Encyclopedia.* Trans. and ed. by David Greenstock. 4 vols. Westminster, MD: Newman Press, 1964-1965.

1351. Nicoll, William Robertson, and Jane T. Stoddart. *The Expositor's Dictionary of Texts, Containing Outlines, Expositions and Illustrations of Bible Texts, with Full References to the Best Homiletic Literature.* New York: George H. Doran Co./ London: Hodder and Stoughton, [1911]. Rept. 2 vols. Grand Rapids, MI: William B. Eerdmans Publishing Co., 1953.

1352. Spurgeon, Charles Haddon. *Spurgeon's Expository Encyclopedia: Sermons by Charles H. Spurgeon, Classified and Arranged for Ready Reference.* 15 vols. Grand Rapids, MI: Baker Book House, 1951.

Bibliographies

1353. Knower, Franklin Howard. *Bibliography of Communication Dissertations in American Schools of Theology.* N.p., 1961. 45 pp.

1354. Litfin, A. Duane, and Haddon W. Robinson, eds. *Recent Homiletical Thought: A Bibliography.* 2 vols. Nashville, TN: Abingdon Press, 1967-83.

1355. Toohey, William, and William D. Thompson, eds. *Recent Homiletical Thought: A Bibliography, 1935-1965.* Nashville & New York: Abingdon Press, 1967. 303 pp.

Professional Associations

Academy of Homiletics
100 Campus View Drive
Lincoln, IL 61656

The Local Church

Bibliographies

1356. Byers, David M., and Bernard Quinn. *Reading for Town and Country Church Workers: An Annotated Bibliography.* Washington, DC: Glenmary Research Center, 1974. 121 pp.

1357. Goreham, Gary A. *The Rural Church in America: A Century of Writings.* New York & London: Garland Publishing, 1990. 272 pp.

1358. James, Gilbert, and Robert G. Wickens, comps. *The Town and Country Church: A Topical Bibliography.* Wilmore, KY: Department of the Church in Society, Asbury Theological Seminary, 1968. 137 pp.

1359. *Laici in Ecclesia: An Ecumenical Bibliography on the Role of the Laity in the Life and Mission of the Church.* Geneva: World Council of Churches, Department of the Laity, 1961.

Pastoral Care

Encyclopedias and Dictionaries

1360. Campbell, Alastair V. *Dictionary of Pastoral Care.* London: SPCK; New York: Crossroad, 1987. 300 pp.

1361. Ferm, Vergilius. *A Dictionary of Pastoral Psychology.* New York: Philosophical Library, 1955. 336 pp.

1362. Hunter, Gerald, ed. *Dictionary of Pastoral Care and Counseling.* Nashville, TN: Abingdon, 1990. 1346 pp.

Bibliographies

1363. *Pastoral Ministers in Time of Death: Bibliography.* Fort Worth, TX: Southwestern Baptist Theological Seminary, Fleming Library, 1964. 18 pp.

1364. *Pastoral Care and Counseling Abstracts.* Vol. 1- . Richmond, VA: Joint Council on Research in Pastoral Care and Counseling, 1972- . Annual.

Directories

1365. *AAPC Directory.* Fairfax, VA: American Association of Pastoral Counselors, 1989-90. 80 pp. Periodically updated.

1366. *ACPE Directory 1988-1989.* Decatur, GA: Association for Clinical Pastoral Education, 1988. 66 pp. Periodically updated.

Professional Centers and Associations

American Association of Christian Counselors
P. O. Box 55712
Jackson, MS 39216

American Association of Pastoral Counselors
9508 A Lee Highway
Fairfax, VA 22031
The Association publishes the *Journal of Pastoral Care.*

American Association of Professional Christian Counselors and Therapists
P. O. Box 5839
Rockville, MD 20855

American Association of Religious Counselors
P. O. Box 10672
Kansas City, MO 64118

American Association of Religious Therapists
7175 S.W. 45th Street, Ste. 303
Ft. Lauderdale, FL 33314

American Board of Examiners in Pastoral Counseling
13014 N. Dale Mabry, Ste. 270
Tampa, FL 33618

Association for Clinical Pastoral Education
1549 Clairmont Road, Ste. 103
Decatur, GA 30033

Association for Clinical Theological Training and Care
St. Mary's House
Church Westcote
Oxford OX7 6SF
United Kingdom
The Association publishes *Contact: The Interdisciplinary Journal of Pastoral Studies.*

Association for Religious and Value Issues in Counseling
c/o Dr. Mary F. Maples
College of Education, Room 213
University of Nevada
Reno, NV 89557

Association of Mental Health Clergy
c/o George E. Doebler
12320 River Oaks Pt.
Knoxville, TN 37922

Christian Association for Psychological Studies
26705 Farmington Road
Farmington Hills, MI 48018

Christian Counseling & Educational Foundation
1790 East Willow Grove Avenue
Laverock, PA 19118
The Foundation publishes the *Journal of Pastoral Practice.*

Commission on Pastoral Research
6722 Patterson Avenue
Richmond, VA 23226
The Commission publishes *Abstracts of Research on Pastoral Care and Counseling*, an annual volume.

Foundation for Religion and Mental Health
30 S. State Road
Briarcliff Manor, NY 10510

International Council for Pastoral Care and Counseling
c/o Rev. David Lyell
St. Mary's College
St. Andrews, Fife, Scotland
The Council publishes the *ICPCC Newsletter.*

United Association of Christian Counselors International
41 Short Street
Harrisburg, PA 77109-1731
The Association publishes the *International Journal of Pastoral Counseling* and *The Professional Christian Counselor*, both quarterlies.

THEOLOGY

Theology, the intellectual task of systematically presenting the teaching of the church about the broad range of subjects from the nature of God and God's revelation to the implication from how one should live, remains a primary task of the Christian life. It is also one of the most exacting fields of Christian scholarship. Theologians must regularly face those issues which seriously divide Christians, and there are few fields within which the priorities of Christianity are so visible.

In assessing the volumes below, the theological perspective of the authors are often the crucial distinction between volumes. One could divide the texts by their origin in one of the three major theological communities, Roman Catholic, liberal Protestant and Evangelical Protestant, though there has been some attempt of Roman Catholics and liberal Protestants to cooperate on joint reference book projects. These reference books, in general, represent the work of the best theological minds in the church, and selecting the best is somewhat subjective. Often the best (and only) way to judge between the volumes below is by coming to know the individual perspective the authors/editors represent.

Encyclopedias and Dictionaries

1367. Angeles, Peter A. *Dictionary of Christian Theology.* San Francisco: Harper & Row, 1985. 210 pp.

1368. Bangs, Carl. *German-English Theological Word List.* Kansas City: The Author, 1952. Rev. ed.: Kansas City: The Author, 1962. 16 pp.

1369. Bigler, Vernon. *Key Words in Christian Thinking: A Guide to Theological Terms and Ideas.* New York: Association Press, 1966. 125 pp.

1370. Bouyer, Louis. *Dictionary of Theology.* Trans. by Charles Underhill Quinn. New York: Desclée, 1965. 470 pp. Originally published in French as *Dictionnaire Théologique.* 2e éd.: Tournai: Desclée, 1963.

1371. Bradley, John P. *Encyclopedic Dictionary of Christian Doctrine.* 3 vols. The Catholic Layman's Library, Vols. 7-9. Gastonia, NC: Good Will Publishers, 1970.

1372. Brewer, Ebenezer Cobham. *A Dictionary of Miracles, Imitative, Realistic and Dogmatic.* Philadelphia: J.B. Lippincott Co., 1885. Rept. Detroit: Gale Research Co., 1966. 582 pp.

1373. Brink, H., et al. *Theologisch Woordenboek.* 3 vols. Roermond: J. J. Romen, 1952-1958.

1374. Buechner, Frederick. *Wishful Thinking: A Theological ABC.* New York: Harper & Row, 1973. 100 pp.

1375. Burnaby, John. *Christian Words and Christian Meanings.* New York: Harper and Brothers/London: Hodder and Stoughton, 1955. 160 pp.

1376. *Catholic Dictionary of Theology.* Vol. 1- . London: Thomas Nelson and Sons, 1962- . Four to five volumes projected.

1377. Crooks, George Richard, and John Fletcher Hurst. *Theological Encyclopaedia and Methodology; on the Basis of Hagenbach.* New York: Phillips and Hunt/ Cincinnati, OH: Walden and Stowe, 1884.

1378. Cully, Iris V., and Kendig Brubaker Cully. *An Introductory Theological Wordbook.* Philadelphia: Westminster Press, 1963. 204 pp.

1379. Davidson, Gustav. *A Dictionary of Angels, Including the Fallen Angels.* New York: Free Press/London: Collier-Macmillan, 1967. 387 pp.

1380. Deferrari, Roy Joseph, and M. Inviolata Barr. *A Lexicon of St. Thomas Aquinas Based on the "Summa Theologica" and Selected Passages of His Other Works.* 5 vols. Washington, DC: Catholic University of America Press, 1948-1953.

1381. Elwell, Walter A. *Evangelical Dictionary of Theology.* Grand Rapids, MI: Baker Book House, 1984. 1204 pp.

1382. Erickson, Millard J. *Concise Dictionary of Christian Theology.* Grand Rapids: Baker, 1984. 1204 pp.

1383. Ferguson, Sinclair B., and David F. Wright, eds. *New Dictionary of Theology.* Downers Grove, IL: InterVarsity Press, 1988. 738 pp.

1384. *Handbook of Theology.* Cleveland: World Publishing Co., 1958. 380 pp. Rept.: New York: New American Library, 1974.

1385. Harrison, Everett F., ed. *Baker's Dictionary of Theology.* Grand Rapids: Baker Book House, 1960. 566 pp.

1386. Harvey, Van A. *A Handbook of Theological Terms.* New York: Macmillan Company, 1964. 253 pp.

1387. Healey, Frances G. *Fifty Key Words in Theology.* Richmond, VA: John Knox Press/London: Lutterworth Press, 1967. 84 pp.

1388. Humphreys, Fisher, and Philip Wise. *A Dictionary of Doctrinal Terms.* Nashville: Broadman Press, 1983. 131 pp.

1389. Komonchak, Joseph A., Mary Collins, and Dermot A. Lane, ed. *New Dictionary of Theology.* Wilmington, DE: Michael Glazier, 1987. 1112 pp.

1390. Lord, Eric, and Donald Whittle. *A Theological Glossary.* Oxford: Religious Education Press, 1969. 134 pp.

1391. Migne, Jacques Paul. *Encyclopédie Théologique. 1-3 Sér. Dictionnaire sur toutes les parties de la science religieuse.* Paris: Migne, 1845-66. 168 pp.

1392. Mosse, Walter M. *A Theological German Vocabulary: German Theological Key Words Illustrated in Quotes from Martin Luther's Bible and the Revised Standard Version.* New York: Macmillan Company, 1955. 148 pp. Rept.: New York: Octagon Books, 1968. 148 pp.

1393. Muller, Richard A. *Dictionary of Latin & Greek Theological Terms.* Grand Rapids, MI: Baker Book House, 1985. 344 pp.

1394. O'Carroll, Michael. *Corpus Christi: An Encyclopedia of the Eucharist.* Wilmington, DE: Michael Glazier, 1988. 221 pp.

1395. ———. *Trinitas: A Theological Encyclopedia of the Holy Trinity.* Wilmington, DE: Michael Glazier, 1987. 220 pp.

1396. ———. *Veni Creator Spiritus: A Theological Encyclopedia of the Holy Spirit.* Collegeville, MN: Liturgical Press, 1990. 232 pp.

1397. Parente, Pietro, et al. *Dictionary of Dogmatic Theology.* Trans. by Emmanuel Doronzo. Milwaukee, WI: Bruce Publishing Co., 1951. 310 pp. Originally published in Italian as: *Dizionario di Teologia Dommatica.* 2. ed. Rome: Editrice Studium, 1945.

1398. Räbiger, J. F. *Encyclopedia of Theology.* Trans. by John MacPherson. 2 vols. Edinburgh: T. & T. Clarke, 1884.

1399. Rahner, Karl. *Encyclopedia of Theology: The Concise Sacramentum Mundi.* New York: Seabury Press, 1975. 1841 pp.

1400. ———, et al. *Sacramentum Mundi: An Encyclopedia of Theology.* 6 vols. New York: Herder & Herder, 1968-70.

1401. ———, and Herbert Vorgrimler. *Concise Theological Dictionary,* 1965. Trans. by Richard Strachan. Freiburg im Breisgau: Herder, 1965/London: Burns and Oates, 1966. Originally published in German as *Kleines Theologisches Wörterbuch,* 5. Aufl. Freiburg im Breisgau: Herder, 1965. 2nd ed. as: *Dictionary of Theology.* New York: Crossroad, 1981. 541 pp.

1402. Richardson, Alan, ed. *A Dictionary of Christian Theology.* Philadelphia: Westminster Press/London: SCM Press, 1969. 364 pp.

1403. ———, and John Bowden, eds. *Westminster Dictionary of Christian Theology.* Philadelphia: Westminster Press, 1983. 614 pp.

1404. Roberti, Francesco, comp. *Dictionary of Moral Theology.* Edited by Pietro Palazzini, trans. by Henry Yannone. Westminster, MD: Newman Press, 1962. 1352 pp. Trans. of *Dizionario di Teologia Morale.* 2. ed.: Rome: Editrice Studium, 1957.

1405. Simcox, Carroll Eugene. *The Words of the Creeds: A Brief Dictionary of Our Faith.* Cincinnati, OH: Forward Movement Publications, 1960. 30 pp.

1406. Stockhammer, Morris, ed. *Thomas Aquinas Dictionary.* New York: Philosophical Library/London: Vision, 1965. 219 pp.

1407. Taylor, Richard S., ed. *Beacon Dictionary of Theology.* Kansas City: Beacon Hill Press of Kansas City, 1983. 559 pp.

1408. *Theological Dictionary of the New Testament.* 10 vols. Grand Rapids, MI: William B. Eerdmans Publishing Company, 1964-76.

1409. Turnbull, Ralph G., ed. *Baker's Dictionary of Practical Theology.* Grand Rapids, MI: Baker Book House, 1967. 467 pp.

1410. Vacant, A., and E. Mangenot. *Dictionnaire de Théologie Catholique.* Paris: Letouzey, 1909-50. 15 Vols. Included in *Encyclopédie des Sciences Religieuses.*

1411. Wetzer, Heinrich Joseph. *Wetzer und Welte's Kirchenlexicon, oder Encyklopädie der katholischen Theologie und ihrer Hülfswissenschaften.* 12 vols. Freiburg im Breisgau: Herder, 1882-1901.

Biographical Material

1412. Ferm, Vergilius Ture Anselm, ed. *Contemporary American Theology: Theological Autobiographies.* 2 vols. New York: Round Table Press, 1932-1933.

Bibliographies

1413. Bauer, Gerhard. *Towards a Theology of Development: An Annotated Bibliography.* Geneva: Committee on Society, Development and Peace, 1970. 201 pp.

1414. Borchardt, C. F. A., and Willem S. Vorster, eds. *South African Theological Bibliography/Sud Afrikaanse Teologiese Bibliografie.* Documenta 22. Pretoria: University of South Africa, 1980. 398 pp.

1415. Bourke, Vernon Joseph. *Thomistic Bibliography, 1920-1940.* St. Louis, MO: The Modern Schoolman, 1945. 312 pp.

1416. Brown, John. *Descriptive List of Religious Books in the English Language Suited for General Use.* Edinburgh: Waugh & Innes, 1827. 92 pp.

1417. Cotrell, Jack. *History of Doctrine: Bibliography for Graduate Studies in the Cincinnati Bible Seminary.* Cincinnati, OH: Cincinnati Bible Seminary.

1418. Crossman, Richard C. *Paul Tillich: A Comprehensive Bibliography.* ATLA Bibliography Series No. 9. Metuchen, NJ: Scarecrow Press, 1983. 193 pp.

1419. *Current Research: Titles of Theses and Dissertations in the Fields of Theology and Religious Studies.* Vol. 1- . Duns, Berwickshire: Institute of Religion and Theology of Great Britain and Ireland, 1974- . Irregular.

1420. Darling, James. *Cyclopaedia Bibliographica: A Library Manual of Theological and General Literature and Guide Books for Authors, Preachers, Students, and Literary Men—Analytical, Bibliographical, and Biographical.* 2 vols. London: The Author, 1854.

1421. Facelina, Raymond. *Liberation and Salvation: International Bibliography 1972-June 1973 Indexed by Computer.* RIC Supplement 6. Strasbourg, France: Cerdic-Publications, 1973. 35 pp.

1422. ————. *African Theology: International Bibliography 1968-June 1977 Indexed by Computer.* RIC Supplement 30. Strasbourg, France: Cerdic-Publications, 1977. 38 pp.

1423. Gasser, Sylvie, and Pierre Beffa. "Theologies from Africa, Asia, and Latin America, including Black Theology: a Bibliography." *The Ecumenical Review* 36, 1 (January 1984): 122-33.

1424. Gillett, Charles Ripley, comp. & ed. *Catalogue of the McAlpin Collection of British History and Theology at the Union Theological Seminary in the City of New York*. 5 vols. New York: UTS, 1927-30.

1425. Hadidian, Dikran, comp. *Bibliography of British Theological Literature 1850-1940.* Pittsburgh, PA: Clifford E. Barbour Library, Pittsburgh Theological Seminary, 1985. 453 pp.

1426. Hurst, John Fletcher. *The Literature of Theology: A Classified Bibliography of Theological and General Religious Literature*. New York: Hunt and Eaton, 1896. Rept.: Boston, MA: Milford House, 1972. 757 pp.

1427. Ibarra, Eduardo. *Holy Spirit: International Bibliography 1972-June 1974 Indexed by Computer*. Strasbourg, France: Cerdic-Publications, 1974. 48 pp.

1428. Kempff, D. *A Bibliography of Calviniana, 1959-1974.* Potchefstroom: Institute for the Advancement of Calvinism/Leiden: E.J. Brill, 1975. 249 pp.

1429. Kepple, Robert J. *Reference Works for Theological Research: An Annotated Selective Bibliographical Guide*. 2nd ed.: Washington: University Press of America, 1981. 283 pp. *Supplement 1981-82.* Philadelphia: Westminister Theological Seminary, 1982. 14 pp.

1430. Kwiran, Manfred. *Index to Literature on Barth, Bonhoeffer and Bultmann.* Basel: Friedreich Reinhardt Verlag, 1977. 506 pp.

1431. *Liberation Theology, Black Theology and the Third World.* Chicago: American Theological Library Association, 1981. 320 pp.

1432. Mills, Watson E. *The Holy Spirit: A Bibliography.* Peabody, MA: Hendrickson, 1988. 192 pp.

1433. Morris, Raymond. *A Theological Book List.* Oxford and Naperville, IL: Theological Education Fund of the International Missionary Council, 1960. 242 pp. *See*: Ward (1448, 1449, 1450). Rept.: Middletown, CT: Greeno, Hadden and Co., 1971.

1434. Muss-Arnolt, William. *Theological and Semitic Literature for the Years 1898-1901: A Supplement to "The American Journal of Theology" and "The American Journal of Semitic Languages and Literatures".* 4 vols. Chicago: n.p., 1898-1902.

1435. Musto, Ronald G. *Liberation Theology: An Annotated Bibliography.* New York: Garland Publishing Company, 1990. c.400 pp.

1436. Noth, Martin. *Developing Lines of Theological Thought in Germany.* Trans. by John Bright. Richmond, VA: Union Theological Seminary, 1963. 18 pp.

1437. O'Brien, Elmer John, ed. *Theology in Transition: A Bibliographical Evaluation of the "Decisive Decade," 1954-1964.* New York: Herder and Herder, 1965. 282 pp.

1438. ———. *Catalogue of Doctoral Dissertations, 1944-1960.* Princeton, NJ: Princeton Theological Seminary, 1962. 119 pp.

1439. Principe, Walter Henry, and Ronald E. Diener. *Bibliographies and Bulletins in Theology.* Toronto: Pontifical Institute of Medieval Studies, 1967. 44 pp.

1440. Robertson, D. B. *Reinhold Niebuhr's Works: A Bibliography.* Boston: G.K. Hall & Co., 1979. 238 pp. Rev. ed: Lanham, MD: University Press of America, 1983. 268 pp.

1441. *Scholars' Choice: Significant Current Theological Literature from Abroad.* No. 1-. Richmond, VA: Union Theological Seminary in Virginia, 1960- . Semiannual.

1442. Smith, Wilbur Moorehead. *A List of Bibliographies of Theological and Biblical Literature Published in Great Britain and America, 1595-1931, with Critical, Biographical and Bibliographical Notes.* Coatesville, PA: The Author, 1931.

1443. Steiner, Urban J. *Contemporary Theology: A Reading Guide.* Collegeville, MN: Liturgical Press, 1965.

1444. *Theologians and Magisterium: International Bibliography 1975-1981.* RIC Supplements 65-66. Strasbourg, France: Cerdic-Publications, 1982.

1445. *Theological and Religious Index.* 2 vols. Harrogate: Theological Abstracting and Bibliographical Services, 1978-1980. Quarterly.

1446. *Union Catalog of the Graduate Theological Union Library.* 15 vols. Berkeley, CA: Graduate Theological Union, 1972.

1447. Vander Marck, William. "Fundamental Theology: A Bibliographical and Critical Survey." *Religious Studies Review* 8, 3 (July 1982): 244-59.

1448. Ward, Arthur Marcus, et al. *A Theological Book List: Supplement 1.* Oxford and Naperville, IL: Theological Education Fund of the International Missionary Council, 1963. 41 pp. *See:* Morris (1433).

1449. ———. *A Theological Book List: Supplement 2.* Oxford and Naperville, IL: Theological Education Fund of the International Missionary Council, 1968. 121 pp.

1450. ———. *A Theological Book List: Supplement 3.* London: Theological Education Fund of the International Missionary Council, 1973.

1451. Washington Theological Coalition. *Union List of Periodicals of Members of the Washington Theological Consortium and Contributing Institutions.* Washington, DC: Catholic University of America Press, 1967. 370 pp. 2nd ed.: Silver Spring, MD: Washington Theological Coalition, 1970.

Guides to Periodical Literature

1452. *TEAM-A Serials: A Union List of Serials Holdings of the Theological Education Association of Mid-America.* Louisville, KY: Southern Baptist Theological Seminary for TEAM-A, 1972. 392 pp.

Resource Centers

Aquinas Center of Theology at Emory
874 Clifton Court Circle #5
Atlanta, GA 30329-4037

Center for Process Studies
1325 N. College Avenue
Claremont, CA 91711

Center for Theological Inquiry
50 Stockton Street
Princeton, NJ 08540

Howard and Edna Hong Kierkegaard Library
St. Olaf College
Northfield, MN 55057
The Library includes a set of Kierkegaard's writings and a replication of his personal library.

Institute for a Theological Future
c/o Dr. Gordon Ingram
P. O. Box 8434
Aspen, CO 81612

International Theological Institute
c/o The American Committee
950 Leonard Street
Grand Rapids, MI 49504

Regis College Library
15 Saint Mary Street
Toronto, ON M4Y 2R5
Canada
The Library houses a collection of writing by and about theologian Bernard Lonergan.

Professional Associations

American Theological Society
North Park Theological Association
3225 W. Foster
Chicago, IL 60625

Association for Theological Studies
P. O. Box 290168
Minneapolis, MN 55429

Association of Disciples for Theological Discussion
c/o Division of Higher Education
11780 Borman Drive, Ste. 100
St. Louis, MO 63146

Bonhoeffer Society
c/o Geffrey B. Kelly
Department of Religion
LaSalle University
20th Street and Olney Avenue
Philadelphia, PA 19141

Catholic Theological Society of America
c/o Mary Hinds
Washington Theological Union
9001 New Hampshire Avenue
Silver Spring, MD 20903

Center for Process Studies
c/o David Griffiths
Claremont School of Religion
Claremont, CA
Periodical: *Process Studies*

College Theology Society
c/o Bill McInerney
Theology Department
Rockhurst College
5225 Troost
Kansas City, MO 64110

Evangelical Theological Society
c/o Reformed Theological Seminary
5422 Clinton Blvd.
Jackson, MS 39209

Karl Barth Society of North America
c/o Steve Crocco
Elmhurst College
190 Prospect Street
Elmhurst, IL 60126

Native American Theological Association
Minnesota Church Center
Room 303
122 W. Franklin Avenue
Minneapolis, MN 55404

North American Paul Tillich Society
c/o H. Frederick Reisz, Jr.
Harvard Divinity School
45 Francis Avenue
Cambridge, MA 02138

Mariology

The study of the role of the Blessed Virgin Mary in theology is a special topic primarily for Roman Catholic theologians, though at least one group which includes non-Catholics (primarily Anglicans and Eastern Orthodox) has been formed. At least some Mariologists also have an interest in the popular devotion of the Virgin which has grown out of the many reports of her appearance (apparitions), Lourdes and Fatima being the most well-known examples. The accounts of her apparitions have also speaked the interest of anthropologists and historians of religion.

Encyclopedias and Dictionaries

1453. Attwater, Donald, comp. *A Dictionary of Mary.* New York: P.J. Kennedy, 1956; London: Longmans, Green and Co., 1957. 312 pp.

1454. O'Carroll, Michael. *Theotokos: A Theological Encyclopedia of the Blessed Virgin Mary.* Wilmington, DE: Michael Glazier, 1982. 378 pp.

Bibliographies

1455. Baumeister, Edmund J., comp. *Booklist of the Marian Library.* 2nd ed.: Dayton, OH: Dayton University, Marian Library, 1949.

1456. Melton, J. Gordon, and George Eberhart. "Marian Apparitions" In George Eberhart. *UFOs and the Extraterrestrial Movement: a Bibliography.* Metuchen, NJ: Scarecrow Press, 1986. Pp. 903-39.

Resource Centers

American Religions Collection
Library
University of California-Santa Barbara
Santa Barbara, CA 93106
The Collection includes a large selection of books, pamphlets, and ephemera concerning the reported apparitions of the Virgin Mary.

Marian Library
University of Dayton
Dayton, OH 45469-0001
The Library houses a 78,000+ volume collection on Mariology.

Mariological Society of America
c/o Marian Library
University of Dayton
Dayton, OH 45469-0001
The Society publishes *Marian Studies* (annual), which carries the proceedings of its yearly meeting.

Ecumenical Society of the Blessed Virgin Mary
423 Fourth Street, N.E.
Washington, DC 20002

WORSHIP AND LITURGY

Broadly speaking, worship encompasses the various means religious believers have developed to acknowledge their relationship to the Divine. For Christians, worship includes act of devotion, the church's ritual and liturgy, and the sacraments (especially baptism and the eucharist), the primary subject of this chapter. In the West, the Roman Catholic Chruch has been a liturgically oriented body and has produced a rich liturgical literature. The Protestant and especially the Free Churches rebelled, in part, against the Roman liturgy, many parts of which they saw as non-biblical if not Pagan in emphasis. They developed a very simple worship style which has not called for the elaboration in books as that of the Roman Church. One exception has been the Church of England which developed a strong liturgical approach through its Prayer book.

Material closely related to worship can be found in the earlier chapter on Mysticism and Spirituality.

General Sources

1457. Jones, Cheslyn, Geoffrey Wainwright, et al., eds. *The Study of the Liturgy.* London: SPCK/New York: Oxford University Press, 1978. 547 pp.

Encyclopedias and Dictionaries

1458. Britt, Matthew. *A Dictionary of the Psalter, Containing the Vocabulary of the Psalms, Hymns, Canticles and Miscellaneous Prayers of the Breviary Psalter.* New York: Benziger, 1928. 299 pp.

1459. Bryant, Al. *Encyclopedia of Devotional Programs for Women's Groups.* Vol. 1— . Grand Rapids, MI: Zondervan Publishing House, 1956- .

1460. Davies, John G., ed. *A Dictionary of Liturgy and Worship.* New York: Macmillan Company/London: SCM Press, 1972. 385 pp. Rept. as: *The Westminster Dictionary of Worship.* Philadelphia: Westminster Press, 1979. Rev. ed. as: *The New Westminster Dictionary of Liturgy and Worship.* Philadelphia: Westminster Press, 1986. 544 pp.

1461. ———. *A Select Liturgical Lexicon.* Ecumenical Studies in Worship No. 14. London: Lutterworth Press, 1965. Rept.: Richmond, VA: John Knox Press, 1966. 146 pp.

1462. Fink, Peter E. *The New Dictionary of Sacramental Liturgy.* Collegeville, MN: The Liturgical Press, 1990. 1352 pp.

1463. Harford, George, and Morley Stevenson, eds. *The Prayer Book Dictionary.* London: Sir I. Pitman & Sons, 1912. 832 pp. Rev. ed.: London: Sir Isaac Pitman and Sons, 1925. 832 pp.

1464. Hoffman, Alexius. *Liturgical Dictionary.* Popular Liturgical Library Series III, No. 1. Collegeville, MN: Liturgical Press, 1928. 186 pp.

1465. Hoskins, Edgar. *Horae Beatae Mariae Virginis; or, Sarum and York Primers, with Kindred Books and Primers of the Reformed Roman Usage together with an Introduction.* London: Longmans, Green and Co., 1901. 577 pp.

1466. Kapsner, Oliver Leonard. *Benedictine Liturgical Books in American Benedictine Libraries: A Progress Checklist Prepared for the Library Science Section of the American Benedictine Academy.* Latrobe, PA: St. Vincent College Library, 1960. 31 pp.

1467. Lang, Jovian P. *Dictionary of the Liturgy.* New York: Catholic Book Publishing Company, 1989. 687 pp.

1468. Lee, Frederick George. *A Glossary of Liturgical and Ecclesiastical Terms.* London: Bernard Quaritch, 1887. Rept.: Detroit, MI: Tower Books, 1971. 452 pp.

1469. Lercaro, Giacomo. *A Small Liturgical Dictionary.* Trans. by J.F. Harwood-Tregear. Collegeville, MN: Liturgical Press/London: Burns and Gates, 1959. 248 pp. Trans. of the 2nd Italian ed. of *Piccolo Dizionario Liturgico.*

1470. Podhradsky, Gerhard. *New Dictionary of the Liturgy.* Trans. by Ronald Walls and Michael Barry and ed. by Lancelot Sheppard. Staten Island, NY: Alba House/London: Geoffrey Chapman, 1967. 268 pp. Originally published in German as *Lexikon der Liturgie.* Innsbruck: Tyrolia Verlag, 1962.

1471. Sartore, Domenico, and Achille M. Triacca. *Nuovo Dizionario di Liturgia.* Milan: Edizioni Paoline, 1984. 1667 pp.

1472. Tatlock, Richard. *A Prayer Book Dictionary: An Explanation, with Examples, of Obsolete, Unusual and Ambiguous Words Commonly Used in the "Book of Common Prayer" of 1662.* London: A.R. Mowbray and Co., 1960.

Bibliographies

1473. Benton, Josiah Henry. *The Book of Common Prayer and Books Connected with Its Origin and Growth: Catalogue of the Collection of Josiah Henry Benton.* Boston, MA: Privately printed, 1910. 83 pp. 2nd ed.: Boston: D.B. Updike, 1914. 142 pp.

1474. *Eucharist: International Bibliography 1975-1984.* RIC Supplements 96-98. Strasbourg, France: Cerdic-Publications, 1985. 184 pp. *See*: Pigault (1482).

1475. *General Catalogue of Printed Books. Liturgies.* London: Trustees of the British Museum, 1962.

1476. Grimes, Ronald L. *Research in Ritual Studies: A Programmatic Essay and Bibliography.* ATLA Bibliography Series No. 14. 1985.

1477. ———. "Sources for the Study of Ritual." *Religious Studies Review* 10, 2 (April 1984): 134-45.

1478. Harrah, Barbara K., and David F. Harrah. *Funeral Services: A Bibliography of Literature on Its Past, Present and Future, the Various Means of Disposition and Memorialization.* Metuchen, NJ: Scarecrow Press, 1976. 383 pp.

1479. Irwin, John C. *American Protestantism's Self-Understanding of Its Worship: A Selected Bibliography.* Bibliographical Lecture Series No. 4. Evanston, IL: Garrett Theological Seminary Library, 1969. 11 pp.

1480. Pfaff, Richard W. *Medieval Latin Liturgy: A Select Bibliography.* Toronto Medieval Bibliographies 9. Toronto: University of Toronto Press, 1982. 129 pp.

1481. Pigault, Gérard, and Jean Schlick. *Baptism: International Bibliography 1971-1973 Indexed by Computer.* RIC Supp. 9. Strasbourg: Cerdic-Publications, 1974. 35 pp.

1482. ———. *Eucharist: International Bibliography 1971-1974 Indexed by Computer.* RIC Supplement 17. Strasbourg, France: Cerdic-Publications, 1975. 44 pp. *See*: (1474).

1483. ———. *Eucharist and Eucharistic Hospitality: International Bibliography 1971-1973 Indexed by Computer.* RIC Supplement 10. Strasbourg, France: Cerdic-Publications, 1974. 39 pp.

1484. Sinclair, Keith Val. *French Devotional Texts of the Middle Ages: A Bibliographic Manuscript Guide.* Westport, CT: Greenwood Press, 1979. 231 pp. First Supplement: 1982. 234 pp. Second Supplement: 1988. 385 pp.

1485. Thompson, Bard. *A Bibliography of Christian Worship.* ATLA Bibliography Series No. 25. Metuchen, NJ: Scarecrow Press, 1989. 830 pp.

1486. Tiller, John Eric. *A Modern Liturgical Bibliography.* Grove Booklet on Ministry and Worship No. 23. Bramcote, Nottinghamshire: Grove Books, 1974. 24 pp.

1487. Travis, Stephen. *Audio-Visual Media: A Guide to Sources of Materials for Christian Education and Worship.* Bramcote, Nottinghamshire: Grove Press, 1972. 16 pp.

1488. Vismans, Thomas Antonius, and Lucas Brinkhoff, comps. *Critical Bibliography of Liturgical Literature.* Trans. by Raymund W. Fitzpatrick and Clifford Howell. Bibliographia ad Usum Seminariorum, Annotated Basic Bibliography Vol. E.1. Nijmegen: Bestelcentrale der VSKB Publishers, 1961. 72 pp.

1489. Weale, William Henry James. *Bibliographia Liturgica: Catalogus Missalium, Ritus Latini ab Anno 1474 Impressorum. Iterum Edidit H. Bohatta.* London: Quaritch, 1928. 380 pp.

Professional Associations

International Society for Liturgical Study and Renewal
P. O. Box 338
214 Ashwood Road
Villanova, PA 19083

North American Academy of Liturgy
c/o David Truemper, Secretary
Valparaiso University
Valparaiso, IN 46383
The Academy publishes *Worship.*

Research/Resource Centers

Institute for Ritual Studies
c/o Rev. Hal Taussug
513 S. 48th Street
Philadelphia, PA 19143

Institute for Ritual, Symbol and World Religions
Maryknoll School of Theology
Maryknoll, NY 10545

North American Liturgy Resources
2110 W. Peoria Avenue
Phoenix, AZ 85029

Notre Dame Center for Pastoral Liturgy
Box 81
1224 Hesburgh Library
Notre Dame, IN 46556
Formerly known as the **Murphy Center for Liturgical Research**, the Center is a unit of the Institute for Pastoral and Social Ministry. It sponsors the **Associates of the Notre Dame Center for Pastoral Liturgy**, a professional organization of Notre Dame graduates.

VI

CHRISTIAN HISTORICAL STUDIES

CHURCH HISTORY: GENERAL SOURCES

Because of its very nature, grounded in historical events at a particular moment in history, Christianity has had a peculiar concern with history. This concern has but grown with the development of critical historical methods during the last two centuries. The materials in this chapter include the basic reference documents which survey the entire period of Christianity's existence and offer international coverage of its life. It also makes note of the basic working tools for the church historian. Subsequent chapters will cover those volumes which limit themselves to one of the more important phases of the church's history and to one of the major denominational families which have developed as the church spread through the populous. The denominational families into which the church divided have been the major structural feature of modern Christianity

---

Encyclopedias and Dictionaries

1490. Baudrillart, Alfred, Albert Vogt, and Urbain Rouzies. *Dictionnaire d'Histoire et de Geographie Ecclésiastiques.* 19 vols. Paris: Letouzey et Ane, Editeurs, 1912- .

1491. Brauer, Jerald C., ed. *The Westminster Dictionary of Church History.* Philadelphia: Westminster Press, 1971. 887 pp.

1492. Buck, Charles. *Theological Dictionary . . . of All Religious Terms . .. of All the Principle Denominations . . . Together with an Accurate Statement of . . . Transactions and Events . . . in Ecclesiastical History.* Philadelphia: J. J. Woodward, 1831, 1832. 624 pp.

1493. O'Brien, T. C. *Corpus Dictionary of Western Churches.* Washington, DC: Corpus Publications, 1970. 820 pp.

1494. Schaff, Philip, ed. *Bibliotheca Symbolica Ecclesiae Universalis. The Creeds of Christendom, with a History and Critical Notes.* 3 vols. New York: Harper and Bros., 1919. Schaff's volumes, give inclusive coverage of the church's creeds historically through the nineteenth century. It has recently been supplemented by Melton's *Encyclopedia of American Religion: Religious Creeds* (567), which includes copies of the numerous new creedal statements written in the twentieth century.

Biographical Material

1495. Barker, William Pierson. *Who's Who in Church History.* Old Tappan, NJ: Fleming H. Revell, 1969. Rept.: Grand Rapids, MI: Baker Book House, 1977. 319 pp.

1496. Bautz, Friedrich Wilhelm. *Biographisch-Bibliographisches Kirchenlexicon.* Vol 1- . Hamm, Germany: Verlag Traugott Bautz, 1975- .

1497. Chenu, Bruno, et al. *The Book of Martyrs.* New York: Crossroads, 1990. 215 pp.

1498. Jamieson, Robert. *Cyclopaedia of Religious Biography: A Series of Memoirs of the Most Eminent Religious Characters of Modern Times, Intended for Family Reading.* London: J.J. Griffin and Co./Glasgow: R. Griffin and Co., 1853.

1499. Moyer, Elgin Sylvester. *The Wycliffe Biographical Dictionary of the Church.* Rev. ed. Chicago: Moody Press, 1982. 449 pp. Originally entitled *Who Was Who in Church History.*

1500. Schaff, Philip, and Samuel Macauley Jackson. *Encyclopedia of Living Divines and Christian Workers of All Denominations in Europe and America.* New York: Funk and Wagnalls Company, 1894. 296 pp. Published as a supplement to Schaff's *A Religious Encyclopedia* (21).

Bibliographies

1501. Case, Shirley Jackson, ed. *A Bibliographical Guide to the History of Christianity.* Chicago: University of Chicago Press, 1931. 265 pp. Rept. New York: Peter Smith, 1951.

1502. Chadwick, Owen. *The History of the Church: A Select Bibliography.* Helps for Students of History No. 66. London: Historical Association, 1962. Rev. ed: 1966. Rev. ed: 1973. 52 pp. First published in 1923.

1503. *Church History: A Selection of Books based on J. P. Whitney's Bibliography [1923].* 2nd. ed.: London: National Book Council, 1930. *See:* Whitney (1509).

1504. Fisher, J. A. *A Select Bibliography of Ecclesiastical History.* Boston, MA: D. C. Heath & Co., 1885. 391 pp.

1505. Gliozzo, Charles A., comp. *A Bibliography of Ecclesiastical History of the French Revolution.* Bibliographia Tripotamopolitana No. 6. Pittsburgh: Pittsburgh Theological Seminary, Clifford E. Barbour Library, [1972].

1506. Oster, Richard. *A Bibliography on Ancient Ephesus.* ATLA Bibliography Series No. 19. Metuchen, NJ: Scarecrow Press, 1987. 181 pp.

1507. Purvis, James D. *Jerusalem, the Holy City: A Bibliography.* ATLA Bibliography Series No. 20. Metuchen, NJ: Scarecrow Press, 1988. 513 pp.

1508. Stokes, Lawrence D. *Medieval and Reformation Germany (to 1664).* Helps for Students of History No. 84. London: Historical Association, 1972.

1509. Whitney, James Pounder. *A Bibliography of Church History.* Historical Association Leaflet No. 55. London: Historical Association, 1923. 44 pp.

Guides to Periodical Literature

1510. *Church History Periodicals: Classified Listing by Call Number.* Cambridge, MA: Harvard University Library, 1970. 959 pp.

Atlases

1511. Emmerich, Heinrich. *Atlas Hierarchicus. Descriptio Geographica et Statistica Ecclesiae Catholicae tum Occidentis tum Orientis.* Mödling: St. Gabriel Verlag, 1968. 76 pp.

1512. Freitag, Anton, et al. *Atlas du Monde Chrétien; L'Expansion du Christianisme à travers les Siècles.* Paris, Bruxelles: Elsevier, 1959. 215 pp. Published in English as: *The Universal Atlas of the Christian World: The Expansion of Christianity through the Centuries.* London: Burns & Oates, 1963. 200 pp.

1513. Jedin, Hubert, Kenneth Scott Latourette, and Jochen Martin. *Atlas zur Kirchengeschichte: die Christlichen Kirchen in Geschichte und Gegenwart.* Freiburg: Herder, 1970. 83+152 pp.

1514. Littell, Franklin Hamlin. *The Macmillan Atlas History of Christianity.* New York: Macmillan Company, 1976.

Historical Studies

American Catholic Historical Association
Catholic University of America
Washington, DC 20064
The Society publishes quarterly *The Catholic Historical Review.*

American Society of Church History
328 Deland Avenue
Indialantic, FL 32903
The Society, founded in the late-nineteenth century, publishes two periodicals: *Church History* and *Church History News Supplement.*

Conference on Faith and History
Indiana State University
Department of History
Terre Haute, IN 47809
The Conference publishes *Fides et Historia* (3/yr.).

Ecclesiastical History Society
Department of History
Westfield College
London NW3 7ST, UK
The Society publishes *Studies in Church History.*

PATRISTICS

The Patristic period, the period of the Church Fathers, includes the post-biblical centuries when the church made the basic formative decisions about its life and belief. It includes the period of the Ecumenical Councils, beginning in 325 C.E., at which important decisions on doctrine, including the definitive doctrine of the Trinity, were hammered out. After the last Ecumenical Council (787 C.E.), the Patristic Era fades into the Medieval period.

While this volume has not tried to include collections of source material, the study of Patristics by definition is in part the study of the writings of the early church leaders and scholars. There now exist a variety of collections of their writings, both collections of the more important writings for use of pastors and interested lay scholars, and more extensive collections in original languages for scholars.

Encyclopedias and Dictionaries

1515. Berardino, Angelo D. *Dizionario di Antichitá Cristiane.* 3 vols. Casale Monf.: Casa Editrice Marietti, 1983.

1516. Cabrol, Fernand, and Henri, Leclerq. *Dictionnaire d'Archéologie chrétienne et de Liturgie.* Paris: Letouzey, 1907-53. 15 Vols. included in *Encyclopédie des Sciences Religieuses.*

1517. Cozens, M. L. *Handbook of Heresies.* New York: Sheed and Ward, 1928. 96 pp. Rev. ed.: 1974. 95 pp.

1518. Dölger, Franz Joseph, et al. *Reallexikon für Antike und Christentum.* 13 vols. Stuttgart, Germany: Hiersemann, 1950-84.

1519. Ferguson, Everett, Michael McHugh, Fred Norris, and David Scholer, eds. *Encyclopedia of Early Christianity.* New York: Garland Publishing, 1990. 983 pp.

1520. Smith, William, and Samuel Cheetham. *Dictionary of Christian Antiquities; Being a Continuation of the "Dictionary of the Bible."* 2 vols. Boston: Little, Brown and Co./London: John Murray, 1875-1880. Rept.: New York: Kraus Reprint, 1968.

Biographical Volumes

1521. Rausch, William G. *The Later Latin Fathers.* London: Duckworth, 1977. 209 pp.

1522. Smith, William, and Henry Wace. *A Dictionary of Christian Biography, Literature, Sects and Doctrines during the First Eight Centuries.* 4 vols. Boston: Little, Brown and Co./London: John Murray, 1877-1887. Rept.: New York: AMS Press, 1967/New York: Kraus Reprint, 1979.

Bibliographies

1523. Allenbach J., et al. *Biblic Patristica.* 4 vols. Paris: Editions du Centre National de la Recherche Scientifique, 1975-87. Supplement. 1982.

1524. Altaner, Berthold. *Patrologie.* Frieburg: Herder, 1978. English ed. as: *Patrology.* Trans. by Hilda C. Graef. 2nd ed.: New York: Herder and Herder, 1961.

1525. *Bibliographica Patristica Internationale Patristische Bibliographie.* Vol. 1- . Berlin: Walter de Gruyter for the Patristische Komision der Axademien der Wissenschaften in der Bundesrepublik Deutschland, 1959- . Annual.

1526. Cayré, F. *Manual of Patrology and History of Theology.* 2 vols. Paris: Society of St. John the Evangelist, 1935.

1527. Dekker, Eligius. *Clavis Patrum Latinorum, Qua in Novum Corpus Christianorum Edendum Optimas Quasque Scriptorum Recensiones a Tertulliano ad Bedam.* Steenburgis: In Abbatia Sancti Petri, 1961. 640 pp.

1528. Geerard, Maurice. *Clavis Patrum Graecorum.* 4 vols. Turnhout: Brepols, 1974-83.

1529. Krüger, Gustav. *History of Early Christian Literature in the First Three Centuries.* Trans. by Charles R. Gillett. New York: Burt Franklin, 1969. 407 pp. Originally published 1875.

1530. Metzger, Bruce. *Index of Articles on the New Testament and the Early Church Published in Festschriften.* Journal of Biblical Literature Monograph Series, Vol. 5.

Philadelphia: Society of Biblical Literature, 1951. *Supplementary Volume.* 1955. 20 pp.

1531. Quasten, Johannes. *Patrology.* 3 vols. Westminster, MD: Newman Press, 1950, 1953, 1960.

1532. Schreiber, John L. *Primitive Christian Traditions: Towards the Historical Structure of Primitive Christianity.* Evanston, IL: Garrett Theological Seminary Library, 1968.

1533. Steidle, Basilius. *Patrologia, seu Historia Antiquae Litteraturae Ecclesiaticae, Usui Scholarum.* Friburgi Brisgoviae: Herder, 1937. 249 pp.

1534. Stewardson, Jerry L. *A Bibliography of Bibliographies on Patristics.* Evanston, IL: Garrett Theological Seminary Library, 1967. 52 pp.

Atlases

1535. Van der Meer, Frederick, and Christine Mohrmann. *Atlas of the Early Christian World.* Trans. by Mary F. Hedlund and H. H. Rowley. New York: Thomas Nelson Company, 1958. 215 pp.

Professional Associations

International Association for Patristic Studies
(Association Internationale d'Etudes Patristiques)
via San Uffizio 25
I-00193 Roma, Italy

North American Patristics Society
c/o Dr. Charles Bobertz
Loyola College of Maryland
4501 N. Charles Street
Baltimore, MD 21210-2699

Resource Centers

American Institute for Patristic and Byzantine Studies
c/o Dr. Constantine N. Tsirpanlis
R. R. 1, Box 353-A, Minuet Lane
Kingston, NY 12401
The Institute sponsors an annual international symposium.

Center for the Study of Religion in the Greco Roman World
Department of Religious Studies
Southern Methodist University
Dallas, TX 75275
Supported by SMU and also affiliated with Dallas University, the Center focuses research on the period from Alexander the Great to Justinian I. It includes work on both ancient Paganism and early Christianity.

Institute for Antiquity and Christianity
Claremont Graduate School
831 N. Dartmouth Avenue
Claremont, CA 91711-6178
Known for its gnostic studies, the institute has a broad research program that centers on the origins of Western civilization in the Middle East.

Institute for the Study of Christian Origins
c/o European Evangelistic Society
2606 Wood Hill Lane
Atlanta, GA 30344

Institute of Christian Oriental Research
Catholic University of America
Mullen Library, Room 18
Washington, DC 20064
The Institute concentrates upon the scientific study of texts related to the history of the churches in the East. It co-sponsors a journal, *Corpus Scriptorium Christianorum Orientalium*, with the University of Louvain, Belgium.

International Center on Christian Origins
c/o Duke University
Durham, NC 27706

MEDIEVAL

The medieval period begins as the great Councils finish their work and as the Western Roman (Catholic) Church and the Eastern Greek (Orthodox) Church begin to show their differences and go their separate ways. The split was formalized in 1054. The period carries to the sixteenth century and the Reformation in the West at which time Protestantism and the Free Church Movement (best exemplified by the Mennonites)emerged. Protestants have long considered the medieval period the Dark Ages and have shown relatively little interest in its study. Hence the field tends to be dominated by Roman Catholic scholarship.

Encyclopedias and Dictionaries

1536. DuBoulay, Francis Robin Houssemayne, comp. *A Handlist of Medieval Ecclesiastical Terms.* Local History Series No. 9. London: National Council of Social Service for the Standing Conference on Local History, 1952.

Bibliographies

1537. Atiya, Aziz Suryal. *The Crusades: Historiography and Bibliography.* Bloomington, IN: Indiana University Press, 1962. 170 pp.

1538. Berkhout, Carl T., and Jeffrey B. Russell. *Medieval Heresies: A Bibliography 1960-1979.* Toronto: Pontifical Institute of Modern Studies, 1981. 201 pp.

1539. Boyle, Leonard E. *A Survey of the Vatican Archives and Its Medieval Holdings.* Subsidia Medievalia 1. Toronto: Pontifical Institute of Medieval Studies, 1972.

1540. Paetow, Louis John. *A Guide to the Study of Medieval History.* Rev. ed. New York: Crofts, 1931.

1541. Pontifical Institute of Medieval Studies Library. *Dictionary Catalogue of the Library of the Pontifical Institute of Medieval Studies.* 5 vols. Boston: G. K. Hall, 1972.

1542. van der Vekene, Emil. *Bibliotheca Bibliographica Historiae Sanctae Inquisitionis.* 2 vols. Vaduz: Topos Verlag, 1982-83.

1543. Walther, Daniel. "A Survey of Recent Research on the Albigensian Cathari." *Church History* 34, 2 (June 1965): 146-77.

Atlases

1544. Anderson, Charles S. *Augsburg Historical Atlas of Christianity in the Middle Ages and Reformation.* Minneapolis, MN: Augsburg Press, 1967. 61 pp.

Resource Centers

Center for Byzantine and Modern Greek Studies
Queens College of City University of New York
Jefferson Hall, Room 303
Flushing, NY 11376
Concentrates research on the history and culture of Greek people from the Byzantine era to the present. The Center publishes the semi-annual *Journal of Modern Hellenism.*

Center for Medieval and Early Renaissance Studies
State University of New York at Binghamton
Binghamton, NY 13901

Center for Medieval and Renaissance Studies
University of California, Los Angeles
212 Royce Hall
405 Hilgard Avenue
Los Angeles, CA 90024
The Center publishes two annual journals: *Viator: Medieval and Renaissance Studies* and *Comitatus.*

Medieval Institute
Western Michigan University
201 Hillside West
Kalamazoo, MI 49008
The Institute supports a significant medieval collection in the university library which includes a collection of Cistercian manuscripts. It publishes *Vox Mediaevalis* and two

monograph series and sponsors the annual International Conference on Medieval Studies. It maintains the CARA Register of North American Medievalists, now containing over 7,000 names.

Medieval Institute
University of Notre Dame
715 Memorial Library
Notre Dame, IN 46556
The Institute's broad research on medieval times includes a concentration on higher education in the Middle Ages. The institute publishes two monograph series in medieval studies, and supports a 60,000+ volume collection in the University's library.

Medieval Studies Institute
Indiana University
Ballantine Hall 642
Bloomington, IN 47401

Pontifical Institute of Mediaeval Studies
University of Toronto
113 St. Joseph Street
Toronto, ON M5S 1J4
The collection at the Institute includes the Etienne Gilson papers. Its broad publication program includes the annual *Mediaeval Studies*, two series of textual studies, and a series in honor of Etienne Gilson.

REFORMATION/PROTESTANTISM

The Reformation of the sixteenth century resulted in the formation of Protestantism, and Protestants have fostered the study of the period. Since most English speaking Christians are Protestants of one kind or another it is not surprising to find writings on the subject in great abundance. The English-speaking Reformation scholars are joined by an equally large number of Lutheran and Reformed scholars in Northern and Western Europe. In recent decades, Roman Catholic scholars of the Counter Reformation and Free Church scholars of the Radical Reformation have seen their insights integrated into the work on the period. Apart from Luther, Zwingli, and Calvin, one sixteenth century character, Thomas More, has also inspired a significant following as noted by the existence of several Thomas More societies.

This chapter contains materials most directly related to the Protestant Movement and the period of the Reformation. Related material can be found elsewhere in this volume especially in the chapters on Christianity in the British Isles and the Mennonites, although referencesappear in the chapters on the denominational families.

Encyclopedias and Dictionaries

1545. Ferm, Vergilius. *A Protestant Dictionary.* New York: Philosophical Library, 1951. 283 pp.

1546. Mönnich, C. W., ed. *Encyclopedie von het Protestantisme.* Amsterdam: Elsevier, 1959. 755 pp.

1547. Riddle, K. Williamson. *A Popular Dictionary of Protestantism.* London: Arco Publications, 1962. 208 pp.

1548. Wright, Charles H. H., and Charles Neil, eds. *A Protestant Dictionary: Containing Articles on the History, Doctrines, and Practices of the Christian Church.* London: Hodder & Stoughton, 1904. 832 pp. New ed.: London: The Harrison Trust, 1933. Rept. Detroit, MI: Gale Research Co., 1971.

Biographical Volumes

1549. Bietenholz, Peter G., and Thomas B. Deutscher, eds. *Contemporaries of Erasmus: A Biographical Register of the Renaissance and Reformation.* 3 vols. Toronto: University of Toronto Press, 1985.

1550. Boehmer, Edward. *Bibliotheca Wiffeniana: Spanish Reformers of Two Centuries from 1520: Their Lives and Writings, According to the Late Benjamin B., Wiffen's Plan and the Use of His Materials.* 3 vols. Strassburg & London: Trübner, 1874-1904. Rept. 3 vols. Burt Franklin Bibliographical and Reference Series No. 32. New York: Burt Franklin, [1971?].

1551. Haag, Eugène, and Émile Haag. *La France Protestante; ou Vies des Protestantes Français qui Se Sont Fait un Nom dans l'Histoire.* 10 vols. Paris: Cherbuliez, 1846-59.

Bibliographies

In addition to the items cited below, several periodicals provide annual bibliographical articles listing the recent published items in various Reformation topics. The *Archiv für Reformationsgeschichte* has a bibliography covering the whole field of Reformation studies. The *Lutherjahrbuch* has included a bibliography of Luther and Lutheran studies in each of its annual issues. The bibliography on the Radical Reformation is regularly updated in *Mennonite Life.* Works concerning the life and thought of two other main reformers, John Calvin (French-speaking Geneva) and Ulrich Zwingli (German-speaking Zurich), are listed in the *Calvin Theological Journal* and *Zwingliana.*

1552. Allison, A. F., and D. M. Rogers. *The Contemporary Printed Literature of the English Counter-Reformation between 1558 and 1640.* Vol. 1. Hant, England: Scolar Press, 1989. 291 pp.

1553. Bächtold, Ans U., George Bührer, and Matthias Senn. "Literatur zur schweizerischen Reformantionsgeschichte." *Zwingliana* Part 1. 16, 1 (1983): 54-66. Part 2. 16, 4 (1984): 97-105.

1554. Bainton, Roland H., and Eric W. Gritsch. *Bibliography of the Continental Reformation: Materials Available in English.* N.p.: American Society of Church History, 1935. Rev. ed.: Hamden, CT: Archon Books, 1972. 220 pp.

1555. Baker, Derek, ed. *The Bibliography of the Reform 1450-1648 Relative to the United Kingdom and Ireland for the Years 1955-1970.* Oxford: Basil Blackwell, 1975. 242 pp.

1556. Bigane, Jack, and Kenneth Hagen. *Annotated Bibliography of Luther Studies, 1967-1976.* Sixteenth Century Bibliography No. 9. St. Louis, MO: Center for Reformation Research, 1977.

1557. Center for Reformation Research. *The Center for Reformation Research Microfilm Holdings from All Periods: A General Finding List.* 8 vols. Sixteenth Century Bibliography Nos. 12-19. St. Louis, MO: Center for Reformation Research, 1977-1979.

1558. ———. *Early Sixteenth Century Roman Catholic Theologians and the German Reformation: A Finding List of CRR Holdings.* Sixteenth Century Bibliography No. 2. St. Louis, MO: Center for Reformation Research, 1975. 55 pp.

1559. ———. *Evangelical Theologians of Württemburg in the Sixteenth Century: A Finding List of CRR Holdings.* Sixteenth Century Bibliography No. 3. St. Louis, MO: Center for Reformation Research, 1975.

1560. ———. *Gnesio-Lutherans, Philippists and Formulators: A Finding List of CRR Holdings.* Sixteenth Century Bibliography No. 8. St. Louis, MO: Center for Reformation Research, 1977.

1561. Daniel, David P. *The Historiography of the Reformation in Slovakia.* Sixteenth Century Bibliography No. 10. St. Louis, MO: Center for Reformation Research, 1977.

1562. Dillenberger, John. "Survey, Literature in Luther Studies, 1950-1955." *Church History* 25, 2 (June 1956): 160-77.

1563. Dowey, Edward A., Jr. "Survey, Continental Reformation: Works of General Interest, Studies in Calvinism Since 1948." *Church History* 24, 4 (December 1955): 360-67.

1564. Edmond, John Philip, comp. *Catalogue of a Collection of Fifteen Hundred Tracts by Martin Luther and His Contemporaries, 1511-1598.* Bibliotheca Lindesiana Collations and Notes No. 7. [Aberdeen], 1903. Rept.: Burt Franklin Bibliographic and Reference Series No. 79. New York: Burt Franklin, [1965?].

1565. Eisenbichler, Konrad, et al., eds. *Bibles, Theological Treatises, and Other Religious Literature 1491-1700 at the Centre for Reformation and Renaissance Studies, Victoria University, Toronto.* Toronto: Centre for Reformation and Renaissance Studies, 1981. 94 pp.

1566. Green, Lowell C. *The Formula of Concord: An Historiographical and Bibliographical Guide.* Sixteenth Century Bibliography No. 11. St. Louis, MO: Center for Reformation Research, 1977.

1567. Grislis, Egil. "Selected Books in Print about Luther—in English and in German, 1983: an Annotated Review." *Consensus* 9 (October 1983): 21-30.

1568. Gruber, L. Franklin. "Documentary Sketch of the Reformation." *Lutheran Church Review.* Part 1. (July 1917): 399-420. Part 2. (October 1917): 541-565. Reprinted separately as a pamphlet.

1569. Hazlett, Ian. "A Working Bibliography of Writings of John Knox." In Robert V. Schnucker, ed. *Calviniana: Ideas and Influence of Jean Calvin.* Kirksville, MO: Sixteenth Century Journal Publishers, 1988. Pp. 185-193.

1570. Hinz, James A., comp. *A Handlist of the Printed Books in the Simmlerische Sammlung (Complete Imprints from Volumes 1-155): Manuscript Collection in the Microfilm Library of the Center for Reformation Research, the Original Located in the Zentralbibliothek in Zürich.* Rev. ed. 2 vols. Sixteenth Century Bibliography Nos. 6-7. St. Louis, MO: Center for Reformation Research, 1976.

1571. Horst, Irvin B. "The Early Reformation in the Netherlands in Recent Historical Writing: a Bibliographical Survey." In Irvin B. Horst. *The Dutch Dissenters.* Leiden: E. J. Brill, 1986. Pp. 207-430.

1572. Huber, Raphael M. "Recent Important Literature Regarding the Catholic Church During the Late Renaissance Period, 1500-1648." *Church History* 10, 1 (March 1941): 3-37.

1573. International Commission of Historical Sciences. *Bibliographie de la Réforme 1450-1648.* Vol. 1- . Leiden: E. J. Brill, 1958- .

1574. Kieffer, George Linn. *List of References on the Reformation in Germany.* Ed. by William Walker Rockwell and Otto Hermann Pannkoke. New York: n.p., 1917.

1575. Kinder, A. Gordon. *Spanish Protestants and Reformers in the Sixteenth Century: A Bibliography.* London: Grant & Cutler, 1983. 108 pp.

1576. McNeill, John T. "Thirty Years of Calvin Study." *Church History* 17, 3 (September 1948): 207-40.

1577. O'Malley, John. *Catholicism in Early Modern Europe: A Guide to Research.* St. Louis, MO: Center for Reformation Research, 1988. 342 pp.

1578. Ozment, Steven E., ed. *Reformation Europe: a Guide to Research.* St. Louis, MO: Center for Reformation Research, 1982. 390 pp.

1579. Pauck, Wilhelm. "The Historiography of the German Reformation during the Past Twenty Years." *Church History* 9, 4 (December 1940): 305-40.

1580. Pegg, Michael A. *A Catalogue of German Reformation Pamphlets (1516-1550) in Swiss Libraries.* Baden-Baden: Valentine Koerner, 1983. 467 pp.

1581. Reu, Johann Michael. *Thirty-five Years of Luther Research.* Chicago: Wartburg Publishing House, 1917. 155 pp. Rept.: New York: AMS Press, [1970]. 155 pp.

1582. Thompson, Bard. "Bucer Study Since 1918." *Church History* 25, 1 (March 1956): 62-82.

1583. ————. "Zwingli Study Since 1918." *Church History* 19, 2 (June 1950): 116-28.

Professional Associations

Reformation Translation Fellowship
1318 Sixth Street
Beaver Falls, PA 15010

Sixteenth Century Studies Council
LB115
Northeast State University
Kirksville, MO 63501
The Council publishes the quarterly, *The Sixteenth Century Journal.*

Society for Reformation Research
c/o Prof. Dr. Gottfried G. Krodel
Valparaiso University
Valparaiso, IN 46383
The Society co-sponsors the annual journal *Archive for Reformation History* with the Swiss-based Verein für Reformationsgeschichte.

Verein für Reformationsgeschichte
c/o Prof. Dr. Han R. Guggisberg
Bruderholzalle 20
CH-4059 Basel, Switzerland
The Verein co-sponsors the annual journal *Archiv für Reformationsgeschichte* with the American-based Society for Reformation Research.

Resource Centers

Caven Library
Knox College
University of Toronto
59 St. George Street
Toronto, ON M5S 2E6
The Library houses a special John Calvin Collection.

Center for Reformation and Renaissance Studies
Victoria University
University of Toronto
71 Queen's Park Crescent
Toronto, ON M5S 1K7

Center for Reformation Research
6477 San Bonita Avenue
St. Louis, MO 63105
(314) 727-6655
The independent Institute publishes a number of resource items for Reformation scholars, many of which are listed above.

John M. Kelly Library
St. Michael's College
University of Toronto
113 St. Joseph Street
Toronto, ON M5S 1J4
The Library houses a special Counter Reformation collection.

Montgomery Library
Westminister Theological Seminary
Chestnut Hill
Philadelphia, PA 19118
The Library houses a special collection on Reformed theology.

Reformation Study Center
2011 Fallen Leaf Road
Los Altos, CA 94022

Thomas More Studies

Amici Thomae Mori
Sezione Italiana
17 Via Patano
20122 Milano, Italy

International Association Amici Thomae Mori
29 Rue Volney, BP808
49005 Angers Cedex, France
or
CRS, 114 Mount Street
London W1Y GA11, UK
or
c/o Brother Michael Grace, .J.
Loyola University
6525 N. Sheridan Road
Chicago, IL 60626
The Society publishes the quarterly *Moreana.*

Japan Thomas More Society
c/o Paul Akio Sawada
Tsukiba University
Sa Kuramura
305 Ibarak 300.31 Japan

Thomas More Society of America
Box 65175
Washington, DC 20035

Thomas Morus Gesellschaft
Hubertushöhe 9
Bensberg
5060 Bergisch-Gladbach, Germany

CHRISTIANITY IN MODERN EUROPE

Christianity in modern Europe has been dominated by the various state churches, but that domination has, since World War II, come under significant challenge by the Evangelical and Pentecostal churches. Religious diversity in Europe now rivals that of North America. Slowly, volumes are appearing which are tracking the new Christian pluralism in Europe. Especially helpful are the directories being produced by MARC (Missions Advanced Research & Communications) Europe. Reference should also be made to the directories of churches in Great Britain, cited below as items (1596-1599).

Directories

1584. Brierley, Peter, comp. *Dansk Kirkehandbog [Danish Christian Handbook].* Bromley, Kent, UK: Scandinavia and MARC Europe, 1989. 48 pp.

1585. ————. *Norske Håndbok for Kirke og Misjon [Norwegian Handbook for Churches and Missions].* Bromley, Kent, UK: Lunde Forlag and MARC Europe, 1990. 64 pp.

1586. ————. *Suomen Kristlliste Kirkot ja yhteisöt. Osa 1" Kirkot [Finnish Christian Handbook Part 1: Churches].* Bromley, Kent, UK: Keskusliitto and MARC Europe, 1988. 63 pp.

1587. *Gele Gids 1985. 2000 Evangelische Adressen.* Putten, Netherlands: Stichting Opwekking, 1985. 124 pp.

1588. Heino, Harri. *The Religious Communities in Finland.* Tampere: Findland: Research Institute of the Lutheran Church in Finland, 1984. 30 pp.

1589. Walters, Philip. *World Christianity: Eastern Europe.* Eastbourne, Sussex (UK): MARC, 1988.

Bibliographies

1590. Mojzes, Paul, comp. *Church and State in Postwar Eastern Europe*. Bibliographies and Indexes in Religious Studies No. 11. New York, etc.: Greenwood Press, 1987. 109 pp.

1591. Wilber, Earl Morse, comp. *A Bibliography of the Pioneers of the Socinian-Unitarian Movement in Modern Christianity in Italy, Switzerland, Germany and Holland.* Rome: Edizioni di Storia e Letteratura, 1950. 80 pp.

CHRISTIANITY IN THE BRITISH ISLES

Scholars in Great Britain, whose history had a direct bearing on the development of Christianity in North America and much of the world formerly a part of the colonial empire, have produced a host of helpful reference tools covering all phases of the life of the British church. The Church of England, of course, went through the Reformation, from which the Anglican tradition received its modern shaping. It competes for attention with the equally important Scottish Presbyterian churches. Throughout the twentieth century, Christianity has continued to splinter and currently only a minority of the population adhere to the Church of England and the older Reformation church bodies. Also, as has been occurring in the rest of the Western world through the twentieth century, the remnants of religious uniformity in the United Kingdom has been disturbed by the emergence of non-Christian religions in strength throughout the country. A fairly recent arrival on the scene, the *UK Christian Handbook* (1597), is beginning to reveal the great diversity that is now the hard fact of British religious life.

Encyclopedias and Dictionaries

1592. Maunder, W. F., ed. *Reviews of United Kingdom Statistical Sources.* Vol. 20, *Religion.* Oxford: Pergamon Press, 1987. 621 pp.

1593. Ollard, Sidney Leslie, Gordon Cross, and Maurice F. Bond, eds. *A Dictionary of English Church History.* London: A. R. Mowbray & Co., 1912. Rev. ed.: 1919. 3rd ed.: New York: Morehouse-Goreham/London: A.R. Mowbray and Co., 1948. 698 pp.

Biographical Volumes

1594. Pine, L. G., ed. *Who's Who in the Free Churches.* London: Shaw Publishing Co., 1951. 500 pp.

1595. Wordsworth, Christopher. *Ecclesiastical Biography; or, Lives of Eminent Men, Connected with the History of Religion in England.* 3rd ed. 1839. 4th ed. 4 vols. London: Francis & John Rivington, 1853.

Directories

1596. *The Body Book: A Directory of Christian Fellowships.* Bromley, Kent, UK: Team Spirit, MARC Europe, 1987. Rev. ed.: 1989. Rev. ed.: 1991. 108 pp.

1597. Brierley, Peter, ed. *UK Christian Handbook.* Vol. 1- . London: Evangelical Alliance and Bible Society/Bromley, Kent, UK: MARC Europe, 1964- . Annual.

1598. *The Master List.* Hockley, Essex, UK: Capstone Publishers, 1988. Rev. ed.: 1989. 3rd ed.: 1990. 173 pp. Updated annually.

1599. McNicol, John. *Free Church Directory.* Morden, Surrey, UK: Crown House Publications, 1968-69. 411 pp.

Bibliographies

1600. Abbott, Wilbur Cortez. *A Bibliography of Oliver Cromwell: A List of Printed Materials Relating to Oliver Cromwell, Together with a List of Portraits and Caricatures.* Cambridge, MA: Harvard University Press, 1929. 551 pp.

1601. Anstruther, Godfrey. *The Seminary Priests: A Dictionary of the Secular Clergy of England and Wales, 1558-1850.* Vol. 1- . Durham, England: Ushaw College/Ware, England: St. Edmund's College, [1969-].

1602. Booty, John E., ed. *The Godly Kingdom of Tudor England: Great Books of the English Reformation.* Wilton, CT: Morehouse-Barlow, c. 1981.

1603. Kenney, James Francis. *The Sources for the Early History of Ireland: An Introduction and Guide. Volume One: Ecclesiastical.* Records of Civilization: Sources and Studies No. 11. New York: Columbia University Press, 1929. Rept. as *The Sources for the Early History of Ireland: Ecclesiastical; An Introduction and Guide.* New York: Octagon Books, 1966.

1604. MacGregor, Malcolm B. *The Sources and Literature of Scottish Church History.* Glasgow: J. McCallum and Co./Philadelphia: University of Pennsylvania Library, 1934. Rept. Merrick, NY: Richmond Publishing Co., 1976. 260 pp.

1605. McHardy, A. K. *The Church in London 1375-1392.* London: London Record Society, 1977. 126 pp.

1606. Milward, Peter. *Religious Controversies of the Elizabethan Age: A Survey of Printed Sources.* Lincoln, NE: University of Nebraska Press, 1977. 202 pp.

1607. ———. *Religious Controversies of the Jacobean Age: A Survey of Printed Sources.* London: Scolar Press, 1978. 264 pp.

1608. Read, Conyers. *Bibliography of British History, Tudor Period, 1485-1603.* Oxford: Clerendon Press 1933. 467 pp.

1609. Sachse, William Lewis, comp. *Restoration England, 1660-1689.* Cambridge, England: Cambridge University Press for the Conference on British Studies, 1971. 115 pp.

1610. Williams, William Proctor. *A Descriptive Catalogue of Seventeenth Century English Religious Literature in the Kansas State University Library.* Manhattan, KS: Kansas State University Library, 1966. 26 pp.

CHRISTIANITY IN NORTH AMERICA

Christianity begins in North America with the arrival of Roman Catholic priests aboard the vessels of the first explorers. The first church seems to have been established by the short-lived French Reformed settlement on the St. John's River near present-day Jacksonville, Florida, in 1564. During colonial time Christianity came to dominate the land not still under the control of the Native Americans, who were gradually pushed aside through the nineteenth century. Today approximately 1000 different Christian denominations are active in North America. They range in size from the Roman Catholic Church with more than 50 million members to small denominations with only a few congregations. The most complete survey of all the denominations is found in Melton (1613). The great majority of North Americans identify themselves as Christians.

Encyclopedias and Dictionaries

1611. Hill, Samuel S., ed. *Encyclopedia of Religion in the South.* Macon, GA: Mercer University Press, 1984. 878 pp.

1612. Mead, Frank S., and Samuel S. Hill. *Handbook of Denominations in the United States.* 1951. 8th ed.: Nashville: Abingdon Press, 1985. 320 pp. Periodically updated.

1613. Melton, J. Gordon. *Encyclopedia of American Religions.* 3rd. ed.: Detroit, MI: Gale Research Company, 1989. 1100 pp.

1614. Reid, Daniel G., Robert D. Linder, Bruce L. Shelley, and Harry S. Stout, eds. *Dictionary of Christianity in America.* Downers Grove, IL: InterVarsity Press, 1990. 1305 pp.

1615. Schenck, Robert L. *Constitutions of American Denominations.* 3 vols. Buffalo, NY: William S. Hein Co., 1984.

Biographical Volumes

1616. Bowden, Henry Warner. *Dictionary of American Religious Biography.* Westport, CT: Greenwood Press, 1977. 572 pp.

1617. Melton, J. Gordon. *Religious Leaders of America.* Detroit, MI: Gale Research Company, 1991. 604 pp.

1618. Nygaard, Norman Eugene, and V. G. Miller, comps. *Who's Who in the Protestant Clergy.* Encino, CA: Nygaard Associates, 1957.

1619. Schwarz, Julius Caesar. *Who's Who in the Clergy.* New York: The Author, 1936. Rev. ed. as: *Religious Leaders of America.* New York: The Author, 1941.

1620. Sprague, William Buell. *Annals of the American Pulpit; or, Commemorative Notices of Distinguished American Clergymen of Various Denominations, from Early Settlement of the Country to the Close of the Year Eighteen Hundred and Fifty-Five.* 9 vols. New York: R. Carter and Brothers, 1857-1869. Rept.: 9 vols. New York: Arno Press, 1969.

Bibliographies

1621. Allison, William Henry. *Inventory of Unpublished Material for American Religious History in Protestant Church Archives and Other Repositories.* Washington, DC: Carnegie Institute of Washington, 1910. 254 pp.

1622. Burr, Nelson R. "Sources for the Study of American Church History in the Library of Congress." *Church History* 22, 3 (September 1953): 227-38.

1623. Carter, Paul A. "Recent Historiography of the Protestant Churches in America." *Church History* 37, 1 (March 1986): 95-107.

1624. Handy, Robert T. "Survey of Recent Literature: American Church History." *Church History* 27, 2 (June 1958): 161-65.

1625. Hogan, Brian F., and Margaret Sanche. "A Current Bibliography of Canadian Church History." In T. Crowley, et al. *The Canadian Catholic Historical Association: Study Sessions, 1984.* Gleuph, ON: Canadian Catholic Historical Association, 1984. Pp. 145-98.

1626. Jackson, Samuel Macauley. "A Bibliography of American Church History." In *American Church History.* Vol. 12. New York: The Christian Literature Company, 1894. Pp. 441-519.

1627. Lindquist, Emory Kempton. *The Protestant Church in Kansas: An Annotated Bibliography.* Wichita, KS: University of Wichita, 1956.

1628. *List of Yearbooks Issued by the Churches.* Washington, DC: Library of Congress, 1926.

1629. Mode, Peter George. *Source Book and Bibliographical Guide for American Church History.* Menasha, WI: George Banta Publishing Co., 1921. Rept.: Boston: J.S. Canner, 1964. 735 pp.

1630. "Recent Articles of Interest [in North American Church History]." *Journal of the Canadian Church Historical Society* 27 (October 1985): 121-25.

1631. Rouseau, Louis. "Religion in French America." Trans. by K. C. Russell. *Religious Studies Review* 10 (January 1984): 33-46.

1632. Rudolph, L. C., and Judith E. Endelman. *Religion in Indiana: A Guide to Historical Resources.* Bloomington, IN: Indiana University Press, 1986. 232 pp.

1633. Tomasi, Silvano M., and Edward C. Stibili. *Italian-Americans and Religion: An Annotated Bibliography.* New York: Center for Migration Studies, 1978. 222 pp.

1634. Wilson, John F., ed. *Church and State in America: A Bibliographical Guide.* 2 vols. New York: Greenwood Press, 1986-87.

Guides to Periodical Literature

1635. *Geo Batten & Co's Directory of the Religious Press of the United States, A List of Nearly All Religious Periodicals, with their Denomination or Class. . . .* New York: George Batten & Co., 1892, 1895, 1897.

1636. *Religious Press Directory.* New York: Joseph E. Wagner, Inc., 1943- .

1637. Richardson, Ernest Cushing, ed. *An Alphabetical Subject Index and Index Encyclopaedia to Periodical Articles on Religion, 1890-1899.* 2 vols. New York: C. Scribner for the Hartford Seminary Press, 1907, 1911.

1638. *Tobias Brothers' German Newspaper Directory . . . also a Separate List of Religious Newspapers.* 2 vols. New York: Tobias Bros., 1885, 1890.

Directories

1639. *Directory.* Associated Church Press. 1956-1757.

1640. *Directory: Chinese Churches, Bible Study Groups and Fellowships in North America.* Paradise, PA: Ambassadors for Christ, 1984-85. 178 pp.

1641. Melton, J. Gordon. *Religious Bodies in the United States: A Directory.* New York: Garland Publishing, 1991. 325 pp.

1642. *Win with Love: A Comprehensive Directory of the Liberated Church.* Berkeley, CA: Free Church Publications. No. 4. 1970. 63 pp. No. 5. 1971. 64 pp.

1643. *Yearbook of American and Canadian Churches.* Ed. 1- . Nashville, TN: Abingdon Press, 1916- . Annual. Variously titled *Federal Council Yearbook, Yearbook of the Churches, Handbook of the Churches,* and *Yearbook of American Churches.*

Statistical Materials

1644. Carroll, H. K. *The Religious Forces of the United States, Enumerated, Classified, and Described on the Basis of the Government Census of 1890.* New York: The Christian Literature Co., 1893. Revised, January 1, 1896, with Additional Tables of Statistics for the five years since the Census of 1890. 478 pp. Rev. ed.: 1912.

1645. ———. *Report on Statistics of Churches in the United States as the Eleventh Census: 1890.* Washington, DC: G. P. O.: Department of the Interior, Census Office, 1894. 812 pp.

1646. ———. *Statistics of the Churches of the United States for 1914.* Bulletin of Church Statistics, No. 68. New York: Federal Council of Churches of Christ in America, 1915.

1647. *Churches and Church Membership in the United States: An Enumeration and Analysis by Counties, States and Regions.* New York: Bureau of Research and Survey, National Council of Churches of Christ in the U.S.A., 1956-58. Unpaged.

1648. Johnson, Douglas W., Paul R. Picard and Bernard Quinn. *Churches & Church Membership in the United States: An Enumeration by Region, State and County.* Washington, DC: Glenmary Research Center, 1974. 237 pp.

1649. Linfield, Harry Sebee. *State Population Census by Faiths: Meaning Reliablity and Value.* New York: Hasid's Bibliographic and Library service, 1938. 71 pp.

1650. Schem, Alexander Jacob. *The American Ecclesiastical Yearbook*. . .. New York: n.p. 1960.

1651. "Statistics of the Churches." *The Independent* 51, 2614 (January 5, 1899): 19-67.

1652. United States Department of Commerce, Bureau of the Census. *Religious Bodies 1890.* Washington, DC: U. S. Goverment Printing Office, 1894. Rev. ed. as *Religious Bodies, 1906.* 2 vols. 1910. Rev. ed. as: *Religious Bodies: 1916.* 2 vols. 1919. Rev. ed. as: *Religious Bodies: 1926.* 2 vols. 1930. Rev. ed. as: *Religious Bodies: 1936.* 2 vols. 1941.

Atlases

1653. Gaustad, Edwin Scott. *Historical Atlas of Religion in America.* 1926. Rev. ed: New York: Harper & Row, 1976. 208 pp.

1654. Halvorson, Peter L. *Atlas of Religious Change in America.* Washington, DC: Glenmary Research Center, 1978. 95 pp.

Archival Depositories

The majority of the archival collections housing materials on North American religion are the archives of the various denominations and are discussed in the chapters under the individual family traditions. The following articles, however, give an overview of some of the more notable archive collections:

1655. Binfield, Edmund L. "Church Archives in the United States and Canada: A Bibliography." *American Archivist* 21, 3 (July 1958): 311-32.

1656. Kirkham, E. Kay. *A Survey of American Church Records for the Period Before the Civil War East of the Mississippi River.* 2 vols. Salt Lake City: Deseret Book Co., 1959, 1960. 3rd rev. ed.: Logan, UT: Everton Pubs., 1971. 4th rev. ed.: Logam, UT: Everton pubs., 1978. 344 pp.

1657. Sweet, William Warren. "Church Archives in the United States." *Church History* 8, 1 (March 1939): 43-53.

AFRO-AMERICAN RELIGION

Afro-American religion has been until recently a neglected part of American religious studies. However, in the post-Martin Luther King, Jr., era, black religious studies have flourished and helpful reference tools are beginning to appear. This area remains one of the most needful areas for further work.

General Resources

1658. Finkelman, Paul, ed. *Religion and Slavery.* Article on American Slavery vol. 16. New York: Garland Publishing, 1989. 670 pp.

1659. Schatz, Walter, ed. *Directory of Afro-American Resources.* New York: R. R. Bowker Company, 1970. 485 pp.

Encyclopedias and Dictionaries

1660. Adams, Revels A. *Cyclopedia of African Methodism in Mississippi.* Natchez, MS: The Author, 1902. 215 pp.

1661. Payne, Wardell J. ed. Directory of African-American Religious Bodies, a Compendium by the Howard University School of Divinity. Washington, DC: Howard University Press, 1991. 361 pp.

1662. Wright, Richard R., Jr. *Centennial Encyclopedia of the African Methodist Episcopal Church.* Vol. 1. Philadelphia: African Methodist Episcopal Church, 1916. Rev. ed. as: *The Encyclopedia of the African Methodist Episcopal Church.* Philadelphia, PA: Book Concern of the AME Church, 1947. 688 pp.

Biographical Volumes

1663. DuPree, Sherry Sherrod. *Biographical Dictionary of African-American Holiness-Pentecostals, 1880-1990.* Washington, DC: Middle Atlantic Regional Press, 1989. 386 pp.

1664. Scally, Sister Mary Anthony. *Negro Catholic Writers, 1900-1943: A Bio-Bibliography.* Detroit, MI: Walter Romig & Company, 1945. 152 pp.

1665. Williams, Ethel L. *Biographical Directory of Negro Ministers.* New York: Scarecrow Press, 1965. 421 pp. Rev. ed. 1970. 605 pp. Rev. ed. Boston: G.K. Hall & Co., 1975. 584 pp.

Bibliographies

1666. Baer, Hans A. "Bibliography on Social Science Literature on Afro-American Religions in the United States." *Review of Religious Research* 39 (1988): 413-30.

1667. Baldwin, Lewis V. *Resources for the Study of Afro-American Religious History: A Guide to Selected North Shore Libraries.* Evanston, IL: The Institute for Black Religious Research, Garrett-Evangelical Seminary Library, 1980. 72 pp.

1668. *Black Methodism: An Introductory Guide to the Literature.* Madison, NJ: General Commission on Archives and History, The United Methodist Church, 1984. 45 pp.

1669. Callender, Jean A. *African Survivals in Caribbean Religion: A Select Bibliography.* Cave Hill, Barbados: University of the West Indies, 1986. 91 pp.

1670. Evans, James H. *Black Theology: A Critical Assessment and Annotated Bibliography.* New York: Greenwood Press, 1987. 205 pp.

1671. Fisher, William Harvey. *Free At Last: A Bibliography of Martin Luther King, Jr.* Metuchen, NJ: Scarecrow Press, 1977.

1672. Gillespie, Bonnie J. "The Black Church and the Black Elderly." *Journal of Religious Studies* 10, 2 (Fall 1983): 19-31.

1673. Harrison, Ira E. *A Selected, Annotated Bibliography on Store-Front Churches and Other Religious Writings.* Syracuse, NY: Syracuse University Youth Development Center, 1962. 29 pp.

1674. Jackson, Giovanna R. *Afro-American Religion and Church and Race Relations.* Bloomington, IN: Indiana University Libraries/Focus: Black America, 1969. 18 pp.

1675. ———. *Black Nationalism.* Bloomington, IN: Indiana University Libraries and Focus: Black America, 1969. 19 pp.

1676. Jackson, Irene V., comp. *Afro-American Religious Music: A Bibliography and a Catalogue of Gospel Music.* Westport, CT: Greenwood Press, 1979.

1677. Jones, Charles Edwin, ed. *Black Holiness.* ATLA Bibliography Series No. 18. Metuchen, NJ: Scarecrow Press, 1987. 422 pp.

1678. Leffall, Dolores C., comp. *The Black Church: An Annotated Bibliography.* Washington, DC: Minority Research Center, [1973].

1679. Melton, J. Gordon. *A Bibliography of Black Methodism.* Evanston, IL: Institute for the Study of American Religion, 1969. 45 pp.

1680. *A Preliminary Guide to Black Materials in the Disciples of Christ Historical Society.* Nashville, TN: Disciples of Christ Historical Society, 1971. 32 pp.

1681. U.S. National Archives and Records Service. *Black Studies: Select Catalog of National Archives and Records Service Microfilm Publications.* Washington, DC: National Archives, 1973.

1682. Williams, Ethel L., and Clifton L. Brown, comps. *Afro-American Religious Studies: A Comprehensive Bibliography with Locations in American Libraries.* Metuchen, NJ: Scarecrow Press, 1972. Rev. ed. as: *The Howard University Bibliography of African and Afro-American Religious Studies: With Locations in American Libraries.* 2nd ed. Wilmington, DE: Scholarly Resources, 1977.

Statistical Materials

1683. Shuster, George, and Robert M. Kearns. *Statistical Profile of Black Catholics.* Washington, DC: Josephite Pastoral Center, 1976. 42 pp.

Black Religious Studies

Afro-American studies flowered in the 1980s and numerous collections were established at libraries across the United States. Among the ones in which religious materials are strongly represented are:

African American Worship Traditions Research Project
Interdenominational Theological Center
671 Beckwith Street, SW
Atlanta, GA 30314
Founded in 1984, the Project explores Afro-American worship from a broad interdisciplinary context.

Black Religious Collection Development Project
Schomberg Center for Research in Black Culture
c/o New York Public Library
515 Malcolm X Blvd.
New York, NY 10037-1801
A major center for the collection of Afro-American materials, the Schomberg also has a significant religious collection.

Black Religious Studies Network
c/o Rev. James T. Roberson, Jr.
3045 Douglas Drive
Yorktown Heights, NY 10598
BRSNET is a computer conferencing network established in 1989.

Black Women in Church and Society
Research/Resource Center
Interdenominational Theological Center
671 Beckwith Street, S.W.
Atlanta, GA 30314
With the cooperation of many of the larger predominantly black Baptist and Methodist denominations, and the United Methodist Church, ITC has become the most important school for black religious studies. While possessing an excellent collection in black studies, it is also unique for its focus on black women.

Black Women in the Church, 1780-1970
Center for African American History and Culture
Temple University
Weiss Hall, Suite B18
Philadelphia, PA 19122
The Center initiated the project on Black church women in 1990.

Charles L. Blockson Afro-American Historical Collection
Temple University
Sullivan Hall, 1st Floor
Philadelphia, PA 19122
The Collection includes Afro-American religious materials, including the papers of AME bishop R. R. Wright, Jr.

R. C. Ransom Memorial Library
Payne Theological Seminary
P. O. Box 474
Wilberforce, OH 45384
Payne is the primary seminary of the African Methodist Episcopal Church and its library has a collection of AME materials. It is supplemented by the collection at the **Rembert Stokes Learning Center** of Wilberforce and the nearby **National Afro-American Museum and Cultural Center**, an independent corporation affiliated with the Ohio Historical Society, also located in Wilberforce.

Research Center on Black Religious Bodies
Howard University School of Divinity
1400 Shepherd Street, NE
Washington, DC 20017
The Center was established in 1985 to produce a research tool, the *Directory of African American Religious Bodies* (1661).

School of Divinity Library
Howard University
500 Howard Place, N.W.
Washington, DC 20059
The special collection on Afro-American religion at the Divinity School Library is supplemented by the large Black history collection at the **Moorland-Spingarn Research Center** also on the Howard campus.

Society for the Study of Black Religion
c/o Howard University School of Divinity
1400 Shepherd Street, NE
Washington, DC 20017
The Society was founded in 1971 by black religious scholars associated with the American Academy of Religion.

W. J. Walls Heritage Hall Archives
Library
Hood Theological Seminary/Livingston College
W. J. Walls Center
100 W. Thomas Street

Salisbury, NC 28144
W. J. Walls had a lengthy and outstanding career as a bishop of the African Methodist Episcopal Zion Church. Following his retirement he became the church historiographer and authored its standard history. The AMEZ Church's archive is located in the **Walls Center** on the campus of the church's seminary/college.

Much of the work on black religious history is being done at centers in the context of more general black studies. For example, those interested in black religious music might make reference to the **Black Music Archives**, 711 Stoney Springs Drive, Baltimore, MD 21210; the **Center for Black Music Research**, Columbia College, 600 South Michigan Avenue, Chicago, IL 60605; and the **Afro-American Arts Institute**, Indiana University, 109 North Jordan Avenue, Bloomington, IN 47405.

CHRISTIANITY IN AFRICA, ASIA, LATIN AMERICA, THE MIDDLE EAST, AND OCEANIA

The nineteenth century was the period of the greatest expansion of Christianity around the world. Both Roman Catholics and Protestants supported a vast missionary program. Much of that program has now disintegrated due to its own success. Missionary churches created in the last century now exist as autonomous Christian churches. In addition the mission programs spawned, as an unexpected and largely unwanted side effect, a host of new independent indigenous churches. The force of these new churches was first recognized in Africa, where literally hundreds of new independent denominations have arisen. Adding to the mix in the non-Western world are the new missionary programs developed by twentieth century Pentecostalism and Evangelicalism, which have created a new wave of missionary endeavor and a host of new denominations.

Few reference tools have yet to be produced which give broad coverage to the distinct waves of Christian emergence outside of Europe and North America. Barrett's *World Christian Encyclopedia*, cited earlier (787), stands as a notable exception. Also, it should be noted, that with the dismantling of the older missionary programs, several of the larger missionary libraries fell into disuse and have not continued to collect current material on missionary Christianity outside of North America and Europe.

The Christian World Mission

Encyclopedias and Dictionaries

1684. Dwight, Henry Otis, et al., eds. *The Encyclopedia of Missions: Descriptive, Historical, Biographical, Statistical.* 2nd ed. New York: Funk and Wagnalls Co., 1904. Rept.: Detroit, MI: Gale Research Co., 1975.

1685. Goddard, Burton L., ed. *The Encyclopedia of Modern Christian Missions; the Agencies.* Camden, NJ: Thomas Nelson and Sons, 1967. 743 pp.

1686. Jackson, Herbert C., ed. *Judaism, Jewish-Christian Relations and the Christian Mission to the Jews: A Selected Bibliography.* New York: Missionary Research Library, [1966]. *See*: (1880) below.

1687. Neill, Stephen Charles, et al., eds. *Concise Dictionary of the Christian World Mission.* Nashville, TN: Abingdon Press; London: United Society for Christian Literature, Lutterworth Press, 1971.

1688. Roberts, W. Dayton, and John A. Stewert. *Mission Handbook.* Grand Rapids, MI: Zondervan Publishing House/Monrovia, CA: MARC, 1989. 481 pp.

Directories

1689. *Directory of Christian Councils.* 1971. Rev. ed.: Geneva: World Council of Churches, 1985. 244 pp. Periodically updated.

1690. *The Great Commission Handbook.* Evanston, IL: SMS Publications. Revised annually. A directory of study for Christian students and missionary work for young adults.

1691. *Mission Handbook.* Monrovia, CA: MARC (Missions Advanced Research & Communications), updated periodically. A directory of missionary agencies based in North America.

1692. Pate, Larry D. *From Every People: A Handbook of Two-Thirds World Missions with Directory/Histories/Analysis.* Monrovia, CA: MARC (Missions Advanced Research & Communications), 1989. 310 pp. A directory of missionary agencies based in Asia, Africa, the Middle East, Latin America, and Oceania.

1693. *Stepping Out: A Guide to Short-Term Missions.* Monrovia, CA: Short-term Missions Advocates, 1987. 144 pp.

1694. Van der Bent, Ans J. *Handbook: Member Churches, World Council of Churches.* Geneva: Switzerland: World Council of Churches, 1982. 281 pp. Rev. ed.: 1985. 289 pp.

Bibliographies

1695. Amistad Research Center. *Author and Added Entry Catalog of the American Missionary Association Archives, with References to Schools and Mission Stations.* 3 vols. Westport, CT: Greenwood Publishing Corporation, 1970.

1696. Anderson, Gerald H., comp. *Bibliography of the Theology of Missions in the Twentieth Century.* 3rd ed. New York: Missionary Research Library, 1966. 119 pp.

1697. *Bibliografia Missionaria.* Vol. 1- . Roma: Pontificia Universitaria di Propaganda Fide, 1935- . Annual.

1698. *Evangelization and Mission: International Bibliography 1975-1982.* RIC Supplements 74-77. Strasbourg, France: Cerdic-Publications, 1982. 312 pp.

1699. Facelina, Raymond. *Evangelization and Mission: International Bibliography 1972 Indexed by Computer.* RIC Supplement 5. Strasbourg, France: Cerdic-Publications, 1973. 36 pp.

1700. ——— and Gérard Pigault. *Evangelization and Mission: International Bibliography 1973-June 1974 Indexed by Computer.* RIC Supplement 15. Strasbourg, France: Cerdic-Publications, 1974. 55 pp.

1701. Hartley, R.W., comp. and ed. *Bibliography on the History and Theology of Missions from the Collection in Leigh College Library, Enfield, N.S.W., Australia.* Leigh College Library Bulletin No. 15. Enfield, New South Wales: Leigh College Library, 1969.

1702. Hering, Hollis W., comp. *Recommended Titles on Missions and Related Subjects.* New York: Committee of Reference and Counsel, [Protestant Foreign Missions Conference of North America], 1925. 29 pp.

1703. Missionary Research Library. *Dictionary Catalog of the Missionary Research Library (New York).* 17 vols. Boston: G.K. Hall and Co., 1967.

1704. ———. *Missionary Biography: An Initial Bibliography.* New York: Missionary Research Library, 1965.

1705. ———. *Selected List of Books and Pamphlets Added to the Collection.* No. 1- . New York: Missionary Research Library, 19- . Irregular.

1706. Person, Laura. *Cumulative List of Doctoral Dissertations and Masters Theses in Foreign Missions and Related Subjects As Reported by the Missionary Research*

Library in the "Occasional Bulletin", 1950-1960. New York: Missionary Research Library, 1961. 36 pp.

1707. Smalley, William Allen. *Selected and Annotated Bibliography of Anthropology for Missionaries.* Rev. ed. Occasional Bulletin of the Missionary Research Library, Vol. 11, No. 1. New York: Missionary Research Library, 1962.

1708. Streit, Robert. *Bibliotheca Missionum.* 30 vols. Freiburg: Herder, 1916-74.

1709. Vriens, Livinius, et al. *Critical Bibliography of Missiology.* Trans. by Deodatus Tummers. Bibliographia ad Usum Seminariorum Vol. 2. Nijmegen: Bestelcentrale der V.S.K.B., 1960.

Guides to Periodical Literature

1710. Byrnes, Paul A., comp. *Current Periodicals in the Missionary Research Library: A Subject List.* New York: Missionary Research Library, 1972.

1711. Ma, John T., comp. *Current Periodicals in the Missionary Research Library, Alphabetical List and Index.* 2nd ed. New York: Missionary Research Library, 1961.

Atlases

1712. Despont, J. *Nouvel Atlas des Missions.* Paris: L'Oeuvre de al Propagation de la Foi, 1951. 59 pp.

Missiology

American Society of Missiology
c/o George R. Hunsberger
Western Theological Seminary
86 E. 12th Street
Holland, MI 49423

Association of Evangelical Professors of Missions
c/o Kenneth B. Mulholland
Columbia Biblical Seminary and Graduate School of Missions
P. O. Box 3122
Columbia, SC 29230

Association of Professors of Missions
c/o Dr. Charles Van Eglen
Fuller Theological Seminary

School of World Missions
Pasadena, CA 91182

International Association for Mission Studies
(Internationale Vereinigung für Missionswissenschaft)
Mittelweg 143
D-2000 Hamburg 13, Germany

Africa

General Sources

1713. Froise, Marjorie, ed. *World Christianity: Southern Africa: A Factual Portrait of the Christian Church in South Africa, Botswana, Lesotho, Namibia, and Swaziland.* Monrovia, CA: Missions Advanced Research and Communications, 1989. 127 pp.

Directories

1714. Eilers, Franz-Josef et al., eds. *Christian Communication Directory Africa.* Communicatio Socialis: Zeitschrift für Publizistik in Kirche und Welt, Beihaft 8. Paderborn: Ferdinand Schöningh for the Catholic Media Council et al., 1980. 544 pp.

Bibliographies

1715. Brownlee, Margaret. *The Lives and Work of South African Missionaries: Bibliography.* N.p.: University of Cape Town Libraries, 1969. 32 pp.

1716. Center for Research Libraries. *Church Missionary Society Archives Relating to Africa and Palestine, 1799-1923: Index to Records on Microfilm at the Center for Research Libraries.* Chicago: Center for Research Libraries, 1968.

1717. Hexham, Irving. "Religion in Southern Africa." *Religious Studies Review* 11, 4 (October 1985): 370-79.

1718. Ofori, Patrick E. *Christianity in Tropical Africa: A Select Annotated Bibliography.* New York: KTO Press, 1977. 461 pp.

1719. Turnbull, C. E. P., comp. *The Work of Missionaries of Die Nederduits Gereformeerde Kerk van Suid-Afrika: An Annotated Bibliography of Materials in the Johannesburg Public and University of Witwatersrand Libraries.* Johannesburg: University of Witwatersrand Dept. of Bibliography, Librarianship and Typography, 1965. 85 pp.

Asia

Directories

1720. Ebisawa, Arimichi, comp. *Christianity in Japan. Part I: 1543-1858.* Tokyo: Committee on Asian Cultural Studies, International Christian University, 1960. 171 pp.

1721. Law, Gail. *Chinese Churches Handbook.* Hong Kong: Chinese Coordination Centre for World Evangelism, 1982. 372 pp.

Bibliographies

1722. Anderson, Gerald H. *Christianity in Southeast Asia: A Bibliographical Guide; An Annotated Bibliography of Selected References in Western Languages.* New York: Missionary Research Library/New Haven, CT: Yale University, Southeast Asian Studies, 1966. 69 pp.

1723. Chao, Johnathan T'ien-en. *A Bibliography of the History of Christianity in China (Preliminary Draft).* CGST Research Project No. 3. Waltham, MA: Faculty-in-Preparation, China Graduate School of Theology, 1970.

1724. Chu, Clayton H. *American Missionaries in China: Books, Articles and Pamphlets Extracted from the Subject Catalog of the Missionary Research Library.* 3 vols. Research Aids for American Far Eastern Policy Studies No. 2. Cambridge, MA: Harvard University Press, 1960.

1725. Crouch, Archie R., et al. *Christianity in China: A Scholar's Guide to Resources in the Libraries and Archives of the United States.* Armonk, NY & London: M.E. Sharpe, 1989. 709 pp.

1726. Ikado, Fujio, and James R. McGovern, comps. *A Bibliography of Christianity in Japan: Protestantism in English Sources (1859-1959).* Tokyo: Committee on Asian Cultural Studies, International Christian University, 1966. 125 pp.

1727. Laurès, John. *Kirishtan Bunko: A Manual of Books and Documents on the Early Christian Mission in Japan; with Special Reference to the Principal Libraries in Japan and More Particularly to the Collection at Sophia University, Tokyo.* 3rd ed. Monumenta Nipponica Monographs No. 5. Tokyo: Sophia University, 1957. 536 pp.

1728. Lee, Helen F. MacRae Parker, comp. *A Bibliography of Korean Relations with Canadians and Other Western Peoples Which Includes a Checklist of Documents and Reports.* Ed. by Doreen E. Fraser. Occasional Paper No. 12. Halifax, NS: School of Library Services, Dalhousie University, 1976. 201 pp.

1729. Marchant, Leslie R. *A Guide to the Archives and Records of Protestant Christian Missions from the British Isles to China 1796-1914.* Nedlands, Western Australia: University of Western Australia Press, 1966. 134 pp.

1730. Price, Francis Wilson. *Selected Bibliography of Books, Pamphlets and Articles on Communist China and the Christian Church in China.* Occasional Bulletin, Vol. 9, No. 8. New York: Missionary Research Library, 1958.

1731. Ronda, James P., and James Axtell. *Indian Missions: A Critical Bibliography.* Bloomington, IN: Indiana University Press for the Newberry Library, 1978.

1732. Yanagita, Tomonobu. *Japan Christian Literature Review: A Comprehensive Subject Listing of Protestant and Catholic Books with over 600 Analytical Reviews.* [Sendai: Seisho Tosho Kankokai, c. 1958].

1733. Yung-Hsiang Lai, John. *Catalog of Protestant Missionary Works in Chinese.* Harvard-Yenching Library. Harvard University. Boston: G. K. Hall, 1980. 339 pp.

Research/Resource Centers

Christian Study Centre for Chinese Religions and Culture
c/o Dr. Peter Lee
6.F Kiu Kin Mission
No. 566 Nathan Road
Kowloon, Hong Kong

Latin America

General Sources

1734. Bessil-Watson, Lisa, comp. *Handbook of the Churches of the Caribbean.* Bridgetown, Barbados: The Cedar Press, 1982. 134 pp.

1735. Borremans, Valentine, with Ivan Illich. *The History of Religiosity in Latin America, ca 1830-1970.* 3 vols. Zug, Switzerland: Inter Documentation Company, n.d. Catalog/index of a collection on microfiche of primary documents on the life of the Roman Catholic Church in Latin America.

Bibliographies

1736. Dahlin, Therrin C., Garry P. Gillum, and Mark L. Grover. *The Catholic Left in Latin America: A Comprehensive Bibliography.* Boston: G. K. Hall, 1981. 410 pp.

1737. Ibarra, Eduardo. *Christianity in Latin America: International Bibliography 1973-1974, Indexed by Computer.* RIC Supplement 22. Strasbourg, France: Cerdic-Publications, 1977. 80 pp.

1738. Sinclair, John H. *Protestantism in Latin America: A Bibliographical Guide.* Austin, TX: The Hispanic American Institute, 1967. 213 pp.

Middle East

General Sources

1739. Horner, Norman A. *A Guide to Christian Churches in the Middle East.* Elkart, IN: Mission Focus, 1989.

Oceania

General Sources

1740. Douglas, Leonora Misende, ed. *World Christianity: Oceania.* Monrovia, CA: Missions Advanced Research and Communications, 1986. 338 pp.

1741. Forman, Charles W. *The Island Churches of the South Pacific: Emergence in the Twentieth Century.* Maryknoll, NY: Orbis Books, 1982. 285 pp.

1742. Guillermo, Merlyn L., and L. P. Verona. *Protestant Churches and Missions in the Philippines.* Manila: World Vision Philippines, [1982]. 374 pp.

1743. Hynd, Douglas. *Australian Christianity in Outline: A Statistical Survey and Directory.* Australia: Lancer Books, 1984.

1744. Von Oeyen, Robert R. *Philippine Evangelical Protestant and Independent Catholic Churches: An Historical Bibliography of Church Records, Publications and Source Material Located in the Greater Manila Area.* Asian Center Bibliography Series No. 1. Quezon City: University of the Philippines, Asian Center, 1970.

VII

CHRISTIAN DEMONINATIONAL FAMILY TRADITIONS

ADVENTISM

The Adventist Movement grew out of the preaching of William Miller (1782-1849), a Baptist preacher who believed that the second coming of Jesus would be in 1843. As a result of the disappointment when Christ failed to return at the appointed hour, and then again the following year, the movement began to splinter into a number of fragments, each with its own interpretation of what had occurred. In the decades to come other issues would divide them, the most important being the keeping of the Sabbath, a practice absorbed from the Seventh Day Baptists. The largest groups which can be traced to the original Millerite impulse are the Seventh-day Adventist Church, the Worldwide Church of God, and the Jehovah's Witnesses.

General Sources

1745. Land, Gary, ed. *Adventism in America.* Grand Rapids, MI: William B. Eerdmans Publishing Company, 1986. 301 pp.

1746. Utt, Richard H. *Your Adventist Neighbors.* Mountain View, CA: Pacific Press Publishing Association, 1978. 64 pp.

Encyclopedias and Dictionaries

1747. Neufeld, Don F., ed. *Seventh-Day Adventist Encyclopedia.* Vol. 10 of Commentary Reference Series. Washington, DC: Review & Herald Publishing Association, 1966. 1452 pp.

Bibliographies

1748. Bergman, Jerry. *Jehovah's Witnesses and Kindred Groups: A Historical Compendium and Bibliography.* Sects & Cults in America Series Vol. 4. New York: Garland Publishing, 1984. 370 pp.

1749. Bjorling, Joel. *The Churches of God, Seventh Day: A Bibliography.* Sects & Cults in America Series Vol. 8. New York: Garland Publishing, 1987. 320 pp.

1750. Patrick, Arthur N. "Seventh-day Adventist History in the South Pacific: A Review of Sources." *The Journal of Religious History* 14, 3 (June 198-): 307-26

1751. Shearer, Gary. *The Advent Christian Church: A Selected Guide to Materials in the Heritage Rooms of the Loma Linda University Libraries.* The Author, 1983. 5 pp.

1752. ———. *Church of God (Abrahamic Faith): A Guide to Materials in the Heritage Rooms of the Loma Linda University Libraries.* The Author, 1983. 2 pp.

1753. ———. *Church of God (Seventh-day): A Guide to Materials in the Heritage Room of the Loma Linda University Libraries.* The Author, 1983. 3 pp.

1754. ———. *The Dark Day of 19 May 1790: A Bibliographical Guide to Materials in the La Sierra Campus Library, Loma Linda University.* The Author, 1983. 2 pp.

1755. ———. *Ellen G. White, Her Life and Teachings and the Gift of Prophecy in the Seventh-day Adventist Church.* Angwin, CA: Ellen G. White/Seventh-day Adventist Heritage Collection, Pacific Union College, 1985.

Part I. *A Bibliographical Guide to Books about Ellen G. White.* 8 pp.

Part II. *A Bibliographical Guide to Theses and Dissertations about Ellen G. White.* 4 pp.

Part III. *A Bibliographical Guide to Periodical Articles about Ellen G. White.* 40 pp.

1756. ———. *The History of the Seventh-day Adventist Church: A Bibliographical Guide to Materials in the La Sierra Campus Library, Loma Linda University.* The Author, 1979. 35 pp.

1757. ———. *The Millerite Movement: A Guide to Materials in the Loma Linda University Library.* The Author, 1979. 12 pp. Supplement 1, 6 pp.

1758. ———. *The SDA Reform Movement: A Selected Guide to Materials in the Heritage Rooms of the Loma Linda University Libraries.* The Author, 1983. 3 pp.

1759. ———. *The Seventh-day Adventist Church and the American Civil War: A Bibliographical Guide to the PUC [Pacific Union College] Library.* The Author, 1984. 2 pp.

1760. ———. *The Seventh-day Adventist Church, Creationism and Evolution: A Bibliographical Guide to the Materials in the Pacific Union College Library, Angwin, California.* The Author, 1984. 25 pp. Supplement No. 1. 1985. 12 pp.

1761. ———. *The Seventh Day Adventist Church in Nepal: A Bibliographical Guide to Materials in the Pacific Union College Library.* The Author, 1984. 2 pp.

1762. ———. *The Year-Day Principle in Prophecy: A Guide to Materials in the Heritage Rooms of Loma Linda University.* The Author, 1982. 2 pp.

Guides to Periodical Literature

1763. *Seventh-day Adventist Periodical Index.* Vol 1- . Loma Linda, CA: Loma Linda University Libraries, 1972- . Issued semi-annually.

Archival Depositories

Advent Christian Church: Archival depositories for the Advent Christian Church can be found in the **Jenks Memorial Collection** at Aurora College in Aurora, Illinois (a far west Chicago suburb) and in the **Dr. Linden J. Carter Library**, Berkshire Christian College in Lenox, Massachusetts.

Church of God (Abrahamic Faith): The Church of God archives is at their headquarters, 131 North Third Street, Oregon, IL 61061.

Church of God (Seventh-Day): Archival holdings are at the Church headquarters, 330 West 152 Avenue, Box 33677, Denver, CO 80233.

Seventh-day Adventist Church: The Seventh-day Adventist Church has several depositories. The Ellen G. White manuscripts and writings are under the care of the **Ellen G. White Estate**, a corporation established in 1915 and whose offices are at the church's headquarters, 6840 Eastern Avenue, N.W., Washington, DC 20012. The Archives of the Seventh-day Adventists General Conference are at 12501 Old Columbia Pike, Silver Spring, MD 20904. Other significant holdings of Adventist materials can be found at Andrews University in Berrien Springs, Michigan; Pacific Union University Library, Angwin, CA 94508; and the **Heritage Room of Loma Linda University**, Loma Linda, CA 92350. The **Department of Archives and Special Collections** at Loma Linda University publishes the quarterly, *Adventist Heritage.*

Jehovah's Witnesses: The archives of the Jehovah's Witnesses is located at their headquarters in Brooklyn, but is generally not open to nonmembers. While there are many large (and for research, significant) private collections, the largest public collections of Witness literature (and that of associated groups with the same historical roots) is in the **American Religions Collection** of the Library of the University of California-Santa Barbara, which also has a collection of Seventh-day Church of God material.

ANGLICANISM

The Anglican tradition developed in the British Isles during the early centuries of Christian presence there, but took its most definitive form after the Church of England broke with the Roman Catholic Church. In the following centuries, as Great Britain built its worldwide empire, the Church of England established missions in all of the Crown colonies. As the colonies became independent countries, so the missions tended to become autonomous churches which kept a fraternal relationship to the Church of England, from whom it derived its apostolic succession and episcopal orders. The relationship finds outward expression in the Lambeth Conference of Bishops of the Anglican Communion which first met in 1867 and the Anglican Consultive Council founded in 1969. Its primary North American representatives are the Episcopal Church and the Anglican Church in Canada. The North American Anglican community has been disrupted over the last two decades by the movement of conservatives to found separate churches, and both countries have numerous Anglican splinter groups.

Church of England and the Worldwide Anglican Communion

Sources immediately below relate to the Church of England and Anglican Churches outside of North America.

General Sources

1764. Neill Stephen. *Anglicanism.* London: Mowbrays, 1977. 421 pp.

Encyclopedias and Dictionaries

1765. *Facts and Figures about the Church of England.* No. 1- . London: Church Information Office, 1959- . Triennial report issued by the Central Board of Finance's Statistics Unit of the Church of England.

1766. Hartford, George, and Morley Stevenson. *The Prayer Book Dictionary.* London: Pitman, 1912. 832 pp.

1767. Ollard, S. L. *A Dictionary of English Church History.* London: A. R. Mowbray & Co., 1912. 698 pp.

Biographical Volumes

1768. Edwards, David Lawrence. *Leaders of the Church of England, 1828-1944.* London: Oxford University Press, 1971. 358 pp.

1769. LeNeve, John. *Fasti Ecclesiae Anglicanae; or A Calendar of the Principal Ecclesiastical Dignitaries in England and Wales, and of the Chief Officers in the Universities of Oxford.* 3 vols. Oxford: Oxford University Press, 1854.

1770. ———. *Fasti Ecclesiae Anglicaae, 1066-1300.* 3 vols. London: Institute of Historical Research/Athlone Press, 1968-1977.

1771. ———. *Fasti Ecclesiae Anglicanae, 1300-1541.* 12 vols. London: University of London, Institute of Historical Research/Athlone Press, 1962-1967.

1772. ———. *Fasti Ecclesiae Anglicanae, 1541-1857.* 5 vols. London: University of London, Institute of Historical Research/Athlone Press, 1969-1979.

1773. Scott, Hew. *Fasti Ecclesiae Scoticanae; The Succession of Ministers in the Church of Scotland from the Reformation.* 7 vols. Edinburgh: Oliver and Boyd, 1915-28. 7 Vols. Vols. 8-10, 1950-81

1774. Watt, Donald Elmslie Robertson. *Fasti Ecclesiae Scoticanae Medii Aevi ad Annum 1638.* 2nd draft. Edinburgh: Smith & Ritchie Ltd., 1969. 411 pp.

Directories

1775. *Church of England Yearbook.* Ed. 1- . London: Church Information Office, 1959- . Annual.

1776. *Church of Scotland Yearbook.* Ed. 1- . Edinburgh: Church of Scotland, Department of Publicity and Publication, 1885- . Annual.

1777. *Crockford's Clerical Dictionary.* London: Oxford University Press, 1858-1983. Biennial.

1778. *Irish Church Directory and Yearbook.* Ed. 1- . Dublin: Church of Ireland Printing and Publishing Co., 1862- . Annual.

Bibliographies

1779. Crumb, Lawrence N. *The Oxford Movement and Its Leaders: A Bibliography of Secondary and Lesser Primary Sources.* ATLA Bibliography Series No. 24. Metuchen, NJ: Scarecrow Press, 1988. 736 pp.

1780. Donaldson, Gordon. *The Sources of Scottish History.* Edinburgh: n.p., 1978. 41 pp.

1781. Fallon, Maura. *Church of Ireland Diocesan Libraries.* Dublin: Library Association of Ireland, 1959.

1782. Macgregor, Malcolm B. *The Sources and Literature of Scottish Church History.* Glascow: McCallum, 1934. 260 pp.

1783. Pollard, Alfred William, et al. *A Short-Title Catalogue of Books Printed in England, Scotland, & Ireland and of English Books Printed Abroad, 1475-1640.* London: The Bibliographical Society, 1926.

1784. Read, E. Anne. *A Checklist of Books, Catalogues and Periodical Articles Relating to the Cathedral Libraries of England.* Oxford: Oxford Bibliographical Society, 1970.

1785. Shropshire, England County Library. *Catalogue of Books from Parochial Libraries in Shropshire.* London: Mansell, 1971. 607 pp.

1786. *Suffolk Parochial Libraries: A Catalogue.* London: Mansell, 1977. 129 pp.

Anglican Religious Orders

General Sources

1787. Anson, Peter Frederick. *The Call of the Cloister: Religious Communities and Kindred Bodies in the Anglican Communion.* 4th ed. London: SPCK, 1964.

1788. Church of England. Advisory Council on the Relation of Bishops and Religious Communities. *Guide to the Religious Communities of the Anglican Communion.* New York: Morehouse-Gorham Co./London: A.R. Mowbray and Co., 1955. 140 pp.

1789. Thomas, Evangeline, CSJ. *Women Religious History Sources: A Guide to Repositories in the United States.* New York: Bowker, 1983. 329 pp.

Episcopal Church (U.S.A.) and the Anglican Church of Canada

General Sources

1790. Armentrout, Donald D. *Episcopal Splinter Groups: A Study of Groups Which Have Left the Episcopal Church, 1873-1985.* Sewanee, TN: School of Theology, The University of the South, 1985. This excellent survey of groups which left the Episcopal Church is supplemented by the coverage in Melton (566) and Ward (1999).

1791. Sydnor, William. *Looking at the Episcopal Church.* Wilton, CT: Morehouse-Barlow Co., 1980. 142 pp.

Encyclopedias and Dictionaries

1792. Benton, Angela Ames, ed. *The Church Cyclopaedia: A Dictionary of Church Doctrine, History, Organization and Ritual, Designed Especially for the Use of the Laity of the Protestant Episcopal Church in the United States of America.* New York: M/H/ Mallory, 1883. Rept. Detroit: Gale Research, 1975.

1793. Crum, Rolfe Pomeroy. *A Dictionary of the Episcopal Church, Compiled from Various Authentic Sources.* 1939. 10th ed.: Baltimore, MD: Trefoil Publishing Society, c. 1953. The *Dictionary* was published annually for many years beginning in 1939 (except for the years during World War II) and regularly revised and enlarged.

1794. Harper, Howard V. *The Episcopalian's Dictionary: Church Beliefs, Terms, Customs and Traditions Explained in Layman's Language.* New York: Seabury Press, 1975. 183 pp.

1795. Wall, John N., Jr. *A New Dictionary for Episcopalians.* Minneapolis, MN: Winston Press, 1985. 179 pp.

Directories

1796. *Episcopal Church Annual.* New York: Morehouse-Gorham, 1830- . Annual. Originally entitled *The Churchman's Almanac*; later *The Living Church Annual.*

1797. *Episcopal Clergy Directory*. Vol. 1- . New York: Church Hymnal Corporation, 1898- . Biennial. Variously entitled *Lloyd's Clerical Directory*, *Stowe's Clerical Directory*, *Clerical Directory of the Protestant Episcopal Church in the United States of America*.

Bibliographies

1798. Sumner, David E. "A Bibliography of Modern Episcopal Church History." *Anglican and Episcopal History* 57, 1 (March 1988): 93-101.

Archival Depositories

Anglican Church of Canada: The Archives of Canadian Anglicanism are located at the Church's headquarters, 600 Jarvis Street, Toronto, ON M4Y 2J6. The Church House Library has a general collection on the Anglican Communion and the Archives holds the records of the church in Canada. Local archival collections are to be found at the diocesan headquarters in Calgary, Montreal, and Vancouver. Archives for Manitoba are in the provincial archives.

Church of England: The archives and historical collection of the Church of England are in the Lambeth Palace Library, London SE1 7JU, England. It holds the records of the Archbishops of Canterbury and the historical records of all of the central institutions of the Church of England with the exception of the General Synod and its subsidiary bodies. Their records are at the Church of England Record Centre, Galleywell Road, Bermandsey, London SE16 3PB.

Episcopal Church: The Historical Society of the Episcopal Church is the official agency for the preservation of archival material and promoting historical research. It publishes a quarterly, *Anglican and Episcopal History*. The Society is headquartered at the Episcopal Theological Seminary of the Southwest, Box 2247, Austin, TX 78767. The libraries of the various church-sponsored seminaries also have collections of Anglican materials, especially Berkeley Divinity School at Yale, New Haven, CT 06510, and General Theological Seminary, 175 Ninth Avenue, New York, NY 10011.

Reformed Episcopal Church: The archives of the Reformed Episcopal Church are at the Cummins Memorial Theological Seminary, 705 Main Street, Summerville, SC 29483. There is also a collection of Church materials at the Reformed Episcopal Church Theological Seminary, 4225 Chestnut Street, Philadelphia, PA 19104.

BAPTISTS

The Baptists emerged in the sixteenth century as the left wing of the Puritan Movement in England, the issues centering upon a rejection of ties to the state and the self-determining role of the local church. These issues were symbolized in the rejection of infant baptism and its replacement by adult believers' baptism. The Baptists experienced spectacular growth in post-Revolutionary America. The Southern Baptist Church is now the largest Protestant Church in the United States and collectively the Baptists are the largest Protestant family group in America, though splintered among a variety of denominations.

General Sources

1799. Baker, Robert A. *A Baptist Sourcebook, with Particular Reference to the Southern Baptists.* Nashville, TN: 1966. 216 pp.

1800. Brackney, William Henry. *The Baptists.* New York: Greenwood Press, 1988. 327 pp. This excellent introductory volume, part of the series on denominational families from Greenwood, includes a survey of the Baptist tradition and sketches of a number of prominent American Baptists.

1801. McBeth, H. Leon. *The Baptist Heritage: Four Centuries of Baptist Witness.* Nashville, TN: Broadman Press, 1987. 850 pp.

Encyclopedias and Dictionaries

1802. Burgess, G. A., and J. T. Ward. *Free Baptist Cyclopedia.* N.p.: Free Baptist Cyclopedia Co., 1889. 724 pp.

1803. Cathcart, William. *The Baptist Encyclopedia, A Dictionary of. . . the Baptist Denomination in All Lands.* 2 vols. Philadelphia: Louis H. Evans, 1881. 1327 pp.

1804. *Encyclopedia of Southern Baptists.* 4 vols. Nashville: Broadman Press, 1958, 1971.

1805. Hayward, Elizabeth. *Index to Names in the Baptist Encyclopedia.* Chester, PA: The American Baptist Historical Society, 1951. 58 pp.

Directories

1806. Hall, A. B., comp. *Primitive Baptist Statistics: Compiled from 1970 Records.* 3 vols. Arab, AL: The Author, 1972.

1807. *Telephone Directory: Southern Baptist Convention, 1989-90.* Nashville, TN: Public Relations Office, SBC, 1989. 77 pp.

Biographical Volumes

1808. George, Timothy, and David S. Dockery, eds. *Baptist Theologians.* Nashville, TN: Broadman Press, 1990. 704 pp.

1809. Graham, B. J. W. *Baptist Biography.* 3 vol. Atlanta, GA: Index Printing Co., I, 1917. 365 pp.; II, 1920. 389 pp. III, 1923. 488 pp.

1810. Harrison, Harold D., ed. *Who's Who Among Free Will Baptists and Encyclopedia of Denomination Information.* Nashville, TN: Randall House, 1978. 493 pp.

1811. *History of Georgia Baptists (with Biographical Compendium).* 1881.

1812. Lasher, George William, ed. *The Ministerial Directory of the Baptist Churches in the United States of America.* Oxford, OH: Ministerial Directory Co., [c. 1899].

Bibliographies

1813. Atkinson, Ernest Edwin. *A Selected Bibliography of Hispanic Baptist History.* Nashville, TN: Southern Baptist Convention, Historical Commission, 1981.

1814. Gill, Athol. *A Bibliography of Baptist Writings on Baptism, 1900-1968.* Bibliographical Aids No. 1. Rüschlikon-Zürich: Baptist Theological Seminary, 1969. 184 pp.

1815. Graham, Balus Joseph Winzer, ed. *Baptist Bibliography.* 3 vols. Atlanta, GA: Index Printing Company, 1917-1923.

1816. McIntyre, Willard Ezra. *Baptist Authors: A Manual for Bibliography, 1500-1914.* Montreal: Industrial and Educational Press, 1914.

1817. Southern Baptist Convention Historical Commission. *Graduate Theses in-Progress in Southern Baptist Theological Seminaries.* Vol 1- . Nashville, TN: Southern Baptist Convention, Historical Commission, 1965- . Irregular.

1818. ———. *Index of Graduate Theses in Baptist Theological Seminaries, 1894-1962.* Nashville, TN: Southern Baptist Convention, 1963.

1819. Southern Baptist Convention Sunday School Board. *Church Library Resource Guide: Books and Audio-Visual Materials Recommended for Church Libraries.* Nashville, TN: Convention Press, 1960.

1820. *Southern Baptist Periodical Index.* Vol. 1- . Nashville, TN: Southern Baptist Convention, Historical Commission, 1965- . Annual.

1821. Southwestern Baptist Theological Seminary. *Essential Books for Christian Ministry: Basic Reading for Pastors, Church Staff Leaders and Laymen.* Fort Worth, TX: Southwestern Baptist Theological Seminary, 1972.

1822. ———. *Union List of Baptist Serials.* Fort Worth, TX: Nemac Publications, 1960.

1823. Starr, Edward A. *A Baptist Bibliography.* 25 vols. Philadelphia: Judson Press, 1947/Chester, PA & Rochester, NY: American Baptist Historical Society, 1952-76.

1824. Whitley, W.T., comp. *A Baptist Bibliography: Being a Register of the Chief Materials for Baptist History, Whether in Manuscript or in Print, Preserved in Great Britain, Ireland, and the Colonies.* 2 vols. London: Kingsgate Press, 1916-1922.

Baptist Studies

Alabama Baptist Historical Society
Samford University
Birmingham, AL 35209
The Society publishes *The Alabama Baptist Historian* twice annually.

Baptist Information and Retrieval System (BIRS)
c/o Historical Commission of the Southern Baptist Convention
127 Ninth Avenue, North
Nashville, TN 37234

National Association of Baptist Professors of Religion
c/o Watson E. Mills
Mercer University
Macon, GA 31207
The Association publishes *Perspectives in Religious Studies*

Archival Depositories

American Baptist Churches in the U.S.A.: The primary archival depositories for the American Baptist Churches in the U.S.A. (formerly the Northern Baptist Convention) are under the care of the **American Baptist Historical Society** whose executive director is at the **American Baptist Archives Center** and the Churches' headquarters complex, Box 851, Valley Forge PA 19482-0851. Two strong archival collections are located at the **American Baptist-Samuel Colgate Historical Library** located in the campus of the **Colgate-Rochester Theological Seminary**, 1100 South Goodman Street, Rochester, New York 14260, and at the **Andover Newton Theological Seminary**, Newton Centre, Massachusetts 02159. Each of the schools sponsored by the Churches has a Baptist collection.

Baptist General Conference: The Baptist General Conference, a body of Swedish heritage, has its archives at **Bethel Theological Seminary**, 3949 Bethel Drive, St. Paul, MN 55112

Baptist Union of Great Britain and Ireland: Historical and archival endeavors among British Baptists is guided by the **Baptist Historical Society**, which may be reached through T. S. H. Elwyn, 148 Greenvale Road, London SE9 1PQ, UK. It publishes the *Baptist Quarterly*.

Canadian Baptists: Most of the Baptist conventions in Canada have placed their historical records in the **Canadian Baptist Archives** at **McMaster Divinity School**, Hamilton, ON L8S 4K1. It includes Baptist material for all of Canada except the Maritime Provinces whose archive is at **Atlantic Baptist College**, Box 6004, Moncton, NB E1C 9L7.

National Association of Free Will Baptists: The National Association's archives are at the **Free Will Baptist Bible College**, 3606 West End Avenue, Nashville, Tennessee 37205.

North American Baptist Conference: The archives of the North American Baptist Conferences are located in the **Kaiser-Ramaker Library** at the **North American Baptist Seminary**, 1321 W. 22nd Street, Sioux Falls, SD 57105-1599.

Primitive Baptists: Elder E. J. Berry established the **Primitive Baptist Library,** Route 2, Elon College, NC 27244, as an archival center for all Primitive Baptist groups. For a number of years he also issued *The Primitive Baptist Library Quarterly*.

Seventh Day Baptists: The **Seventh Day Baptist Historical Society** and the archives for the Seventh Day Baptist Convent are located at the headquarters complex, 3120 Kennedy Road, (mailing address: Box 1678), Janesville, WI 53547. A second strong collection of Seventh Day Baptist material is at **Alfred University**, Alfred, NY 14802, formerly affiliated with the church.

Southern Baptist Convention: The principal Southern Baptist Convention archives is located at the convention's headquarters complex, 901 Commerce Street, Ste. 400, Nashville, Tennessee. It is under the care of the Historical Commission of the SBC. The Commission, together with its auxiliary, the **Southern Baptist Historical Society,** publishes the quarterly *Baptist History and Heritage*. The Commission issues a pamphlet, "Resources for Meeting Heritage Needs," which details its publications and services.

Strong Southern Baptist collections can be found at the Conventions's seminaries, especially **Southern Baptist Theological Seminary**, Louisville, Kentucky, and Baylor University, Waco, Texas. **Southwestern Baptist Theological Seminary** in Waco, Texas, has the papers of a number of outstanding Baptists including B. H. Carroll, L. R. Scarborough, and George Washington Truett.

Possibly the most well-known Southern Baptist of this century is evangelist Billy Graham. His association has established a library of materials documenting his career at its headquarters, 1300 Harmon Place, Minneapolis, MN 55403. Southern Baptist Theological Seminary has a Billy Graham Room with a special collection of material on his ministry.

BRETHREN (CHURCH OF THE BRETHREN)

The Brethren Church emerged in the early eighteenth century as a Pietist movement in Germany. During their first generation they moved to Pennsylvania and over the centuries since have frequently made common cause with the Mennonites. Like them, the Brethren were "Plain People" in their dress, opposed to the state church ideal, and pacifist in their ethical orientation.

Encyclopedias and Dictionaries

1825. Durnbaugh, Donald F., ed. *The Brethren Encyclopedia.* 3 vols. Philadelphia, PA: and Oak Brook, IL: The Brethren Encyclopedia, Inc., 1983-84.

Biographical Volumes

1826. Cable, W. Arthur, and Homer F. Sanger. *Educational Blue Book and Directory of the Church of the Brethren, 1708-1923.* 1923. 656 pp.

Bibliographies

1827. Doll, Eugene E., and Anneliese M. Funke. *The Ephrata Cloister: An Annotated Bibliography.* Philadelphia, PA: Carl Shurz Memorial Foundation, 1946. 128 pp.

1828. Durnbaugh, Donald F. *Guide to Research in Brethren History.* Elgin, IL: Brethren Press and Church of the Brethren Historical Committee, 1968. 12 pp.; Rev. ed.: Elgin, IL: Church of the Brethren General Board, 1977. 16 pp.

1829. ———. "A Second Supplement to the Brethren Bibliography." *Brethren Life and Thought* 15, 4 (Autumn 1970): 187-204.

1830. ———. "Supplement and Index to the Brethren Bibliography." *Brethren Life and Thought* 11, 2 (Spring 1966): 37-54.

1831. ———, and Lawrence Schultz. *A Brethren Bibliography, 1713-1963.* Elgin, IL: Brethren Press, 1964. 177 pp. Reprinted from a special issue of *Brethren Life and Thought* 9, 1/2 (Winter/Spring 1964): 3-177.

1832. Flory, John S. *Literary Activity of the German Baptist Brethren in the Eighteenth Century.* Elgin, IL: Brethren Publishing House, 1908. 333 pp. Originally written as a Ph.D dissertation at the University of Virginia.

1833. Harley, Chester I. "A Study of the Yearbook of the Church of the Brethren." *Schwezenau* 1 (October 1939): 13-61.

1834. Heckman, Marlin L. "Articles of Brethren Historical Interest in Non-Brethren Journals: A Preliminary List." *Brethren Life and Thought* 15, 4 (Autumn 1970): 211-13.

1835. Ogden, Galen B. *A Bibliography of Brethren Publications.* B.D. Thesis, Bethany Biblical Seminary, 1941. Rev. ed. published in: *Schwarzenau* 3 (January 1942): 58-116.

1836. Sappington, Roger E. "Bibliography of Theses on the Church of the Brethren." *Brethren Life and Thought* 15, 4 (Autumn 1970): 205-210.

1837. ———. "Historical Notes—Eighteenth Century Non-Brethren Sources of Brethren History." *Brethren Life and Thought* 2, 1 (Winter 1957): 75-78.

Archives/Research Centers

Bethany Theological Seminary
Butterfield and Meyers Road
Oak Brook, IL 60521

Brethren Historical Library and Archives
1451 Dundee Avenue
Elgin, IL 60120

Juniata College
Library
Huntington, PA 16652

Morgan Library
Grace Theological Seminary
200 Seminary Drive
Winona Lake, IN 46590
Included in the collection of the Morgan Library are the archives for the Fellowship of Grace Brethren Churches and the papers of evangelist Billy Sunday.

Young Center for the Study of Anabaptist and Pietist Groups
One Alpha Drive
Elizabethtown College
Elizabethtown, PA 17022-2298
The Center fosters study of the Amish, Mennonite and Brethren traditions.

CHRISTIAN CHURCH

The Christian Church exists in three main branches: the Christian Church (Disciples of Christ), the Churches of Christ, and the Christian Church and Churches of Christ. It grew out of the early nineteenth century move to restore primitive Christianity (hence its being referred to as the Restoration Movement) by a number of ministers, most prominently Barton Stone, Thomas Campbell, and Alexander Campbell. The issue of the designation of their group as just Christians, without denominational names, was important to them, hence the problem of specific names as the group divided throughout the twentieth century. For a survey of the family and its various segments, see Melton (566).

General Sources

1838. Dowling, Enos. *The Restoration Movement.* Lincoln, IL: Lincoln Christian College, Alumni Publishing Fund, 1964. 128 pp.

1839. McAllister, Lester G., and William E. Tucker. *Journey of Faith.* St. Louis, MO: Bethany Press, 1975.

Bibliographies

1840. *Preliminary Guide to Black Materials in the Disciples of Christ Historical Society.* Nashville, TN: Disciples of Christ Historical Society, 1971. 32 pp.

1841. Spencer, Claude Elbert, comp. *An Author Catalog of Disciples of Christ and Related Religious Groups.* Canton, MO: Disciples of Christ Historical Society, 1946. 367 pp.

1842. ———. *Theses Concerning the Disciples of Christ and Related Religious Groups.* 2nd ed. Nashville, TN: Disciples of Christ Historical Society, 1964. 94 pp.

Guides to Periodical Literature

1843. *The Christian-Evangelist Index, 1863-1958.* 3 vols. Nashville, TN: Christian Board of Publication and Disciples of Christ Historical Society, 1962.

1844. *Christian Standard Index, 1866-1966.* 6 vols. Nashville, TN: Disciples of Christ Historical Society, 1972.

1845. Spencer, Claude Elbert, comp. *Periodicals of the Disciples of Christ and Related Groups.* Canton, MO: Disciples of Christ Historical Society, 1943.

Archival Depositories

Christian Church (Disciples of Christ): The **Disciples of Christ Historical Society**, 1101 Nineteenth Avenue, S., Nashville, TN 37212, attempts to be a central archive for the Disciples of Christ, as well as the larger Restoration Movement, which includes the Churches of Christ and the Christian Churches and Churches of Christ. It also publishes a quarterly, *Discipliana*. Other collections are located at the church's schools, especially **Christian Theological Seminary**, Indianapolis, IN 46208; **Lexington Theological Seminary**, Lexington, KY 40508; The **Disciples Divinity House** at the University of Chicago, Chicago, IL 60637; **Texas Christian University**, Fort Worth, TX 76219; and **Culver-Stockton College**, Canton, MO 63435. The church had its beginning in the Cane Ridge Meeting House near Paris, Kentucky. The House is preserved by the **Cane Ridge Preservation Project**, which publishes the quarterly newsletter, the *Cane Ridge Bulletin*, 1655 Cane Ridge Road, Paris, KY 40261.

Christian Churches and Churches of Christ: Prior to this present generation, the history of the Christian Churches and Churches of Christ was at one with the Christian Church (Disciples of Christ). Among the schools with significant archival materials which have adhered to this, the newest branch of the movement, is **Lincoln Christian College and Seminary**, 100 Campus View Drive, Box 178, Lincoln, IL 62656.

Churches of Christ: The loosely organized Churches of Christ have no official archive, but collections have been built at the libraries of their several schools, especially **Abilene Christian University**, Abilene, Texas 79699; **David Lipscomb University**, Nashville, TN 37204; **Harding Graduate School of Religion**, 100 Cherry Road, Memphis, Tennessee 38117; and **Pepperdine University**, Malibu, CA 90265.

CONGREGATIONALISM/ UNITED CHURCH OF CHRIST

Congregationalism emerged as the form of government which the New England Puritans (most of whom had been Presbyterians) assumed in the seventeenth century in Massachusetts and Connecticut. Affirming the autonomy of the local congregation, the church eventually formed a General Council of Congregational Churches as a denominational administrative umbrella. In the twentieth century, the church has been dominated by liberal Protestant forces and became committed to the ecumenical movement. Through two mergers in 1931 and 1957, it emerged as the United Church of Christ, and now shares its heritage with the previous Evangelical and Reformed Church, an American by-product of the Prussian Church Union which united Lutheran and Reformed churches in Prussia. The Congregational Church has had a role in the religious intellectual leadership in America far beyond its relative size.

General Sources

1846. Horton, Douglas. *The United Church of Christ.* New York: Thomas Nelson, 1962.

1847. Youngs, J. William T. *The Congregationalists.* New York: Greenwood Press, 1990. 376 pp. Includes an overview of the Congregational stream of the history of the United Church of Christ and biographical sketches of a number of prominent leaders.

Biographical Volumes

1848. Peel, Albert. *The Congregational Two Hundred, 1530-1948.* London: Independent Press, [1948].

1849. *Who's Who in Congregationalism: An Authoritative Reference Work and Guide to the Careers of Ministers and Lay Officials of the Congregational Churches.* London: Shaw Publishing Co., 1933- .

Bibliographies

1850. Dexter, Henry Martyn. *The Congregationalism of the Last Three Hundred Years As Seen in Its Literature; With Special Reference to Certain Recondite, Neglected or Disputed Passages.* 2 vols. in 1. London: Hodder and Stoughton, [1879]; New York: Harper and Brothers, 1880. Rept.: 2 vols. New York: Burt Franklin, 1970.

1851. Keiling, Hanns Peter, comp. *The Formation of the United Church of Christ (U.S.A.): A Bibliography.* Bibliographia Tripotamopolitana No. 2. Pittsburgh: Pittsburgh Theological Seminary, Clifford E. Barbour Library, 1970. Unpaged.

Atlases

1852. Goddard, Carolyn E. ed. *On the Trail of the United Church of Christ: A Historical Atlas of the United Church of Christ.* New York: United Church Press, 1981. 127 pp.

Archival Depositories

United Church of Christ: The United Church of Christ tradition emphasizes intellectual activity and has produced a literature far beyond what might be expected by its relatively small constituency. In general, the **Historical Council of the United Church of Christ**, 105 Madison Avenue, New York, NY 10016, guides the network of its varied historical and archival work. The Church's Archives is located at **Lancaster Theological Seminary,** 555 W. James Street, Lancaster, PA 17603 (also one of the two headquarters of the **Evangelical and Reformed Historical Society**). The **Eden Archives,** the other location of the Evangelical and Reformed Historical Society), is at **Eden Theological Seminary**, 475 E. Lockwood Avenue, Webster Groves, MO 63119. The **Congregational Library** is managed by the **American Congregational Association**. Its 100,000 volume library is at 14 Beacon Street, Boston, MA 02108. Strong representative UCC collections are also at the **Chicago Theological Seminary**, 5757 University Avenue, Chicago, IL 60637; The **Divinity Library, Yale University**, New Haven, CT 06520; the **Library of Hartford Theological Seminary**, Hartford, CT 06105; and the **Library at Harvard Divinity School**, Cambridge, MA 02138.

United Church of Canada: The United Church of Canada was founded as a merger in 1925 of the Congregational Church with the Canadian branches of the Methodist and Presbyterian Churches. The primary archive of the Church is located at **Victoria University,** Birge Carnegie Building, 75 Queen's Park Crescent E., Toronto, ON M5S 1K7. The archives for the Maritime Provinces is at the **Atlantic School of Theology,** 640 Franklyn Street, Halifax, NS B3H 3B5.

EASTERN ORTHODOXY

Often referred to as the churches of Oriental Christianity, the Eastern Orthodox churches continue the Middle Eastern and Greek Apostolic tradition, and are proud of being located in the lands of the Christian New Testament. They find a spiritual unity by their adherence to the Nicene Creed and spiritual (though by no means organizational) unity in communion with the Ecumenical Patriarchate, whose seat is at Istanbul. There are major divisions among the Oriental churches. During the Patristic Era, the churches were rent with theological and ethnic controversy which led to dissent by the Egyptian, Ethiopian, Armenian, and Chaldean churches which persist to this day. During the twentieth century, conservative factions who reject both the adoption of the modern Western calendar and the developing ecumenical relations between the Ecumenical Patriarchate and Rome have formed. Also, in the West, separate church jurisdictions have been founded by groups opposed to cooperation with the Communist governments that controlled most of the lands traditionally dominated by Eastern Orthodoxy.

Encyclopedias and Dictionaries

1853. Clarke, Boden. *Lords Temporal & Lords Spiritual: A Chronological Checklist of the Popes, Patriarchs, Katholikoi, and Independent Archbishops and Metropolitans of the Autocephalous Monarchical Churches of the Christian East and West.* San Bernadino, CA: Borgo Press, 1985. 136 pp.

1854. Demetrakopolous, George H. *Dictionary of Orthodox Theology: A Summary of the Beliefs, Practices and History of the Eastern Orthodox Church.* New York: Philosophical Library, 1964.

1855. Langford-James, Richard Lloyd. *A Dictionary of the Eastern Orthodox Church.* London: Faith Press, 1923. 144 pp.

1856. Patrinacos, Nicon D. *A Dictionary of Greek Orthodoxy.* Pleasantville, NY: Hellenic Heritage Publications, 1984. 391 pp.

Directories

1857. *A Directory of Western Rite Orthodox Parishes including Clergy and Publications.* Akron, OH: Eastern Christian Press, 1986. 55 pp.

1858. *Eastern Orthodox World Directory.* Ed. 1- . Boston: Brandon Press, 1968- .

1859. Haiek, Joseph R. *Arab American Almanac.* Glendale, CA: News Circle Publishing Co., 3rd ed. 1984. Periodically updated.

1860. *Handbook of American Orthodoxy.* Cincinnati, OH: Forward Movement Publications, 1972. 191 pp.

1861. *Parishes and Clergy of the Orthodox, and Other Eastern Churches of North and South America, together with the Parishes and Clergy of the Polish National Catholic Church.* Buffalo: NY: Joint Commission on Cooperation with Eastern and Old Catholic Churches of the General Commission of the Protestant Episcopal Church, 1964/65. 187 pp. Rev. ed.: 1967/68. 184 pp. Rev. ed.: 1970/71. 208 pp.

1862. R. and E. Research Associates. *Eastern Orthodox Church Directory of the United States.* Ed. 1- . San Francisco: Robert D. Reed, 1968- . Various titles and imprints; originally *Orthodox Church Directory of the United States.*

1863. *Yearbook of the Orthodox Churches.* München, Germany: Verlag Alex Proc, 1978. 30 pp. Periodically updated.

Bibliographies

1864. Attwater, Donald. *A List of Books about the Eastern Churches.* Newport, RI: St. Leo Shop, 1960. 221 pp.

1865. Bonk, Jon. *An Annotated Classified Bibliography of English Literature Pertaining to the Ethiopian Orthodox Church.* ATLA Bibliography Series No. 11. Metuchen, NJ: Scarecrow Press, 1984. 132 pp.

1866. Brandreth, Henry R.T. *An Outline Guide to the Study of Eastern Christendom.* London: SPCK, 1951. 34 pp.

1867. *List of the Writings of Professors of the Russian Orthodox Theological Institute in Paris, 1948-1954.* Paris: [Russian Orthodox Theological Institute, 1954?].

1868. Petersen, Paul D. *Eastern Christianity: A Bibliography Selected from the ATLA Religion Database.* Rev. ed. Chicago: American Theological Library Association, 1984. 781 pp.

1869. Remnek, Miranda Beaven. *The Russian Orthodox Church: A Preliminary Survey of Library Materials at the University of California, Berkeley.* Berkeley, CA: Center for Slavic and East European Studies, 1988. 104 pp.

1870. Schmemann, Alexander. *Russian Theology, 1920-1965: A Bibliographical Survey.* Richmond, VA: Union Theological Seminary in Virginia, 1966. 49 pp.

1871. Smith, Barbara. *Preliminary Survey of the Documents in the Archives of the Russian Orthodox Church in Alaska.* Boulder, CO: Western Interstate Commission for Higher Education, 1974. 135 pp.

Professional Associations

Orthodox Theological Society of America
c/o Rev. Thomas Fitzgerald
Holy Cross School of Theology
50 Goddard Avenue
Brookline, MA 02146
The society publishes a monthly *Bulletin.*

Archival Depositories

Greek Orthodox Archdiocese of North and South America: The Greek Orthodox Church archives are at the church's headquarters 8-10 E. 79th Street, New York 10021, however, **Holy Cross Greek Orthodox School of Theology**, 50 Goddard Avenue, Brookline, MA 02146, has a large collection of Orthodox materials.

Orthodox Church in America: The archives of the Orthodox Church in America (formerly the Russian Orthodox Church) are located at the headquarters Box 675, Syosset, NY 11791. Significant Eastern Orthodox collections can be found at the Church's several seminaries.

Ukrainian Orthodox Church of the U.S.A.: The Ukrainian Orthodox Church has developed a headquarters complex at South Bound Brook, New Jersey, that includes its seminary, a library archive facility, and a museum of Ukrainian culture.

Research/Resource Centers

Cultural Centre Library
St. Vladimir's Ukrainian Orthodox Church
404 Meredith Road, N.E.
Calgary, AB T2E 5A6

Hellenic College
Holy Cross School of Theology
Library
50 Goddard Avenue
Brookline, MA 02146
The Library which serves both the college and seminary is especially strong in Orthodox theology.

Institute for Eastern Orthodox Studies
3011 Roe Drive
Houston, TX 77087
The Institute is an independent center with a Ukrainian orientation affiliated with the Eastern Orthodox Diocese of Houston and All Texas (an independent Orthodox jurisdiction) and under the direction of Bishop Vladika Makarios.

St. Innocent Veniaminov Research Institute
St. Herman's Theological Seminary
414 Mission Road
Kodiak, AK 99615
The Institute holds an archival collection on the Russian Orthodox Church, especially in its Alaskan work and early American phase.

St. Nerses Shnorhali Library
Armenian Apostolic Church of America
138 E. 39th Street
New York, NY 10016
This library, located at the headquarters of the Armenian Apostolic Church of America, has a collection on Armenian Christianity and an additional special collection of Armenian literature.

Ukrainian Canadian Research and Documentation Centre
St. Vladimir Institute
620 Spadina Avenue
Toronto, ON M5S 2H4

EVANGELICALISM/FUNDAMENTALISM

Fundamentalism emerged in the late nineteenth century as a variety of new forces began to change the larger Protestant churches. Among the most cited factor was the emergence of a new scientific worldview which denied the literal truth of the Genesis account of creation and a new social philosophy which looked to the building of the kingdom of God by consciously changing the basic structures of society, especially its economics. Fundamentalists were largely driven out of the mainline churches in the 1930s and reorganized in new denominations, primarily Baptist and Presbyterian in tradition. Evangelicalism began as a movement to bridge the chasm which had developed between Fundamentalism and the culture. It affirmed most of the Fundamentalist essentials, but wished to carry on a debate with the larger Christian world.

Little recognized out of scholarly Evangelical circles, a British movement, the Plymouth Brethren, had a significant influence in shaping Fundamentalism and this large but largely invisible movement now forms a core segment of Evangelicalism.

Bibliographies

1872. Blumhofer, Edith L., and Joel A. Carpenter. *Evangelicalism in Twentieth-Century America: A Guide to the Sources.* New York: Garland Publishing, 1990. 250 pp.

1873. Branson, Mark Lau. *The Reader's Guide to the Best Evangelical Books.* New York: Harper & Row, 1982. 224 pp.

1874. Carpenter, Joel A., ed. *Fundamentalism in American Religion 1880-1950.* 45 vols. New York: Garland Publishing, 1988.

1875. Ehlert, Arnold D. *A Bibliographic History of Dispensationalism.* Grand Rapids, MI: Baker Book House, 1965. 110 pp.

1876. ————. *Brethren Writers: A Checklist with an Introduction to Brethren Literature and Additional Lists.* BCH Bibliographic Series No.3. Grand Rapids, MI: Baker Book House, 1969. 83 pp.

1877. Grier, William James. *The Best Books: A Guide to Christian Literature.* London: Banner of Truth Trust, 1968. 175 pp.

1878. Magnuson, Norris A., and William G. Travis. *American Evangelicalism: An Annotated Bibliography.* West Cornwall, CT: Locust Hill Press, 1990. 495 pp.

1879. Merchant, Harish D., ed. *Encounter with Books: A Guide to Christian Reading.* Downers Grove, IL: InterVarsity Press, 1970.

1880. Pruter, Karl. *Jewish Christians in the United States.* Sects & Cults in America Series Vol. 7. New York: Garland Publishing, 1987. 208 pp.

Guides to Periodical Literature

1881. *Christian Periodical Index: An Index to Subjects, Authors and Book Reviews.* Vol. 1- . West Seneca, NY: Christian Librarian's Fellowship, 1959- .
Issued quarterly with cumulative volumes every three years.

Jesus People Movement

Bibliographies

1882. Jorstad, Erling. "A Review of Sources and Interpretations of the Jesus Movement." *Lutheran Quarterly* 25 (1973): 295-303.

1883. Pritchett, W. Douglas. *The Children of God/Family of Love: An Annotated Bibliography.* Sects & Cults in America Series Vol. 5. New York: Garland Publshing, 1985. 177 pp.

1884. Zimmerman, Marie. *Jesus Movement: International Bibliography 1972 Indexed by Computer.* RIC Supplement 4. Strasbourg, France: Cerdic-Publications, 1973. 36 pp.

Evangelical Studies

Institute for the Study of American Evangelicals
Wheaton College
Wheaton, IL 60187
The Institute supports the study of Evangelical Christianity in America, holds conferences, and publishes the *Evangelical Studies Bulletin* (semi-annual).

Research Centers/Archival Depositories

Billy Graham Center
Wheaton College
Wheaton, IL 60187-5593
The Billy Graham Center at Wheaton College promotes the study of Christian world evangelization. It houses an extensive archive of source material on Christian world missions and evangelism. The Center publishes a quarterly newsletter, *Center Line*, and the Archive issues *From the Archives of the Billy Graham Center* (semi-annual). One section of the center, the Institute for Prison Ministries, is specifically concerned with prison evangelism.

Bob Jones University
Greenville, SC 29614
Along with its general collection of Fundamentalist Christian materials, the University has an outstanding Christian Music Library.

Emmaus Bible College Library
2570 Asbury Road
Dubuque, IA 52001-3044
Emmaus has the largest publicly accessible collection of Plymouth Brethren material.

Goddard Library
Gordon-Conwell Theological Seminary
130 Essex Street, No. 583
South Hamilton, MA 01982-2361
A leading Evangelical school, the seminary library has a broad collection of conservative Protestant materials. It also houses a special collection of rare Bibles, and the Mercer Collection of Assyrio-Babylonian materials.

Lincoln Memorial Library
Northeastern Bible College
12 Oak Lane
Essex Fells, NJ 07021
The Library houses the Cleveland Collection of Jewish evangelism materials.

Moody Bible Institute Library
820 N. LaSalle Street
Chicago, IL 60610
The library has a large collection of conservative fundamentalist Protestant literature which includes special holdings on Dwight L. Moody, for whom the school is named, and one of the few collections of materials on Jewish evangelism, a missional enterprise the school has nurtured.

Philadelphia College of the Bible Library
200 Manor Avenue
Langhorne, PA 19047-2992
Among the special collections in the library is the C. I. Scofield Library of Biblical Studies. Scofield wrote the notes for the famous study Bible which bears its name.

Turpin Library
Dallas Theological Seminary
3909 Swiss Avenue
Dallas, TX 75204
A leading Fundamentalist school, the seminary library has a broad collection of fundamentalist theological and biblical writings.

FRIENDS (QUAKERS)

The Society of Friends was founded by George Fox who had begun to preach in England in 1647. His experience of inner illumination became determinative of the course of the movement which grew up around him and became known for the members search for guidance from the inner Spirit. The movement also became known for its pacifist stance and for its plain dress. Brought to America, the Quakers prospered in Pennsylvania and made important contributions to the traditions of religious freedom.

General Sources

1885. Barbour, Hugh, and J. William Frost. *The Quakers.* New York: Greenwood Press, 1988. 407 pp.

Directories

1886. *Finding Friends Around the World.* London: Friends World Committee for Consultation, periodically updated.

1887. *WCC Friends Directory of Meetings and Churches in the Section of the Americas.* Philadelphia: Friends World Committee for Consultation, periodically updated.

Bibliographies

1888. Friends Literature Committee. *A Guide to Quaker Literature.* London: Bannisdale Press [1952]. 24 pp.

1889. Green, Joseph J. *Quaker Records; Being an Index to "The Annual Monitor" 1813-92.* London: Hicks, 1894. 458 pp.

1890. Smith, Joseph. *Biblioteca Anti-Quakeriana: or, A Catalogue of Books Adverse to the Society of Friends, Alphabetically Arranged with Biographical Notices of the Authors, Together with the Answers which Have Been Given to Some of Them by Friends and Others.* London: Joseph Smith, 1873. 474 pp. Rept.: New York: Kraus Reprint, 1968. 474 pp.

1891. ———. *Biblioteca Quakeristica: A Bibliography of Miscellaneous Literature Relating to the Friends (Quakers), Chiefly Written by Persons Not Members of Their Society; Also Publications by Authors in Some Way Connected; and Biographical Notices.* London: Joseph Smith, 1883. 32 pp. Rept.: New York: Kraus Reprint, 1968. 32 pp.

1892. ———. *A Descriptive Catalogue of Friends' Books, or Books Written by Members of the Society of Friends, Commonly Called Quakers, from the First Rise to the Present Time, Interspersed with Critical Remarks and Biographical Notices.* 3 vols. London: Joseph Smith, 1867-1893. Rept.: New York: Kraus Reprint, 1970.

1893. Swarthmore College. Friends Historical Library. *Catalog of the Book and Serials Collection of the Friends Historical Library of Swarthmore College.* 6 vols. Boston: G. K., Hall, 1982.

Archival Depositories/Research Centers

Edmund Stanley Library
Friends University
2100 University Avenue
Wichita, KS 67213
The Edmund Stanley Library houses the archives of the Kansas Yearly Meeting and a special collection documenting Quaker work among Native Americans.

Friends' Historical Library
Swarthmore College
Swarthmore, PA 19081
The Swarthmore collection of Friends materials rivals that of Haverford College. It also houses a large Peace Collection that includes the papers of A. J. Muste and archival material of the Fellowship of Reconciliation.

Quaker Collection
Lilly Library
Earlham College
Richmond, IN 47374
The Lilly Library Collection is especially valuable for its documentation of the large Indian Quaker community.

Treasure Room and Quaker Collection
Haverford College Library
Haverford, PA 19041
The library houses one of the largest collections of Quaker books and archival materials in North America.

HOLINESS

The Holiness movement emerged in the context of nineteenth-century American Methodism. Methodist founder John Wesley had emphasized the biblical admonition to "become perfect." That aspect of Methodism had been less emphasized in the early decades of the nineteenth century, but found its supporters as the decades came and went. After the Civil War, a revival of Holiness theology swept through the Methodist churches. It emphasized the possibility of God making the believer perfect in love as an instantaneous act of the Holy Spirit. Before the end of the century, splits began to occur as Methodist leadership became hostile to the movement. Independent churches and associations began to form and a set of new Holiness denominations came into existence.

Directories

1894. *Directory of the Nazarene Churches in Australia, British Isles, Canada, Mexico and the United States, Including the Location of Some Holiness Camp Meetings with Approximate Dates.* Wollaston, MA: E.N.C. Press, 1963.

1895. *Salvation Army Yearbook.* London: Salvationist Publishing and Supplies, 1906— . Annual.

Bibliographies

1896. Bundy, David D. *Keswick: A Bibliographic Introduction to the Higher Life Movements.* Wilmore, KY: Asbury Theological Seminary, 1975. 89 pp. Rept. in: Donald W. Dayton, ed. *The Higher Christian Life: A Bibliographical Overview.* New New York: Garland Publishing, 1985. 201 pp.

1897. Dayton, Donald W. *The American Holiness Movement: A Bibliographic Introduction.* Wilmore, KY: Asbury Theological Seminary, B. L. Fisher Library, 1971

59 pp. Rept. in: Donald W. Dayton, *The Higher Christian Life: A Bibliographical Overview.* New York: Garland Publishing, 1985. 201 pp.

1898. Jones, Charles Edwin, ed. *A Guide to the Study of the Holiness Movement.* ATLA Bibliography Series No. 1. Metuchen, NJ: Scarecrow Press, 1974. 946 pp.

1899. Miller, William Charles. *Holiness Works: A Bibliography.* Kansas City, MO: Nazarene Publishing House, 1986. 120 pp.

1900. Moyles, R.G. *A Bibliography of Salvation Army Literature in English (1875-1987).* Texts and Studies in Religion Vol. 38. Lewiston, NY: Edwin Mellen Press, 1988. 209 pp.

1901. Nazarene Theological Seminary. *Master Bibliography of Holiness Works.* Kansas City, MO: Beacon Hill Press of Kansas City, 1965. 45 pp.

1902. Simmons, Randall C., ed., with Cliff A. Pemble. *Nazarene Biography Index.* Napa, ID: Northwest Nazarene College, 1984. 146 pp.

1903. Walls, Francine E. *The Free Methodist Church: A Bibliography.* Winona Lake, IN: Free Methodist Historical Center, 1977. 102 pp.

Archival Depositories

Asbury College is one of the oldest Holiness schools, having been founded in 1890 and the theological seminary in 1923. The **B. L. Fisher Library** at Asbury Theological Seminary, Wilmore, KY 40390, has one of the better collections of Holiness literature in existence. The independent Seminary is officially approved by both the Free Methodist Church and the Wesleyan Church.

Church of the Nazarene: The Archive of the Church of the Nazarene is located at the Church's headquarters 6401 The Paseo, Kansas City, MO 64131. A significant collection of Holiness materials is located at the **William Broadhurst Library,** Nazarene Theological Seminary, 1700 East Meyer Blvd., Kansas City, MO 64131.

Free Methodist Church: The Free Methodist Church archives are located at the **Marston Memorial Historical Library,** 777 North High School Road, Indianapolis, IN 46214. The papers of Free Methodist founder Benjamin T. Roberts are housed at the **Kenneth B. Keating Library,** Roberts Wesleyan College, 2301 Westside Drive, Rochester, NY 14624.

Kentucky Mountain Holiness Association: The **Gilson Library** of the Association sponsored Kentucky Mountain Bible Institute includes a special collection of Holiness literature.

Salvation Army: The **Archives and Research Center** of the Salvation Army is located at 145 W. 15th Street, New York, NY 10011.

Wesleyan Church: The **Archives and Historical Library** of the Wesleyan Church is located at the church's headquarters, 8050 Castleway Dr., Box 59434, Indianapolis, IN 46250.

LATTER-DAY SAINTS

The Latter-day Saint movement began in the 1820s with the experiences of Joseph Smith, Jr., who claimed contact with God the Father and Jesus Christ and who received a series of new revelations including the *Book of Mormon*, which tells a story of the people of pre-Columbian America in a language reminiscent of the Bible, and the *Doctrine and Covenants*, a set of on-going revelations received during Smith's lifetime. Following his assassination in 1844, the movement splintered, though the overwhelming majority of Latter-day Saints are to be found in one of the two larger churches, the Church of Jesus Christ of Latter-day Saints and the Reorganized Church of Latter Day Saints.

The Church of Jesus Christ of Latter-day Saints settled in Utah in the 1850s and built a unique American culture. Its academic institutions have taken their place in the scholarly world and have done a fine job of documenting Latter-day Saint life and providing reference tools to assist pursuits in Mormon studies.

Encyclopedias and Dictionaries

1904. Brooks, Melvin R. *L.D.S. Reference Encyclopedia.* Salt Lake City: Bookcraft, 1960.

1905. Ludlow, Daniel L. *The Encyclopedia of Mormonism.* 5 vols. New York: Macmillan Publishing Company, 1991.

1906. Shields, Steven L. *Divergent Paths of the Restoration.* 1975. 2nd ed. 1975. 3rd ed. 1982. 4th ed.: Los Angeles: Restoration Research, 1990. 336 pp.
The standard survey of the many splinter groups of the Latter-day Saint Movement.

Biographical Volumes

1907. Jenson, Andrew. *Latter Day Saints Biographical Encyclopedia.* 4 vols. Andrew Jenson History Co., 1901. Rept.: Salt Lake City, UT: Western Epics, 1971.

1908. Van Wagoner, Richard S., and Steven C. Walker. *A Book of Mormons.* Salt Lake City, UT: Signature Books, 1982. 454 pp.

Directories

1909. Van Nest, Albert. *A Directory of the "Restored Gospel" Churches.* Evanston, IL: Institute for the Study of American Religion, 1983. 32 pp.

Bibliographies

A running bibliography of current Mormon writings is carried annually in *Brigham Young University Studies.* Occasional bibliographical articles are also to be found in *Dialogue* and the *Journal of Mormon History.*

1910. Alexander, Thomas G., and James B. Allen. "The Mormons in the Mountain West: A Selected Bibliography." *Arizona and the West* 9 (Winter 1967): 365-84.

1911. Arrington, Leonard J. "Scholarly Studies of Mormonism in the Twentieth Century." *Dialogue* 1, 1 (Spring 1966): 15-32.

1912. Brigham Young University, College of Religious Instruction. *A Catalogue of Theses and Dissertations Concerning the Church of Jesus Christ of Latter-Day Saints, Mormonism and Utah.* Provo, UT: Brigham Young University, 1971. 742 pp.

1913. Bitton, Davis. *Guide to Mormon Diaries and Autobiographies.* Provo, UT: Brigham Young University Press, 1977. 417 pp.

1914. Clement, Russell T. *Mormons in the Pacific: A Bibliography.* Laie, HI: Inst. for Polynesian Studies, 1981. 239 pp.

1915. Flake, Chad. *A Mormon Bibliography, 1830-1930; Books, Pamphlets, Periodicals, and Broadsides relating to the First Century of Mormonism.* Salt Lake City, UT: University of Utah Press, 1978. 825 pp.

1916. Kirkpatrick, L. H., ed. *Holdings of the University of Utah and the Church of Jesus Christ of Latter-day Saints.* Salt Lake City, UT: University of Utah Library, Widtsoe Collection. 1954. 285 pp.

1917. Mauss, Armand L. "Sociological Perspectives on the Mormon Subculture." *Annual Review of Sociology* 10 (1984): 437-60.

1918. ———, and Jeffrey R. Franks. "Comprehensive Bibliography of Social Science Literature on the Mormons." *Review of Religious Research* 26 (1984): 73-115.

1919. *Mormon Americana.* (1960-1981?). Issued through the 1960s and 1970s, this semi-monthly periodical listed new publications by and about the Latter-day Saints.

1920. Poll, Richard D. "Nauvoo and the New Mormon History: A Bibliographical Survey." *Journal of Mormon History* 5 (1978): 105-23.

1921. Shields, Steven L. *The Latter Day Saint Churches: An Annotated Bibliography.* Sects & Cults in America Series Vol. 11. New York: Garland Publishing, 1987. 617 pp.

Guides to Periodical Literature

1922. Butt, Newbern Isaac, ed. *Indexes to First Periodicals of the Church of Jesus Christ of Latter-Day Saints: Evening and Morning Star, vols. 1-2 (1832-1834); L.D.S. Messenger and Advocate, vols. 1-3 (1834-1836); Elders' Journal, vol. 1 (1837-1838) Pub. at Kirkland, Ohio, and Far West, Missouri.* Provo, UT: Brigham Young University, 1960.

1923. *Index to Mormonism in Periodical Literature.* Vol. 1- . Salt Lake City: Church of Jesus Christ of Latter-Day Saints, Historical Department, 1976- . Annual with quincennial and decennial cumulations.

1924. *Index to Periodicals of the Church of Jesus Christ of Latter-Day Saints.* Cumulative ed. Vol. 1- . Salt Lake City: Church of Jesus Christ of Latter-Day Saints, 1961- . Annual with decennial cumulations.

Mormon Studies

Church of Jesus Christ of Latter-day Saints: The archives of the Church of Jesus Christ of Latter-day Saints is located in the Historian's Office of the church headquarters, 50 East Temple Street, Salt Lake City, UT 84150. There is also a collection of historical materials in the **Genealogical Society** Office at the same address. The largest collection of publicly accessible material is at the **Harold B. Lee Library** of Brigham Young University in Provo, Utah 84602. The **Sunstone Foundation** sponsors the Sunstone Collection, part of the larger **Marriot Library Archives** at the University of Utah, Salt Lake City.

Reorganized Church of Jesus Christ of Latter Day Saints: The Reorganized Church archives and historical library is at their headquarters, The Auditorium, Box 1059, Independence, MO 64051. There is also a significant collection at **Graceland College**, Lamoni, IA 50140.

During the 1980s, Mormon historical studies began a flourishing period which has not ended. Work is focused in several organizations and publications.

Mormon History Association
P. O. Box 7010
University Station
Provo, UT 84602
Besides holding regular meetings, the primary focus of Mormon studies, the Association publishes the quarterly *Journal of Mormon History*.

Dialogue Foundation
202 West 300 North
Salt Lake City, UT 84103
The Foundation publishes the quarterly *Dialogue: A Journal of Mormon Thought*.

John Whitmer Historical Association
Graceland College
Lamoni, IA 50140
This unofficial body, is the major arena for studies by Reorganized Church historians. It publishes quarterly *The John Whitmer Historical Association Journal*.

Joseph Fielding Smith Institute for Church History
Brigham Young University
127 Knight Magnum Building
Provo, UT 84602
The Institute supports research in Mormon history.

Religious Research Center
Brigham Young University
156 Joseph Smith Building
Provo, UT 84602
As part of a broad program of research in religious studies, the Center sponsors research on Latter-day Saint history and archeological endeavors into the background of the *Book of Mormon*.

Sunstone Foundation
331 South Rio Grande Street, Ste. 30
Salt Lake City, UT 84101-1136
The Foundation sponsors regular conferences and publishes *Sunstone Magazine*

Utah State Historical Society Library
300 Rio Grande
Salt Lake City, UT 84101
The Society's Library houses a special collection on the Latter-day Saints.

LUTHERANISM

Lutheranism grew out of the reforms initiated by Martin Luther in the sixteenth century. Unable to resolve their problems with the Roman Catholic Church, Luther's supporters went their separated way. Materials on the early phase of the movement will be found above in the chapter on the Reformation and Protestantism. Material in this chapter is limited to more contemporary materials concerning Lutheranism in the last two centuries and the present-day Lutheran churches, especially those in North America.

Encyclopedias and Dictionaries

1925. Bodensieck, Julius, ed. *The Encyclopedia of the Lutheran Church.* 3 vols. Minneapolis, MN: Augsburg Publishing House, 1965.

1926. *Evangelisches Kirken Lexikon.* Göttingen, Germany: Vanderhoeck & Ruprecht, 1956, 1961.

1927. Lieder, Walter. *Lutheran Dictionary.* St. Louis, MO: Concordia Publishing House, [1952].

1928. Lueker, Erwin L., ed. *Lutheran Cyclopedia.* St. Louis, MO: Concordia Publishing House, 1954. Rev. ed.: St. Louis, MO: Concordia Publishing House, 1975. 845 pp.

1929. Wentz, Abdel Ross. *Lutheran Churches of the World.* Geneva: Lutheran World Convention, 1952.

1930. *Where Are the Lutherans? A County-by-County Statistical Summary of Lutheran Congregations and Their Members for Each of the 50 States in the United States.* Minneapolis: Commission for a New Lutheran Church, Augsburg Publishing House, 1984. 366 pp.

Directories

1931. Bachmann, Mercia Brennen. *Lutheran Mission Directory.* Geneva, Switzerland: Lutheran World Federation, 1982. 421 pp.

1932. *Lutheran Churches of the World.* Minneapolis, MN: Augsburg Publishing House, 1957. 333 pp.

1933. *Lutheran Directory.* Berlin: Lutheraisches Verlaghaus, 1963. Part 1. Lutheran Churches of the World. Part 2. Lutheran World Federation. Supple.: Geneva: Lutheran World Federation, Information Bureau, 1975.

1934. *Lutheran World Almanac and Encyclopedia.* 8 vols. New York: Lutheran Publicity Bureau, 1921-1937.

Biographical Volumes

1935. Jensen, John Martin, et al., comps. *A Biographical Directory of Pastors of the American Lutheran Church.* Minneapolis, MN: Augsburg Publishing House, 1962. 857 pp.

1936. Malmin, Rasmus, et al., trans. & eds. *Who's Who among Pastors in All the Norwegian Lutheran Synods in America, 1843-1927.* 1914. 3rd ed.: Minneapolis, MN: Augsburg Publishing House, 1928. 662 pp.

1937. Mickelson, Arnold R., ed. *A Biographical Directory of Clergymen of the American Lutheran Church.* Minneapolis, MN: Augsburg Publishing House, 1972.

1938. Miller, Lillian, and Gerald Giving, comps. *A Biographical Directory of Pastors of the American Lutheran Church: Supplement, Listing Pastors of the Lutheran Free Church.* Minneapolis, MN: Augsburg Publishing House, 1963.

Bibliographies

1939. Wiederaenders, Robert C. *A Bibliography of American Lutheranism, 1624-1850. Arranged Alphabetically.* N.p., n.d.

Guides to Periodical Literature

1940. ———. *Periodicals of the ALC, 1930-1960, and Antecedent Bodies (A Preliminary Checklist).* Dubuque, IA: Archives of the Wartburg Theological Seminary, 1969.

Archival Depositories

Apostolic Lutheran Church: The Archive for Lutherans of Finnish descent is located at the Finnish-American Historical Archives, Hancock, MI 49930. There is also a collection of Finnish Lutheran material at the **Finnish-American Historical Archives**, Suomi College, Hancock, MI 49930-1882.

Evangelical Lutheran Church in America (1988): The Archives of Cooperative Lutheranism, which serves the largest Lutheran Church in the United States, is located in the Church headquarters, 8765 Higgins Road, Chicago, IL 60631. Significant collections of Lutheran materials can be found at the several church colleges and seminaries, most of which have unique holdings representative of the particular synod which gave it birth before the numerous mergers of the twentieth century led to the united church which exists today. The best collections are at the **Lutheran School of Theology**, 1100 East 55th Street, Chicago, IL 60615; the **Lutheran Archives Center at Philadelphia** (at the Lutheran Theological Seminary), 7301 Germantown Avenue, Philadelphia, PA 19119; **Wartburg Theological Seminary**, 333 Wartburg Place, Dubuque, IA 52001; **Lutheran Theological Seminary**, Gettysburg, PA 17325; **Lutheran Theological Southern Seminary**, 4201 N. Main, Street, Columbia, SC 29203; and **Wittemburg University**, P. O. Box 720, Springfield, OH 45501.

Archives of the Norwegian antecedents of the ELCA are at **Luther Northwestern Seminary Library**, 2375 Como Avenue, St. Paul, MN 55108. Those of the Danish Lutherans can be found at the **Danish Immigrant Archives** in the Library of Grandview College, 137-51 Grandview Avenue, Des Moines, IA 50316. The archive of the Deaconess Movement, pioneered in the United States by the Lutherans, are to be found at the **Lutheran Deaconess Community Library**, 801 Merion Square Road, Gladwyne, PA 19035.

Lutheran Church-Missouri Synod: The Missouri Synod has been the most accomplished and sophisticated preservers of history. The **Concordia Historical Institute**, on the campus of Concordia Theological Seminary, is among the best archival establishments in America. The Institute operates under the guidance of the Synod's Department of Archives and History, 801 DeMun Avenue, St. Louis, MO 63105. The Institute also houses the archives of several of the smaller Lutheran bodies: the National Evangelical Lutheran Church, and the Synod of Evangelical Lutheran Churches.

Wisconsin Evangelical Lutheran Synod: The Synod's archives are located at the **Wisconsin Lutheran Seminary,** 11831 N. Seminary Drive, 65W, Mequin, WI 53092.

MENNONITE/AMISH

The Mennonite and Amish churches continue the Radical Reformation thrust begun in Switzerland by the Swiss Brethren. As the Protestant Reformation began, the Swiss Brethren asked for a more thorough reform that included the Christian church's separation from its entanglements with the state. Persecuted out of their homeland, the movement survived in Holland and reorganized under the leadership of Menno Simons, by whose name the group began to be known.

Largely surviving in America, in Pennsylvania, the Mennonites' conservative culture and separation from government and many common social activities led to their becoming a most distinctive subculture in the American religious milieu. They also possessed a strong sense of history and have devoted a significant amount of their energy to historical and genealogical studies. Some of their recent historical studies have been in response to the tourist industry which has moved into Lancaster County, Pennsylvania, and turned the heart of Mennonite/Amish country into a tourist center using the Amish horse-and-buggy image as a dominant theme.

General Sources

1941. Luthy, David. *Amish Settlements Across America.* Aylmer, ON: Pathway Publishers, 1985. 12 pp.

Encyclopedias and Dictionaries

1942. Hege, Christian, and Christian Neff. *Mennonitisches Lexicon.* 4 vols. Frankfurt am Main: The Authors, 1913-7.

1943. *The Mennonite Encyclopedia.* 4 vols. Scottdale, PA: The Mennonite Publishing House, 1955-1959.

Directories

1944. *Amish Directory of the Lancaster County Family.* Gordonville, PA: Pequea Publishers, 1988. 42 pp.

1945. Beiler, Benjamin K., comp. *Old Order [Amish and Mennonite] Shop and Service Directory.* Lancaster, PA: The Author, 1988. 52 pp. Vol. 2. 1989. 54 pp. Vol. 3, 1990. 41 pp.

1946. Cross, Harold E., comp. *Ohio Amish Directory, Holmes County and Vicinity.* Baltimore, MD: The Author, 1965. 262 pp.

1947. *The Lancaster County Family Register.* Gordonville, PA: Pequea Publishers, 1988. 148 pp. A directory of Old Order Amish families and churches.

1948. *The Mennonite Christian Brotherhood Congregations.* Ephrata, PA: Grace Press, 1970. 140 pp.

1949. *The Old Order Mennonite Directory.* Ephrata, PA: The Home Messenger, 1976. 78 pp.

1950. [Stauffer, Mrs. Paul Z. (Louella)]. *Record of Members of the Stauffer Mennonite Church at the Present Time.* Gordonville, PA: Gordonville Print Shop, 1977. Rev. ed.: 1990.

Biographical

1951. *Who's Who Among the Mennonites.* [Newton, KS: A Warkentin], 1937.

1952. *Who's Who in the Free Churches and Other Denominations.* Vol 1- . London: Shaw Publishing Co., 1951- .

Bibliographies

Supplementing the several excellent bibliographical studies cited below is an annual bibliographical update of Mennonite literature carried in *Mennonite Life*, the quarterly from Bethel College in Newton, Kansas.

1953. Bender, Harold Stauffer. *Two Centuries of American Mennonite Literature: A Bibliography of Mennonitica American, 1727-1928.* Goshen, IN: Mennonite Historical Society, Goshen College, 1929. 181 pp.

1954. Hillerbrand, Hans Joachim. *A Bibliography of Anabaptism 1520-1630.* Elkhart, IL: Institute of Mennonite Studies, 1962. 281 pp.

1955. ———. *A Bibliography of Anabaptism 1520-1630: A Sequel, 1962-1974.* Sixteenth Century Bibliography No. 1. St, Louis, MO: Center for Reformation Research, 1975.

1956. Hostetler, John A. *Annotated Bibliography on the Amish: An Annotated Bibliography of Source Materials Pertaining to the Old Order Amish Mennonites.* Scottdale, PA: Mennonite Publishing House, 1951. 100 pp.

1957. Ressler, Martin E. *An Annotated Bibliography of Mennonite Hymnals and Songbooks, 1742-1986.* Lancaster, PA: Privately published, 1987. 117 pp.

1958. Riley, Marvin P. *The Hutterite Brethren: An Annotated Bibliography with Special Reference to South Dakota Hutterite Colonies.* Brookings, SD: South Dakota State University, 1965. 188 pp.

1959. Scrag, Dale R., John D. Thiesen, and David A. Haury. *The Mennonites: A Brief Guide to Information.* North Newton, KS: Bethel College, 1888. 20 pp.

1960. Smartley, Willard M., and Cornelius J. Dyck, eds. *Annotated Bibliography of Mennonite Writings on War and Peace: 1930-1980.* Scottdale, PA & Kitchener, ON: Herald Press, 1987. 740 pp.

1961. Smucker, Donovan E. *The Sociology of Canadian Mennonites, Hutterites, and Amish: A Bibliography with Annotations.* Waterloo, Ont.: Wilfrid Laurier University Press, 1977. 232 pp. Vol. 2.: *The Sociology of Mennonites, Hutterites and Amish, 1977-1990.* 1991. 198 pp.

1962. Springer, Nelson P., and A. J. Klassen, comps. *Mennonite Bibliography, 1631-1961.* 2 vols. Scottdale, PA: Herald Press, 1977.

Archival Depositories/Resource Centers

Though a relatively small group, the Mennonite/Amish community possess a strong sense of their own history, which has spawned an interest in historical research that rivals that of the Jewish community and an interest in genealogy that compares to Latter-day Saints. In that regard they have created a number of archival/historical/genealogical research centers. Besides the North American centers listed below, there are Mennonite archival centers in Brazil, Germany, the Netherlands, and Paraguay.

Associated Mennonite Biblical Seminaries Library
3003 Benham Avenue
Elkhart, IN 46514
The Library houses one of the larger collections of Mennonite literature.

Freeman Academy Historical Library
748 S. Main Street
Freeman, SD 57209

The Historical Center
HCR 3
Richfield, PA 17086

Illinois Mennonite Historical Library and Genealogical Library/Archives
P. O. Box 819
Metamora, IL 61548

Lancaster Mennonite Historical Society
2215 Millstream Road
Lancaster, PA 17602
The Society publishes the quarterly, *Pennsylvania Mennonite Heritage*.

Menno Simons Historical Library and Archives
Eastern Mennonite College
Harrisonburg, VA 22801

Mennonite Historical Library
Bluffton College
Bluffton, OH 45817

Mennonite Historical Library
Goshen College
Goshen, IN 46526-9989
Goshen College is the headquarters for the **Historical Committee of the Mennonite Church** and houses the **Archives of the Mennonite Church**, the largest of the several Mennonite groups.

Mennonite Historical Library and Archives of Eastern Pennsylvania
The Meeting House
Box 82, 565 Yoder
Harleysville, PA 19438
The Library, formerly located in Lansdale, Pennsylvania, is supported by the Mennonite Historians of Eastern Pennsylvania and publishes the *MHEP Newsletter*.

Mennonite Historical Society of Iowa
Box 576
Kalona, IA 52247

Mennonite Information Center
2209 Millstream Road
Lancaster, PA 17602-1494
The Center seeks to provide information on Mennonite and Amish religious life to an increasingly tourist-oriented situation in eastern Pennsylvania.

Mennonite Library and Archives
Bethel College
North Newton, KS 67117

Muddy Creek Farm Library
N. Muddy Creek Road
R. 3
Denver, PA 17517

Pacific Coast Conference Archives
Western Mennonite School
9045 Wallace Road, N.W.
Salem, OR 97304

The People's Place
Main Street
Intercourse, PA 17534
Located in the heart of the tourist-oriented section of Lancaster County, Pennsylvania, The People's Place attempts to educate the general public about the Old Order groups in the area. In that endeavor, it operates a museum, gives public programs and publishes a set of booklets under the imprint "Good Books."

Amish/Mennonite-Canada

Amish Historical Library
Rte. 4
Aylmer, ON N5H 2R3

Mennonite Archival Association
Colombia Bible College
2940 Clearbrook Road
Clearbrook, BC
Canada V2T 2Z8

Mennonite Archives of Ontario
Conrad Grebel College
Waterloo, ON N2L 3G6

Mennonite Educational Institute, Archives
4081 Clearbrook Road
Clearbrook, BC
Canada V2T 3X8

Mennonite Heritage Center Archives
600 Shaftesbury Blvd.
Winnipeg, MB R3P 0M4

Mennonite Historical Society of Alberta
76 Skyline NE
Calgary, AL T2K 5X7

Rosthern Junior College Archives
Rosthern Junior College
Rosthern, SK S0K 3R0

Mennonite Brethren

Center for Mennonite Brethren Studies
4824 East Butler
Fresno, CA 93727-5097
The Center is located on the campus of the Mennonite Brethren Theological Seminary.

Center for Mennonite Brethren Studies
Tabor College
Hillsboro, KS 67063

Center for Mennonite Brethren Studies in Canada
169 Riverton Avenue
Winnipeg, MB
Canada R2L 2E5

Brethren in Christ

Archives of the Brethren in Christ Church
Messiah College
Grantham, PA 17027

METHODISM

Methodism began as a revival movement within the Church of England in the 1740s. It was founded by John Wesley, an Anglican minister, assisted by his brother Charles Wesley, one of the great hymn writers of Christianity. While Wesley never left the Church of England, the American Methodists became independent following the Revolutionary War and the British separated formally in the early nineteenth century. During the nineteenth century, its missionary impulse took the movement worldwide.

The United Methodist Church, the largest Methodist body in North America, has been able to bring together five of the larger Methodist bodies of the nineteenth century: the Methodist Episcopal Church, the Methodist Episcopal Church, South, the Methodist Protestant Church, the United Brethren in Christ, and the Evangelical Association. In the nineteenth century, Methodists also gave birth to the Holiness movement and Pentecostal movement. Two of the most important Methodist groups, the Free Methodist Church and the Wesleyan Church are considered in the chapter on Holiness Churches. See the chapter on Pentecostalism for those groups with Methodist roots.

Methodists have been known for their methodical record keeping and the journals of several Methodist churches, and their constituent organizations have done a thorough job of detailing their progress, membership and finances since the earliest days of the movement. Note: Materials related to Afro-American Methodists have been grouped together with other sources in the chapter on Afro-American Religion (1659-1683) above.

General Sources

1963. Allen, Charles L. *Meet the Methodists: An Introduction to the Methodist Church*. Nashville, TN: Abingdon, 1986. 92 pp.

1964. Washburn, Paul. *United Methodist Primer*. Nashville, TN: Tidings, 1969. 108 pp.

Encyclopedias and Dictionaries

1965. Cornish, George H. *Cyclopedia of Methodism in Canada.* 2 vols. 1881.

1966. Harmon, Nolan B., ed. *Encyclopedia of World Methodism.* 2 vols. Nashville, TN: United Methodist Publishing House, 1974.

1967. Simpson, Matthew, ed. *Cyclopedia of Methodism; Embracing Sketches of the Rise, Progress and Present Condition, with Biographical Notice and Numerous Illustrations.* 5th rev. ed. Philadelphia: L.H. Everts, 1882.

1968. Waltz, Alan. *A Dictionary for United Methodists.* Nashville, TN: Abingdon Press, 1991. 208 pp.

Biographies

1969. Clark, Elmer Talmadge, ed. *Who's Who in Methodism.* Chicago: A.N. Marquis Co., 1952.

1970. Howell, Clinton T. *Prominent Personalities in American Methodism.* Birmingham, AL: The Author, 1945. 512 pp.

1971. Leary, William, comp. *Ministers and Circuits in the Primitive Methodist Church, a Directory* [for Great Britain]. Loughborough, UK: Teamprint, 1990. 266 pp.

1972. Leete, Frederick De Land. *Methodist Bishops: Personal Notes and Bibliography, with Quotations from Unpublished Writings and Reminiscences.* Nashville, TN: Parthenon Press, 1948.

1973. *The Methodist Who's Who.* London: Charles H. Kelly, 1910- .

1974. Thompson, H. A. *Our Bishops.* Chicago: Elder Publishing Company, 1889. 631 pp.

1975. *Who's Who in American Methodism.* Vol. 1- . New York: E.B. Treat and Co., 1916- . Various imprints.

1976. *Who's Who in Methodism: An Encyclopaedia of the Personnel and Departments, Ministerial and Lay, in the United Church of Methodism.* London: The Methodist Times and Leader (Methodist Publications), 1933- .

1977. *Who's Who in Pan-Methodism.* Vol. 1- . Nashville, TN: Parthenon Press, 1940— .

1978. *Who's Who in the Methodist Church.* Nashville: Abingdon Press, 1966. 1482 pp.

Directories

1979. Methodist Publishing House, comp. *Directory of World Methodist Publishing.* Nashville, TN: Methodist Publishing House, 1972. 33 pp. 4th rev. ed.: 1990. 83 pp.

Bibliographies

1980. Baker, Frank, comp. *A Union Catalogue of the Publications of John and Charles Wesley.* Durham, NC: Duke University Divinity School, 1966. 230 pp.

1981. Blanchard, Thomas. *Catalogue of Books Published by J. Wesley and the Preachers in Connexion with Him.* London: Corceaux, 1816. 16 pp.

1982. Cammack, Eleanore, comp. *Indiana Methodism: A Bibliography of Printed and Archival Holdings in the Archives of DePauw University and Indianan Methodism.* Greencastle, IN: DePauw University and the Conferences of Indiana Methodism, 1964.

1983. Green, Richard. *Anti-Methodist Publications Issued during the Eighteenth Century.* London: C.H. Kelly, 1902. 175 pp. Rept. Detroit, MI: Gale Research Co., 1966. 175 pp.

1984. ———. *The Works of John and Charles Wesley: A Bibliography, Containing an Exact Account of All the Publications Issued by the Brothers Wesley, Arranged in Chronological Order, with a List of the Early Editions and Descriptive and Illustrative Notes.* London: C. H. Kelly, 1896. 291 pp. Rept: London: Methodist Publishing House, 1906. 291 pp.

1985. Hatcher, Stephen, comp. *A Primitive Methodist Bibliography.* Leigh-on-Sea, Essex, UK: Laurie Gage Books, 1980.

1986. Jarboe, Betty M. *John and Charles Wesley: A Bibliography.* ATLA Bibliography Series No. 22. Metuchen, NJ: Scarecrow Press, 1987. 422 pp.

1987. Little, Brooks Bivens, ed. *Methodist Union Catalogue of History, Biography, Disciplines, and Hymnals.* Preliminary ed. Lake Junaluska, NC: Association of Methodist Historical Societies, 1967. 478 pp.

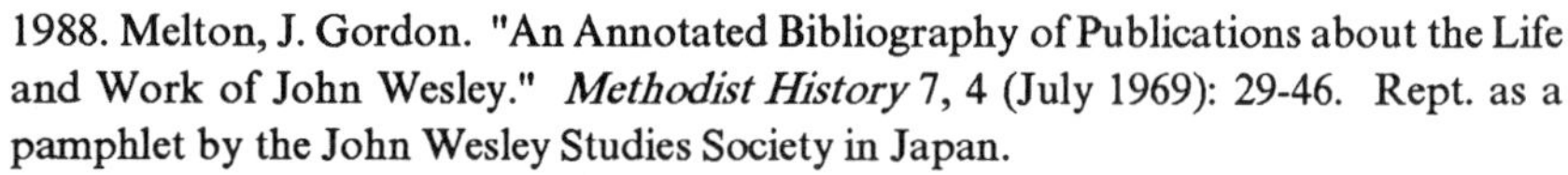
1988. Melton, J. Gordon. "An Annotated Bibliography of Publications about the Life and Work of John Wesley." *Methodist History* 7, 4 (July 1969): 29-46. Rept. as a pamphlet by the John Wesley Studies Society in Japan.

1989. ———. *The Disciplines (Church Manuals) of United Methodism and Related Churches compiled from the Holdings of the Institute for the Study of American Religion.* Evanston, IL: Institute for the Study of American Religion, 1983. 10 pp.

1990. Norwood, Frederick A. "A Bicentennial Appraisal of United Methodist Historical Literature." *American Theological Library Association Proceedings* 38 (1884): 75-92.

1991. ———. "Methodist Historical Studies, 1930-1959." *Church History* Part 1. 28 (1959): 391-417. Part 2. 29 (1960): 74-88.

1992. ———. "Wesleyan and Methodist Historical Studies, 1960-1970: A Bibliographical Article." *Church History* 40, 2 (June 1971): 182-99.

1993. Osborn, G. *Outlines of Wesleyan Bibliography; or, A Record of Methodist Literature from the Beginning.* London: Wesleyan Conference Office, 1869. 220 pp.

1994. Rowe, Kenneth E., ed. *Methodist Union Catalogue: Pre 1976 Imprints.* Vol 1- . Metuchen, NJ: Scarecrow Press, 1975- . To date 6 volumes (A through I) have appeared of a projected 20-volume series.

1995. ———. *United Methodist Studies Basic Bibliographies.* Nashville, TN: Abingdon Press, 1982. 40 pp.

Guides to Periodical Literature

1996. Batsel, John D., and Lyda K. Batsel, comps. *Union List of Methodist Serials, 1773-1973.* Evanston, IL: Prepared in Cooperation with the Commission on Archives and History of the United Methodist Church, the United Methodist Librarians' Fellowship and Garrett Theological Seminary, 1974.

1997. *United Methodist Periodical Index.* 20 vols. Nashville, TN: United Methodist Publishing House, 1961-1980. Quarterly with quincennial cumulations. Originally entitled *Methodist Periodical Index.*

Archival Depositories

Evangelical Congregational Church: The ECC derives from the Evangelical Association, one branch of the German Methodist tradition. The Church's national offices are located at the **Evangelical Congregational Church Center**, 121 S. College, Myerstown, Pennsylvania. The Archives are housed at the Center and the Historical Society is headquartered there. The Church's college is across the street from the Center.

United Methodist Church: During the 1970s, the several archives of United Methodism (remnants of the various church bodies which have merged to create the United church) were brought together in an official archives which was established on the campus of Drew University, Madison, NJ 07490. The archive is under the direction of the church's **General Commission on Archives and History**. Supplementing the Archive collection is the large collection of Methodistica in the Library at Drew University.

Significant Methodist collections are to be found at the several seminaries of the United Methodist Church, especially the older ones such as the **New England Methodist Historical Library** at the Boston University School of Theology, 745 Commonwealth Avenue, Boston, MA 02215; the **United Library of Garrett-Evangelical and Seabury-Western Theological Seminaries**, 2121 Sheridan Road, Evanston, IL 60201; **Pitts Theology Library**, at Candler School of Theology, Emory University, Atlanta, GA 30322; **Duke Divinity School Library**, Durham, NC 27706; and **Bridwell Library Center for Methodist Studies** at Perkins School of Theology, Southern Methodist University, Dallas, TX 75275.

A **Center for United Evangelical Brethren Studies** has been established at United Theological Seminary, 1810 Harvard Blvd., Dayton, OH 45406, and a German Methodist Collection is located at the **Nippert Memorial Library of the Cincinnati Historical Society**, Eden Park, Cincinnati, OH 45402. Black Methodist Studies have found a focus at **Interdenominational Theological Center Library**, 671 Beckwith Street, Atlanta, GA 30314.

Wesley Theological Seminary, 4500 Massachusetts Avenue, Washington, DC 20016, was the ministerial training school for the Methodist Protestant Church, which merged into United Methodism in 1929. The Library houses the best collection of MPC materials.

Apart from the seminaries, two United Methodist archival collections of note are located at the **United Methodist Historical Library**, Beeghley Library, Ohio Wesleyan University, Delaware, OH 43015, and Indiana United Methodist Archives, at the **Roy O. West Library**, DePauw University, Greencastle, IN 46135. Two church agencies with special program agendas also keep an archival collection: **The Upper**

Room Library, 1908 Grand Avenue, Nashville, TN 37203, and the World Methodist Council, Box 518, Lake Junaluska, NC 28745.

Methodist Studies

The United Methodist Church's **General Commission on Archives and History** guides and promotes historical study throughout the church. It publishes the quarterly, *Methodist History*, and sponsors the **Historical Society of the United Methodist Church**. *The Historian's Digest*, formerly the newsletter of the Commission, was adopted by the Society at its founding in 1988 as its newsletter. Annual conference Commissions on Archives and History are active locally and most have established archives for the records of the conferences and their individual congregations.

While never known for their theological work, there is a very real interest among some Methodists for theological pursuits.

John Wesley Theological Institute
c/o Ted E. Rodd
82 Woodside Road
Riverside, IL 60546

Wesley Historical Society
c/o Wesley Historical Society Library
Suthlands College
Wimbledon Parkside
London SW19
The Wesley Historical Society is the major British organization focusing upon Methodist history.

Wesleyan Theological Society
c/o Asbury Theological Seminary
Wilmore, KY 40390
Founded in 1965, the Society publishes the *Wesleyan Theological Journal*. It tends to be conservative (but not fundamentalist) and holiness (but not exclusively) in its perspective.

World Methodist Historical Society
P. O. Box 127
Madison, NJ 07940
The Society is affiliated with the World Methodist Council and publishes the *Historical Bulletin*.

MORAVIANS

The Moravians trace their history to the followers of Czechoslovakian reformer John Hus (1369-1414). Their movement all but died and was revived by refugees living on the estate of Count von Zinzendorf in Saxony. Here they became the fountainhead of a Pietist (dutiful and devotional) revival which had its primary manifestation in England as Methodism. The Moravians have been devoted historians and support on-going Moravian historical work at their two church centers.

Moravian Studies

Moravian Archives-Northern Province
41 W. Locust Street
Bethlehem, PA 18018
or
Moravian Archives-Southern Province
4 E. Bank Street
Winston-Salem, NC 27101-5307
Both provinces of the Moravian Church keep excellent archives. The Southern Archives issues a quarterly *The Moravian Archives News.*

Moravian Music Foundation
Peter Memorial Library
20 Cascade Avenue
Winston-Salem, NC 27127
Music was a vital part of Moravian life and has led to the establishment of one of the major centers for the study of religious music.

Reeves Library
Moravian College and Theological Seminary
Main Street at Elizabeth Avenue
Bethlehem, PA 18018
Bethlehem is also home to the Church's seminary, whose library also houses a substantial Moravian collection.

OLD CATHOLICISM

Strictly speaking, Old Catholicism is the movement which emerged in response to the declaration of papal infallibility during the First Vatican Council. These churches derive their episcopal orders and are in communion with the Old Catholic Church of Utrecht (Netherlands). There is only one church in North America currently in communion with Utrecht, the Polish National Catholic Church.

The term Old Catholicism has also, in the English-speaking world, become more generalized to include a host of independent Catholic, Orthodox, and Anglican churches which have (or claim to have) valid Apostolic orders yet are not recognized by any of the larger churches for which such orders are a treasured possession. While some of these churches have orders derived from Utrecht, none is currently in communion with it. These smaller independent churches have proliferated greatly during the last generation.

Biographical Material

1998. Bain, Alan. *Bishops Irregular.* Bristol, UK: The Author, 1985. 233 pp.

1999. Ward, Gary L. *Independent Bishops: An International Directory.* Detroit, MI; Apogee Books, 1990. 524 pp.

Directories

2000. Pruter, Karl, ed. *A Directory of Autocephalous Bishops.* Highlandsville, MO: St. Willibrord Press, 1988-89. 56 pp. Supple. 7 pp. Supple. 1990-91. 65 pp. Supple. 1991. 16 pp.

2001. ———, comp. *A Directory of Priests Serving the Autocephalous Churches in the Apostolic Succession.* Highlandsville, MO: St. Willibrord's Press, 1991. 64 pp.

Bibliographies

2002. Pruter, Karl, and J. Gordon Melton. *The Old Catholic Sourcebook.* Sects & Cults in America Series Vol. 3. New York: Garland Publishing, 1983. 254 pp.

2003. Wielewinski, Bernard, comp. & ed. *Polish National Catholic Church, Independent Movements, Old Catholic Church and Related Items: An Annotated Bibliography.* New York: Columbia University Press, 1990. 751 pp.

Archival Depositories

Only two publicly accessible archival depositories of significance for Old Catholicism exist in North America. The Polish National Catholic Church's archives are under the guidance of its **Commission on History and Archives,** 1031 Cedar Avenue, Scranton, PA 18505.

A more general collection assembled by Old Catholic bishops Karl Pruter and Alan Bain has been deposited at the **American Religions Collection** at the University of California—Santa Barbara.

PENTECOSTALISM

Pentecostalism is a movement which emerged out of the Holiness movement at the beginning of the twentieth century. It followed the general teachings of the Holiness movement but emphasized the experience of the baptism of the Holy Spirit. It believes that as a sign that a believer has received the baptism, s/he will speak in tongues. Objects of derision during the first half of the century, Pentecostals have become a mass movement in the post-World War II era and have forced the older churches to take notice of them.

Encyclopedias

2004. Burgess, Stanley M., and Gary B. McGee, eds. *Dictionary of Pentecostal and Charismatic Movements.* Grand Rapids, MI: Zondervan Publishing House, 1988. 914 pp.

Bibliographies

2005. Dayton, Donald W., ed. *The Higher Christian Life: A Bibliographical Overview.* New York: Garland Publishing Publishing, 1985. 201 pp.

2006. Faupel, David W. *The American Pentecostal Movement: A Bibliographical Essay.* Wilmore, KY: Asbury Theological Seminary, B. L. Fisher Library, 1972. 56 pp. Rept. in Donald W. Dayton. *The Higher Christian Life: A Bibliographical Overview.* New York: Garland Publishing, 1975. 201 pp. *See:* (2005).

2007. Ibarra, Eduardo. *Holy Spirit: International Bibliography 1972-June 1974 Indexed by Computer.* Strasbourg, France: Cerdic-Publications, 1974. 48 pp.

2008. Jones, Charles Edwin, ed. *A Guide to the Study of the Pentecostal Movement.* ATLA Bibliography Series No. 6. 2 vols. Metuchen, NJ: Scarecrow Press and the American Theological Library Association, 1983.

2009. Martin, Ira Jay. *Glossolalia, the Gift of Tongues: A Bibliography.* Cleveland, TN: Pathway Press, 1970. 72 pp.

2010. Mills, Watson E. *Charismatic Religion in Modern Research: A Bibliography.* NABPR Bibliographic Series No. 1. Macon, GA: Mercer University Press, 1985. 178 pp.

2011. ———. *Glossolalia: A Bibliography.* Studies in the Bible and Early Christianity Vol. 6. New York: Edwin Mellen Press, 1985. 129 pp.

Archival Depositories

Two major archival collections of Pentecostal literature and artifacts exist. The **Assemblies of God Archives** is located in the church's headquarters complex, 1445 Boonville Avenue, Springfield, MO 65802. It publishes the quarterly *Assemblies of God Heritage.*

The **Holy Spirit Research Center** at Oral Roberts University Library, 7777 S. Lewis, Tulsa, OK 74171, has built an impressive archive which is more broadly representative of the Pentecostal movement and includes a special emphasis upon divine healing. The Center has published a number of bibliographies on Pentecostalism.

The major center for records of the Holiness Pentecostal church is at **Lee College**, Cleveland, the school of the Church of God (Cleveland, Tennessee), and **Emmanuel College**, Franklin Springs, Georgia, the school of the International Pentecostal Holiness Church.

In Canada, the **Lorne Philip Hudson Memorial Library** at Western Pentecostal Bible College houses the "Archive for Pentecostal Studies."

Pentecostal Studies

Society for Pentecostal Studies
c/o Peter Hoken
P. O. Box 2671
Gaithersburg, MD 20879
The Society publishes *Pneuma* (2/year).

PRESBYTERIAN/REFORMED

The Presbyterian and Reformed Churches trace their history to the Reformation in Switzerland, primarily that in Geneva under John Calvin. On the European continent, the name Reformed was generally used and in the United States, churches of the Reformed tradition usually have an ethnic background from France, Germany, Hungary, the Netherlands, or Switzerland. In the British Isles, the Reformed movement was known as Presbyterianism and gained its greatest success in Scotland. In both cases, it is a learned tradition which has produced some of Protestantism's finest theologians. *Note*: material relevant to the Reformed/ Presbyterian tradition, especially its continental roots, is to be found above in the chapter on the Reformation and Protestantism.

Encyclopedias and Dictionaries

2012. Nevin, Alfred, ed. *Encyclopedia of the Presbyterian Church in the United States of America: Including the Northern and Southern Assemblies.* Philadelphia: Presbyterian Encyclopedia Publishing Co., 1884. 1248 pp.

Biographical Material

2013. Evans, Joseph. *Biographical Dictionary of Ministers and Preachers of the Welsh Calvinist Methodist Body or Presbyterians of Wales.* Carnarvon: D. O'Brien Owen, 1907. 338 pp.

2014. Scott, E.C., comp. *Ministerial Directory of the Presbyterian Church, U.S. 1861-1941.* Rev. and supplemented 1942-1950. Atlanta, GA: Hubbard Printing Co., 1980. 798 pp.

2015. VandenBerge, Peter N., ed. *Historical Directory of the Reformed Church in America, 1628-1965.* New Brunswick, NJ: Reformed Church in America, Commission on History, [1966].

2016. Witherspoon, Eugene Daniel, Jr., comp. *Ministerial Directory of the Presbyterian Church, U.S., 1861-1967.* Doraville, GA: Foot and Davies, 1967.

Bibliographical

2017. Benedetto, Robert. *Guide to the Manuscript Collections of the Presbyterian Church, U.S.* New York: Greenwood Press, 1990. 570 pp.

2018. *An Index of Book Reviews of Southern Presbyteriana Published between 1800 and 1945.* Austin, TX: Austin Presbyterian Theological Seminary, Library, 1960.

2019. Parker, Harold M., Jr., comp. *Bibliography of Published Articles on American Presbyterianism, 1901-1980.* Bibliographies and Indexes in Religious Studies No. 4. Westport, CT: Greenwood Press, 1985. 261 pp.

2020. Prince, Harold B. *A Presbyterian Bibliography.* ATLA Bibliography Series No. 8. Metuchen, NJ: Scarecrow Press, 1983. 466 pp.

2021. Spence, Thomas Hugh. *Catalogues of Presbyterian and Reformed Institutions. I. As Historical Sources. II. In the Historical Foundation.* Montreat, NC: Historical Foundation Publications, 1952.

2022. Trinterud, Leonard J. *A Bibliography of American Presbyterianism during the Colonial Period.* Philadelphia: Presbyterian Historical Society, 1968.

2023. Verner, Beryl Anne, comp. *Huguenots in South Africa: A Bibliography.* Cape Town, South Africa: University of Cape Town School of Librarianship, 1967. 44 pp.

Archival Depositories

Christian Reformed Church: The major depository of Christian Reformed material is at **Calvin College**, Grand Rapids, MI 49056.

Cumberland Presbyterian Church: The **Historical Foundation of the Cumberland Presbyterian Church** is located at the headquarters building, 1978 Union Avenue, Memphis, TN 38104. It cooperates with the Presbyterian Church (USA) in publishing *American Presbyterians and the Journal of Presbyterian History.*

Churches of God, General Conference: The Churches of God grew out of a split in the German Reformed Church (now part of the United Church of Christ). Records of the Church are to be found at the Library of the **Winebrenner Theological Seminary**, 701 E. Melrose Avenue, Box 478, Findley, OH 45839-0478.

Presbyterian Church in America: The archives of the Presbyterian Church in America is located at the Buswell Library, **Covenant Theological Seminary**, 12330 Conway Road, St. Louis, MO 63141.

Presbyterian Church (USA): The primary archive of the Presbyterian Church (USA) is at the **Presbyterian Historical Association** and Department of History, 425 Lombard Street, Philadelphia, PA 19147 (formerly the history and archive center for the United Presbyterian Church in the U.S.A.). It publishes the quarterly *American Presbyterians and Journal of Presbyterian History*. A second center for the Department of History is at the **Historical Foundation**, Montreat, NC 28757 (formerly the center for the Presbyterian Church in the U.S.). Strong collections of Presbyterian materials are found at the church's several seminaries, especially at the **Speer Library** of Princeton Theological Seminary, Princeton, NJ 08540, the **Library of the Union Theological Seminary in Virginia**, 3401 Brook Road, Richmond, Virginia 23227, and **McCormack Theological Seminary**, 800 W. Belden, Chicago, IL 60614.

The Huguenot [French Reformed] tradition has largely been absorbed into the Presbyterian Church (U.S.A.) however, three historical organizations keep the memory of their contribution (including the founding of the first Protestant Church in what is now the United States) alive. The **Huguenot Historical Society** maintains a Library at 88 Huguenot Street, Box 339, New Paltz, NY 12561. The Library of the **Huguenot Society of America** is in Manhattan at 122 E. 58th Street, New York, NY 10022. Southern Huguenots can find material at the Library of the **Huguenot Society of South Carolina**, 21 Queen Street, Charleston, SC 29401.

Reformed Church in America: The archives of the oldest continuously existing Protestant church in America is located at **New Brunswick Theological Seminary,** New Brunswick, NJ 08901. It is under the guidance of the Church's Commission on History.

Reformed Presbyterian Church in North America: The archives of the Reformed Presbyterian church and the particular tradition of Scottish Presbyterianism it continues can be found in the **Reformed Presbyterian Theological Seminary Library**, 7418 Penn Avenue, Pittsburgh, PA 15208.

ROMAN CATHOLICISM

The Roman Catholic Church holds a special position in Christendom. It is the oldest and largest church in North America and the largest single church organization among Christians worldwide. Because of its antiquity and its international scope, many items of direct relevance to the Western Roman tradition are to be found above in the different chapters on church history. For example, the chapter on the medieval church is almost totally Roman Catholic related.

Not surprisingly, of the several denominations in the United States, the Roman Church has produced the largest number of reference books. In this regard, special note should be made of James Patrick McCabe's *Critical Guide to Catholic Reference Books* (2144), now in its third edition (1988), each has become increasingly more exhaustive and has supplied a needed bibliographical control over the field. This chapter is limited to reference books about the Roman Catholic Church, as opposed to books produced by Catholic authors and/or books presenting the Roman Catholic Church's perspective on various issues or general reference books which also cover the Roman Church. Also, for convenience the material on the church in North America has been separated.

General Information

2024. Deedy, John G. *The Catholic Fact Book.* Chicago: Thomas More Press, 1986. 412 pp.

2025. Hassan, Bernard. *The American Catholic Catalog.* San Francisco: Harper & Row, 1980. 274 pp.

2026. Klein, Peter. *Catholic Source Book.* Worthington, MN: The Printers, 1980. 2nd ed.: 1981. 3rd ed.: 1985. 370 pp.

2027. Scharp, Heinrich. *How the Catholic Church Is Governed.* Glen Rock, NJ: Deus Books, 1960. 128 pp.

Encyclopedias and Dictionaries

2028. Addis, William Edward, and Thomas Arnold. *A Catholic Dictionary Containing Some Account of the Doctrine, Discipline, Rites, Ceremonies, Councils and Religious Orders of the Catholic Church.* 1886. 17th ed. Rev. by T.B. Scannell et al. London: Routledge and Kegan Paul, 1960. 860 pp.

2029. Attwater, Donald, ed. *The Catholic Encyclopaedic Dictionary.* 1931. Rev. ed as: *A Catholic Dictionary.* New York: Macmillan Company, 1961. 552 pp.

2030. Bowden, Charles Henry. *Short Dictionary of Catholicism.* New York: Philosophical Library, 1958.

2031. Broderick, Robert C. *The Catholic Encyclopedia.* Nashville & New York: Thomas Nelson, 1976. 603 pp. Rev. ed., 1987. 613 pp.

2032. ———. *The Concise Catholic Dictionary.* Milwaukee: Bruce Publishing Company, 1944. 195 pp. Rev. ed. as *The Catholic Concise Encyclopedia.* St. Paul, MN: Catechetical Guild Educational Society, 1957. Later rev. ed. as *Catholic Concise Dictionary.* Rev. by Placid Hermann and Marion Alphonse Habig. Chicago: Franciscan Herald Press, 1966. 330 pp.

2033. *Catholic Encyclopedia Dictionary; Containing 8500 Articles on the Beliefs, Devotions, Rites, Symbolism, Tradition and History of the Church; Her Laws, Organizations, Dioceses, Missions, Institutions, Religions, Orders, Saints; Her Part in Promoting Art, Science, Education and Social Welfare.* Comp. and ed. under the direction of the editors of the Catholic Encyclopedia. New York: Gilmary Society, 1941. 1095 pp.

2034. *Catholic Encyclopedia for School and Home.* 13 vols. New York: McGraw-Hill Book Co., 1965-1968.

2035. *Catholic Encyclopedia for School and Home. The Contemporary Church [Supplement].* New York: Grolier, 1974. 264 pp.

2036. *Catholic Reference Encyclopedia.* 6 vols. N.p. Catholic Educational Guild, 1968.

2037. Daniel-Rops, Henri, ed. *The Twentieth Century Encyclopedia of Catholicism.* 150 vols. New York: Hawthorn Books, 1958-1968.

2038. *Enciclopedia Cattolica.* 12 vols. Città del Vaticano: Enciclopedia Cattolica, 1949-54.

2039. Evans, Illtud, et al., eds. *The New Library of Catholic Knowledge.* 12 vols. New York: Hawthorn Books, 1963-64.

2040. Foy, Felician A., and Rose M. Avato. *A Concise Guide to the Catholic Church.* Huntington, IN: Our Sunday Visitor, 1984. 158 pp.

2041. Hardon, John A. *Modern Catholic Dictionary.* Garden City, NY: Doubleday & Company, 1980. 635 pp.

2042. Hendrikx, E., van, J. C. Doenson, and W. Bocxe., eds. *Encyclopaede van het Katholicisme.* 3 vols. Antwerp, Belgium: 't Groeit, 1955-56.

2043. *Guide to Catholic Italy: With a Dictionary of Church Terminology.* Washington, DC: Catholic War Veterans of the U.S.A., 1950. 1373 pp.

2044. Hebermann, Charles George, et al., eds. *Catholic Encyclopedia.* 16 vols. New York: The Encyclopedia Press and the Gilmary Society, 1907-1922. Supplement, 1922. Supplement, 1958.

2045. Kühner, Hans. *Encyclopedia of the Papacy.* Trans. by Kenneth J. Northcott. New York: Philosophical Library, [1958]; London: Peter Owen, [1959]. 249 pp. Originally published in German as *Lexikon der Päbste von Petrus bis Pius XII.* Zürich: W. Classen, 1956.

2046. Maryknoll Sisters of St. Dominic, eds. *The Catholic Heritage Encyclopedia.* Union City, NJ: J. J. Crawley, 1966.

2047. McDonald, William J., ed. *New Catholic Encyclopedia: An International Work of Reference on the Teachings, History Organization and Activities of the Catholic Church and on All Institutions, Religions, Philosophies and Scientific and Cultural Developments Affecting the Catholic Church from Its Beginning to the Present.* 17 vols. New York: McGraw-Hill, 1967-1979.

2048. Nevins, Albert J., ed. *Maryknoll Catholic Dictionary.* New York: Grosset & Dunlap, 1965. 710 pp.

2049. Pallen, Conde B., and John J. Wynne, eds. *The New Catholic Dictionary.* New York: Universal Knowledge Foundation, 1929. 1078 pp.

2050. Pegis, Jessie Corrigan. *A Practical Catholic Dictionary.* Garden City, NY: Hanover House, 1957. 258 pp. Rept.: New York: All Saints, 1961. 258 pp.

2051. Pfeiffer, Harold A. *The Catholic Picture Dictionary.* New York: Duell, Sloan and Pearce, 1948. 156 pp.

2052. Quin, Mabel, ed. *Virtue's Catholic Encyclopedia.* 3 vols. London: Virtue, 1965. Rev. ed. as *The New Catholic People's Encyclopedia.* Ed. by Edward G. Finnegan. 3 vols. Chicago: Catholic Press, 1973.

2053. Sheppard, Lancelot Capel, ed. *Twentieth Century Catholicism: A Periodic Supplement to the Twentieth Century Encyclopedia of Catholicism.* No. 1. New York: Hawthorn Books, 1965.

Directories

2054. *The Book of Catholic Names and Numbers.* Pierpont, NY: Catholic Heritage Press, 1980. 168 pp.

2055. *Catholic Almanac.* Vol. 1- . Huntington, IN: Our Sunday Visitor, 1904- . Updated annually.

2056. *Catholic Directory.* Vol. 1- . London: Associated Catholic Publications, 1837- . Annual.

2057. *Catholic Directory for Scotland.* Vol. 1- . Glasgow: John S. Burns and Sons, 1828- . Annual.

2058. *Catholic Press Directory.* Rockville Centre, NY: Catholic Press Association, 1923-. Published annually. Includes list of Roman Catholic periodicals.

2059. *Catholic Press in India: Directory.* Bombay: St. Xavier's College, Institute of Communication Arts, 1976.

2060. *Catholic Year Book.* Vol. 1- . London: Burns, Oates and Washbourne, 1950- . Annual.

2061. *CCC Guide to Media Resources.* Washington: Catholic Communications Campaign, periodically updated.

2062. Eilers, Franz-Josef, and Wilhelm Herzog, eds. *Catholic Press Directory Africa/Asia.* Communicatio Socialis: Zeitschrift für Publizistik in Kirche und Welt, Beihaft 4. Paderborn: Ferdinand Schöningh, 1975.

2063. Elesser, Suzanne P., ed. *Preparing Laity for the Ministry 1986: A Directory of Programs in Catholic Dioceses throughout the United States.* Washington, DC: United States Catholic Conference, 1986. Unpaged.

2064. *Irish Catholic Directory.* Vol. 1- . London: Associated Catholic Publications, 1838- . Annual.

2065. *Official Catholic Directory 1988.* Vol. 1- . New York: P.J. Kennedy & Sons, 1886- . Published annually. Various titles and imprints.

2066. Willging, Eugene Paul, and Dorothy E. Lynn. *A Handbook of American Catholic Societies.* Scranton, PA: Catholic Library Association, 1940.

Biographical Volumes

2067. *American Catholic Who's Who.* Vol. 1- . Washington, DC: National Catholic News Service, 1935- . Biennial.

2068. Attwater, Donald. *A Dictionary of the Popes from Peter to Pius XII.* London: Burns, Oates & Washbourne, 1939.

2069. ———. *Martyrs from St. Stephen to John Tung.* New York: Sheed and Ward, 1957. 236 pp.

2070. Bransom, Charles N., Jr. *Ordinations of U.S. Catholic Bishops 1790-1989: A Chronological List.* N.p.: U.S. Catholic Conference, 1990. 277 pp.

2071. Brown, Stephen James Meredith, comp. *An Index of Catholic Biographies.* Dublin: Central Catholic Library Association, 1930. 2nd ed. as *International Index of Catholic Biographies.* London: Burns, Oates and Washbourne, 1935. 287 pp.

2072. Brusher, Joseph Stanislaus. *Popes Through the Ages.* Princeton, NJ: Van Nostrand, 1959. 530 pp.

2073. *Catholic Encyclopedia and Its Makers.* New York: The Encyclopedia Press, 1917.

2074. *Catholic Who's Who.* Vols. 1-35. London: Burns and Oates, 1908-1952. Annual. Originally entitled *Catholic Who's Who and Yearbook.*

2075. Code, Joseph Bernard. *American Bishops, 1964-1970.* St. Louis, MO: Wexford Press, [c. 1970]. 25 pp.

2076. ———. *Dictionary of the American Hierarchy, 1789-1964.* New York: J.F. Wagner, 1964. Rept.: New York: Free Press, 1967.

2077. Delaney, John J. *Dictionary of American Catholic Biography.* Garden City, NY: Doubleday, 1984. 621 pp.

2078. Delaney, John J., and James Edward Tobin. *Dictionary of Catholic Biography.* Garden City, NY: Doubleday and Co., 1961. 1245 pp.

2079. *Directory of Catholic Communications Personnel.* Washington, DC: Office of Public Affairs, NCCB/USCC, 1987. 44 pp.

2080. Finn, Brendan A. *Twenty-Four American Cardinals: Biographical Sketches of Those Princes of the Catholic Church Who Either Were Born in America or Served There at Some Time.* Boston: B. Humphries, 1948. 475 pp.

2081. Hoehn, Matthew, ed. *Catholic Authors: Contemporary Biographical Sketches.* 2 vols. Newark, New Jersey: St. Mary's Abbey, 1948, 1952. Rept.: (first vol.). Detroit: Gale Research Co., 1981.

2082. Kelly, J. N. D. *The Oxford Dictionary of Popes.* Oxford: Oxford University Press, 1986. 347 pp.

2083. Kirk, John. *Biographies of English Catholics in the Eighteenth Century.* London: Burns and Oates, 1909.

2084. Liederbach, Clarence A. *America's Thousand Bishops: From 1513 to 1974, from Abromowicz to Zuroweste.* St. Mary's College Historical Series. Cleveland, OH: Dillon/Liederbach, 1974. 67 pp.

2085. ———. *Canada's Bishops: From 1120-1975, from Allen to Yelle.* St. Mary's Historical Series. Cleveland, OH: Dillon/Liederbach, 1975. 64 pp.

2086. National Catholic Welfare Conference. *A Pictorial Directory of the Hierarchy of the United States.* Washington, DC: National Catholic Welfare Conference, 1962. 86 pp.

2087. O'Donnell, John Hugh. *The Catholic Hierarchy of the United States, 1790-1922.* Catholic University of America Studies in American Church History Vol. 4. Washington, DC: Catholic University of America Press, 1922. Rept.: New York: AMS Press, 1974. 223 pp.

2088. Reuss, Francis Xavier. *Biographical Cyclopedia of the Catholic Hierarchy of the United States, 1748-1898: A Book for Reference in the Matter of Dates, Places and Persons in the Records of Our Bishops, Abbots and Monsignors.* Milwaukee, WI: Wiltzius & Co., 1898.

2089. Taylor, S. S., and L. Melsheimer, eds. *Europe: A Biographical Dictionary, Containing about 5500 Biographies of Prominent Personalities in the Catholic World.* Who's Who in the Catholic World Vol. 1. Düsseldorf: L. Schwann Verlag, 1967.

2090. Thornton, Francis Beauchesne. *Our American Princes: The Story of the Seventeen American Cardinals.* New York: G.P. Putnam's Sons, 1963. 319 pp.

2091. Willging, Eugene Paul, and Dorothy E. Lynn. *A Handbook of American Catholics.* Scranton, PA: Catholic Library Association. 24 pp.

Biographical Volumes: The Saints

2092. Attwater, Donald, comp. *A Dictionary of Saints; Based on Butler's "Lives of the Saints", Complete Ed.* New York: P. J. Kennedy; London: Burns & Oates, 1958. 280 pp.

2093. ———. *The Penguin Dictionary of the Saints.* Baltimore, MD: Penguin Books, 1965. 362 pp.

2094. ———. *Saints of the East.* New York: P.J. Kennedy, 1963. 190 pp.

2095. *Book of Saints: A Dictionary of Persons Canonized or Beatified by the Catholic Church.* Comp. by the Benedictine Monks of St. Augustine's Abbey, Ramsgate. 5th ed. New York: Thomas Y. Crowell, 1966. 740 pp. Published in England as *Book of Saints: A Dictionary of Servants of God Canonized by the Catholic Church.* 5th ed. London: Adams and Charles Black, 1966. 740 pp.

2096. Butler, Alban. *Butler's Lives of the Saints.* 4 Vols. New York: Kenedy, 1963.

2097. Coulson, John, ed. *The Saints: A Concise Biographical Dictionary.* New York: Hawthorn Books/London: Burns and Oates, 1958. 496 pp.

2098. Delaney, John J. *Dictionary of Saints.* Garden City, NY: Doubleday and Company, 1980.

2099. Dunbar, Agnes Baillie Cunninghame. *A Dictionary of Saintly Women.* 2 vols. London: G. Bell and Sons, 1904-1905.

2100. *Encyclopedia of Catholic Saints.* 12 vols. Philadelphia: Chilton Books, 1966.

2101. Engelbert, Omer. *The Lives of the Saints.* Trans. by Christopher and Anne Jackson Freemantle. New York: D. McKay Co./London: Thames and Hudson, [1951]. First published in 1911.

2102. Farmer, David Hugh. *The Oxford Dictionary of the Saints.* Oxford: Clarendon Press, 1978. 435 pp. 2nd ed.: Oxford: Oxford University Press, 1987. 478 pp.

2103. Holweck, Frederick George. *A Biographical Dictionary of the Saints, with a General Introduction on Hagiology.* St. Louis, MO: B. Herder Book Co., 1924. Rept. Detroit, MI: Gale Research Co., 1969.

Bibliographies/Indices

2104. Alhadef, John Joseph, comp. *National Bibliography of Theological Titles in Catholic Libraries.* Vol. 1- Los Gatos, CA: Alma College, 1965- .

2105. Allison, Anthony Francis, and David M. Rogers. *A Catalogue of Catholic Books in English Printed Abroad or Secretly in England, 1558-1640.* 2 vols. Biographical Studies, vol. 3, nos. 3-4. Bognor Regis: Arundel Press, 1956. Rept. London: William Dawson & Sons, 1964. 187 pp.

2106. Assunta, Maria, ed. *The Church in the World: A Bibliography Compiled by Students of the Course on the Church at Saint Mary's College, Notre Dame, Indiana.* Cincinnati, OH: CSC Press, 1963.

2107. Bernard, Jack F., and John J. Delaney. *A Guide to Catholic Reading: A Practical Handbook for the Reader on Every Aspect of Catholic Literature with Descriptions of More than 750 Books of Catholic Interest.* Garden City, NY: Doubleday and Company, 1966. 392 pp.

2108. *Best Sellers: The Monthly Book Review.* Vol. 1- . Scranton, PA: University of Scranton, 1941- . Monthly.

2109. *Bibliographie catholique, revue critique des ouvrages de religion, de philosophie, d'histoire, de littérarie, d'éducation.* Paris: Bureau de la Bibliographie catholique, 1841-89. 80 v. Monthly.

2110. *Bibliography of the Catholic Church Representing Holdings of American Libraries Reported to the "National Union Catalog" in the Library of Congress.* London: Mansell Information/Publishing, 1970. 527 pp.

2111. Blum, Fred, ed. *Theses and Dissertations: A Bibliographical Listing, Keyword Index and Author Index.* Washington, DC: Catholic University of America Press, 1970. 548 pp. Covers the years 1961-67.

2112. *Bollettino Bibliografico Internazionale.* Vol. 1 . Roma: Pia Società di San Paolo, 1948- .

2113. Boyle, Leonard E. *A Survey of the Vatican Archives and Its Medieval Holdings.* Pontifical Institute of Medieval Studies Subsidia Mediaevalia, No. 1. Toronto: Pontifical Institute of Medieval Studies, 1972.

2114. Brown, Stephen James Meredith. *An Introduction to Catholic Booklore.* Catholic Bibliographical Series, No. 4. London: Burns, Oates and Washbourne, 1933. 105 pp.

2115. Byrns, Lois. *Recusant Books in America, 1559-1640.* New York: P. Kavenaugh Hand-Press, 1959.

2116. Cadden, John Paul. *The Historiography of the American Catholic Church, 1785-1943.* Washington, DC: Catholic University of America Press, 1944. 122 pp.

2117. Carlen, Sister Mary Claudia, I.H.M. "Bibliography of Catholic Bibliographies." Unpublished in the Archives of Marygrove College Library, Detroit, MI.

2118. ———. comp. *A Guide to the Encyclicals of the Roman Pontiffs from Leo XIII to the Present Day (1878-1937).* New York: H.W. Wilson, 1939. 247 pp. Rept. Ann Arbor, MI: University Microfilms, 1964.

2119. *Catalogue of All Catholic Books in English.* New York: Benzinger Brothers, 1912. 183 pp.

2120. *Catholic Book Review.* Vol. 1- . Ottawa: Paul T. Harris, 1947- . Issued bimonthly.

2121. *The Catholic Bookman: International Survey of Catholic Literature.* 7 Vols. Grosse Point, MI: Walter Romig and Company, 1937-44. Issued monthly through 1939 and then bi-monthly. Superseded by the *Catholic Periodical and Literature Index* and the *Religious Book Review.*

2122. Catholic Library Association. *Catholic Supplement to the Standard Catalog for High School Libraries.* New York: H. W. Wilson Company, 8th ed., 1962. A listing of Roman Catholic books for high school age readers selected by a committee of the Catholic Library Association chaired by Clara C. Glenn.

2123. ———. *C.L.A. Booklist.* Haverford, PA: Catholic Library Association, 1942-1970. 28 vols. Annual. Originally entitled *The Catholic Booklist.*

2124. ———. High School Libraries Section. *C.L.A. Basic Reference Books for Catholic High School Libraries.* 2nd ed. Haverford, PA: Catholic Library Association, 1963. 47 pp.

2125. Catholic Library Service. *Catalog and Basic List of Essential First-Purchase Books.* New York: Paulist Press, 1962. 152 pp.

2126. *Catholic Library World.* Vol. 1- Haverford, PA: Catholic Library Association, 1929- . Ten issues annually. There is an annual review of religious reference books.

2127. *Catholic Magazine Index.* 3 vols. Detroit, MI: Walter Romig and Company, July/Dec. 1937-July/Dec. 1938.

2128. Catholic University of America. *Theses and Dissertations: A Bibliographical Listing, Keyword Index and Author Index.* Cumulation, 1961-1967. Ed. by Fred Blum. Washington, DC: Catholic University of America Press, 1970. 548 pp.

2129. *A Century of Religious Studies: Faculty and Dissertations.* Washington, DC: School of Religious Studies, Catholic University of America, 1989.

2130. Clancy, Thomas H. *English Catholic Books, 1641-1700: A Bibliography.* Chicago: Loyola University Press, 1974. 157 pp. Continues the work begun by Allison (2105).

2131. Dahlin, Therrin C., Gary P. Gillum, and Mark L. Grover. *The Catholic Left in Latin America: A Comprehensive Bibliography.* Reference Publications in Latin America Series. Boston: G. K. Hall, 1981. 410 pp.

2132. Diocese of Cashel Library. *Catalogue of the Cashel Diocesan Library, County Tipperary, Republic of Ireland.* Boston: G.K. Hall, 1973.

2133. Dollen, Charles, comp. *Vatican II: A Bibliography.* Metuchen, NJ: Scarecrow Press, 1969. 208 pp.

2134. Ellis, John Tracy. *A Guide to American Catholic History.* Milwaukee: Bruce Publishing Co., 1959. 147 pp. Rev. ed.: with John Trisco. Santa Barbara, CA: ABC-Clio Information Services, 1982. 265 pp.

2135. ———. *A Select Bibliography of the History of the Catholic Church in the United States.* New York: Declan X. McMullen Co., 1947. 96 pp.

2136. Finotti, Joseph Maria. *Biblographia Catholica Americana: A List of Works Written by Catholic Authors and Published in the United States. Part 1, from 1784 to 1820 Inclusive.* New York: Catholic Publication House, 1872. 318 pp. Rept. Burt Franklin Biblio. and Ref. Series Vol. 401. New York: Burt Franklin, 1971. 318 pp.

2137. Gillow, Joseph. *A Literary and Biographical History, or Bibliographical Dictionary, of the English Catholics from the Breach with Rome to the Present Time.*

5 vols. New York: Catholic Publication Society; London: Burns and Oates, [1885-1902]. Rept. Burt Franklin Bibliography and Reference Series Vol. 25. New York: Burt Franklin, 1961.

2138. Grace, Melania, and Gilbert Charles Peterson, comps. *Books for Catholic Colleges: A Supplement to Shaw's "List of Books for College Libraries."* Chicago: American Library Association, 1948. 134 pp. Supplement as: Grace, Melania, Gilbert Charles Peterson and Redmond Ambrose Burke. *Books for Catholic Colleges, 1948-1949.* Chicago: American Library Association, 1950. 57 pp. Supplement as: Grace, Melania and Louis A. Ryan. *Books for Catholic Colleges, 1950-1952.* Chicago: IL: American Library Association, 1954.

2139. Haley, Emile Louise, comp. *Books by Catholic Authors in the Cleveland Public Library: An Annotated List.* Cleveland, OH: Cleveland Public Library, 1911. 232 pp.

2140. Hansen, Eric C. *Nineteenth-Century European Catholicism: A Bibliography of Secondary Works in English.* New York: Garland Publishing, 1989. 558 pp.

2141. *Index for the Complete Works of the United States Catholic Historical Society, 1884-1966.* N.p.: n.d.[1967]. 441 pp.

2142. Kenneally, Finbar. *United States Documents in the Propaganda Fide Archives: A Calendar.* Academy of American Franciscan History, First Series Vol. 1- . Washington, DC: Academy of American Franciscan History, 1966- .

2143. Lewis, Clifford Merle, ed. *Focus: Catholic Background Reading for the Orientation of College and University Students.* Washington, DC: National Newman Club Federation, 1956.

2144. McCabe, James Patrick. *Critical Guide to Catholic Reference Books.* Litton, CO: Libraries Unlimited, 1971. 287 pp. 2nd. ed.: 1980. 282 pp. 3rd ed.: Englewood, CO: Libraries Unlimited, 1989. 323 pp.

2145. McCoy, James Comly. *Jesuit Relations of Canada, 1632-1673: A Bibliography.* Paris: A Rayu, 1937. 310 pp. Rept.: New York: Burt Franklin, 1972. 310 pp.

2146. Maddrell, Jane G. *Bibliography of Catholic Books Published during 1948—Listed According to Subject.* Kansas City, KS: Bibliographic Publishing Co., 1949. Only one issue of what was to be an annual volume.

2147. Matochik, Michael J. *Catholicism and Anti-Catholicism: A Title List from the Microfische Collection, Pamphlets in American History, Group IV.* Sanford, CT: Microfilming Corporation of America, 1982. 127 pp.

2148. Menendez, Albert J. *The Catholic Novel: An Annotated Bibliography.* New York: Garland Publishing, 1948. 344 pp.

2149. ———. *The Road to Rome: An Annotated Bibliography.* New York: Garland Publishing, 1986. 152 pp.

2150. Merrill, William Stetson. *Catholic Authorship in the American Colonies before 1784.* Washington, DC: [Catholic University of America Press], 1971. 18 pp.

2151. Mierzwinski, Theophil J., comp. *What Do You Think of the Priest? A Bibliography of the Catholic Priesthood.* New York: Exposition Press, 1972. 95 pp.

2152. Musto, Ronald G. *The Peace Tradition in the Catholic Church: An Annotated Bibliography.* New York: Garland Publishing, 1987. 624 pp.

2153. O'Malley, Charles D., and personnel of the W.P.A., comp. *The Sutro Library Catalogue of Works on the Catholic Church by Spanish, Portuguese, and Spanish-American Writers before 1800.* Bibliographical Series No. 3, Pt 1. Sacramento, CA: State Library, 1941.

2154. Parsons, Wilfred. *Early Catholic Americana: A List of Books and Other Works by Catholic Authors in the United States, 1729-1830.* New York: Macmillan Company, 1939. Rept. Boston: Milford House, 1973. 282 pp.

2155. ———. *List of Additions and Corrections to Early Catholic America: Contributions of French Translations (1724-1820) by Forest Bowe.* New York: Franco-Americana, 1952. 101 pp.

2156. Pilley, Catherine M., ed. *Guide to Catholic Literature.* 8 vols. Haverford, PA: Catholic Library Association. 1940-1968.

2157. Pollen, John Hungerford, ed. *Sources for the History of Roman Catholics in England, Ireland and Scotland from the Reformation Period to That of Emancipation, 1533 to 1795.* Helps for Students of History No. 39. New York: Macmillan Company/ London: SPCK, 1921.

2158. Pontifical Institute of Medieval Studies. *Dictionary Catalogue of the Pontifical Institute of Medieval Studies.* 5 vols. Boston, MA: G.K. Hall & Co., 1972.

2159. *Publications in Print: A Descriptive Index Complete with Subject Title and Cross-Reference.* Washington, DC: National Conference of Catholic Bishops/United States Catholic Conference, 1991. Periodically updated.

2160. *Recusant Books of St. Mary's, Oscott.* Vol. 1- . New Oscott, Sutton Coldfield, UK: St. Mary's Seminary, 1964- . Four volumes each covering a selected historical period from 1518 to the present are projected.

2161. Regis, Mary, ed. *The Catholic Bookman's Guide: A Critical Evaluation of Catholic Literature.* New York: Hawthorne Books, 1962. 638 pp.

2162. Seger, Mary C. *Church Polity and American Politics: Issues in Contemporary American Catholicism.* New York: Garland Publishing, 1989. c.300 pp.

2163. Smyth, Donald, et al. *Focus: An Annotated Bibliography of Catholic Reading.* Washington, DC: National Newman Club Federation, 1962. 134 pp.

2164. Snyderwine, L. Thomas. *Researching the Development of Lay Leadership in the Catholic Church since Vatican II: Bibliographical Abstracts.* Roman Catholic Studies Vol. 1. Lewiston, NY: Edwin Mellen Press, 1987. 192 pp.

2165. Stanley, Mary E., trans. *The Books Published by the Vatican Library, 1885-1947: An Illustrated Analytic Catalogue.* Vatican City: Apostolic Library, 1947. 183 pp.

2166. Vismans, Thomas A., and Lucas Brinkhoff. *Critical Bibliography of Liturgical Literature.* English ed. trans. from German by Raymond W. Fitzpatrick and Clifford Howell. Nijmegen: Bestelcentrale der V.S.K.B. Publications, 1961. 72 pp.

2167. Vollmer, Edward R. *The Catholic Church in America: An Historical Bibliography.* New York: Scarecrow Press, 1956. 354 pp. Rev. ed. 1963. 399 pp.

2168. Weber, Francis J. *A Select Guide to California Catholic History.* Los Angeles: Westernlore Press, 1966. 227 pp.

2169. ———. *A Select Bibliography to California Catholic Literature, 1856-1974.* Los Angeles: Dawson's Book Shop, 1974. 70 pp.

2170. Weigle, Marta, comp. *A Penitente Bibliography.* Albuquerque, NM: University of New Mexico Press, 1976. 162 pp.

2171. Willging, Eugene Paul, comp. *Catalog of Catholic Paperback Books.* 5 vols. New York: Catholic Book Merchandiser, 1961-1966.

2172. ———. *The Index to Catholic Pamphlets in the English Language.* 6 vols. Washington, DC: Catholic University of America Press, 1937-1953.

Guides to Periodical Literature

2173. *The Catholic Periodical and Literature Index: A Cumulative Author-Subject Index to a Selective List of Catholic Periodicals and an Author-Title-Subject Bibliography of Adult Books by Catholics with a Selection of Catholic-Interest Books by Other Authors.* Edited by Natalie A. Logan. Vol. 1- . Haverford, PA: Catholic Library Association, 1930- . Issued bi-monthly with biennial cumulative issues. Volumes 1-13 as *The Catholic Periodical Index.*

2174. Fitzgerald, Catherine Anita. *A Union List of Catholic Periodicals in Catholic Institutions on the Pacific Coast.* Ann Arbor, MI: Edwards Brothers, 1957.

2175. Gaines, Stanley J., comp. *Publisher's Guide: Catholic Journals, Academic and Professional.* River Forest, IL: Commission on Journals, Academic and Professional, 1961. 85 pp.

2176. Lucey, William Leo. *An Introduction to American Catholic Magazines.* [Philadelphia, PA: n.p. 1952?]

2177. Weber, Francis J. *A Select Bibliographical Guide to California Catholic Periodical Literature, 1844-1973.* Los Angeles: Dawson's Book Shop, [1973].

2178. Willging, Eugene Paul, and Herta Hatzfeld, comps. *Catholic Serials of the Nineteenth Century in the United States: A Descriptive Bibliography and Union List. Second Series.* Vol. 1- . Washington, DC: Catholic University of America, 1959- .

Statistics

2179. Quinn, Bernard, and John Feister. *Apostolic Regions of the United States, 1971.* Washington, DC: Glenmary Research Center, 1978. 53 pp.

2180. ———. *Distribution of Catholic Priests in the United States, 1971.* Washington, DC: Glenmary Research Center, 1975. 35 pp.

Roman Catholic Orders

Encyclopedias and Dictionaries

2181. Hélyot, Pierre. *Dictionnaire des Ordres Religieux.* Paris: Migne, 1859-63. 4 Vols.

2182. Pelliccia, Guerrino, and Giancarlo Rocca. *Dizionario degli Istituti di Perfezione.* 7 vols. Roma: Ed. Paoline, 1974-83.

Biographical Volumes

2183. Code, Joseph Bernard. *Great American Foundresses.* New York: Macmillan, 1929. Rept.: Freeport, NY: Books for Libraries, 1968. Rept. as: *The Veil is Lifted.* Milwaukee, WI: Bruce Publishing Co., 1932.

2184. Knowles, David, et al., eds. *The Heads of Religious Houses, England and Wales, 940-1216.* Cambridge, England: Cambridge University Press, 1972.

Directories

2185. Anson, Peter Frederick. *The Religious Orders and Congregations of Great Britain and Ireland.* Worcester, England: Stanbrook Abbey Press, 1949.

2186. *CARA Formation Directory for Women Religious and Religious Brothers, 1989-1990.* Washington, DC: Center for Applied Research in the Apostolate, 1989- . Updated regularly.

2187. *CARA Seminary Directory 1984: US Catholic Institutions for the Training of Candidates for the Priesthood.* Washington, DC: Center for Applied Research in the Apostolate, 1984. 108 pp.

2188. Cowan, Ian Borthwick, and David Edward Easson. *Medieval Religious Houses, Scotland. With an Appendix on the Houses in the Isle of Man.* 2nd ed. London: Longman Group, 1976.

2189. Dehey, Elinor Tong. *Religious Orders of Women in the United States: Catholic; Accounts of Their Origin, Works and Most Important Institutions, Interwoven with Histories of Many Famous Foundresses.* Rev. ed.: [Hammond, IN: W. B. Conkey Co., c. 1930].

2190. *Directory of Religious Orders, Congregations and Societies of Great Britain and Ireland.* Glasgow: J.S. Burns, 1955- . Annual.

2191. *Guide to Religious Communities for Women.* Chicago: National Sisters Vocation Conference, 1981. 445 pp.

2192. Gwynn, Aubrey Osborn, and Richard Neville Hadcock. *Medieval Religious Houses: Ireland; with an Appendix to Early Sites.* Harlow: Longmans, Green, 1970.

2193. Holub, William, ed. *Ministries for the Lord: A Resource Guide and Directory of Church Vocations for Men, 1979-1980.* New York: Paulist Press, 1978.

2194. Kapsner, Oliver Leonard, ed. *Catholic Religious Orders: Listing Conventional and Full Names in English, Foreign Language, and Latin, also Abbreviations, Date and Country of Origin and Founders.* 1948. 2nd ed.: Collegeville, MN: St. John's Abbey Press, 1957.

2195. Knowles, David, and Richard Neville Hadcock. *Medieval Religious Houses, England and Wales.* New ed. London: Longmans, Green and Co., 1971/New York: St. Martin's Press, 1972.

2196. McCarthy, Thomas Patrick. *Guide to the Catholic Sisterhoods in the United States.* 5th ed. Washington, DC: Catholic University of America Press, 1964.

2197. O'Hara, Magdalen, ed. *Directory of Women Religious in the United States 1985.* Wilmington, DE: Michael Glazier, 1985. 989 pp.

2198. Rudder, Victor L., Jr. *Guide to Religious Ministries for Catholic Men and Women.* 11th annual ed.: New Rochelle, NY: Catholic News Pub. Co., 1990. 200 pp. Regularly updated.

Bibliographies

2199. Adams, Eleanor Burnham. *A Bio-Bibliography of Franciscan Authors in Colonial Central America.* Washington, DC: Academy of American Franciscan History, 1953. 97 pp.

2200. Bangert, William V. *A Bibliographical Essay on the History of the Society of Jesus: Books in English.* Study Aids on Jesuit Topics No. 6. St. Louis, MO: Institute of Jesuit Sources, 1976. 75 pp.

2201. Constable, Giles. *Medieval Monasticism: A Select Bibliography.* Toronto & Buffalo: University of Toronto Press, 1976. 171 pp.

2202. Facelina, Raymond, and Marie Zimmerman. *Religious Life: International Bibliography 1972-June 1973 Indexed by Computer.* RIC Supplement 8. Strasbourg, France: Cerdic-Publications, 1973. 42 pp.

2203. Harmer, Sister Mary Fabian. *Books for Religious Sisters: A General Bibliography.* Washington, DC: Catholic University Press of America, 1963. 184 pp.

2204. Kapsner, Oliver L., comp. *A Benedictine Bibliography: An Author-Subject Union List.* 2 vols. 2nd ed. Collegeville, MN: St. John's Abbey Press, 1962.

2205. McCoy, James Comly. *Jesuit Relations of Canada, 1632-1673: A Bibliography.* Paris: A. Rau, 1937. Rept.: Burt Franklin Bibliography and Reference Series Vol. 456. New York: Burt Franklin, 1972.

2206. Morgan, John H. *Aging in the Religious Life: A Comprehensive Bibliography, 1960-75.* Wichita, KS: Institute on Ministry and the Elderly, 1977.

2207. Pigault, Gérard. *Christian Communities: International Bibliography 1972-June 1974 Indexed by Computer.* RIC Supplement 16. Strasbourg, France: Cerdic-Publications, 1974. 40 pp.

2208. Polgár, László. *Bibliography of the History of the Society of Jesus.* Sources and Studies for the History of the Jesuits Vol. 1. Rome: Jesuit Historical Institute/St. Louis, MO: St. Louis University, 1967. 207 pp.

2209. St. John's University Library. *Checklist of Manuscripts Microfilmed for the Monastic Manuscript Microfilm Library.* Vol. 1- . Collegeville, MN: St. John's University Library, 1967- .

2210. Smet, Joachim, and Gervase Toelle, comps. *Catalog of the Carmelitana Collection, Whitefriars Hall.* [Washington, DC: Whitefriars Hall, 1959]. 381 pp.

2211. Sutcliffe, Edmund F., comp. *Bibliography of the English Province of the Society of Jesus 1773-1953.* London: Manresa Press, 1957. 247 pp.

2212. Thomas, Evangeline, CSJ, ed. *Women Religious History Sources: A Guide to Repositories in the United States.* New York & London: R. R. Bowker, 1983. 329 pp.

2213. Walter, Frank Keller, and Virginia Doneghy, comps. *Jesuit Relations and Other Americana in the Library of James F. Bell: A Catalogue.* Minneapolis, MN: University of Minnesota Press, [1950]. 419 pp.

Canon Law

Encyclopedias and Dictionaries

2214. Naz, R., et al., eds. *Dictionnaire de Droit Canonique, Contenant tous les Terms du droit Canonique, avec un Summaire de l'Histoire et des Institutions et de l'État Actuel de la Discipline.* Paris: Letouzey et Ané, 1935- .

2215. Köstler, Rudolf. *Wörterbuch zum Codex juris Canonici.* München: J. Kosel and F. Pustet, 1927-29. 379 pp.

2216. Roussos, E. *Lexilogion Ekklésiastikou Dikaiou.* 2 vols. Athens: 1948-49.

2217. Trudel, P. *Dictionary of Canon Law.* St. Louis, MO: B. Herder Book Co., 1919.

Bibliographies

2218. Cunningham, Richard G. *An Annotated Bibliography of the Work of the Canon Law Society of America, 1965-1980.* Washington, DC: Canon Law Society of America, 1982. 121 pp.

2219. Ferreira-Ibarra, Dario C., comp. *The Canon Law Collection of the Library of Congress: A General Bibliography with Selective Annotations.* Washington, DC: Library of Congress, 1981. 210 pp.

2220. Sheridan, Leslie W. *Bibliography on Canon Law, 1965-1971.* Tarlton Law Library Legal Bibliography No. 6. Austin, TX: University of Texas, School of Law, 1971. 801 pp.

2221. Zimmerman, Marie. *Church and State in France: Book Index 1801-1979.* RIC Supplements 45-46. Strasbourg, France: Cerdic-Publications, 1980. 92 pp.

2222. ———. *Marriage and Code of Canon Law: International Documentation 1975-1983.* RIC Supplements 84-85. Strasbourg, France: Cerdic-Publications, 1983. 160 pp.

2223. ———. *Revision of the Code of Canon Law: International Bibliography 1965-1977 Indexed by Computer.* RIC Supplement 29. Strasbourg, France: Cerdic-Publications, 1977. 46 pp.

Guides to Periodical Literature

2224. *Canon Law Abstracts: A Half Yearly Review of Periodical Literature in Canon Law.* Vol. 1- . Edinburgh: Canon Law Society of Great Britain, 1959- . Semi-annual.

Roman Catholic Studies

Academy of American Franciscan History
1712 Euclid Ave.
Berkeley, CA 94709

Academy of Catholic Hispanic Theologians of the United States
1050 N. Clark Street
El Paso, TX 79905

American Catholic Historical Association
Catholic University of America
Washington, DC 20064
The Association publishes the quarterly *The Catholic Historical Review.*

American Catholic Historical Society
263 South Fourth
Philadelphia, PA 19106

American Catholic Philosophical Association
Catholic University of America
Washington, DC 20064

American Catholic Psychological Association
c/o American Psychological Association
1200 17th Street, N.W.
Washington, DC 20036

Canon Law Society of America
1933 Spielbusch Avenue
Toledo, OH 43624

Catholic Biblical Association
Catholic University of America
Washington, DC 20064

Catholic Theological Society of America
c/o Mary Hins
Catholic University of America
Washington, DC 20064

Cushwa Center for the Study of American Catholicism
University of Notre Dame
Notre Dame, IN 46556
The Center publishes the *American Catholic Studies Newsletter*

Fellowship of Catholic Scholars
c/o Msgr. George A. Kelly
St. John's University
Jamaica, NY 11439

Institute of Formative Spirituality
Duquesne University
Pittsburgh, PA 15219

United States Catholic Historical Society
3 Downing Drive
East Brunswick, NJ 08816
The Society publishes the quarterly *The U. S. Catholic Historian.*

Archival Depositories

As large and as old as the Roman Catholic Church in America is, it is not surprising that its archival material is scattered among a number of its many schools and centers. The main depositories, however, are to be found at some of its older and more prominent institutions of higher learning. Among the prominent Roman Catholic institutions are those created by the religious orders, and for the women's order, an excellent guide of archival holdings exists.

2225. Thomas, Evangeline, CSJ, ed. *Women Religious History Sources: A Guide to Repositories in the United States.* New York: R. R. Bowker Company, 1983. 329 pp.

Other prominent archival depositories include:

Archives of the America Catholic Historical Society of Philadelphia
St. Charles Boromeo Seminary
Overbrook
Philadelphia, PA 19151

Department of Archives and Manuscripts
Catholic University of America
Washington, DC 20017

Georgetown University
Washington, DC 20007

St. Mary's Seminary and University
Roland Park
Baltimore, MD 21210

University of Notre Dame Archives
Box 512
Notre Dame, IN 46556

St. Louis University
St. Louis, MO 63103

UNITARIANS / UNIVERSALISTS

The Unitarian Universalist Association has a unique place in North American religion. Its two constituent bodies were for many years Christian in orientation and played a significant role in the development of American Christianity. However, in recent decades the church has, at the national level, taken itself out of the Christian community. On the local level its ministers still move among professional circles with clergy colleagues in Christian ministerial associations. The richness of Unitarian history, centered upon intellectual achievement, has produced a rich literature and the historians to appreciate it.

General Sources

2226. Robinson, David. *The Unitarians and the Universalists.* Westport, CT: Greenwood Press, 1985. 368 pp.

Biographical Volumes

2227. Eliot, Samuel A. *Heralds of a Liberal Faith.* 4 vols. Boston, MA: American Unitarian Association, 1910-52.

2228. Ware, William. *American Unitarian Biography.* 2 vols. Boston, MA: James Munroe, 1850.

Bibliographies

2229. Godbey, John C. *A Bibliography of Unitarian Universalist History.* Chicago: Meadville Lombard Theological Seminary, 1982.

2230. Myerson, Joel, ed. *The Transcendentalists: A Review of Research and Criticism.* New York: Modern Language Association, 1984. 534 pp.

2231. Seeberg, Alan. "Recent Scholarship in American Universalism: A Bibliographical Essay." *Church History* 41, 4 (December 1972): 513-23.

Archival Depositories

The Unitarian-Universalist Association, formed in 1961, located its archives in the Association headquarters building, 25 Beacon Street, Boston, MA 02108. Significant collections of books and documents relative to the history of Unitarianism and Universalism can also be found at Harvard Divinity School Library, 45 Francis Street, Cambridge, MA 02138; Meadville Theological School, 5701 S. Woodlawn Avenue, Chicago, IL 60637, and the **Rhode Island Historical Society**, Providence, RI.

A special collection of UUA material is housed in the **Universalist Unitarian Genealogical Society**, 10605 Lakespring Way, Hunt Valley, MD 21030, which maintains a 1,300 volume library and extensive biographical files on UUA members and ministers.

VIII

ESOTERIC/NEW AGE/OCCULT RELIGION

GENERAL METAPHYSICAL/OCCULT SOURCES

Modern esoteric religion continues the major longstanding alternative to Christianity in Western society. While rooted in pre-Christian Paganism, it had its strongest expression in Gnosticism and Neo-Platonic philosophy, elements of which, especially Neo-Platonism, have reappeared over the centuries. Frequently, esoteric thought and the people who held such notions suffered the fate of the loser in the West's ideological battles as representatives of the dominant faith denounced esotericism and on occasion persecuted its followers. It survived, however, by founding creative ways to interact with Christianity and assuming numerous disguises in order to find acceptance. In the eighteenth century, a marked esoteric revival emerged concurrently with the rise of religious liberties.

Esoteric studies are only beginning to reach some degree of sophistication, and the history of occult religions are just now being integrated into the history of Western culture and world religions. As the esoteric revival gained popular support, many scholars dismissed the "occult" as merely a return to superstition and unworthy of serious study as a genuine religious movement. That has changed somewhat with the development of a pluralistic religious community in the West and the making of common cause between the esoteric and Eastern religions.

In spite of the "outsider" position inhabited by esoteric religions, a host of reference books have been produced which have helped to organize the subject and offer some bibliographical control. Many, like the majority of Christian books, simply systematize the beliefs and teachings of esotericists. A second important group examines the peculiar (and often outlandish) assertions put forth by some esoteric faiths that claim to be based upon scientifically demonstratable facts. Parapsychology developed as a new scientific discipline to examine those claims and some spokespersons for the establishment, opposed both to the rise of esotericism and the publicizing of its "scientific" claims, have been passionate in their denunciation of even the work of parapsychology.

As with the early sections of this *Sourcebook*, the material is arranged in a way which moves from the general to the particular. It also concentrates on the religious (or spiritual, as some would insist) rather than the purely secular claims, though the occult is inherently religious in nature. Thus parapsychology is treated in cursory fashion, as is ufology. Anomalistics, i.e., the study of scientific anomalies, seems beyond the subject matter of this text. Given the facts that between a quarter and a third of the population in the West are believers in astrology and reincarnation, and that more than 20 percent have practiced some form of meditation, suggests that there are more metaphysically inclined people than there are Methodists, Presbyterians, or Episcopalians. The occult is no longer just a socially marginal belief system, but a strong minority viewpoint that is making a home for itself in the middle of the culture.

Encyclopedias and Dictionaries

2232. Abbot, A. E. *A Dictionary of the Occult Sciences.* London: Emerson Press, 1960. 176 pp.

2233. Bessy, Maurice. *A Pictorial History of Magic and the Supernatural.* London: Spring Books, 1964. 317 pp.

2234. Bletzer, June G. *The Donning International Encyclopedic Psychic Dictionary.* Norfolk, VA: The Donning Company, 1986. 875 pp.

2235. Cattell, Ann. *A Dictionary of Esoteric Words.* New York: Citadel Press, 1967. 128 pp.

2236. Cavendish, Richard. *Encyclopedia of the Unexplained.* New York: McGraw-Hill Book Company, 1974. 304 pp.

2237. ———, ed. *Man, Myth and Magic.* 24 vols. New York: Marshall Cavendish Corp., 1978.

2238. Chambers, Howard V. *An Occult Dictionary for the Millions.* Los Angeles: Sherbourne Press, Inc. 1966. 160 pp.

2239. Chaplin, J. P. *Dictionary of the Occult and Paranormal.* New York: Dell Publishing Company, 1976. 176 pp.

2240. Cohen, Daniel. *The Encyclopedia of the Strange.* New York: Dorset Press, 1985. 291 pp.

2241. Day, Harvey. *Occult Illustrated Dictionary.* New York: Oxford University Press, 1976. 156 pp.

2242. De Givry, Emile Grillot. *Illustrated Anthology of Sorcery, Magic and Alchemy.* New York: Causeway A & W Visual Library, 1973. 995 pp.

2243. De Purucker, Gottfried. *Occult Glossary.* Pasadena, CA: Theosophical University Press, 1933. 193 pp.

2244. Dunwich, Gerina. *The Concise Lexicon of the Occult.* New York: Carol Publishing Group, 1990. 211 pp.

2245. Fodor, Nandor. *Encyclopedia of Psychic Science.* N.p.: University Books, 1966. 416 pp.

2246. Franklyn, Julian. *A Dictionary of the Occult.* New York: Causeway Books, 1973. 301 pp.

2247. Gettings, Fred. *Dictionary of Occult, Hermetic and Alchemical Sigils.* London, Boman and Henley: Routledge & Kegan Paul, 1981. 410 pp.

2248. Gibson, Walter B., and Litzka R. Gibson. *The Complete Illustrated Book of Divination and Prophecy.*

2249. ————. *The Complete Illustrated Book on the Psychic Sciences.* Garden City, NY: Doubleday and Company, 1966. 403 pp.

2250. Godwin, David. *Cabalistic Encyclopedia.* St. Paul, MN: Llewellyn Press, 1979. 101 pp.

2251. Introvigne, Massimo. *Il Cappello del Mago. I Nuovi Movimenti Magici dallo Spiritismo al Satanismo.* Milano: Sugar Co., 1990. 487 pp.

2252. Poinsot, M. C. *The Encyclopedia of the Occult Sciences.* New York: Robert M. McBride and Company, 1939. 496 pp.

2253. Riland, George. *The New Steinerbooks Dictionary of the Paranormal.* New York: Warner Books, 1980. 358 pp.

2254. Shepard, Leslie, ed. *Encyclopedia of Occultism and Parapsychology.* 2 vols. with supplements. Detroit: Gale Research Co., 1978, 1980, 1981; 2nd ed.: 3 Vols. 1984-85, 1987.

2255. Spence, Lewis. *An Encyclopedia of Occultism.* New Hyde Park, NY: University Books, 1906. 440 pp. Superseded by Shepard (2254).

2256. Waite, Arthur Edward. *The Occult Sciences.* Secaucus, NJ: University Books, 1974. 292 pp.

2257. Walker, Benjamin. *Man and the Beast Within: The Encyclopedia of the Occult, the Esoteric and the Supernatural.* New York: Stein and Day, 1977. 343 pp.

2258. Wedeck, Harry. *Dictionary of Magic.* New York: Philosophical Library, 1956. 105 pp.

2259. ———. *Dictionary of the Occult.* New York: Philosophical Library, 1956. 105 pp.

2260. Zolar. *The Encyclopedia of Ancient and Forbidden Knowledge.* Los Angeles: Nash Publishing Company, 1907. 394 pp.

Biographical Volumes

2261. Dalmor, E. R. *Quien Fue y Quien es en Ocultismo.* Buenos Aires, Argentina: Kier S.A., 1989. 972 pp.

2262. Finch, W. J., and Elizabeth Finch. *Who's Who in the Psychic World.* Phoenix, AZ: Esoteric Publications/Psychic Register Intl., 1971. 184 pp. 2nd edit., 1973. 240 pp.

2263. Hartmann, William C. *Who's Who in Occultism, New Thought, Psychism and Spiritualism.* Jamaica, NY: The Occult Press, 1925. 196 pp. 2nd ed.: 1927. 350 pp. Rev. ed.: 1930. 176 pp. Rev. ed. 1931. 186 pp.

Directories

No comprehension of the growth of the occult world is possible without some apprehension of the large number of professional occultists, groups, book and supply houses and publications that exist. While no directory on the national scene even approaches completeness, a search through several of the directories listed blow will begin to give you the idea. The directory of Chicago (Melton, 2282) is the only attempt at a complete city directory, but comparable listings could be compiled in any metropolitan area. These directories will also help you locate local representatives on occult groups of interest.

The New Age movement made the creation of networks between individuals, organizations and communities a central focus of its activity and has thusly raised the production of directories to a new level. *See*: the chapter on the New Age movement below.

2264. Bloomfield, Frena. *The Occult World of Hong Kong.* Hong Kong: Hoi Kwong Priest Co., 1980. 133 pp.

2265. Cushing, A. I. *The International "Mystery Schools" Directory.* Boston: A.C. Publications, 1970. 34 unnumbered pages.

2266. Drury, Nevill, and Gregory Tillet. *Other Temples Other Gods: The Occult in Australia.* Sydney, Australia: Hodder and Stoughton, 1980. 254 pp.

2267. *The International Psychic Register.* Ed. by Donald McQuaid. Vol 1- . Erie, PA: Ornion Press, 1977- . Editions for 1977, 1978, and 1979 are known to have appeared.

2268. *The Q Directory.* London: Aquariana. 1978-79. 105 pp. London: Pallas Aquariana 1980-81. 117 pp. #4, London: The Neopantheist Society, n.d. 119 pp.

2269. Rodway, Howard. *The Psychic Directory: The Comprehensive Guide to Practicing Psychics in the UK.* London: Futura, 1984. 178 pp.

2270. *Spirals Directory of Occult Resources* (DOOR). Grastonbury, UK: Spiral Publications. Updated quarterly.

2271. Wilcox, Laird. *Directory of the Occult and Paranormal.* Kansas City, MO: Editorial Research Service, 1981. 26 pp. Rev. ed. as: *Guide to the American Occult.* Olathe, KS: The Author, 1987. 84 pp.

2272. Yeterian, Dixie, Sandra Johnson, and Jacqueline Sparks. *The Psychic Bluebook.* Lompoc, CA: Near Horizons, 1978. 156 pp.

Directories-North America

2273. Brandon, Jim. *Weird America: A Guide to Places of Mystery in the United States.* New York, NY: E. P. Dutton, 1978. 257 pp.

2274. *Chicago Psychic Guide.* Chicago: Astro Occult Book Store, 1975. 30 pp. Rev. ed. as: *Chicagoland and Midwest Psychic Guide.* Chicago: Mystic Church and Healing Center, 1976. 27 pp. Rev. ed. as: Techter, David, and Elinor Jaksto. *Astro-Psychic Guide.* Chicago: Gemini Publications, 1978. 38 pp.

2275. Griggs, Edward N. C., and Gerald N. Born *Occult Bookstores and Supplies Directory.* Chicago, IL: Stonehenge Books, 1977. 27 pp.

2276. Harris, Jay, and Susan Harris. *Visions and Reflections: Psychic America, 1776-1976.* Scottsdale, AZ: Omega Productions, 1976. 39 pp.

2277. Hartman, William C. *Who's Who in Occult Psychic and Spiritual Realms.* Jamaica, NY: The Occult Press, 1925. 136 pp. Rev. ed. as: *Hartman's International Directory of Psychic Science and Spiritualism.* Jamaica, NY: The Occult Press, 1930. 176 pp. 2nd edition, Jamaica, NY: The Occult Press, 1931. 186 pp.

2278. Holzer, Hans. *The Directory of the Occult.* Chicago, IL: Henry Regnery Co., 1974. 224 pp.

2279. Kaczmarek, Dale. *The Greater Chicagoland Psychic Directory.* Chicago: The Author, 1986. 10 pp. Rev. ed.: 1987-88. 12 pp.

2280. ————. *International Directory of Psychic Sciences.* Chicago: The Author, 1985. 8 pp. Rev. ed.: 1986. 21 pp. Rev. ed.: 1987. 26 pp.

2281. Larsen, Miriam C. *Where Are The Psychics?* Dallas, TX: Miriam C. Larsen, 1985. 535 pp.

2282. Melton, J. Gordon. "The Chicago Psychic/Metaphysical/Occult New Age Community: A Directory and Guide." In *Psychic Chicago* by Brad Steiger. Garden City, New York: Doubleday and Company, 1976. Pp. 161-86.

2283. *Occult Publications Directory.* [Chicago, IL]: Ghost Research Society, 1987. 10 pp.

2284. Regush, June, and Nicolas, Regush. *PSI, The Other World Catalogue: The Comprehensive Guide to the Dimensions of Psychic Phenomena.* New York: Putnam, 1974/Toronto: Longman, 1974. 320 pp.

2285. Stewart, Louis. *Life Forces: A Contemporary Guide to the Cult and Occult.* Kansas City: Andrews and McMeep Inc., 1979. 613 pp.

2286. Werner, Elizabeth. *Directory of Psychic Arts and Sciences.* Burbank, CA: Inner-Space Interpreters, 1974. 40 pp.

2287. White, A. Sandra. *The Seeker's Guide to Groups and Societies.* Central Valley, NY: Aurea Publications, 1964. 109 pp. Rev. ed: Allenhurt, NJ: Aurea Publ., 1969. 110 pp. New edition: 1970.

Bibliographies

2288. Abbot, A. E. *A Guide to Occult Books and Sacred Writings of the Ages.* London: Emerson Press, 1963. 64 pp. Anthroposophical in orientation.

2289. *Bibliographia et l'Annulaire International des Sciences Psychophysiques et Occultes.* Paris, 1940.

2290. *Bibliotheca Esoterica.* Paris, 1940.

2291. Caillet, Albert L. *Manuel Bibliographique des Sciences Psychiques ou Occultes.* 3 vols. Paris: Lucien Dorbon, 1913.

2292. Carlson, E. A. *Foreteckning Oefver Literatue Angaende Spiritism.* Stockholm: 1902.

2293. Carrington, Hereward. "The Occult Readers Guide." *Fate* 4 (May-June 1951): pp. 54-61

2294. Claire, Thomas C. *Occult Bibliography: An Annotated List of Books Published in English, 1971-1975.* Metuchen, NJ: Scarecrow Press, 1978. 454 pp.

2295. ———. *Occult/Paranormal Bibliography: An Annotated List of Books Published in English, 1976 through 1981.* Metuchen, NJ: Scarecrow Press, 1984. 561 pp.

2296. Delaney Oliver J. "The Occult: Diabolica to Alchemists." *R Q [Research Quarterly]* 11 (1971): 7-14.

2297. Durville, H. *Bibliographie du Magnetisme et des Sciences Occultes.* Paris: 1895.

2298. Encausse, G. *Bibliographie Methodique de la Science Occulte (Livres Moderns).* Paris: 1892.

2299. Galbreath, Robert. "The History of Modern Occultism: A Bibliographical Survey." *Journal of Popular Culture* 5 (1971): 725-54. Rept. in: Robert Galbreath, ed. *The Occult: Studies and Evaluations.* Bowling Green, OH: Bowling Green University Popular Press, 1972. pp. 98-126.

2300. ———. "Occult and the Supernatural." In *Handbook of American Popular Culture* edited by M. Thomas Inge. 2 vols. Westport CT: Greenwood Press, 1980.

2301. Gardner, F. Leigh. *A Catalogue Raisoné of Works on the Occult Sciences.* 3 vols. London: The Author, 1903-1923. Rev. ed.: Vol. I. Rosicrucian Books. 1923. 101 pp. Abridged ed.: Vol. I. 1923. 33 pp. Rept. in: Paul Allen, ed. *A Christian Rosenkruetz Anthology.* Blauvelt, NY: Rudolf Steiner Publications, 1968. Pp. 600-33.

2302. Graesse, J.G.T. *Bibliotheca Magica et Pneumatica.* Leipzig, 1843.

2303. Hall, Manly Palmer. *Great Books on Religion and Esoteric Philosophy.* Los Angeles: Philosophical Research Society, 1966. 85 pp.

2304. Hyre, K. M., and Goodman, Eli. *Price Guide to the Occult and Related Subjects.* Los Angeles, CA: Reference Guides, Inc., 1967. 379 pp.

2305. Kies, Cosette N. *The Occult in the Western World: An Annotated Bibliography.* Hamden, CT: Library Professional Publ., 1986. 233 pp.

2306. King, Clyde S. *Psychic and Religious Phenomena Limited: A Bibliographical Index.* Westport, CT: Greenwood Press, 1978. 245 pp.

2307. Lenglet, Dufresnoy N. *Recueil de Dissertations Anciennes et Nouvelles sur les Apparitions, les Visions et les Songes.* Avignon and Paris, 1751-52.

2308. Mandrou, Robert. *Magistrats et Sorciers en France au XVII Siecle.* Paris; Biblioteque Chacornac, 1900. 254 pp.

2309. Midelfort, H. C. Erik. "Witchcraft, Magic, and the Occult." In Steven Ozment, ed. *Reformation Europe: A Guide to Research.* St. Louis, MO: Center for Reformation Research, 1987. pp. 183-210.

2310. Roth-Scholtuzius, F. *Catalogus Rariorum Librorum et Manuscriptorum Magico-Cabbalistico-Chymicorum.* Col, I. Herrenstadii, 1732.

2311. *Sciences Secretes,* Moscow, 1970.

2312. T.S. "Bibliography." *The Spiritual Magazine* I, March 1, 1876. pp. 127-144. II, August 1, 1867. pp. 336-384.

2313. Werner, Elizabeth M. *Guide to Occult Tape Recordings.* Burbank, CA: Inner Space Interpreters Services, 1976. 48 pp. 2nd edition, Burbank, CA: Inner Space Interpreters Services, 1977. 20 pp.

2314. Westrum, Ron. "A Bibliography of Anomalies with Some Cautionary Remarks," Chicago, 1976. A paper presented to the 1976 Meeting of the Popular Culture Association. 12 pp. Mimeo.

2315. Wilcox, Laird. *Astrology, Mysticism, and the Occult: A Critical Bibliography.* Kansas City, MO: Editorial Research Service, 1980. 29 pp.

2316. Yve-Plessis, R. *Essai D'Une Bibliographie Française Methodique et Raisonnee de la Sorcellerie et dela Possession Demoniaque.*

Guides to Periodical Literature

2317. Werner, Elizabeth M. *Directory of Psychic Science Periodicals.* Burbank: Inner Space Interpreters, 1973. 20 pp. Rev. ed. as: *Guide to Occult Periodicals.* 1974. 25 pp. Rev. ed.: 1975. 40 pp. Rev. ed., 1976. 48 pp. Rev. ed.: 1977. 63 pp. 8th. ed. as: *International Guide to PSI Periodicals.* 1981/82. 68 pp.

Book Catalogues

The vacuum created by the lack of bibliographies has been filled in part by the published catalogues of retail occult outlets and the sales lists of publishers. Some, like de Laurence's catalog, have become valued collector's items.

2318. *Beltane Occult Supplies and Books/Catalog.* Seattle, WA: Beltane, 1406 A.N.E. 50th Street, 98105), 1974. 20 unnumbered pages.

2319. *Bookpeople: Subject Catalog.* Berkeley, CA: Bookpeople, 1988. 346pp.

2320. *De Laurence's Catalog of Books for Mystics.* Chicago: The de Laurence Co., Inc., 1949. 576 pp.

2321. *More Light!* Vancouver, B.C., Canada: Banyan Books, 1974. 192 pp. *More Light* 3, 1976. 48 pp.

2322. *The New Leaf Catalog of Books for Growth and Change: A Reader's Guide.* Atlanta, GA: New Leaf Publishing Co., 1990. 560 pp.

2323. *New Leaf Metaphysics.* Atlanta, GA: New Leaf Publishing Co., 1988. 470 pp.

2324. Popenoe, Cris. *Books For Inner Development/The Yes! Guide.* Washington, D.C.: Yes! Bookshop (1035 31st Street, N.W. 20007) 1976. 383 pp. Supplements 1-11. 1982-83.

Professional Associations

The Hermetic Aacdemy
c/o Dr. James S. Cutsinger
Department of Religious Studies
University of South Carolina
Columbia, SC 29208
The Academy emerged out of the still continuing Group on Esotericism and Perennialism of the American Academy of Religion

Archive/Research Centers

While there are a number of outstanding specialized collections on particular aspects of the occult and related topics, the largest general research-level collection of materials on the occult and its broad manifestation, especially in the contemporary West, is in the **American Religions Collection** at the Library of the University of California-Santa Barbara. This collection, gathered over the last generation, brings together secondary sources with an extensive primary source collection in all aspects of nineteenth and twentieth century occultism, with especially strong coverage of astrology, contemporary Wicca (Witchcraft) and magic(k), Swedenborgianism, and flying saucers. The book collection is supplemented with extensive files of pamphlets, brochures, and newspaper clippings which are the backup collection for the *Encyclopedia of American Religions* (566) and the *New Age Encyclopedia* (2388). The collection began in 1985 with donation of the library of the Institute for the Study of American Religion and have been complemented by the libraries of the J. F. Rowny Publishing Co., the former Aquarian Ministry, several private collections, and continued accessions.

A second significant publicly accessible collection which covers the psychic/esoteric/occult is the 55,000 volume collection of the **Association for Research and Development**, Box 595, Virginia Beach, VA 23451. This collection has been built to support the Association's research program on the reading of psychic/seer Edgar Cayce. The library houses the transcripts of the Cayce readings, and a large general collection, notable for a 3,000 volume collection on the lost continent of Atlantis and a complete set of the works of spiritualist Andrew Jackson Davis.

Other publicly available collections include:

As-You-Like-It-Library
915 E. Pine Street, Rm. 401
Seattle, WA 98122
This independent library includes approximately 12,000 volumes. It is open to the public and offers mail order services.

IAO Research Centre
P. O. Box 5265, Sta. A
Toronto, ON M5W 1N5
This 12,000+ volume library is open to the public.

Merton J. Mandeville Collection
Education and Social Science Library
University of Illinois
1408 W. Gregory Drive
Urbana, IL 61801

ASTROLOGY

Surveys over this generation have regularly reported a significant percentage of the population who profess a belief in astrology. The art has experienced a steady revival in the West in spite of anti-fortune-telling laws in most states and public attacks from both scientists and Christian ministers. Some efforts at bibliographical control of the literature is just beginning. However, there are several reference sources available which can provide a handle on the field.

Encyclopedias and Dictionaries

2325. Carter, Charles E. O. *An Encyclopedia of Psychological Astrology.* London: W. Foulsham & Co. Ltd., 1924; 2nd edit., 1926. 187 pp.

2326. deVore, Nicholas. *Encyclopedia of Astrology.* Totowa, NJ: Littlefield, Adams and Co., 1976. 435 pp.

2327. Fleming-Mitchell, Leslie. *Astrology Terms.* Philadelphia, PA: Running Press, 1977. 102 pp.

2328. Francis, James Jason, comp. *A New English Astrological Thesaurus.* Lakemont, GA: CSA Press, 1977. 131 pp.

2329. Gettings, Fred. *Dictionary of Astrology.* London: Routledge & Kegan Paul, 1985. 365 pp.

2330. Hall, Manly Palmer. *Astrological Keywords.* Los Angeles, CA: Philosophical Research Society, 1966. 229 pp.

2331. Lee, Dal. *Dictionary of Astrology.* New York: Coronet Communications and Constellation International, 1968. 250 pp.; Rept.: New York: Paperback Library, 1968. 250 pp.

2332. Partridge, A. E. *Dictionary of Astrological Terms and Explanations.* Seattle: Dorothy Hughes, 1933. 30 pp.

2333. Sepharial, [Walter Gorn Old]. *New Dictionary of Astrology.* New York: Arco Publishing Company, 1963. 158 pp.

2334. Wedeck, Harry. *Dictionary of Astrology.* Secaucus, NJ: Citadel Press, 1973. 189 pp.

2335. Wilson, James. *A Complete Dictionary of Astrology.* Boston, MA: A. H. Rolfe & Co., 1885. 406 pp. Rept.: Mokelumne Hill, CA: Health Research, 1971. 406pp.

Directories

2336. *Astrology Directory.* [Chicago, IL]: Ghost Research Society, 1987. 19 pp.

2337. Glenn, Jeannette Yvonne. *"Who's Who" United States Directory of Professional Astrologers.* Riverside, CA: Anno Press, 1976. 186 pp.

2338. *The International Directory of Astrologers and Psychics.* Myrtle Beach, SC: CAR/LO Publications, 1979. 280 pp.

2339. Marks, Tracy. *Directory of New England Astrologers.* Natick, MA: Sagittarius Rising, 1978. 133 pp.

2340. *Michigan Astrologer: A Guide.* Flat Rock, MI: The Michigan Astrologer, 1977. 60 pp.

2341. Modin, E. Dee. *Astrological Directory 1953 - 1954.* Seattle, WA: Hermes Press, 1953. 175 pp.

2342. Vance, Charles Burce, and Clyde Beauregarde Vance. *International Astrological Register.* Fresno, CA: Fresno Astrology Book Center, 1974-75. 130 pp.

2343. Weingarten, N. Henry. *The NASO International Astrological Directory.* New York, NY: National Astrological Society, 1977-78. 68 pp. New York, NY: National Astrological Society, 1980-81. 94 pp. New York, NY: National Astrological Society, 1982-83. 80 pp.

2344. Wilkerson, Karen, Joan A. Piszak, and James A. Eshelman. *The Registry of Sidereal Astrologers.* Placentia, CA: Founders of R.O.S.A., 1975. 36 pp.

Bibliographies

2345. *Astrology Books in Print.* Rockport, MA: Para Research, 1981. 121 pp.

2346. Gardner, F. Leigh. *A Catalogue Raisonné of Works on the Occult Sciences.* II. *Astrology.* London: The Author, 1911. 164 pp.

2347. Truzzi, Marcello. "Scientific Studies of Classical Astrology." *Zetetic Scholar* 1, 2 (1978): 79-87.

2348. Melton, J. Gordon. *A Bibliography of Astrology in America, 1840-1940.* Santa Barbara, CA: Institute for the Study of American Religion, 1990. 21 pp.

DIVINATORY TECHNIQUES

Apart from Astrology, there are a number of techniques which have been used in the past for divination and which are in process of being changed by the New Age movement into "transformational tools." They include palmistry, the Tarot, and tea leaf reading. Handwriting analysis, while still used by some for divinatory purposes, has arisen out of the cluster of divination practices to develop a more "scientific" form as a non-divinatory practice.

2349. Bright, J. S. *The Dictionary of Palmistry.* New York: Bell Publishing Co., 1958. 184 pp.

2350. Butler, Bill. *Dictionary of the Tarot.* New York: Schocken Books, 1975. 254 pp.

2351. Kaplan, Stuart R. *Encyclopedia of the Tarot.* New York: U. S. Games Systems, 1978. 387 pp.

2352. Truzzi, Marcello. "Debunking Biorhythms." *Zetetic Scholar* 1, 1 (1978): 47.

FLYING SAUCERS/UFOS

The study of UFOs is not a religious subject and those in control of it are not particularly religiously inclined people. However, the appearance of strange unidentified objects in the sky has provoked a religious response in the form of claims of contact with extraterrestrials whose message is essentially religious. These claims have led to the formation of a number of flying saucer contactee groups. The only attempt to survey these groups is contained in Melton (566). The volumes listed below survey ufology and regularly include material on the contactees, if just to note their difference from the scientific work of discerning the nature of UFOs. Special mention should be made of Eberhart (2363), whose bibliography provides exhaustive coverage of the field, while Melton and Eberhart (2366) updates the contactee chapter.

Dictionaries/Encyclopedias

2353. Clark, Jerome. *UFOs in the 1980s.* Volume One of *The UFO Encyclopedia.* Detroit: Apogee, 1990. 234 pp.

2354. Sachs, Margaret. *The UFO Encyclopedia.* New York: Perigee, 1980. 408 pp.

2355. Spencer, John, comp. and ed. *The UFO Encyclopedia.* London: Headline, 1991. 340 pp.

2356. Story, Ronald D. *The Encyclopedia of UFOs.* Garden City, NY: Doubleday & Company, 1980. 440 pp.

Biographical Volumes

2357. Boyd, Robert D. *Who's Who in UFOlogy.* Mobile, AL: The Author, 1988. 267 pp.

Directories

2358. *UFO Research Directory of Organizations and Publications for the 1980s.* Willowdale, ON: SS&S Publications, 1980. 27 pp.

2359. *Ufology Directory.* [Chicago, IL]: Ghost Research Society, 1987. 13 pp.

Bibliographies

2360. Brennan, Norman. *Flying Saucer Books and Pamphlets in English: A Biographical Checklist.* The Author, [n.d.]. 94 pp.

2361. Catoe, Lynn E. *UFOs and Related Subjects: An Annotated Bibliography.* Arlington, VA: Air Force Office of Scientific Research/Office of Aerospace Research, USAF, 1969. 401 pp.

2362. Eberhart, George M. *A Survey of Ufologists and Their Use of the Library.* Evanston, IL: Center for UFO Studies, 1978. 24 pp.

2363. ———. *UFOs and the Extraterrestrial Contact Movement.* 2 vols. Metuchen, NJ: Scarecrow Press, 1986.

2364. Keel, John A. "The Flying Saucer Subculture." *Journal of Popular Culture* 8 (1975): 871-95.

2365. MacDonald, Howard Brenton. *Flying Saucers and Space Ships.* New York, NY: Flying Saucer News Co., n.d. 6 pp.

2366. Melton, J. Gordon, and George Eberhart, comps. *The Flying Saucer Contactee Movement: 1950-1990.* Santa Barbara, CA: Santa Barbara Centre for Humanistic Studies, 1990. 46 pp.

2367. Morison, Robert Kingsley. *UFO Book Index 1977.* London, GB: Ascent, 1977. 8 pp.

2368. Page, Henrietta M. *Flying Saucers...A Bibliography.* Foxboro, MA: The Author, 1st edit., 1968, 17 pp.; 2nd edition, 1975, 18 pp.

2369. Rasmussen, Richard Michael. *UFO Bibliography.* La Mesa, CA.: Rasmussen Publications, 1975. 24 pp.

2370. ———. *The UFO Literature.* Jefferson, North Carolina, London: McFarland & Co., 1985. 263 pp.

2371. Sable, Martin H. *Exobiology: A Research Guide.* Brighton, MI: Green Oak Press, 1978. 324 pp.

2372. ———. *UFO Guide/1947-1967.* Beverley Hills, CA: Rainbow Press Company, 1967. 100 pp.

2373. Smith, Marcie S. *Congressional Research Service: The UFO Enigma.* Washington, DC: The Library of Congress, 1st edit., Feb 18, 1976. 2nd edition., Mar 9, 1976. 45 pp.

Guides to Periodical Literature

2374. Barker, Gray. *A UFO Guide to FATE Magazine.* Clarksburg, WV: Saucerian Press, 1981. 100 pp.

Archives/Study Centers

The largest publicly available collection of UFO literature is at the **J. Allen Hynek Center for UFO Studies** (CUFOS), Chicago, IL 60659. Along with its many books, it has received the archives from the National Investigations Committee on Aerial Phenomena (NICAP) and the Aerial Phenomena Research Organization (APRO), two of the most important early UFO investigation organizations. A similar large collection is to be found in the **American Religions Collection** at the University of California-Santa Barbara. The latter differs from the CUFOS collection in its concentration on the ancient astronaut and contactee movements, the arena in which UFOs and religion have their most interesting interaction. There is also a UFO collection housed at the manuscript department of the *American Philosophical Society*, 105 S. Fifth Street, Philadelphia, PA 19106. It consists of approximately 100 feet of material.

FREEMASONRY/SECRET SOCIETIES

During the period of the emergence of modern occultism in the eighteenth and nineteenth century, Freemasonry and related secret societies, such as the Rosicrucians, played an important role in the spreading of occult metaphysics. Their role was clearly recognized in the nineteenth century when a lengthy battle was fought by the churches against Freemasonry, a battle kept alive by a few churches such as the Roman Catholic Church and the Lutheran Church-Missouri Synod. The role of Freemasonry in opening the culture to the occult is a significant theme yet to be explored by scholars.

Encyclopedias and Dictionaries

2375. Beha, Ernest. *A Comprehensive Dictionary of Freemasonry.* London: Arco Publications, 1962; New York: Citadel Press, 1963.

2376. Heckethorn, Charles William. *The Secret Societies of All Ages and Countries.* 2 vols. 1875. Rev. ed. 1897. Rept.: New Hyde Park, NY: University Books, 1965.

2377. Macoy, Robert. *General History, Cyclopedia and Dictionary of Freemasonry.* New York: Masonic Publishing Company, 1871. 700 pp.

2378. Preuss, Arthur. *A Dictionary of Secret and Other Societies.* St. Louis, MO: R. Herder Book Co., 1924. 543 pp.

2379. Whalen, William. *Handbook of Secret Organizations.* Milwaukee, WI: Bruce Publishing Company, 1966. 169 pp.

Bibliographies

2380. Gardner, F. Leigh. *Freemasonry: A Catalogue of Lodge Histories.* London: The Author, 1912. 37 pp.

2381. Plummer, George Windslow. *A Masonic Compendium to the Sacred Books and Early Literature of the East.* New York: Oriental Foundation, 1918. 67 pp.

2382. U.S. Library of Congress. *Freemasons and Freemasonry: A Bibliography Extracted from Volume 184 of "The National Union Catalog, Pre-1956 Imprints".* London: Mansell Publishing, 1973.

Directories

2383. *List of Lodges Masonic.* Bloomington, IL: Pantagraph Print and Stationary Co., 1970. 288 pp.

NEW AGE MOVEMENT

The New Age movement, though it has roots that go back to nineteenth-century theosophy, began in England in the 1960s among a number of theosophically inspired groups who came to believe that the world was about to go through a great change occasioned by the influx of a new wave of spiritual energy. That energy, caused by the arrival of the astrological Aquarian Age, would bring a new era of peace and well-being. The coming transformation of the culture was signaled by the transformation each of the New Age proponents had experienced and the new transformative techniques, most from various Eastern religions, which they had learned and adapted for Western audiences.

From England, the New Age movement spread across the European continent and on to North America, Africa and Australia. It has become the most successful occult movement in modern history and has had a lasting role in moving the occult into middle class society.

Somewhat anti-hierarchical in their thinking, New Agers have tended to form horizontal networks of people otherwise free to form the New Age as they please, rather than strong leader-oriented organizations. Directories are the essential tool in creating and nurturing a network over a period of time, and the New Age directories provide the best entry into the community.

Encyclopedias and Dictionaries

2384. Campbell, Eileen, and J. H. Brennan. *The Aquarian Guide to the New Age.* Wellingborough, UK: Aquarian Press, 1990. 352 pp.

2385. Harvey, David. *Thorson's Complete Guide to Alternative Living.* Wellingborough, UK: Thorsons Publishing Group, 1986. 316 pp.

2386. Holroyd, Stuart. *The Arkana Dictionary of New Perspectives.* London: Arkana, 1989. 250 pp.

2387. Jack, Alex, ed. *The New Age Dictionary.* Brookline, MA: Kanthaka Press, 1976. 224 pp.

2388. Melton, J. Gordon, Jerome Clark, and Aidan A. Kelly. *New Age Encyclopedia.* Detroit, MI: Gale Research Company, 1990. 586 pp. Paperback ed. as: *New Age Almanac.* Detroit, MI: Visible Ink Press, 1991. 479 pp.

Directories

2389. Adams, Robert. *The New Times Network: Groups and Centers for Personal Growth.* London: Routledge & Kegan Paul, 1982. 148 pp.

2390. Biteaux, Armand. *The New Consciousness.* Willets, CA: Oliver Press, 1975. 168 pp.

2391. Body, Mind and Spirit, Editors of. *The New Age Catalogue.* New York: Dolphin/Doubleday, 1988. 244 pp.

2392. Cott MacPhail, Carolyn. *Choices and Connections: The First Catalog of the Global Family.* Boulder, CO: Human Potential Resources Inc., 1987.

2393. Friedlander, Ira. *Year One Catalog: A Spiritual Directory for the New Age.* New York: Harper & Row, 1972. 152 pp. Covers, CA, New York, Boston only.

2394. Gardner, Richard. *Alternative America.* Cambridge, MA: (Box 134, Harvard Square), 1976. Unpaged. Rev. ed.: 1984. Unpaged

2395. Hooper, Judith, and Dick Teresi. *Would the Buddha Wear a Walkman?: A Catalogue of Revolutionary Tools for Higher Consciousness.* New York: Simon & Schuster, 1990. 255 pp.

2396. Ingenito, Marcio Gervase. *National New Age Yellow Pages.* Fullerton, CA: National New Age Yellow Page, 1987. 197 pp. Rev. ed.: Fullerton, CA: Highgate House, 1988. 252 pp.

2397. *International Cooperation Directory.* Northridge, CA: International Cooperation Council, 1966. 2nd ed.: 1967/68. 51 pp. 4th ed.: 1970. 72 pp. 7th ed.: 1973. 140 pp. 8th ed.: 1974. 160 pp. 9th ed.: 228 pp. 9th ed.: Supplement, 1975. 135 pp. 10th ed.: ed. by Louis Acheson. 1976. 256 pp. 13th ed. as: *Directory For A New World.* Santa Monica, CA: International Cooperation Council, 1979. 334 pp.

2398. Krapf, Vickie. *Directory of Alternative Services.* Kansas City, MO: Vickie Krapf, 1987. 20 pp.

2399. Lande, Nathaniel. *Mindstyles/Lifestyles.* Los Angeles; Price/Stern/Sloan, 1976. 495 pp.

2400. Lipnack, Jessica, and Jeffery Stamps. *Networking: The First Report and Directory.* Garden City, NY: Dolphin/Doubleday, 1982. 398 pp.

2401. Logan, Elizabeth A. *Crystal Cosmos Network Directory.* Winnipeg, MB: Crystal Cosmos Network, 1986. 43 pp. Rev. ed.: 1988. 175 pp.

2402. *The New Age Guide.* Los Angeles: Llewellyn Publications, 1959. 52 pp.

2403. New Age Journal, Editors of. *Guide to New Age Living.* Vol 1- . Brighton, MA: New Age Journal, 1989- . Published Annually. Title varies as: *New Age Sourcebook.*

2404. *The New Consciousness Sourcebook: Spiritual Community Guide #5.* Berkeley, CA: Spiritual Community Publications, 1982. Spiritual Guide #6. Pomona, CA: Arcline Publ., 1985. 208 pp. *See also*: (2410-2411)

2405. *A Pilgrim's Guide to Planet Earth: A Traveler's Handbook and New Age Directory.* San Rafael, CA: Spiritual Community Publications, 1981. 320 pp.

2406. Regush, Nicholas and June. *The New Consciousness Catalogue.* New York: G.P. Putnam's Sons, 1979. 159 pp.

2407. Russell, Marie. *The Natural Yellow Pages.* N. Miami, FL: The Natural Yellow Page, 1988. 72 pp.

2408. Ryan, Tim, and Rae Jappinen. *The Whole Again Resource Guide.* Santa Barbara, CA: Source Net, 1982. 315 pp.

2409. [Shapiro], Joshua. *Journeys of an Aquarian Age Networker.* Palo Alto, CA: New Life Printing Co., 1982. 333 pp.

2410. *Spiritual Community Guide: The New Consciousness Source Book.* San Rafael, CA: Spiritual Community, 1978. 256 pp. *See also* (2404)

2411. *Spiritual Community Guide for North America.* San Rafael, CA: Spiritual Community (Box 1080, 94902), 1972. 192 pp. 3rd printing April, 1973, 208 pp. 1974, 192 pp. 1978. 256 pp. East West Spiritual Community Supplement 1973, 112 pp. Issued periodically by the followers of Yogi Bhajan. *See also* (2404)

Directories-North America: Regional

2412. *Bohdi Tree Bookstore Directory Guide to Community Resources.* Los Angeles, CA: Real Moon House, 1984. 26 pp. 2nd ed.: Los Angeles, CA: Real Moon House, 1985. 34 pp. 3rd ed.: Los Angeles, CA: Old Oak Grove Press, 1986. 38 pp. 4th ed.: Los Angeles, CA: Old Oak Grove Press, 1988. 41 pp.

2413. Cara. *Directory of the Occult and Psychic Phenomena.* Houston, TX: Cara's (P.O. Box 20272), [n.d.]. 64 unnumbered pages.

2414. Cocciardi, Carol, and Mary Erickson. *The Psychic Yellow Pages.* Saratoga, CA: Out of the Sky, 1977. 177 pp.

2415. *Colorado Resource Guide.* Denver, CO: Together Books, 1990. 17 pp.

2416. Cutler, David, and Curtiss Hoffman, eds. *Aquarian Unity Directory of Massachusetts.* Waltham: MA: Servers of the Great Ones, 1972. 91 pp.

2417. Greenwood, Patti Normandy. *Metaphysical Florida: A Spiritual Traveler's Directory.* Sarasota, FL: Pineapple Press, 1991.

2418. McLaughlin, Corinne, and Gordon Davidson. *New England Network of Light Directory.* Amherst, MA: Sirius Community, 1983. 40 pp. Rev. ed.: 1983. 43 pp.

2419. McQuaid, Donald *The International Psychic Register.* Erie, PA: Ornion Press, 1978. 60 pp. 2nd edition, Erie, PA: Ornion Press, 1979. 92 pp.

2420. Micelli, Elenore. *Devi Dasi's Directory to Spiritual Groups and Activities in Florida.* Miami, FL: The Author, 1979. 40 pp.

2421. *Network of Light Directory* [Washington, DC, Area and Neighboring States]. Chevy Chase, MD: Network of Light, 1983. 71 pp.

2422. *New Age Resource Directory: for the Chicago Area.* Elk Grove Village, IL: New Age Resource Directory, 1987/1988.27 pp.

2423. *New Age Service Directory for Southeastern Michigan 1982.* Detroit, MI: New Age Service Directory, 1981. 52 pp.

2424. *New Age, Metaphysical and Wholistic Florida Directory.* Clearwater, FL: DynamicLife Publilcations, 1990. 108 pp.

2425. Powers, Linda. *New Age Directory.* Virginia Beach, VA: Crystal Clear Publications, 1989. 36 pp.

2426. Shapiro, Joshua. *Directory of New Age Resources (Southern California).* Los Gatos, CA: J. S. Aquarian Networking, 1985. 32 pp.

2427. *Southern California's New Age Telephone Book.* Hollywood, CA: New Age Telephone Book, 1988. 160 pp. Rev. ed.: 1989. 96 pp.

2428. Werner, Elizabeth W. *California Directory of PSI Services.* Burbank, CA: Inner Space Interpreters, 1977. 52 pp. Burbank, CA: Inner Space Interpreters, 1978. 116 pp.

Directories-Europe

2429. *The Aquarius Guide.* 1981. 4th ed.: London: UFON Publications, 1984. 24 pp. Published annually for several years.

2430. Bourgeois, Isabelle. *Le Guide de l'Occulte.* Paris, France: Philippe Lebaud, 1990. 268 pp.

2431. Brady, Kate. *The London Guide to Mind Body & Spirit.* London: Brainwave, 1988. 206 pp. *See also* (713).

2432. Button, John, comp. *Green Pages: A Directory of Natural Products, Services, Resources and Ideas.* London: Macdonald Optima, 1988. 320 pp.

2433. *Connexions New Age: Kontakte zur spirituellen Szene Herausgegeben von Brita Dahlberg.* Klingelbach: Mandala Verlag Peter Meyer, 1987. 314 pp.

2434. *Connexions Schweiz: Ein Reise-Addressbuch mit Infos, Tips, Kontackten herausgegeben von Netzwerk für Selbstverwaltung.* Klingelbach: Mandala Verlag Peter Meyer, 1986. 288 pp.

2435. *Connexions Südeurope: Infos/Tips/Kontakte: Schweiz, Italien, Portugal, Spanien, Greichenland, Österreich, Frankreich.* Klingelbach: Mandala Verlag Peter Meyer, 1985. 304 pp.

2436. *Guida Internationale dell'Età dell'Acquario.* Torino, Italy: Bresci Editore, 1975. 318 pp. This directory is kept updated through the issues of the quarterly *L'Età dell'Acquario,* Via Lamarmora 37, 10128 Torino, Italy.

2437. *New Life Directory.* Forest of Dean, Glos., UK: Soluna Publications, 1982. 89 pp.

2438. Saunders, Nicolas, asssisted by Ann Cucksey. *Alternative London.* London: The Author, 1970. 192 pp. Periodically updated.

Bibliographies

2439. Beddoes, Thomas P. *Reincarnation and Christian Tradition/An Annotated Bibliography.* Washington, DC: PhD Dissertation, Catholic University of America, 1970. 190 pp.

2440. *Books of Light.* Columbus, OH: Ariel Press, 1986. 160 pp.

PARAPSYCHOLOGY/PSYCHICAL RESEARCH

Psychical research emerged in the nineteenth century to test scientifically the claims made by Spiritualists and moved on to become the science of psychical experience. Parapsychologists have developed a wide range of attitudes, from complete skepticism about any claims of paranormal reality to complete belief in the psychic realm. Parapsychology, a twentieth century daughter of psychical research, emphasized laboratory experimental work more than psychical research. While parapsychology is not necessarily religious, the occult has relied upon psychical research and parapsychology to provide them at least a modest scientific authority, and a knowledge of psychical research is integral to understanding the appeal of the occult.

General Sources

2441. Ashby, Robert H. *The Guidebook for the Study of Psychical Research.* New York: Samuel Weiser, Inc., 1972. 190 pp.

Encyclopedias

2442. Berger, Arthur S., and Joyce Berger. *The Encyclopedia of Parapsychology and Psychical Research.* New York: Paragon House, 1991. 554 pp.

2443. Garrison, Omar V. *The Encyclopedia of Prophecy.* Secaucus, NJ: Citadel Press, 1979. 225 pp.

Biographical Volumes

2444. Berger, Arthur S. *Lives and Letters in American Parapsychology.* New York: McFarland, 1988. 381 pp.

2445. Pleasants, Helene, ed. *Biographical Dictionary of Parapsychology.* New York, NY: Garrett Publ., 1964. 371 pp.

Bibliographies

2446. Clark, Jerome. "Bibliography of Skeptical and Debunking Articles in Fate Magazine, 1975-September 1981." *Zetetic Scholar* 8 (July 1981): 76-77.

2447. Hansen, George P. "Bibliography of Bibliographies on Dowsing." *Zetetic Scholar* 7 (December 1980): 101-105.

2448. Kelly, Ivan W. "Debunking Biorhythms: A Supplement." *Zetetic Scholar* 10 (December 1982): 148.

2449. *Library Catalog of the Society for Psychical Research.* London: Society for Psychical Research, 1927-33.

2450. Lockard, Robert R., and Ray Hyman. "Basic Annotated Bibliography [of books critical of occult belief]." *Skeptical Inquirer* Part 1. 3, 4 (Summer 1979): 66-71. Part 2. 4, 1 (Fall 1979). Part 3. 4, 2 (Summer 1979/1980): 98-101.

2451. Morgan, S. R. *Index To Psychic Science.* Swarthmore, PA: [n.p.], 1950. 117 pp.

2452. Ring, Kenneth. *Annotated Reading List.* Stamford, CT: Association for Transpersonal Psychology, n.d., 30 pp.

2453. *Surveys of Soviet Bloc Scientific and Technical Literature: Soviet Parapsychology.* ATD Work Assignment No. 38. Task 3. Washington, DC: Aerospeace Technology Division, Library of Congress, 1964. 17 pp.

2454. Techter, David. *A Bibliography and Index of Psychical Research and Related Topics for the Years.....1962....1963....1964.* 3 vols. Chicago: Privately published, 1963-1965.

2455. Truzzi, Marcello. "A Bibliography on Firewalking." *Zetetic Scholar* 11 (August 1983): 105-108.

2456. ————. "Chinese Parapsychology: A Bibliography of English Language Items." *Zetetic Scholar* 10 (December 1982): 143-145.; Part II: 12/13 (1987): 58-60.

2457. ————. "Crank, Crackpot, or Genius? Pseudoscience or Science Revolution? A Bibliographic Guide to the Debate." *Zetetic Scholar* 1, 1 (1978): 20-22. Supplement: 1, 2 (1978): 66.

2458. ———. "The Powers of Negative Thinking, or Debunking the Paranormal: A Basic Book List." *Zetetic Scholar* 1, 1 (1878): 35-38. Supplement: 1, 2 (1978): 66.

2459. ———, and Ray Hyman. "Uri Geller & the Scientists: A Basic Bibliography." *Zetetic Scholar* 1, 1 (1978): 39-46. Supplement: 1, 2 (1978): 66.

2460. White, Rhea A. *Parapsychology: A Reading and Buying Guide to the Best Books in Print.* Dix Hills, NY: Parapsychology Sources of Information. 4th ed.: 1990. 113 pp.

2461. ———. *Parapsychology: Sources on Application and Implications.* Dix Hills, NY; Parapsychology Sources of Information Center, ; 2nd ed.: 1989. 115 pp.

2462. ———. *Surveys in Parapsychology.* Metuchen, NJ: The Scarecrow Press, 1976. 484 pp.

2463. White, Rhea, and Roger I. Anderson. *On Being Psychic: A Reading Guide.* Dix Hills, NY: Parapsychology Sources of Information Center, 1989. 150 pp.

2464. ———. *Psychic Experiences: A Bibliography.* Dix Hills, NY: Parapsychology Sources of information Center, 1990. 147 pp.

2465. White, Rhea A., and Laura A. Dale. *Parapsychology in Print 1971-72.* New York: The Library of the American Society for Psychical Research, n.d. 74 pp.

2466. ———. *Parapsychology: Sources of Information.* Metuchen, NJ: The Scarecrow Press, 1973. 303 pp.

2467. Zorab, George. *Bibliography of Parapsychology.* New York: Parapsychology Foundation, 1957. 127 pp.

2468. Zusne, Leonard. "'Fingertip Sight.' A Bibliography." *Zetetic Scholar* 10 (December 1982): 35-42.

Guides to Periodical Literature

2469. White, Rhea A. *Parapsychology Abstracts International.* Vol. 1- . Dix Hills, NY: Parapsychology Sources of Information Center, 1983- . Semi-annual.

Professional Associations

Academy of Religion and Psychical Research
P. O. Box 614
Bloomfield, CT 06002
Periodical(s): *The Journal of Religion and Psychical Research*

Committee for the Scientific Examination of the Claims of the Paranormal
1203 Kensington Avenue
Buffalo, NY 14215
The Committee publishes the *Skeptical Inquirer* (q). The Inquirer carries occasional bibliographies of articles on various occult and psychic articles though carefully selected on their negative approach to the subject.

SATANISM

Satanism, the worship of the Devil, made its appearance in the writings of Catholic Inquisitors in the fifteenth century. No documented cases of Satanism occur, until the court of Louis XIV of France. Since that time isolated instances of it have occurred while a wealth of imaginative lore has been created about it. Since the formation of the Church of Satan in 1966, Devil worship has enjoyed a mild renaissance. More significant than the number of people caught up in Satanism, however, were the numbers who participated in a still continuing wave of anti-Satanism, which has produced a whole new set of Satanic lore.

Of the books below, the volume by Carlson, et al., deals with the current wave of Satanism, while the other volumes are more authoritative about more traditional forms of Devil worship.

General Sources

2470. Carlson, Shawn, with Gerry O'Sullivan, April A. Masche, and D. D. Hudson Frew. *Satanism in America.* El Cerrito, CA: The Author, 1989. 121 pp. Rev. ed: El Cerrito, CA: Gaia Press, 89. 283 pp.

Encyclopedias and Dictionaries

2471. Baskin, Wade. *Dictionary of Satanism.* New York: Philosophical Library, 1972. 352 pp.

2472. Gettings, Fred. *Dictionary of Demons: A Guide to Demons and Demonologists in Occult Lore.* North Pomfret, VT: Trafalgar Square Publishing, 1988. 256 pp.

SPIRITUALISM/CHANNELING/MEDIUMSHIP

Modern Spiritualism began in the 1840s when different people began to claim an ability to prove the continuation of life after death by communicating with the "spirits" of the deceased. Central to the belief and practice of Spiritualism was the medium, the person who could, either in an entranced state or awake, communicate with the spirit world. The popular movement gradually was formed around churches and church associations and, while ignored through the twentieth century, has continued as a vital movement with numerous congregations around the United States.

A new form of Spiritualism, largely disconnected in its origins from the older Spiritualist movement, emerged in the 1970s. It was called channeling. It centered, not upon the contact with the recently dead, with the intent to prove life-after-death, but upon contact with entities believed to be highly evolved beings who lectured audiences on subjects ranging from religion and philosophy to world politics and social behavior. The process of channeling teachings from evolved beings is far older than modern Spiritualism, but its modern form began in the late 1880s with the channeling of the book *Oahspe*. Contemporary channelers have absorbed much from the Human Potential movement and Eastern religious thought.

Encyclopedias and Dictionaries

2473. Blunson, Norman. *A Popular Dictionary of Spiritualism*. New York: The Citadel Press, 1963. 256 pp.

2474. Wedeck, Harry E., and Wade Baskin. *Dictionary of Spiritualism*. New York: Philosophical Library, 1971. 376 pp.

Biographical Volumes

2475. Awtry, Marilyn J., and Paula M. Vogt. *Who's Who in Spiritualism of Yesteryear*. 2 vols. N.p.: SAM Inc., 1981.

2476. Cutlip, Audea. *Pioneers of Modern Spiritualism.* 4 vols. Milwaukee, WI: National Spiritualist Association of Churches, n.d.

Directories

2477. Westen, Ron. *Channelers: A New Age Directory.* New York: Perigee, 1988. 224 pp.

Bibliographies

2478. Bjorling, Joel. *Mediumship and Channeling: A Bibliography.* Sects & Cults in America Series Vol. 15. New York: Garland Publishing, 1989. c.350 pp.

2479. *Catalogue of the Library of the Marylebourne Spiritualist Association.* London: Marylebourne House, 1939. 175 pp.

2480. Lovi, Henrietta. *Best Books on Spirit Phenomena.* Boston: Richard G. Badger/ The Gorham Press, 1925. 94 pp.

2481. Zaretsky, Irving I. *Bibliography on Spirit Possession and Spirit Mediumship.* Evanston, IL: Northwestern University Press, 1966. 106 pp.

2482. Zaretsky, Irving I., and Cynthia Shambaugh. *Spirit Possession and Spirit Mediumship in Africa and Afro-America: An Annotated Bibliography.* New York: Garland Publishing, 1978. 443 pp.

EMANUEL SWEDENBORG AND THE CHURCH OF THE NEW JERUSALEM

Seer Emanuel Swedenborg stands at the fountainhead of the modern occult revival. Working through the 1700s, he was for many years in contact with angels who, he claimed, taught him about the nature of the universe and gave him the key to unlock the true meaning of the Bible. After his death his followers organized a church built around the ideas in his writings. Within the Swedenborgian movement, numerous books have been produced to assist both those in and those outside the church to understand the voluminous writings Swedenborg left behind.

Encyclopedias and Dictionaries

2483. Henderson, W. *Our New Church Vocabulary.* Bryn Athyn, PA: General Church press, [1966]. Reprinted for items in *New Church Life* from January 1961 through June 1966.

2484. Nicholson G., comp. *A Dictionary of Correspondences, Representatives, and Significances, derived from the Word of the Lord, Extracted from the Writings of Emanuel Swedenborg.* 1800. 13th ed. Boston, MA: Massachusetts New Church Union, 1931.

2485. Rose, Frank. *Words in Swedenborg and Their Meaning in Modern English.* Bryn Athyn: General Church Press, 1985.

2486. Sechrist, Alice Spiers, comp. *A Dictionary of Biblical Imagery.* New York: Swedenborg Foundation, 1973. Supersedes Nicholson (2484).

Bibliographies

2487. Blackmar, Franklin. *A Bibliography of Publications by Swedenborgians.* Boston, MA: Massachusetts New Church Union, 1977.

2488. Hyde, James. *A Bibliography of the Works of Emanuel Swedenborg, Original and Translations.* London: Swedenborg Society, 1906.

2489. Woofenden, William Ross. *Swedenborg Researcher's Manual.* Bryn Athyn, PA: Swedenborg Scientific Association, 1988. 366 pp.

Archives/Research Centers

Woofenden (2489) notes four primary centers with research-level Swedenborgian collections. Two are at the headquarters of the two larger Swedenborgian churches, the **General Church of the New Jerusalem**, Bryn Athyn, Pennsylvania, and the **General Convention of the New Church**. The 100,000 volume **Swedenborg Library of the Academy of the New Church**, 2815 Huntington Pike, Bryn Athyn, PA 19009, operated by the General Church, includes a complete collection of Swedenborg's writings, books about him and his thought, and books he referred to in his writings. The Academy Library has also put together a special collection which duplicates Swedenborg's personal library at the time of his death. The **Swedenborg School of Religion**, 48 Sargent Street, Newton, MA 02158, operated by the General Convention, features the Swedenborgian collection of William James, who was raised as a Swedenborgian. The **Swedenborg Foundation**, 139 E. 23rd Street, New York, NY 10010, has a Swedenborgiana collection unique for its collection of pictures relevant to Swedenborg. The fourth significant collection of Swedenborgiana is at **Urbana College**, Urbana Ohio, a small college founded in 1850 by midwestern members of the New Church.

Outside of North America, significant Swedenborgian collections can be found at:

The Swedenborg Society
20 Bloomsbury Way
London WC1A 2TH
England

The Swedenborg Verlag
Apollostrasse 2
CH 8032 Zurich, Switzerland

Swedenborg Library & Enquiry Centre
4 Shirley Road
Roseville, New South Wales 2069
Australia
Roseville is a Sydney suburb.

THEOSOPHY

The Theosophical Society was founded in 1875. As its objectives were clarified, the Society saw as its purposes, the following:

1) to form a nucleus of the Universal Brotherhood of Humanity without distinction of race, creed, sex, caste, or color.

2) to encourage the study of comparative religion, philosophy, and science.

3) to investigate the unexplained laws of nature and the powers latent in man.

The society became a worldwide international organization within its first generation and has done more to spread the modern occult revival than any other body. Many modern occult groups originated among theosophists (such as the Anthroposophical Society founded by Rudolf Steiner and the Arcane School founded by Alice Bailey) and others were inspired by reading its vast literature.

Encyclopedias and Dictionaries

2490. Besterman, Theodore. *A Dictionary of Theosophy.* London: Theosophical Publishing House, 1927. 147 pp.

2491. Blavatsky, H.P. *Theosophical Glossary.* London: Theosophical Pub. Society, 1892. 389 pp. Rept: Los Angeles: Theosophy Co., 1973. 389 pp.

Bibliographies

2492. Babbel, Ulrich, and Craig Giddens, comps. *Bibliographical Reference List of Rudolf Steiner's Work in English Translation.* Vol. 1. London: Rudolf Steiner Press, 1977. 51 pp.

2493. Benjamin, Elsie. *Search and Find: Theosphical Reference Index (Following the Blavatsky Tradition).* San Diego, CA: Point Loma Publications, 1978. 155pp.

2494. Besterman, Theodore. *A Bibliography of Annie Besant.* London: The Theosophical Society in England, 1924. 114 pp.

2495. Brown, Lauren R. *The Point Loma Theosophical Society: A List of Publications, 1898-1942.* La Jolla, CA: Friends of the UCSD Library, University of California, San Diego, 1977. 132pp.

2496. Gomes, Michael. *Theosophy in the Nineteenth Century: An Annotated Bibliography.* New York: Garland Publications, 1992. Forthcoming.

2497. Guignette, Jean-Paul. *Bibliography of H. P. Blavatsky.* London: Theosophical History Centre, 1987. 12pp.

2498. *Olcott Library and Research Center.* Wheaton, IL: The Theosophical Society in America, n.d. Unpaged. A massive catalog of holdings published in the early 1980s.

2499. *Theosophical Publications and Importations.* Wheaton, IL: Theosophical Press, 1930. 113 pp.

Professional Organizations

Theosophical History Foundation
c/o Dr. James Santucci
Department of Religious Studies
California State University
Fullerton, CA 92634-9480
The Foundation publishes *Theosophical History* (q).

Archives/Research Centers

Theosophists has been a very book-oriented community and along with an active publishing program established libraries to make theosophically inclined material available to the public. There are three main theosophical libraries currently open. The **Olcott Library** at the headquarters of the Theosophical Society in America (the group aligned to the international theosophical movement headquartered in Adyar, Madras India) is located in a far-west Chicago suburb: Box 270, Wheaton, IL 60189. The library at **Krotona Institute**, Krotona 2, Ojai, California, is associated with the Wheaton organization. Both libraries are open to the public and non-theosophists may obtain borrowing privileges for a modest fee. An equally fine library is maintained by the **Theosophical Society**, P. O. Bin C, Pasadena, CA 91109. It is open every afternoon during the week for public use. All three libraries have an extensive collection of theosophical periodicals and writings of the early leaders.

British Theosophists maintain an archive and library at their headquarters at 25 Gloucester Street, London. The archives of the international society, of course, are at the headquarters in Adyar, India.

Rudolf Steiner left Theosophy and formed the Anthroposophical Society, the headquarters of which were established at Dornach, Switzerland. The **Rudolf Steiner Library**, RD 2, Box 215, Ghent, NY 12075, has a complete set of Steiner's works in both German and English (as far as they have been translated), and many Anthroposophical books in its 15,000 volume collection. A similar library is supported by the **Anthroposophical Society of Canada**, 81 Lawton Blvd., Toronto, ON M4V 1Z6. A small library is maintained by the **Anthroposophical Society in Hawaii**, 2514 Alaula Way, Honolulu, HI 96822.

WITCHCRAFT/MAGICK

Magick, in the sense it is used by its serious practitioners today, is the art and science of causing change to occur by an act of the will through the command of the unseen forces which underlie the visible world. This definition, drawn from Aleister Crowley, points to a new sophisticated approach to the belief in magical forces that defines the community of magicians and Witches. Wicca, Witchcraft, a new Neo-Pagan nature worshipping religion, now forms the largest segment of the magical community. While drawing upon the images of medieval Witchcraft, it is in fact a modern attempt to reconstruct the old pre-Christian European pagan religion in a modern form.

In working in this field, one must be aware of the confusion concerning the term "Witchcraft," which is used to refer to a variety of different phenomena and to distinct movements which otherwise have no connection with each other and hold little or no common beliefs. The most common error is to identify the Witchcraft of the Middle Ages with contemporary Witchcraft.

Much of modern Wicca interacts with the New Age community and utilizes their practice of networking. Hence the community has produced a number of directories which serve as entry points for the more public side of the craft.

Encyclopedias and Dictionaries

2500. de Placy, Colli. *Dictionary of Witchcraft.* Trans. by Wade Baskin. New York: Castle Books, 1965. Originally published as *Dictionary of Demonology.*

2501. Guiley, Rosemary Ellen. *The Encyclopedia of Witches and Witchcraft.* New York: Facts on File, 1989. 421 pp.

2502. Robbins, R. H. *The Encyclopedia of Witchcraft and Demonology.* New York: Crown, 1959.

Bibliographies

2503. del Cervo, Diane M. *Witchcraft in Europe and America: Guide to the Microfilm Collection.* Woodbridge, CT: Research Publications, 1983. 111 pp.

2504. Field, Wendy Elizabeth. *Witchcraft, Sorcery and Divination in Sub-Sahara Africa: A Bibliography of the Most Important Works.* Johannesburg, So. Af.: University of the Witwatersrand, 1971. 29 pp.

2505. Midelfort, H.C. Erik. "Recent Witch Hunting Research, or Where Do We Go From Here?" *Papers of the Bibliographical Society of America* 62 (1968): 373-420.

2506. Nugent, Donald. "Witchcraft Studies, 1959-1971: A Bibliographical Survey" in *The Occult: Studies and Evaluations*, ed. by Robert Galbreath. Bowling Green, OH: Bowling Green University Popular Press, 1972. pp. 82-97.

Witchcraft in North America

Biographical Volumes

2507. *Crossroads: A Who's Who of the Magickal Community.* Idaho Springs, CO: Witching Well Education and Research Center, 1988. Unpaged.

2508. Ericson, Eric. *The World, the Flesh, the Devil: A Biographical Dictionary of Witches.* New York: Mayflower Books, 1981. 284 pp.

Directories

2509. *The Branches Directory.* Mt. Horeb, WI: Three Sisters, 1988. 21 pp.

2510. *Directory of Canadian Pagan Resources.* Toronto: Obscure Pagan Press/Pagans for Peace, 1987. 2nd ed.: 1989.

2511. Fox, Selena. *Circle Guide to Wicca and Pagan Resources.* Madison, WI: A Circle Publ., 1979. 113 pp. 2nd edition, Madison, WI: A Circle Publ., 1980. 133 pp. 3rd edition, Madison, WI: A Circle Publ., 1981. 133 pp. 4th edition, Mt. Horeb, WI, 1984. 139 pp. 5th ed.: 1987. 153 pp.

2512. ———. *Circle Guide to Wisconsin.* Madison, WI: Circle Holistic New Age Resource Center, 1979. 40 pp.

2513. ———. *Magickal Contacts.* Madison, WI: A Circle Publ., Supplement to Circle Guide to Wicca and Pagan Resources, 1981. 52 pp.

2514. Gawr, Ruddlwm, ed. *Pagan/Occult/New Age Directory.* Atlanta, GA: Pagan Grove Press, 1978. 40 pp. *Supplement.* 1978 12 pp. Rev. ed. as: *1980 Pagan Occult New Age Directory.* Athens, GA: Pagan Grove Press, 1980.

2515. *Nemeton Directory.* Oakland, CA: Nemeton, 1973.

2516. *The New Broom's Directory of Contacts.* Dallas, TX: The New Broom, 1974. 8 pp.

2517. "Paganism in North America/Yellow Pages Directory." Published annually in the *Green Egg* (P.O. Box 2953, St. Louis, MO 63130). Last appearance August 1, 1975 (Vol. 7, No. 64).

Bibliographies

2518. Keeney, Steven H. "Witchcraft in Colonial Connecticut and Massachusetts: An Annotated Bibliography." *Bulletin of Bibliography and Magazine Notes* 33, 2 (1976): 61-72.

2519. Melton, J. Gordon. *Magic, Witchcraft, and Paganism in America: A Bibliography.* New York & London: Garland Publishing, 1982. 231 pp.

Ritual Magick

2520. Fitzgerald, Edward Noel. "Works of Aleister Crowley Published or Privately Printed: A Bibliographical List." In Charles Richard Crammel, *Aleister Crowley: The Man, the Mage, the Poet.* London: Richards Press, 1951.

2521. Galbreath, Robert. "Arthur Edward Waite/Occult Scholar and Christian Mystic/A Chronological Bibliography." *Bulletin of Bibliography* 30, 2 (April-June 1973) 55-61.

2522. Gilbert, R. A. *A. E. Waite: A Bibliography.* Wellingborough, Northamptonshire, UK: Aquarian Press, 1983. 192 pp.

2523. Parfitt, Will, and A. Drylie. *A Crowley Cross-Index.* Avon, England: ZRO, 1976. 36 pp.

2524. Sims, G. F. *Magick: Books by the Master Therion.* Rare Book Catalogue No. 12. Harrow, 1951.

2525. Smith, Timothy D'Arch. "The Books of the Beast': Prolegomena to a Bibliography of Aleister Crowley." In Timothy D'Arch Smith. *The Books of the Beast: Essays on Aleister Crowley, Montegue Summers, Francis Barrett and Others.* Wellingborough, Northamptonshire, UK: Crucible, 1987. Pp. 13-48.

2526. Yorke, Gerald. "Bibliography of the Works of Aleister Crowley." In John Symonds. *The Great Beast.* London: Rider, 1951. Note: The bibliography was cut from the paperback edition.

Directories

2527. Ward, Ken. *Occult Directory.* Saskatoon, SK: The Author, 1973. 2nd. ed. 1975. 17 pp. 10 Supplements, 1 to 3 pages each.

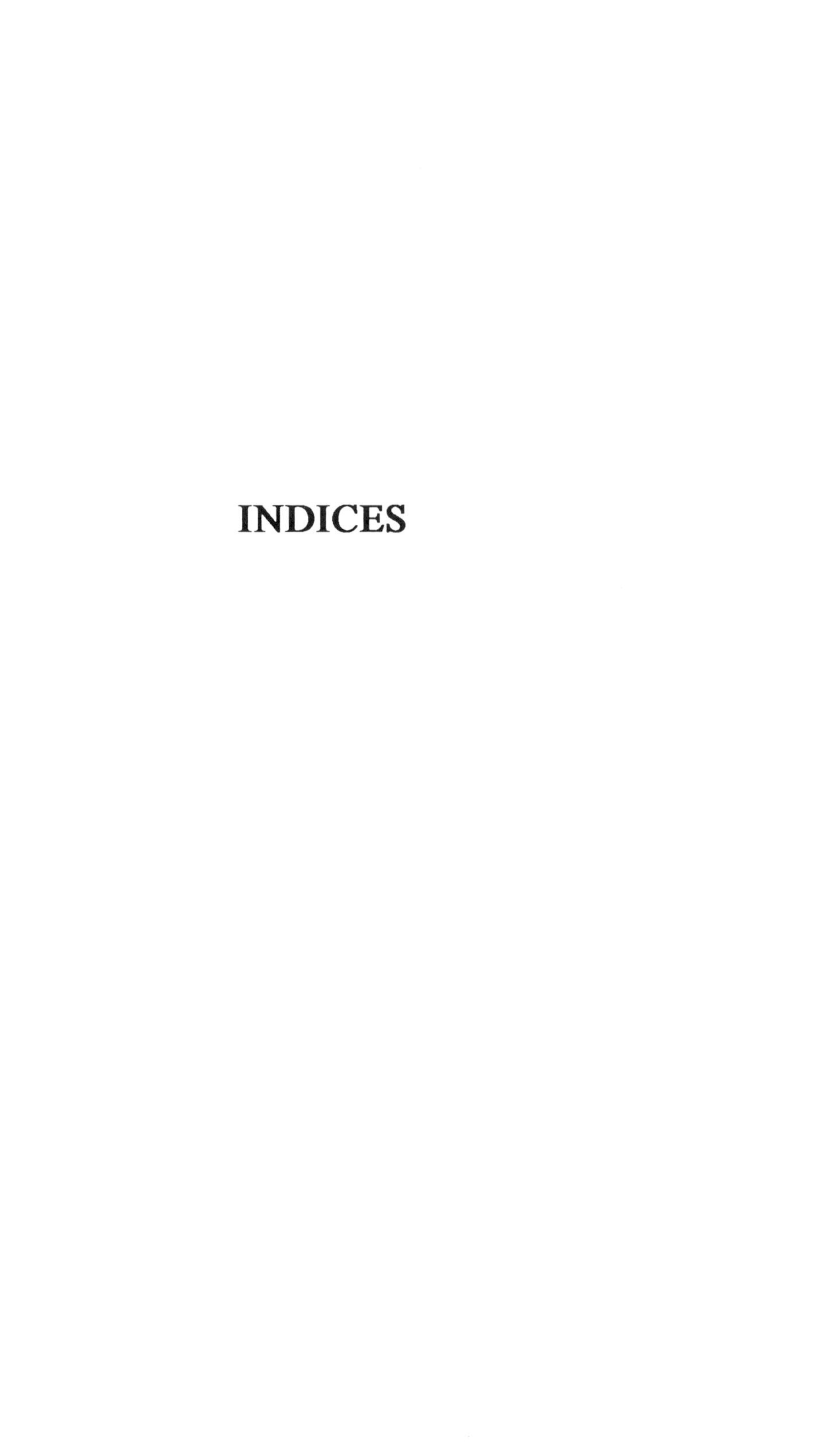

INDICES

TITLE INDEX

A

B

C

D

E

F

G

H

J

K

L

M

N

O

P

Q

R

S

T

U

V

W

AUTHOR INDEX

This index includes all authors, editors, translators and compilers mentioned in the text.

A

B

D

E

F

G

H

I

J

K

M

N

O

P

Q

R

S

T

U

V

W

Y

Z

ORGANIZATIONS INDEX

A

B

C

D

I

J

N

O

P

T

U

V

W

Y

SUBJECT INDEX

N

O

P

Q

R

S